Emerging Challenges of Globalization

# Emerging Challenges of Globalization and Development

EDITED BY
**SURINDER KUMAR**
**FAHIMUDDIN**

Northern Regional Centre
Indian Council of Social Science Research, New Delhi

GIDS
Giri Institute of Development Studies, Lucknow

**RAWAT PUBLICATIONS**
Jaipur • New Delhi • Bangalore • Guwahati • Kolkata

ISBN 978-81-316-0884-5



The publication of this book was financially supported by the Northern Regional Centre, ICSSR. The opinions expressed and the research finding are those of the contributors; the NRC accepts no responsibility for the same.



*Published by*
Prem Rawat for **Rawat Publications**
Satyam Apts, Sector 3, Jawahar Nagar, Jaipur 302 004 (India)
Phone: 0141 265 1748 / 7006 Fax: 0141 265 1748
E-mail: info@rawatbooks.com
Website: www.rawatbooks.com

*New Delhi Office*
4858/24, Ansari Road, Daryaganj, New Delhi 110 002
Phone: 011 2326 3290

Also at *Bangalore, Guwahati* and *Kolkata*

Typeset by Rawat Computers, Jaipur
Printed at Chaman Enterprises, New Delhi

# Contents

# Preface

The ICSSR-Northern Regional Centre of Indian Council of Social Sciences, New Delhi, in collaboration with Giri Institute of Development Studies, Lucknow, organized a three-day Second Northern Regional Social Science Congress at Giri Institute of Development Studies, during 27–28 February and 1 March 2014. The purpose of regional Congress was to provide a platform and opportunity to young, regional scholars of social sciences to meet and exchange their ideas, undertake research and share their findings with leading academics and experts. The research papers presented in the Congress were critiqued by the experts and individual scholars were encouraged to revise their papers in the light of suggestions given by the experts, discussants and other participants. Panel discussions on selected themes and special lectures were organized in the course of Congress for the benefit of young participants in the Congress. The scholars from the Northern region of the country which included the National Capital Territory of Delhi, Madhya Pradesh, Chattisgarh, Uttar Pradesh, Uttarakhand and Rajasthan, were invited to contribute their papers on different themes of the Congress.

Following themes were selected for the Second North Regional Social Science Congress: (i) State, Market and Globalization (ii) Group Inequalities and Marginalization (iii) Environment: The Regional Context (iv) Urbanization, Migration and Informal Sector (v) Public Policies and Institutional Change (vi) Democracy and Representation and (vii) Gender, Culture and Power. It may be noted that first three themes focus on implications of globalization and market oriented growth path on emerging economic inequalities and socio-economic marginalization of some sections of the society and their impact on the growth process on the one hand and environment and ecology on the other. Next theme addresses issues emerging from new growth path on urbanization and social sectors in the world in general and India in particular. Next two themes examine emerging issues in relation to participation in democratic institutions and consequent changes in power relations. The last topic examines how new cultural and power relations are impacting gender related issues in the society. In all, 44 papers were presented during the Congress. The Congress organized two panel discussions, one on 'Radical Movements in India: Issues and Challenges' and the other on 'Demographic Issues'. A decision to publish these papers in book form was taken. However, to ensure the quality of book, subject experts examined the papers and found 24 papers qualitatively worth inclusion in the book. Hence, the present book is a collection of the papers selected by the experts. It is expected that the issues raised in the introduction and research papers will further stimulate research, and provide a road map for creative thinking on social issues and approaches to research and analysis in social sciences in India.

We are sincerely grateful to Prof. Amit Bhaduri for his inspiring inaugural address and for according permission to publish its transcript. We are sure it will show a way to younger generations of social scientists how to be orginal thinkers and do socially meaningful research. We would like to accord our sense of gratitude to the authors of papers who first contributed the papers and later took the pain of revising their papers. We are happy to put on record our appreciation for Prof. Dhruv Raina, Regional Director, Northern Regional Centre of ICSSR, and other officials, particularly to Sh. Shreekant Khandewale, for their contribution and continous support at each step in organizing the Congress and bringing out this book. Thanks are also due to the faculty members of Giri Institute of Development Studies, Lucknow, who helped us in successful organization of the Congress.

Finally we are thankful to the panel of experts who visualized the issues for the seminar and scrutinized the papers for publication. We appreciate the contribution of Dr Animesh Roy along with others in transcription of inaugural address by Prof. Amit Bhaduri. Our profound thanks are due to Dr Ramnik Mohan, former Associate Professor of MD University, Rohtak, for taking up the painstaking task of editing all the papers. Thanks are also due to Mr Shivakar Tiwari for his painstaking help to complete the missing references.

Finally, Rawat Publications, Jaipur, deserve our gratitude for the publication of this book.

**Surinder Kumar**
**Fahimuddin**

# Contributors

**Amit Bhaduri** has been Professor Emeritus at Jawaharlal Nehru University, Delhi. He was Professor of Political Economy at the University of Pavia. He has held various academic assignments in different institutes and organizations in India and abroad.

**B.N. Prasad**, Professor and Head, Sociology and Social Anthropology Division, A.N. Sinha Institute of Social Studies, Patna.

**Bhavya Maheshwari**, Faculty Member, Department of Business Economics, Jiwaji University, Gwalior, Madhya Pradesh.

**Gangotri Mishra**, Research Scholar, Jiwaji University, Gwalior, Madhya Pradesh.

**Virendra B. Shahare**, Assistant Professor, Department of Social Work, Jamia Millia Islamia, New Delhi.

**Khushbu Rani Gupta**, M.Phil Scholar, National University of Educational Planning and Administration, New Delhi.

**Binay Kumar Pathak**, Doctoral Candidate, Zakir Husain Centre for Educational Studies, School of Social Sciences, Jawaharlal Nehru University, New Delhi.

**Nivedita Sarkar**, Research Scholar, National University of Educational Planning and Administration, New Delhi.

**Devesh Vijay,** Fellow, Nehru Memorial Museum and Library, New Delhi and Associate Professor, Zakir Husain Delhi College, University of Delhi.

**Archana Pandey**, Research Scholar, Department of History, Babasaheb Bhimrao Ambedkar University, Lucknow.

**Rukmani**, Research Scholar, Centre for the Study of Law and Governance, Jawaharlal Nehru University, New Delhi.

**Pragya Pandey**, Research Scholar, Centre for Indo-Pacific Studies, School of International Relations, Jawaharlal Nehru University, New Delhi.

**Sujeet Kumar**, Research Scholar, Centre for the Study of Law and Governance, Jawaharlal Nehru University, New Delhi.

**Sumit Kumar**, Research Scholar, National University of Educational Planning and Administration, New Delhi.

**Akram Hannan** Research Scholar, Department of Geography, Aligarh Muslim University, Aligarh.

**Hemant Kumar Varshney**, Deputy Director, Institute of Applied Manpower Research, Delhi.

**Anuneeta Mitra**, Research Scholar, National University of Education Planning and Administration (NUEPA), New Delhi.

**Amardeep Kumar**, M.Phil Student (2012–14), National University of Education Planning and Administration, New Delhi.

**Shraddha Srivastava**, Research Scholar, Department of Sociology, Faculty of Social Sciences, BHU, Varanasi.

**Swadhin Mondal**, Assistant Professor, Institute for Studies in Industrial Development, New Delhi.

**Diksha Jha**, Research Scholar, Centre for the Study of Law and Governance, Jawaharlal Nehru University, New Delhi.

**Sandeep Bhatt**, Principal-in-charge, Karamveer Vidyapeeth, Khanda, Madhya Pradesh.

**Karabi Chetia**, Research Scholar, Centre for the Study of Law and Governance, Jawaharlal Nehru University, New Delhi.

**Ranjana Upadhyay**, Research Scholar, Department of Political Science, Babasaheb Bhimrao Ambedkar University, Lucknow.

**Sunita Sangar**, National Centre for Women, National Mission for Empowerment of Women, Ministry of Women and Child Development, Government of India, New Delhi.

# Introduction

Globalization, liberalization and privatization in the last three decades have triggered tremendous forces of socio-economic transformation in various countries the world over. Further stimulus was provided by the new scientific discoveries and inventions which led to emergence of Information and Communiation Technologies, their application to production processes and means of transport which have deeply affected all the walks of life in the economic, social and political organization of various national economies in the world. This has led to accelerated pace of economic growth in various countries, finance capital ruling supreme. However, fast economic growth based on market driven economic principles of production and distribution of income have led to increased inter-regional and interpersonal disparities in the world which have recently led to deep economic and financial crisis engulfing the world since 2007. Further, environmental unsustainability of such a growth process is also threatening the very existence of mankind. Various countries are at different levels of socio-economic development and the new growth process has a profound influence and has been ushering in far-reaching changes in political and social institutions of various countries. The process of change has brought about lot of tensions in the existing social, economic and political institutions in various countries.

It is in this scenario that a set of emerging socio-economic and political issues in contemporary India were identified for the young social scientists to grapple with and write and present research papers under the direct supervision of the panel of experts. It has been noted that existing theories of social sciences are inadequate to provide adequate explanation to the fast changing and emerging realities. In fact, social sciences in the world are at the cross-roads! In social science teaching and research, three key questions need to be addressed: how far compartmentalization of social science into various water tight disciplines like economics, political science, sociology etc. in terms of subject matter has added to the explanatory power of social sciences? How far the commonly used methods of analysis are adequate to explain the socio-economic processes. What are the limitations of these methods of analysis? Are issues raised and methods of analysis constrained by latent ideological considerations or assumptions? Clarity over these issues will go a long way in improving the quality of teaching and research in social sciences in India.

A lot of discomfort is being exhibited by various scholars about the validity of compartmentalization of social science into various disciplines. Explanatory power of discipline-based partial theories is being questioned. Constraints of structural functional approach to research are becoming self obvious. It has also been reported that statistical techniques are being grossly abused in social science research and in fact most of the research in social sciences in general and economics in particular have become research on testing of the explanatory power of statistical/econometric methods than to provide plausible explanation to any socio-economic phenomenon. Prof. Amit Bhaduri, in a very inspiring inaugural address specially designed to address the concerns of young scholars, 'How to Do Social Science Research', opined by sharing his experience in theory building in social sciences and made some profound observations. The address is a brilliant exercise in training young scholars to be original thinkers in formulation and analysis of research problems. The transcript of the inaugural address is being included as a chapter in the book. However, a summary of the arguments in simplified words is provided as follows: he lamented that some of his brilliant students who were technologically sophisticated went to USA, enrolled in the best universities and conducted some trivial research and such research being carried out in western universities continues to have ill influence on research being carried out in Indian universities and institutes. He argued that aspiring research students should go to the field, observe the socio-economic reality and formulate the research problems. Such research problems are far more genuine and meaningful than to locate problems in most of the debates being carried out in western journals and books. He illustrated this observation by example of his most important contributions to social science research recognized world over, namely his formulations of 'semi-feudal relations in Indian agriculture' in 1970s and his recent formulation of development process in India, 'development by dispossession'. He further argued that young students should observe socio-economic process as they are unfolding in India. Another example he gave was that in most of the industrial production in India, most of the labour was not wage labour but family labour and therefore its character and issues were different from that of western labour class. Such formulations have profound implications for theory of wage determination, labour movements and framing of labour laws. Further, Bhaduri argued that employment maximization than growth rate of GDP/output should be the objective of economic development in the country.

In this book, 24 research papers have been included. The papers have been organized under eight themes.

(i) Challenges Before Social Sciences (ii) The State Market and Globalization, (iii) Group Inequalities and Marginalization, (iv) Environment: The Regional Context, (v) Urbanization, Migration and Informal Sector, (vi) Public Policies and Institutional Change, (vii) Democracy and Representation, and (viii) Gender, Culture and Power.

The first section consists of two papers. The first is the inaugural address, 'How to Do Social Science Research', and the second is the paper presented by Prof. B.N. Prasad in the panel discussion on Radical Movement in India.

**B.N. Prasad**, in his paper entitled 'Democracy, Development and Subaltern: Radical Agrarian Movement in Bihar', has examined the socio-economic processes unleased after India's independence and emergence of subaltern agrarian movements in India. He has observed that rural society witnessed three dominant forms of socio-economic developments: through legislative measures by the Indian state, Gandhian way, and main stream Communist model. Legislative measures were meant to eliminate feudal mode of exploitation and courage development of capitalism in agriculture. Zamindari abolition and related policies created two contradictory trends in agrarian relations: resourceful tenants who could pay compensation got ownership rights and the poor tenants who could not pay, were evicted and became non-owning proletariats. This led to sharpening of conflicts between newly emerging proprietary classes and pauperized proletarianized masses. Proprietary classes launched movements to extract assistance and facilities from the state and the poor and dispossessed masses launched struggles against various types of exploitations, terror and violence. Gandhian way of social reconstruction started by Vinoba Bhave with *bhoodan* and *gramdan* movement after a good start lost its steam. Mainstream political parties formed *Khet Mazdur* organizations but achieved little as due to expediency of electoral politics could not work against rich and middle farmers due to fear of losing their support base. This led to emergence of CPI (ML) party advocating for direct action against the proprietary classes taking inspiration from Telangana struggle using extra-constitutional means. Initially, movement was of open confrontation with state machinery which was soon replaced by 'Guerrilla Warfare'. Naxalite movement in Bihar has two phases. First phase was from 1967 to 1971 and the second phase began in 1973 especially after Emergency in 1977. In mid-1980s, landed gentry launched caste *senas* to maintain their hegemonic position. Various radical groups with their mass fronts have organized rural poor around issues of fair wages and just share in share cropping arrangements. Struggles were not only against economic oppression but also against social humiliation, dignity of labourers and women. Prasad concludes his paper with the observation that miscarriage of development interventions initiated by State, Gandhian movements and mainstream Left parties provided propitious ground for rise and sustainance of extra-parliamentary agrarian struggles in the state. Maoist movement revolves around bacsic issues for socio-economic and political emancipation of toiling masses, which is fundamental duty of democratic system.

**Bhavya Maheshwari and Gangotri Mishra**, in their paper on 'Globalization and the Indian Capital Market', have highlighted that the Indian Capital Market has experienced significant development since the start of globalization in 1990s. On the basis of SEBI data, authors have found that a total of 3,683 companies entered the primary capital market by issuing equities at par and 2,326 companies placed their equities with premium. The banking sector was the front runner in tapping capital through primary market. The major sectors which tapped capital were textile, power, telecommunication and IT. All these sectors placed their equities in the market with capital size of more than 100 crores. A total of 5,237 private sector companies entered the capital market while only 87 public sector companies tapped the capital market during 1997–2013. Out of total capital raised, only one-fourth was tapped by the public sector companies during 1997–98 to 2012–2013. It was also found that no public sector undertaking tapped the capital market during 1997–98 to 2012–2013. The annual share price index rapidly rose from 730 to 16,569 during the year 1993–2012. The share price index also changed 80 per cent in 1995 over previous year index value, showing that globalization has proved as a hallmark of development for the Indian capital market. India also witnessed radical change in foreign investment inflows during 1994–2013. Thus, the authors have tried to explain that globalization has acted as a driver for the growth of Indian Capital Market.

**Virendra B. Shahare**, in his paper on 'Livelihood Issues and Inequality among Dalits in the Era of Globalization', has argued that rapid changes at the macro and micro levels that India witnessed since the initiation of globalization has contributed to the instability of livelihood system of Dalits in rural areas. Agriculture supports the livelihood of around 70 per cent of Dalits in rural areas which is becoming unsuitable to support their livelihood due to decreasing land size and owning of poor quality of land. Most of the Dalits, throughout the country, work as labourers for ₹ 15 to ₹ 35 per day which is much lower than the prescribed minimum wages. The author has found that during 1948 to 1970, 34.9 million acres of land was distributed among landless farmers, out of it, Dalits got only 0.5 per cent. The livelihood of Dalits has been adversely impacted wherever Special Economic Zones (SEZ) have been created. The data showed that 400 SEZs have been approved during 1991 to 2010 and 1,25,000 hectares of land was to be acquired. It has been estimated that around 82,000 Dalit families were displaced and lost work. Thus, the author argues that the slowdown in agriculture both in productivity and changing cropping pattern, increase in distress migration, changing consumption pattern and government policies and financing of industrial houses have surely undermined livelihood options of Dalits. The author is of the view that an integrated, multi dimensional approach to poverty reduction and upliftment of Dalit is crucial to preserve the livelihood system of Dalits.

**Khushbu Rani Gupta**, in her paper on 'Private Unaided School, Elite Spaces and Disadvantaged Children: How Inclusive is the RTE Act, 2009?' has critically analysed the inclusive approach manifested in the Right of Children to

Free and Compulsory Education Act, 2009. The main objective of the paper is to look into the social exclusion of children belonging to Economically Weaker Section (EWS) under the provision of 25 per cent reservation in private unaided schools in Delhi. The investigation was done on the basis of primary data collected from 20 private unaided schools, selected from four zones of Delhi. The respondents were students, teachers, parents and principals of schools of nursery and KG grades. The findings have highlighted that the children from the EWS and disadvantaged groups are denied admission by the schools on one pretext and the other as schools have no accountability. The study finds that the social positioning and identities of the children from the EWS and disadvantaged category within schools are in contradiction with the conditions these children have in their homes. Hence, these children face the problem of adjustment with the children from well off families. She has finally argued that 25 per cent reservation for children from the EWS and disadvantaged background requires a framework of accountability on the part of schools to ensure that such children are not excluded.

**Binay Kumar Pathak**, in his paper on 'Cost and Pricing of Higher Education: Emerging Concerns for Equity and Affordability', has examined the reasons for rising cost of higher education. The one reason, he has attributed to the hiking of fee by the public funded higher education institutions to meet the target of own resource generation as prescribed by Birla-Ambani and Narayan Murthi committees. The other is the relatively higher fee charged by the private higher education institutions to cover the cost of providing higher education. Moreover, various Bills are also pending in the Parliament for providing greater space to private institutions in higher education and encouraging public-private partnership in public funded higher education institutions. The author has raised serious objections to the Tenth Five Year Plan proposal to facilitate higher education by registering it as companies, thereby enabling higher education to shed mask of 'not for profit institution'. In view of rising cost of higher education in public and private institutions, author has suggested that it is desirable now that the policies governing higher education should be framed with proper understanding of higher education in accordance with the goal of social equity and excellence.

**Nivedita Sarkar**, in her paper on 'Inequalities in Participation in Higher Education in India: Role of Household Characteristics', has analysed the pattern of participation of males and females from different social groups, localities and a household's economic status in higher education. She has also attempted to find out the extent of household characteristics responsible for determining whether or not to participate in higher education. The analysis is based on the unit level schedule–25.2, used in the 64th Round of NSS survey conducted in the year 2007–08. She has used information about educational participation and expenditure of persons belonging to the age group of 5–29 years. The findings have revealed three results. One of them is that the household's economic condition plays a crucial role in determining the participation in higher education. The educational profile of the head of the household, particularly of female-headed households, has emerged as an important variable in determining the participation in higher education. The caste did not emerge as determining factor rather it is a critical opportunity for upward mobility for socially backward students.

**Devesh Vijay**, in his paper on 'Transitions in Livelihoods: Long-Term Study of a Slum in East Delhi', has examined the changes in occupational and employment patterns in a slum called Aradhaknagar, located in the periphery of Delhi with the help of quantitative and ethnographic evidences gathered by him since 1988 through repeated field visits, surveys and tracking of family history. The study has found that the type of occupations in the slum economy have changed considerably over the years. The employment in the unorganized sector has also grown considerably in recent years. There has been considerable increase in casualization of work. One noticeable change is evident that the proportion of earning women workers in total women has risen in the slum and the biggest rise has been in the number of domestic maids. This could be due to increased demand of domestic maids in surrounding middle class homes in which more educated women are going out for work and have become open in allowing Dalit women inside their homes. The author has acknowledged that the findings of the paper cannot be generalized to all slums in Delhi because it is small case study but it throws light on the changing dynamics of occupations and employment in slums.

**Archana Pandey**, in her paper on 'A Losing Battle with Development and Human Indifference: A Case of Gomti River in Lucknow', has highlighted the fact that rivers in India are facing multiple problems of sever pollution, over extraction, deforestation in their catchment areas, encroachment, dams and barrages. She has taken Gomti river as a case study to argue her viewpoint. From industrial waste to domestic discharge, river Gomti has become a flowing dumping yard for the 15 small and big towns located in its catchment area. The river collects large amount of human and industrial pollutants as it flows through the highly populous areas. The author has suggested that barrage should be constructed so that extra water could flow regularly over its gates and decline in water quality could be stopped. She has also suggested that awareness about clean Gomti should be spread among the people.

**Rukmani** has conducted a study 'Governing the Forest Resources: A Case Study of Uttarakhand'. The objective of the study is to assess the role of Van Panchayats and Joint Forest Management Committees in the protection of forests. She has highlighted the important role of local institutions in protecting the forest resources in the region but her study has found that bureaucratic interventions have increased in the functional areas of these local institutions. Local institutions have been subjected to dictates of bureaucracy rather than framing and implementing own plans to protect the forests. Hence, she feels that a lot of changes are required to strive for right balance of effectiveness, efficiency, equity and sustainability in the management of forests. She has suggested that there is a need to strengthen the capacity of Van Panchayats and Joint Forest Management Committees in the management of forest in Uttarakhand.

**Pragya Pandey**, in her paper on 'Emerging Environmental Security Threats to the Maritime Security in the Indian Ocean Region: Challenges and Responses', has highlighted the strategic location of Indian Ocean (IO) and the excessive exploitation of its natural resources, maritime pollution, dumping of nuclear waste, natural disasters, weak bio-security, adverse impact on fisheries and other marine biology and threat to food security are some of the major issues Indian Ocean is facing today. She has expressed the view that these threats must be taken as global security challenges and be dealt with not by any single country but by a focussed and coordinated approach by the consortium of the countries in which India can play a leading role.

**Sujeet Kumar**, in his paper on 'Urbanization and Slum Dwellers: A Study of NGOs in Delhi's Slum', has highlighted the key features of various interventions by the Non-Governmental Organizations (NGOs) in Jehangirpuri slums in northern Delhi. He has argued that new paradigm poses several challenges to urban development schemes. The NGOs' presence in these slums is gradually depoliticizing slum dwellers and weakening their potential in asking state to solve their problems. The NGOs are found to be fulfilling the requirement of their funding agencies rather than genuinely helping slum dwellers. The author has argued against the role of strong and vibrant NGOs, as an alternative of the state. He is of the view that excessive NGO involvement in slums will weaken the collective voice of the slum dwellers because the state will become neutral to the issues of slums as NGOs assume replacing state role among slum dwellers.

**Sumit Kumar**, in his paper on 'Decision of Migration: A Case Sudy of Students from Bihar Enrolled in University of Delhi', has examined the nature of decision-making of students for migration from Bihar to Delhi and tried to highlight the factors which have played a role in the process of migration. The study is based on the survey of 26 students who were from Bihar and enrolled in non-professional courses in Dayal Singh College of Delhi. The study has found that decision to migrate to Delhi University from Bihar is multi-layered and these layers are: (i) decision to migrate, (ii) selection of destination, (iii) selection of university, (iv) selection of college and (v) selection of course. But since the decisions are found to be very subjective, any sequence of layers cannot be generalized. The author has found that decision of migration for higher education is neither taken exclusively by individual or by a household but it is actually a mixed decision. In some cases, an individual is seen to have taken decision while in other cases parents, siblings and relatives take the decision of migration for higher education. However, author has pointed out that decision taken by the individuals is most important factor in migration of students from Bihar to Delhi for higher education.

**Akram Hannan**, in his paper on 'Dimensions of Urban Female Educational Status and its Linkages in Eastern Uttar Pradesh', has highlighted that male, female and total literacy rates have increased in India (36.14, 43.46 and 39.54 percentage points, respectively), Uttar Pradesh (42.57, 46.76 and 44.32 percentage points, respectively) and Eastern Uttar Pradesh (48.67, 48.30 and 48.35 percentage points, respectively) during 1971 and 2011. He has attributed it to the rapid rise in the number of elementary educational institutions and to various government programmes like Sarva Shiksha Abhiyan (SSA) and Mid-Day Meal (MDM). The trend in urban female educational status during 1971–2011 also showed upward move at primary, middle, high school, intermediate, graduate and technical and non-technical levels. The author has worked out correlation between the status of urban female education and 30 independent variables with the assumption that linear relationship exists in all cases. The analysis has led to the broader conclusion that the percentage of urban population, population density and female workers in primary, secondary and tertiary occupations are the chief indicators which influence the percentage distribution of female education at different levels in Eastern Uttar Pradesh. The author has suggested a number of measures to further increase female education in Eastern Uttar Pradesh.

**Hemant Kumar Varshney**, in his paper on 'Gender Disparity in Literacy in India: Reflections from Census Data', has analysed the gender disparity in literacy at all India and state levels. He has found that the annual growth rate in female literacy rate was 1.87 per cent as against 0.72 per cent of male literacy during 2001–2011. It has resulted in considerable gap between male and female literacy at all India level. He has found that all states/UTs had achieved more than 50 per cent of male literacy in 1991 and 14 states/UTs had more than 75 per cent of female literacy in 1991 and this increased to 25 states in 2001 and 2011. All the states/UTs had achieved more than 50 per cent female literacy by 2011. The author has found that most states in India, including Kerala, have more literate males than literate females but states where literacy rate is low also has higher gap in male and female literacy. The analysis has revealed that in Indian society, increase in male literacy is followed by the increase in female literacy which has resulted in decrease in gender disparity in literacy. Hence, to reduce disparity in gender literacy, holistic approach needs to be adopted. Focus on female literacy alone may not give desired results, views the author.

**Anuneeta Mitra**, in her paper on 'Benefit Incidence Analysis of Public Spending on Education in India', has analysed, on the basis of NSS 64th Round of 2007–08 data, the distribution of subsidy among five quintile groups (poorest-quintile–1, poor-quintile–2, middle-quintile–3, upper middle-quintile–4 and rich-quintile–5) and three levels of education (elementary, secondary and higher) across 15 major states in India. She has carried out Benefit Incidence Analysis to assess that how government subsidy affects the distribution of welfare in the population. The author has found that the distribution of subsidy across three levels of education, state-wise and over quintile groups, has been pro-poor at the elementary level. In case of secondary level, distribution was varied across states with Assam, Gujarat, Haryana, Kerala and Punjab, distribution was skewed in favour of the richest. The distribution of subsidy for higher level of education was found pro-rich, with high levels of inequality in Gujarat followed by Haryana. The results, on the all India basis, have shown a pro-rich distribution of subsidy at the higher level of education and pro-poor distribution at the elementary educational level. The state-wise analysis has shown varied results, indicating the impact of implementation of different policies across states. The study contains a good review of literature on the Benefit Incidence Analysis.

**Amardeep Kumar**, in his paper on 'Participation of Mahadalit Students in Higher Education: A Case Study in Gaya District of Bihar', has analysed the government policies to promote higher education among Mahadalit students and intra community variations in enrollment of Mahadalit students in higher education. The Bihar State Mahadalit Commission, 1972 has identified 22 castes among dalits as Mahadalits. The author argues that though policy of reservation for SCs/STs is in place but Mahadalits should be given reservation in central jobs and services. He has found that out of 22 castes, only six castes namely Dhobi, Chamar, Pasi, Bhuiya, Mehtar and Musahar could reach higher education but the caste like Bhuiya, which has more than 50 per cent of population among Mahadalits, could reach very little to higher education. The other Mahadalit castes could not reach higher education at all. In the light of findings in the paper, the author has expressed the view that there is need to take more substantive measures at all levels of education for ensuring greater access of Mahadalit students to higher education.

**Shraddha Srivastava**, in her paper on 'Child Nutrition in National Food Security Bill (2013): Some Evidences', has explored the emerging problem of Integrated Child Development Scheme (ICDS) on the basis of primary data collected in two villages of Faizabad district of Uttar Pradesh. She has also used the Comptroller and Auditor General (CAG) Report–2011, to support her findings. She has found serious lacunae in the implementation of ICDS scheme in both villages. The reason, she has attributed, is the fact that ICDS and MDM schemes are being implemented without taking into account the changes in income, attitude and awareness levels of rural population. Hence, there is divergence between implementation of both schemes and ground realities. In the light of shortcomings noticed in the implementation of ICDS scheme, author has suggested to take drastic steps to improve the implementation of ICDS so that nutritional deficiency of vulnerable children in the age of 0–6 years could be minimized.

**Swadhin Mondal**, in his paper on 'Progressive Horizontal and Vertical Equity in Healthcare Financing in India', has analysed the impact of health policy changes on the equity of health financing among households, using NSS data of 50th (1993–94), 61st (2004–05), 66th (2009–10) and 68th (2011–12) Rounds, on the basis of index of Fairness of Financial Contribution (FFC), as proposed by the WHO. He has also examined the factors influencing equity in health financing. He has argued that the present healthcare payment structure is fair in meeting out-of-pocket payment component on part of the poor. This implies that poor people are paying lower share of out-of-pocket payment now than earlier as compared to high income groups. The findings suggest that government funded healthcare services as well as government sponsored healthcare programmes (NRHM, RSBY, etc.) have higher impact on low income groups and these programmes have greater equity in meeting out-of-pocket spending. The study has highlighted the fact that the overall policy changes made by the Government of India especially after 2005 onwards has positive impact on equity in meeting out-of-pocket payment. The author has argued that the expansion of new health policies among non-poor can reduce inequity in meeting out-of pocket payment.

**Dikha Jha**, in her study on 'Democracy and Pluralism: Immigrant Incorporation and Citizenship', has provided a detail account of democracy and pluralism and the place of immigrants in a territory bounded by polity who are generally termed as aliens, refugees and non-citizens. She has attempted to collate three concepts, namely citizenship, pluralism and democracy, by arguing for immigrants' incorporation into the fold of citizenship. Her arguments are based on some important scholarly works of democratic theorists and civic republicans who have advocated that once an individual enters into the territorial field of a polity and is subjected to its laws like the other citizens, then he/she would have a rightful claim over citizenship rights in that polity. She has argued that this approach needs to make way for a more inclusive way out where diversity, plurality and individuality of different kinds are given space and democracy assumes a more broad and inclusive understanding. The focus of the paper is to present immigrant incorporation in a democratic set-up which enhances the virtues of pluralism and make democracy a more inclusive concept.

**Sandeep Bhatt**, in in his paper on 'New Media in India: An Overview of Internet and Mobile Technologies', has examined the role of media as a tool of communication and in developing cultural understanding among the people. He has explained the growth of different types of media over a period of time and the role of internet which has emerged since 1960s in the USA. He has also emphasized the role of mobile phones in communication. In new media revolution, Facebook, Twitter and YouTube have emerged as powerful tools of social networking. He has argued for the greater use of websites for knowledge gathering and social networking.

**Karabi Chetia**, in her study on 'Minorities within Autonomous Areas', has argued that politics of identity among minorities has mobilized them to demand for self rule and autonomy in governance. This happens when minorities feel that they do not get equal respect in the society. Though there are number of identity groups in the society who demand equal status but her study has focussed on the ethnic identity only. She has explained how the ethnic groups lag behind on various socio-economic aspects and demand reservation in jobs, in educational institutions, reservation in politics and self-governance/autonomy. She has argued that increasing inequalities, migration and demographic changes have prompted the elites among the minorities to demand for separate system of governance for them. She has observed that these factors have also contributed to rising conflict among various groups. She has endorsed the views of some scholars who have advocated that minorities should be given economic upliftment, identity preservation and relative autonomy to govern them. By doing so, she argues, that demand of the minorities for their cultural preservation and economic backwardness would be met.

**Ranjana Upadhyay**, in her paper on 'Women, Power and Culture', has explained the concept of socialization of culture from birth till death. She has argued that crimes against women are the cultural products. She has argued that it is the cultural factors that have prohibited the females from getting education and unequal sharing of power in comparison to the males. She has supported her arguments on the basis of analysis of the data of Census and Election Commission of India. She has put up her argument further by noting that if a girl has restricted birth, treated unequally even as an innocent child, forbidden from education, her mobility is banned, she is subjected to severe forms of exploitation and when these acts are legitimized by our cultural beliefs, such a type of culture must be rejected.

**Sunita Sangar** in her article 'Enabling Women Entrepreneurs through MSMEs: A Road Map for their Economic Empowerment' has argued the need for encouraging women entrepreneurs in the micro, small and medium enterprises (MSMEs). She has based her arguments on the basis of growth of women entrepreneurs in MSME sector, their contribution and current government schemes which encourage the promotion of women entrepreneurs in MSME sector. Sunita has also examined various problems being faced by the women entrepreneurs in MSME sector and the need to promote women entrepreneurs in MSME sector of rural areas. She is of the view that women entrepreneurs should be further strengthened through the convergence of existing schemes/policies of the government to improve their knowledge and further encourage them to set up MSME units.

On the basis of the above reviews, it becomes evident that the papers have covered a large gamut of issues associated with the socio-economic development of our society. The paper writers, who are mostly young scholars, deserve appreciation for their efforts.

We are hopeful that the present book will be of immense use to young researchers in the process of learning about 'how to think creatively and do original research'. The readers will also get new ideas from these papers to carry out further research in various areas of social importance.

**Surinder Kumar**
**Fahimuddin**

# Part 1

## Challenges Before Social Sciences

# 1

# How to Do Social Science Research?

**AMIT BHADURI**

I am very grateful to all of you and especially to Prof. Surinder Kumar, whom I had known as Surinder, a student who was very enthusiastic, and later as a professor in Chandigarh and elsewhere. I am grateful for this opportunity to speak particularly to a new generation of social scientists on 'How To Do Social Science Research'? How should it be changing in India? By profession, I have been an economist, at times a mathematical model builder. However, as I live in India, I have a great interest in the problems around us, and I increasingly realize how much I have changed over time in terms of 'how to do economics'. I want to tell you a little bit about this because I think this might also give you an idea about how my particular experience interacts with how to do research. It may not be the only way of doing research but it is at least a possible way of doing research.

I begin with a negative note. One of the tragedies I have had as a Professor in JNU and in many other developing countries like Mexico and briefly in Africa, East Europe and so on, is that some of the best students I spotted in the class in terms of their academic abilities, invariably almost all landed in America. Many are doing in my view quite trivial research to gain academic acceptance in universities like Harvard, MIT and Stanford. But if you examine the way they study for example 'poverty', it is, to put it politely, misleading so far as India is concerned. Our actual problems are not identified and the mere symptom of poverty is treated as the disease.

Now I say this not to criticize them but I think it needs to be said because it had a rather bad effect on Indian social science research. The bad effect is that certain things are made into a respectable topics of research while other probably more pressing things are considered vague and sidelined as not worth doing. I admit it is largely a failure of people like me because we have not been sufficiently persuasive, intellectually, to change the paradigm of research in India. However, at the same time, the reward system of doing research particularly relevant for poor countries like India and against the going orthodoxy is relatively small. And yet, conditions for research in social sciences are better today, and allows those with a passion to understand society to continue. It is not writing papers and seminars, but this passion that can beat all odds and produce original and technically innovative research.

Prof. Surinder Kumar has mentioned about a paper written by me long years ago on 'semi-feudalism'. Many such research problems are around us; but increasingly it becomes more and more difficult to get it through in respectable international journals. And, most of field-based survey lack the ability to bring out the essence of the survey using the necessary technique and being innovative. Contrast this with the fact that one can write on something rather trivial and use relatively new techniques and can publish in standard international journals. Increasingly this is the dominating trend among students who are technologically sophisticated and know some algebra and econometrics. But in terms of a sense of the problem, in terms of seriousness of trying to understand a problem, particularly arising in our social context, they have no interest. Indeed, many, after a few years in America, actually begin to presume that these problems should not be taken seriously because they cannot solve these problems neatly in a standard way: instead take a problem which will quickly get you a PhD degree, see a publication and so on.

I want to illustrate with a research problem which has long been with me, at least for the last 10 years; and I have been trying, not very successfully, to grapple with it. It continues with me. I have published a few pieces here and there but far from having a comprehensive view of the problem. This is the problem which classically Marxist type of economists call the problem of 'Primitive Accumulation'. But in simpler term today, you can call this the problem of 'Development with Dispossession', meaning thereby that we bring development in the country but, at the same time, we have lot of dispossessed people who are not only displaced from their land but from their livelihood.

There is not much to learn in terms of analytics from books except cross country historical experiences in this respect. The actual alternative I have always believed is some first-hand experience and trying to think from the first principles without being suffocated by bookish excesses. New ideas may come from actually going to these areas. I chose Chhattisgarh, one of the so-called extremists affected or Maoist areas of Dantewada. I travelled in these areas and went into the interior areas of Odisha and Jharkhand to understand through comparison, the commonalities and differences in the process of development by dispossession in India. It is a picture, which for our own sake, we need to understand better. This is not the only dispossession that I witnessed. I also want to talk about the Narmada area and Nandigram. While groping I even wrote a short piece on development and displacement in *Economic and Political Weekly* descrbing it ironically as 'developmental terrorism', because governments talk so much about terrorism.

I think that something is happening in the vibrant popular politics of India in various ways in this area of development and dispossession. We owe it to our society to understand better and that is what Northern Regional Social Science Congress (NRSSC) can do for all of us by focusing on this aspect.

Now, let me say, about the way I look at what I call the problem of 'Development with Dispossession'. It would help to contrast this against the problem debated by two of my former distinguished colleagues at Delhi School of Economics over growth-oriented versus social welfare-oriented development strategy. I cannot help feeling that the kind of debate on development is shadow boxing that bypasses all awkward questions, the question of who wields power and how in our society.

Let me explain it by giving just one example. Think about the problem of 'Development with Dispossession'. What is it? If you give somebody a modern industry employment, say in steel factory or some other sort of proper employment, it will roughly lead to an increase in output per worker by five–six times. For instance, according to the data of the TATAs published in the *Financial Times*, London, Tata Steel increased output per worker by 10 times over a period of about eight years. Although the productivity and labour output went up, the Tata decreased employment to half. If you actually generate this type of employment by taking away land from people in Chhattisgarh-Lohandigudda or from other parts of Jharkhand, then for one person you employ, you produce eight times the output but you only use half the labour force, as in Tata employment. If you increase both employment and output by six times, it will add to growth;but if you employ dispossessed labour force by six times, it will not have an increase in output per head. What the Tata will actually be doing is that it will increase the output per head but decrease the number of livelihoods in 'natural economy'. Their land taken, very few are left with alternative livelihoods. Is it just a problem of sacrifice the poor for higher growth with minimal welfare measures?

If you read the so-called 'Arthur Lewis Model', it tends to give a false picture which was spread over 80 to 90 years period when industrialization happened in Western Europe. If you take India's representative democracy, you will immediately see that in the above example, 10 people are thrown out of job and only one or two are given employment on an average. So what happens to remaining eight or nine? No books will tell you about it. If we go to these places mentioned before, we will see that most of the time, these people are not having jobs in the rural economy. I went to Narmada area and met a boatman having no job now. He informed me that he used to run a boat and his children used to get sand from that area, sold it to market and made a living. But now he has nothing to make a living from. In such a situation, where a lot of people are dispossessed without a livelihood, most of them continue to live there (constituting the core of poverty), and others who are a little bit better in health, younger and educated come over to cities. This is the beginning of the growth of 'Informal Sector' in India.

Now, look at the broad Indian statistics. On an average, India had a growth rate of about 8 per cent until recently. China, the other very high growing country, had a growth rate of 10–11 per cent. However, India's regular employment grew by less than half per cent, and China's employment grew at

1.1 per cent. In other words, these two countries had a high growth of output but very little growth in employment; and most of the growth in output was the result of high growth in output per worker, as in the Tata example. The workers employed with Tata and Bajaj produce much more. If we look at the output of all big Indian firms, we will see that their output per worker has increased by around five–six times, at times or even more but increase in employment has been negligible. The Economic Survey which is a very respectable government data source says that despite all these years of liberalization and globalization, employment in private sector hardly could absorb the labour shed by the public sector. Employment has basically grown very little. We have had development induced displacement with jobless growth. Its consequences have spilled over to the informal sector.

Now what is this 'Informal Sector'? This is the topic of research which I hope some of you take up first through direct surveys to arrive at a more coherent picture. I don't think anyone as yet has much clue about what the Informal Sector is, except that we see it around sprawling around us in cities.

I would venture some characterizations. The first, which conforms to statistics is that, perhaps, more than 50 per cent are self-employed. What does it mean? It means that you can neither say they are wage earners, nor are they profit earners. In case you do not know, this is also now a characteristic of the labour force, perhaps less pronounced in advanced capitalist countries like Germany and a little bit less in France and Italy. There are very large number of self-employed people, most of them are very poor, while some others, a very small section like lawyers, doctors and consultants at the other end, are quite rich. So self-employed is neither in wage labour category nor profit earner, and not all necessarily poor.

The second most important characteristic is that the 'labour unit' is different. When I say that I have got a factory job, what does it mean? It means that I am a contract worker who works for 8–12 hours in a day. I may be heavily exploited, I may not be that heavily exploited but I work for some hours and get wage for it. If we look at the most of the self-employed people, let's say a tea shop owner, the whole labour unit will be the family. In India, you find increasingly piece rate work, a rule rather than exception I think. The whole family works for a given piece of work. Together the family makes a living. If we go outside the cities and look at all the small enterprises in almost any part of India, we will find it more common. Earlier, typically the wife would bring the food, husband would work in field a gender division of labour; but now it is all mixed up in the family labour unit working together with implication for child labour, school hours etc. So the labour unit has changed. It is now the family work rather than an individual effort. It is self-employment neither for profit nor wage category pure.

Since we are in the Giri Institute of Development Studies, Lucknow, we should specially know that it has one very significant implication for traditional labour movements, 'why the grip of political parties and traditional trade unions has weakened over the current labour movements'. A few days ago, I went to Maruti where a long standing struggle was making a history. I talked to some of them who lost their jobs, and I found that none of them belongs to any one of the strict CPI/CPM kind of trade unions, and the others are even less relevant. I come from Bengal, and I know this is even more so when I talked to workers in Bengal. 'The people are losing their politics' that is what we were told. There are very good economic, political and democratic reasons for it. Traditional textbooks will tell you where 'exploitation' comes from. If the neo-classical textbooks say that it is 'marginal productivity of labour', Marxists would say that it is the 'exploitation', in *Capital, Volume-I* of Marx, in the long hours of work. If one pays a labour for six hours and makes him to do 10 hours of work, remaining four hours is the profit. Now, already what I have said, if you just think a minute about it, you will see how it does not work. A small self-employed unit in the informal sector works very long hours, but not one person. They work very long hours but the long hours are done by the family. The small children come back from school and do a couple of hours of work. When husband is not at home, the wife does supplementary income earning through 'chiken' embroidery work in Lucknow. Somebody else takes it to the shop which sub-contracted it and so on. It indicates that you have long hours of work but divided over the whole family although not equally distributed. This is where part of the 'exploitation' and part of the 'profit' of the corporate sector might come from.

The phenomenal growth in corporate sector can be explained only partially from corporate profit that comes from labour exploitation. We are a poor country, we have many disadvantages. However, the government policy in last 20 years has consciously been to give investment incentive to the private corporate sector. The policy is, we will give them virtually free, relatively cheap natural resources – water, land, sea coast, mountain and forest, etc. It naturally got mingled with corruption, like Coal-Gate, 2-G, etc. But one of the conscious policy of our way of liberalization and globalization (and to a large extent China's way) was this: as we start with a disadvantage, we will give these 'cheap' natural resources to our local firms, to our local big business at relatively low rates and this will allow them to invest and compete globally. There is actually a 'paradoxical stride on statistics' but not once you begin to understand what is going on in the process. What happens is that the corporate profit has increased over three to five times in last 20 years. However, if you look at their wealth, it has increased close to 150 times! That is how there has been a phenomenal growth in terms of new dollar multi-billionaires in UP, Gujarat, West Bengal, etc. everywhere irrespective of political party in power. Now what is involved here is something which is quite interesting and which I think has a deep political implications that we have to understand. When you give cheap resources to corporations, it is not much profit, their profit increases to some extent but leave that out as a relatively minor economic matter. More important is the fact that their wealth increase manifold within a short span of time through natural resource transfer. This is where corporate wealth rather than corporate profit is largely made, not by exploiting labour on the shop floor. These labours are still relatively better off compared to those who are dispossessed. If someone is lucky enough to speak some English, he gets a job in corporate sector like in

Bangalore without even having great qualifications and get pretty well off with a share of corporate profit. And his salary may become a lakh of rupees per month, virtually for very simple qualification. He gets a share of those cheap natural resources which are transferred to the corporate. Labour, which Lenin at one stage called 'Labour Aristocracy', does not get the imperialist benefits from outside but from inside the country through colonization of territories of the dispossessed. From my impressionistic guess of a few areas I have visited, about one-third of them are in informal sector. The rest are left in the villages and much worse off. And this is roughly the pattern of 'development with dispossession'. The figure going around is some 20 million people were displaced over last 35–40 years, about half a million per year. Now if this figure is roughly true, we have a large section of citizens in India's representative democracy who are forced out of any development. And some 40–50 per cent are tribals.

Now if we think in terms of what is happening to our democracy, it is not simply corruption but what is happening is something quite different. Marginalization is taking place, of a whole class of people, by changing the livelihood structure of India. This is where we have to come back, because earlier the livelihood structure used to be based largely on natural economy but at the same time it was very largely ecology based. People collected a little bit of forest products; there had been common grazing land for animals, collection of fishes and things of that sort. Look at Punjab and Haryana region, this has almost disappeared. This kind of supporting, about one-third to one-fourth of income with these kinds of livelihoods dwindles. This would be an excellent research topic to find out how natural resource-based income is going down in India over time; or in other words, how all these natural resources, common property resources which used to provide a substantial part of the income in the poorer areas on an average from the few samples which we have, are steadily going down over time. I have been looking for a good study but it does not seem to exist. Often common land belongs to the state and is the easiest land to take over. And this is the marginalization which is going on in terms of loss of livelihood and common property resources. A few of these affected people who are much organized are joining various extremists' movement out of despair. Otherwise, they just linger on. And this is what Prof. Surinder started by saying whether we can do things better with MGNREGA? I don't think government can do it. However, if we can have an 'employment focused growth', for which we should be campaigning, only then we can substitute it. I made some calculations quite seriously during the period of India's high economic growth that suppose we try to transit in 15 years' time to a situation where employment will be provided to almost every able bodied person. You can actually get a growth of 6 per cent over a period of 15 years or so, provided this employment can be productively done. India can do it. This government, IAS and Prime Minister or even the forthcoming Prime Minister can't do it from the above. You can do it only when you allow the villagers to decide what is to be done. The villagers will decide whether they will have a primary school or not have a primary school; have a watershed or not have a watershed. This has to be locally done. This is what I observed when Arvind Kejriwal and I started travelling in many of the panchayats together to see as to what extent it is feasible before he became famous. I have written a book *Development with Dignity* which has only claimed fame of best seller but failed to achieve anything else!

I talked to several MPs and requested one MP to implement the employment guarantee scheme in his area and to allow the villagers, local community and gram sabhas to decide on distribution of money or investment. He listened to me and asked me not to talk like a fool despite being educated with higher degrees! He went on by saying that he did a lot to reach at that level as a Member of Parliament and what would happen to him if he implemented the scheme? It is true that there is a tremendous amount of corruption. Therefore, the local-based schemes which are locally supported to some extent must be decided by the local people.

The failure of the many of development models supported by the big leaders like Anna Hazare, Medha Patekar and Baba Amte in their respective areas is that each of these models has a big leader who does this. Hence, it is not a replicable model at all. Replicable models are those in which local people decide and bring the benefits. There is one example in the world which I have witnessed and where I used to be a professor once. That is Norway where the local people actually did this. The great success of the social democracy in Scandinavian countries in 1920s and 1930s was actually the outcome of people's active participation in decision-making locally about what they wanted. If they did not want a particular thing, they gave in writing about that as a local body. And this actually worked in the early years of Scandinavian social democracy. The second thing which they did was, and which I am going to end by saying, that they decided not to pay 'higher personal wages' but higher 'social wages' through public works. Initially, the social democrats decided to provide social wages by sending all children to local schools and ensured that local schools would be of good quality through personal interests of the parents. It also mandated that anybody who was a representative of the people would travel for work in public transport. In Delhi, this idea was converted into a joke by the Chief Minister of Delhi who claimed he was against VIP culture and went public on whether he should stay in a bigger or smaller house, both absurdly large for 'aam admi' and then increased the salary some four times of all his elected party colleagues! What we need instead is what social democracy did in Scandinavian countries. For 10 to 20 years their popularity was based on the notion that if you are an elected representative of people, you will have to use only public amenities, schools, transport, etc. If the representatives of the people travel by bus or if their children study in local schools, you will immediately see how things will begin to change. These things are not very difficult to do, but it is easier to talk of corruption, terrorism or class struggle, while the corporate sector monopolizes natural resources through their model of development with the help of the state apparatus.

# 2

# Democracy, Development and Subaltern

## *Radical Agrarian Movement in Bihar*

**B.N. PRASAD**

Historically Indian rural society has witnessed three dominant ways of social development: through legislative measures by the Indian State, Gandhian way of social reconstruction, and mainstream Communist model. These models will be analysed separately to assess structural limitations and their resultant impact on beyond institutional agrarian struggles for socio-economic equity and social justice.

India inherited massive poverty, galloping unemployment, staggering infrastructure, stagnating economy, and starving millions from her colonial regime. After Independence it was an urgent need to 'decolonize' the country and revitalize the Indian economy. First postcolonial national agenda was 'decolonization' and 'economic modernization' to achieve self-reliance, elimination of poverty and unemployment. The new national agenda was guided by twin imperatives of nation-building and state-maintenance, as depicted by the Nehruvian approach (Kumar, 1989: 89). The Indian state accepted capitalist postulates as the axis of economic development and modernization (Desai, 1961 and 1969). Leadership adopted this path to achieve: (i) national integration, (ii) self-reliance, and (iii) rapid economic growth (Nehru, 1958). In order to realize the twin objectives of 'decolonization' and 'development', Indian State initiated various measures which brought about perceptible changes in socio-economic and political structure of agrarian India.

### Agrarian Transformation in Independent India

Withdrawal of colonial power brought about far-reaching changes in the Indian society in general and primary sector in particular. Modern Indian State became more uniform and cohesive, both politically and administratively. Central and state governments implemented multi-pronged measures to transform agrarian society. Introduction of adult franchise and Panchayati Raj transformed political life of the people. Whereas, Land Reform Measures, National Extension Services, Community Development Programmes, legislative measures to eliminate feudal mode of exploitations and development of agriculture on capitalist line, all were directed to change the economic structure of rural India (Desai, 1986: 16–19).

Zamindari abolition and related policies created two contradictory trends in the agrarian structure. As per government rules, the tenants could secure ownership of land by paying compensation to concerned landlords, which was often beyond the capacity of poor tenants. As a result, majority of the poor tenants denied ownership, lost tenurial security and became non-owning proletariat. On the other side, rich tenants not only acquired bulk of the ownership, due to better economic status, but also accepted capitalist postulates as the axis of agrarian development and modernisation. Thus, government measures created an expanding class of capitalist land owners. On the other, started the process of proletarianization of poor tenants and sub-tenants, thereby converting them into a new kind of bonded labour rooted in capitalist mode of production. This, in turn, sharply changed agrarian class relations and played decisive role in shaping social profile of rural India (ibid.).

Modern Indian agrarian classes can be divided into four major categories: rich farmers and landlords comprising 7 per cent of Indian population possess 50 per cent of total land. Middle farmers possess 30 per cent land and constitute 19 per cent of the population. Whereas poor farmers possess 17 per cent but comprising 30 per cent of the population, and agricultural labourers have just 2 per cent of land but they form 44 per cent of Indian population (ibid., 22). These figures show that 7 per cent of dominant rural population possess 50 per cent of total cultivable land, as against 74 per cent of lower population having a meagre of 19 per cent. Still the data do not provide clear picture of horrifying agrarian situation, which should be viewed in terms of the quality of lands; dry and wet, together with other factors. As per estimates of NSSO (48th and 59th rounds); almost 61 per cent of Indian rural households are either landless or having less than 1 acre of land, which is 73.50 per cent in the case of Bihar (Rawal, 2008: 46); 70th round of NSSO estimates show that extent of landlessness at all India level is 42.2 per cent which is 49.5 per cent in the case of Bihar. Inequality of ownership has further deteriorated over the years.

Bihar, the second most populous state, is economically one of the most backward and least growing regions of India. Rural population of the state has marginally declined from 89.5 per cent in 2001 to 88.7 per cent in 2011, but at the all India level this figure has substantially declined from 72.2 per cent to 68.8 per cent during the same period (Census of India, 2001 and 2011). Thus, Bihar with almost 89 per cent of rural population is one of the most 'ruralized' states of the country, where large segment of its population is dependent on agrarian sector for their livelihoods. But among the major states of India, Bihar has the lowest per capita (rural) income from agriculture, and lowest per capita foodgrains production. In almost all respects of agricultural development, Bihar is near bottom among the Indian states (Sharma, 1987: 26). Reasons for this extreme backwardness are both institutional and technological. Industrial base is quite weak in the state. There had been hardly any industrial growth in last four and a half odd decades. Bihar which had achieved an average annual growth rate of 18 per cent in industrial employment during 1951–61, slide down to 0.7 per cent during 1961–81 (ibid., 22). Even in the recent years, share of manufacturing sector in the state economy has been quite low, i.e. 5.31 per cent during 1993–94, which has further declined to 3.13 per cent in 2004–05. Similarly, share of total secondary sector has also declined from 9.92 per cent in 1993–94 to 9.02 per cent in 2004–05 (Economic Survey, 2007: 5). This trend shows that rural population of the state has been excessively depending on primary sector. This is also evident from the fact that, work force in agrarian sector in Bihar is 73.5 per cent as against 54.6 per cent in India in 2011. In the non-agrarian sector work participation is 26.5 per cent in Bihar, much lower than the all Indian figure of 45.4 per cent during the same period (Census of India, 2011). Above trend has obvious impact on agrarian sector of the state. Due to massive rural population, weak industrial base and stagnating agriculture, pressure on land is quite high, which led to continued division and sub-division of land and deteriorating landman ratio. This resulted into emergence of huge landless and unemployed rural population, which in turn sharpened the agrarian class contradiction.

However, with increasing number of agrarian proletariat and deepening of their hardship, they became more and more desperate. Under the impact of new politico-economic and other forces, lower strata are becoming aware of the true nature of their problems. This led to sharpening conflicts among and between newly emerging proprietary classes and pauperised and proletarianized masses. This in turn, resulted in various types of agrarian struggles. These struggles can be broadly divided into two distinct categories. The movements launched by newly emerged proprietary classes, together with prosperous middle peasant and streamlined landlords. The main aim is to secure more assistance and facilities from the government, and derive maximum benefits from developmental measures. The second category of movements, launched by agrarian poor, is where agrarian proletariat acquired central place (Desai, 1986: 32). These movements are directed against proprietary classes and various forms of exploitations, terror and violence. These are qualitatively different from movements of the first category. Struggles of rural poor not only question efficacy and morality of modern socio-economic framework, but also expose inability of developmental measures to mitigate their vulnerable conditions (Desai, 1969: 24). These struggles exhort for radical social change and transfer of power from dominant class to the toiling masses, i.e. movements seek change *beyond* the institutional framework.

Historically, agrarian movements are not a recent phenomenon in Bihar. There were isolated cases of peasant uprisings, such as Santhal insurrection of 1855–56, Munda uprising of 1899–1901 and Indigo riots of 1867, 1877 and 1907 (Sinha, 1965). By the end of 1920, peasantry of Bihar were not only getting aware of their right on land, but also becoming integral part of the anti-colonial struggle. It was more so because peasant's land question was inextricably linked with nationalist movement (Johnson, 1962). Gandhiji was aware about vital reality that peasant nationalism could be used to overthrow British regime. It was due to this fact that Gandhi launched first Non-Cooperation movement in 1921, after two successful experiments with peasant question – Champaran Satyagraha (Prasad, 1949: 24) and Khera Gujarat (Hardiman, 1977: 72).

## Gandhian Way of Social Reconstruction

Gandhi's 'non-violent approach' falls in the realm of social change and progress coupled with social equity: 'Sarvodaya and Antodaya' (Gandhi, 1967 and 1909). *Ashrams* were the centres of action and practice to train cadre for social reconstruction. Voluntary works were carried out on the basis of self-renunciation and constructive actions (Thomson, 1993: 38–39). Non-violent passive resistance *(satyagraha)* proved to be an effective experiment for collective consolidation of social forces against injustice and for reconstruction of society.

Gandhi came to India in 1915 with his experience of non-violent struggle and *satyagraha* in South Africa, which remained focal point of his socio-political movement. His first involvement with mass movement in India was Champaran Farmers movement in 1917, against injustice. This laid foundation of anti-British struggle, which was subsequently known as the Gandhian movement. In Champaran, he courageously defied the order of the British government and became hero for thousands of the people who witnessed this defiance.

Achārya Vinoba Bhave carried out Gandhi's unfinished task of reconstruction of villages for *Gram Swaraj*, which is poor man's *swaraj* where, 'no one is to be the first and none the last' (Gandhi, 1956: 76 and 100).

## Post-Gandhian Social Mobilization for Rural Reconstruction

After Gandhi; Vinoba Bhave emerged as the most important leader of the non-violence philosophy for social reconstruction. His *Sarvodaya* approach was for the development of society in general and rural society in particular, which was in tune with the Gandhian model of rural reconstruction. This philosophy was based on the proposition that land of the village is a common resource accessible to all for productive use. As natural leader of the *Sarvodaya* movement, he established *Akhil Bhartiya Sarva Seva Sangh* (ABSSS, here on wards) in 1948. Viewing inequality as the most serious problem, he started a campaign of land gift from Pochampalli in Telangana of Andhra Pradesh for redistribution of land among the poor on 18 April 1951. This campaign received wider attention and developed into *Bhoodan* and *Gramdan* movement (Iyengar, 2007). All the constructive organizations: Charkha Sangh, Talimi Sangh, Khadhi and Gramodyog Sangh, Harijan Sevak Sangh, etc. were integrated to work for *Bhoodan* movement. Basic idea behind this merger was to integrate constructive work programmes with the movement, and the programmes should come through movement, which may sustain for longer time to rebuild society.

*Bhoodan* movement found its origin in the Telangana movement, where poor peasants and landless labourers had launched powerful armed struggle against landlords on land question from 1946. Many landlords had lost their life, and were restless for a mediator to save their life at a cost of few hectares of land. Vinoba was very much aware of the inequality in land distribution and inherent contradiction therein. He took initiatives to resolve this contradiction through gift campaign – *Bhoodan.* Vinoba succeeded in persuasion of the poor peasants to compromise with landlords *in lieu of* land gift. This event provided a clue to Vinoba to resolve land question through gift campaign. He then launched land gift campaign in other parts of the country, response to which was very encouraging. Gandhian took it as a starting point of non-violent revolution to solve the most complicated land issue of India. They did not see any possibility of initiating simultaneous process of non-violent struggle for rural reconstruction other than Bhoodan. This movement was well-received by the people of India. In conference of ABSSS at Sevapuri, UP movement was declared as the movement of ABSSS, and all the activists of the ABSSS were involved in the movement (Rahi, 1977). All other activities were sidelined, which ultimately were allowed to die their natural death. The second phase of *Bhoodan* was started as *Gramdan* (gift of village) at Mangroth in UP on 24 April 1952, to dissolve ownership of land in the village assembly, 'Gramdan was foundation over which superstructures of khadi and Shanti Sena had to be erected, thus completing building of village swaraj' (Choudhary, 1970: 66). Gradually this campaign reached to the block, district, and state (Bihar) level. The objective of the movement was to establish a Sarvodaya order of direct and participatory democracy, which alone can ensure freedom, equality, and justice to all the members of the community (Deo, 1962). *Toofan Gramdan* (village gift storm) was started to achieve a wider coverage of *Gramdan. Bhoodan* movement was at its peak from 1951 to 1957, like a reminiscent of political movements led by Gandhi. But in terms of realization, against the target of 50 million acres, the movement's achievement was modest. Only 4.3 million acres could be received in *Bhoodan* as *dana,* which was 8.53 per cent of total target (Iyengar, 2007: 407). One of the major criticisms of the movement is that donors had cheated the movement by donating such land that were either unfit for cultivation or was under serious dispute about titles. More than 44 per cent of donated land was not available for redistribution and cultivation. Further, land redistribution norm of Bhoodan movement was 5 acres per landless family. But data suggests that the all India average land per grantee was 2.63 acres (ibid., 410). Thus, the movement, by and large, failed to redistribute land to landless families as per the norms originally envisaged. When the radical posture of *Bhoodan-Gramdan* reached its stagnation because negotiation and persuasion became almost difficult (Deo, 1962: 3), Vinoba launched *Sulabh Gramdan* (simplified gift) campaign after Raipur Conference of ABSSS in 1963 to attract donors to part with one-twentieth land for *Bhoodan.* These campaigns reached their climax in 1969 at Rajgir Conference of ABSSS in Bihar. In this conference, Vinoba stopped his direct guidance and involvement in this campaign and asked workers to continue their work on their own. *Bhoodan-Gramdan* had broadly three phases: (i) *Prapti* (receipt of gift), (ii) *Pushti* (follow-up for verification), and (iii) *Nirman* (course of reconstruction) (ibid., 6). Most of the Gandhian organizations were actively engaged in constructive works of Gramdan area for village development (Choudhary, 19970: 29).

*Bhoodan* achieved its historic targets, which could not be found elsewhere in the world (Chandra, 1997: 98). Initially it sounded as a panacea for most of the stalwarts of peace movement to resolve the issues of inequality in distribution of land. It was achieved to the extent land was received (quality of land and litigations of titles were in question). But task of distribution of land was given to government, which caused alienation of Sarvodaya workers and poor peasants both. Beneficiaries were identified by government agencies, but any inconsistency emerging out of distribution process went to the discredit to Sarvodaya workers. Thus *Bhoodan* movement, which was initiated as *Karuna,* ultimately converted into *Kanoon*; and more often than not in every state *Kanoon* did not adhere to *Karuna.* Moreover, vision of *Pushti* and *Nirman* was yet to be developed adequately among workers. Therefore, to sustain *Bhoodan-Gramdan* movement became difficult even in the lifetime of Vinoba, and he took retreat from Saharsa (Bihar). Later this movement was reduced to insignificance and now it is not even acknowledged as a measure of land reforms (Gangrade, 1997: 93–95). Furthermore, noble idea of integrating all constructive programmes for Bhoodan and extract programmes from the movement could not be realized. As a result, effectiveness of the organization was lost because of discontinuity. Vinoba himself raised many issues related to assessment of the outcome (Bhave, 2000: 10).

India has a long tradition to build non-violent and peaceful progressive society. Since the ages of Vedas, to Buddha, Kabir, and till the Gandhian way of social reconstruction, all are in continuity with great Indian tradition. *Bhoodan* movement generated social consciousness on land issue, but could not be sustained due to inherent contradictions. Movement was lost in the process, largely because of half-backed plan of land gift campaign and lack of subsequent follow-up actions. The struggle came under severe criticism by the communists, who put forward alternative thesis for agrarian social transformation.

## Role of Mainstream Political Parties

A number of upsurges erupted in the country in 1930s and particularly after Second World War. Struggles launched by Kisan Sabha against Tenancy Bill and Bakasht movement, Telangana and Srikakulam struggles, anti-feudal struggles in princely states, were some of them. Many parties were formed to guard the interest of rural poor – beginning from Kisan Sabha, to the *Khet Mazdur* Union led by CPI, Bihar Provincial Khet Mazdur Sabha by Jagjiwan Ram, Khet Mazdur Panchayat by Socialists, All India Khetihar Mazdur Sangha by Congress, Sarvodaya movement, etc. yet they all failed to redress basic economic hardships of the agrarian poor. However, Vinoba Bhave's *Bhoodan* was to be the *Sarvodaya* answer to Communist challenge on the land problem and was meant to achieve what legislative actions could not do. Although *Bhoodan-Gramdan* movement generated a social awareness about agrarian issue in India, but in terms of its announced aims, the movement was an abortive experiment (Oommen, 1972).

Even Indian Communists rarely accorded sufficient weight to the poor peasants and landless labourers in their organizational strategy and revolutionary mobilisation. A.K. Gopalan (1968), veteran peasant leader of CPM emphasized: 'We have to make landless labourers the hub of our activities. Reluctance to take up their specific demands, fearing that this will drive the rich and middle peasants away from us, will have to be given up ... (Gopalan, 1968)'. CPI also stressed somewhat similar unity strategy (Communist Party of India, 1967: 220). Thus, all political parties – Congress, Socialist, Communists – shared a common predilection, i.e. making the widest possible social constituency. This may be the logical corollary of involvement in electoral politics, where political expediency is the primary motive rather than ideological commitment (Oommen, 1985: 10). It is this violent reality of the countryside that radical ideology and movement found propitious grounds in late 1960s and early 1970s (Sengupta, 1982a).

In postcolonial era, struggle of Dalit labourers *(mazdur)* have intensified throughout India since 1966–67, which are different from *kisan's* anti-*zamindari* struggle. Demands of new struggle are those that have been demands of the *Mazdur* movement from the beginning – statutory minimum wages, end of forced labour and *vethbegar,* redistribution of excess land, prestige of rural poor, etc. The minusculer peasant revolt in Naxalbari (1967) was a pointer to the proposition that neither *Sarvodaya* approach nor legislative process (in which communists had begun to participate after abandoning the tactic of armed struggle) had solved the agrarian problem. There have been many Naxalbari since. These struggles not only reject the Indian Parliamentary system, but also use extra-constitutional means to achieve the People's Democratic Revolution through People's War linked to an agrarian programme (Banerjee, 1984: ii-iii). However, Maoist perspective in Indian Communist movement began with Telangana struggle. Over 20 years later, re-emergence of Maoist trend in the 'Naxalbari', albeit in changed context, marks the return of 'Telangana line'. Naxalite sparks in West Bengal prepared propitious ground for agrarian radicalism in Bihar as well.

## Bihar Peasantry and Maoist Movement

With the formation of CPI (M-L) Party on Lenin's birth anniversary (22 April 1969), tactics of Communist revolutionaries took a new cutting edge in different parts of the country. Party emerged in Bihar as well and tried to utilize turmoil among poor agrarian class. Naxalite movement in the state has two phases. First phase was from 1967 to 1971. During these years, Naxalite presence was marked in north and southern parts of Bihar. Second phase that began in 1973, influence of the movement is greater in central and south-central regions of the state. But in current phase, especially in post-emergency period, the struggle is most intense and vigorous in central Bihar.

## First Phase of the Movement

Radical activities started in Bihar even before the formation of CPI (ML). First such activity was reported in July 1967 in Thankurganj of Prnea district in north

Bihar (The Indian Nation, 1967). But first activity under the leadership of CPI (ML) was started in April 1969 at a village called Gangapur of Muzaffarpur district in north Bihar. Very soon Gangapur emerged as an epitome of fighting peasantry. Within a short span of time movement spread like wildfire in north Bihar and Chotanagpur.[1]

## Radical Activities in North Bihar

Struggle in Muzaffarpur district (Gangapur) had origin in a movement on economic issue, launched by Kisan Sangram Samiti and backed by Bihar State Coordination Committee of Communist Revolutionaries. Samiti seized land of local landlord, Bijli Singh; and harvested *Arahar* crops from the land. Landlord not only attacked peasants with his henchmen but also instituted cases. Unlike past, this time leaders of the movement refused to surrender before the authority and went underground. This was followed by the phase of intense organization by the Samiti and preparation of peasantry for future armed struggle (Singh, 1969). Police camps were set-up in the area and thousands of armed policemen were let loose on the villagers. In Harkesh village, on 23 August 1969, thousands of peasants fought a pitched battle with police and managed to rescue some of their comrades earlier arrested by police.

With direct intervention of State's machinery, leaders of movement felt that phase of open confrontation and pitched battles with landlords and police combined was over. 'Guerrilla Warfare' seemed to be the viable alternative. With change in tactics struggle assumed some sort of sharpness. Revolutionaries stepped up their 'annihilation campaign' and stressed for underground activities. Police, landlords, moneylenders continued to be the targets of 'annihilation campaign.' In Mushahari, by September 1969, guerrillas conducted three attacks in a small period of one and a half months, killed 5 and injured 15 landlords and their agents, burnt land notes and documents of land deeds worth lakhs of rupees, seized landlords' properties (ibid.). Rebels intensified their struggle and carried out attacks in two other places – Paru and Baruraj, in Muzaffarpur district. By June 1969, police force cracked down upon rebels and tried to implement 'encirclement' and 'suppression' policy. Now leadership changed its tactics; smaller guerrilla units were the need of the hour.

The struggle reached up to Dharbhanga and Saharsa district of north Bihar, borders of Bihar and Nepal. This had strategic advantages. During that period, peasant struggles under the leadership of Maoist Communists were also taking place in Nepal. Across Bihar border in the east, in Naxalite area, North Bengal-Bihar Border Regional Committee of CPI (ML) was active during first phase of the movement. Their activities were spilling over into Purnea district. During 1950s, Purnea had witnessed militant movement of peasantry, particularly of sharecroppers, under leadership of CPI and socialists. But the movement was lost by 1960s as it was locked up in the labyrinth of legalism under CPI leadership. In 1970s, Naxalite movement made little headway in this district. On 4 November 1970, nearly 400 military-police launched operation in Munger district, where seven big landlords and moneylenders had been killed earlier.

Large scale operations and arrests followed throughout the state. By January 1971, police had thrown about 1,500 CPI (ML) alleged activists and sympathizers behind bars, 200 of them were from Jamshedpur, the steel town, where party was trying to build its units among the workers (Banerjee, 1980: 288).

## Naxalite Activities in Chotanagpur

During first phase of the movement, West Bengal-Bihar Border Regional Committee of CPI (ML) was active. Its area of operation extended up to Santhalpargana, Birbhum, Singhbhum and deep southern parts of Bihar. Their activities were concentrated mainly among tribal population, but it had strong base among workers, especially in steel town of Jamshedpur. Ranchi and Singhbhum districts were stormy centres during early part of 1970s. It is important to note that Chotanagpur region remained centre of turbulent uprisings throughout the 19th century. In 1820s, *Ho* tribal rose against British rulers, local moneylenders and landlords. *Oraons* rebelled in 1820, 1832 and 1890. *Kol* organized an insurrection in 1831–32, which was mainly directed against government officials and private moneylenders (Datta, 1970: 39). Most interesting aspect of these struggles was that the tactics adopted by the rebels foreshadow in many respects the methods of 'guerrilla warfare' fashioned by Mao-Tsetung. It was in these areas that Naxalites found fertile ground and penetrated among tribal population. Quite interestingly, Naxalbari, where first uprising took place in 1967, was also inhabited by Santhal tribe.

Hills of Chotanagpur caught headlines of the daily newspapers in May 1970, when 54 revolutionary young men and women were arrested by Bihar Police, along with a British lady Miss Mary Tyler, in Jaduguda jungle (Banerjee, 1980: 218). Jamshedpur emerged as 'Little Calcutta' mainly because of growing radical activities in the town. S.N. Singh, a trade union leader in the steel town, provided local leadership and important Naxalite leaders from Midnapur helped in establishing radical ideology and activity in the town. By 1970, three-fourth of police machinery was engaged in tackling Naxalites and only one-fourth was left to look after routine jobs (ibid.: 72). In rural areas of Singhbhum, Naxalites were active in the region bordering Gopiballavpur of West Bengal. This led to posting of two companies of Bihar military police all through areas bordering West Bengal. After Singhbhum, Ranchi was second stormy centre of radical activities in Chotanagpur during 1970s. There were four main areas of their activities – Kolebira in Simdega sub-division, bordering Orissa; Mandar, Burmu and Khelar on Palamu-Hazaribagh border; Silli on Ranchi-Purulia road, and Ranchi town itself. In Dhanbad district, Naxalites were active among student community mainly during 1970–71. In BIT-Sindri many movements had been organized. Students of Jharia took out a procession to protest against police firing in Calcutta University in September 1970. Besides killing landlords, moneylenders, threatening several *kulaks* in rural areas, number of government offices and properties had been damaged by radicals of the region. By 1970, all districts of Bihar, barring Bhojpur and central Bihar, had seen indignant landless peasants and impatient students taking up arms. Between January–July 1970, police arrested 954 Naxalite suspects, number being highest at 468 in Singhbhum district, followed by Muzaffarpur with 170, Munger 102 and Champaran with 88 (Sinha, 1977: 270).

First phase of the movement started petering out by 1971. Rapid expansion of base areas, formation and expansion of people's militia, politicization and arming guerrilla squads are some of the most important conditions for success of radical movements. In spite of courage and devotion shown by rank-and-file, the movement failed on several fronts. It appears that in almost all places, Naxalites failed to mobilize substantial number of poor and landless peasants. As a result, number of guerrilla squads remained static and masses of peasantry remained passive spectators. Naxalite activity could not move beyond the stage of individual annihilation. Formation of People's Liberation Army, mobilization of toiling masses and transforming them into a people's militia, collection of firearms, and formation of guerrilla squads remained elusive. Even so influence of the movement was confined to few pockets of power. Thus, first phase of the movement came to an early end by 1972 under might force of Indian State, and above strategically mistakes (Banerjee, 1984: 357–58).

But, ever growing tension and contradictions could not be contained for long by state power and concession policy of the government. By 1973, Central Bihar[2] started sending green signals to Maoism. *Chauri* incident in Bhojpur district, transformed the district from 'Haryana' of Bihar to 'Naxalbari' of the state (Sinha, 1975). The year 1974 marked an upswing in Naxalite activities. Encounters took place more frequently than before. By 1975, nine out of 16 blocks of Bhojpur were under effective control of Naxalism [CPI (ML) Document, 1986: 26].

## Radical Struggle in Central Bihar

The spread of Maoist activities in the region came at a time when in other areas movement was petering out. Bitter peasant-police encounter at Chauri village of Bhojpur district in May 1973 made the existence of radical struggle led by Maoists a common knowledge (Mukherjee and Kala, 1978). In the current phase, Bhojpur emerged as an epicentre of Bihar, from where revolutionary peasant movement has proliferated in other parts of the state.

### *Maoist Activities in Bhojpur*

Construction of Sone Canal in 19th century and relative modernization of agriculture in the region led to two consequences – emergence of *Junker* and *Kulak* elements and loosening of 'patron-client' relationship, and differentiation within peasantry and depeasantization at the lowest level. This led to emergence of huge army of unemployed landless labourers. Some of them were absorbed in primary sector as contractual labour, but majority of them were forced to external migration for subsistence. This process had impact at two levels. At the economic level, it led to development of 'money-order' economy, and at socio-cultural level, this led to exposure to the 'more modern non-rural world.' This in turn, heightened the sense of relative deprivation among toiling masses, perception about extent of their misery and search of their social identity. Together with above factors, higher level of literacy (Das, 1983: 250) and militancy as dominant way of life in the area (Jha et al., 1985: 22) easily opened doors for radical politics and ideology. Influential Naxalite leaders, like Satyanarayan Singh, Kesho Prasad Singh, etc. were joined by grassroot leader Jagdish Mahto, who had been forced into Naxalism by landlords' themselves (Das, 1983: 248–49). They organized mass meetings, demonstrations and rallies to protest against oppression of Harijans and poor peasants. Thus, discontents of marginalized masses got interwoven with Marxist-Leninist-Maoist ideology, which led trail of violence in Bhojpur.

Naxalite activities in Bhojpur began to occur in Sahar area since 1971. Ekwari was starting point, but Chauri incidence caught headlines of major newspapers and transformed the district into Naxalbari of Bihar. The state supported landlords and proclaimed that it was ready to fight 'insurgency' in Bhojpur. Excessive police repression was launched on poor and landless labourers, mostly Musahars and Chamars (Mukherjee and Yadav, 1980: 121–25).

The year 1974 witnessed growing radical activities and peasant-police encounters took place more frequently than before. In 1974, 80 cases were recorded compared to eight, seven and 10 in 1971, 1972 and 1973. But 1975 was the bloodiest year in the district. Police-peasant encounters in Hanuman Chapra and Piro on 3 April, Dullamchak and Sahar on 14 April, Bahuara on 2 July, Bahubandh and Sahar on 28 November left a lingering trail of blood. Intensity and magnitude of the movement can be gauged by the fact that in Sahar block entire population of poor peasants and agricultural labourers had believed to have joined movement. Till 10 July 1975, *thana*-wise villages under grip of the movement were: Sahar-39, Sandesh-29, Piro-23, Tarai-15, Jagdishpur–6, Nawanagar–6, Udwantnagar–6, and Berhampur–5.

National emergency had been imposed in 1975. This provided the state force a *carte blanche*. It could arrest anyone, kill and ransack any village, without the least fear of exposure in press or of democratic opinion. It was during that period Bhojpur police launched 'Operation Thunder' in May 1976 (CPI (ML) Document, 1986: 24). Motive was to liquidate Naxalites and their strongholds. Most of important leaders – Jagdish Mahto, Rameshwar Ahir, Fagu Mahto, Chamku Musahar Rajendra Yadav, Narayan Kavi were killed. Leaders like Prabhu Harijan and Rameshwar Dusadh were detained. Simultaneously, there emerged well-knit landlord syndicates, which terrorized peasants into submission and cut off potential sources of recruitment for movement (Kala, Maharaj and Mukherjee, 1986). Movement suffered severe losses and lost much of its intensity by 1976.

In the wake of lifting of the black curtain of emergency, central Bihar region saw veritable upheaval of peasantry. According to critics of 'Total Revolution', JP movement contributed substantially towards Maoist struggle in post-Emergency period. Rank-and-files of JP movement got totally disillusioned with the democratic revolution. This was an abortive experiment in terms of its announced goals. Maoist movement was taking its firm roots in central Bihar, during the same period. This attracted a large number of middle class youth, who formed the backbone of 1974 movement. Many of them are today important functionaries of Maoist parties and its mass organizations.

This is evident from the fact that central Bihar region saw a renewed peasant activism during 1977–80. These years saw emergence of a host of mass organizations, such as Bihar Pradesh Kisan Sabha, Indian People's Front, Sangharsha Samitis, Jan Kalyan Samitis, Mazdoor-Kisan Sangharsha Samitis, etc. in different parts of rural Bihar [CPI (ML) Document, 1986: 172]. With these new initiatives movement revitalized itself, and by 1981–82, it took 26 out of 38 districts of Bihar under its fold, with different degrees of intensity. The movement engulfed 52 blocks of the states, out of which 41 are located in seven contiguous districts of central Bihar. Intensity and magnitude of movement transformed the region into 'The Flaming Fields of Bihar (ibid., 67).

It is interesting to note that during the same period landed gentry launched *caste senas* to maintain their hegemonic position, which was effectively threatened by Naxalite onslaught in central Bihar region. Bhoomi Sena, Lorik Sena, Kuer Sena, Brahmarshi Sena, etc. were formed mostly in mid-1980s.

## Threat to Hegemony and Roots of the Movement

Statutory minimum wage, redistribution of surplus and *gair mazarua* land, *izzat* (prestige) of rural poor and quest to participate in electoral process are some of the main issues of Maoist movement in the region. Radical assertion of toiling masses has brought forward these issues and contested feudal forms of exploitation. Maoist groups are not only enforcing fair wages and just shares in *bataidari,* but also social humiliation of Dalits and *samant vichar* of *maliks* has been successfully challenged. Let us focus upon kind of challenges put forward by Maoist movement in the region.

## Economic Threat

Fair wages, equitable share in *bataidari* and redistribution of surplus land are most important economic agenda of Maoist Movement. Both categories of agricultural labourers (*lagua* and *chhutta)* worked within a highly exploitative framework of production relations. In many parts of central Bihar wages were very low. For example, normal daily wage in Rohtas was 4 kg of rice, whereas in Patna, Gaya and Jehanabad wages varied from 2 kg to 2.5 kg of rice, a *harwaha's* wages were even lower (PUDR Report, 1992: 9). Variations in wages depend upon ability of landed gentry to arrest the rise in wages as well as to prevent migration of the agricultural labourers. This ability depends upon organized strength of dominant landowners and extent to which they can exercise this power. On the other side, various radical groups with their mass fronts have organized rural poor around issues of fair wages and just shares in *bataidari,* and posed formidable challenge to landed gentry of the region. The 1980s saw a considerable expansion of Maoist's influence in central Bihar. One of the possible explanations may be that most of the mass fronts of radical groups were formed in post-emergency period [CPI (ML), Party Unity Report, 1993: 12–13]. It is also interesting to note that almost all Senas of landed gentry came into existence in 1980s. However, real wages for male and female both started rising by early 1970s. The rise was quite pronounced from 1970–71 to 1988–89: 55.2 per cent increase for male and 74.3 per cent for female (Sharma, 1987: 16). Maoist organizations have been instrumental through numerous strikes and struggles (PUDR Report, 1992: 16).

Amount of grains, quantity of *sattu* (coarse grain or pulses which are roasted and grounded) and size of *panja*[3] are three main issues of wage struggle in the region. Places where struggle for higher wages has been own, size of *panja* has become a contentious issue. Due to increasing cost of production, landlords are shifting towards *bataidari* system of production. Now, struggles in these areas are centred on just and equitable shares between *bataidars* and *maliks*. *Bataidars* demand that landowners should provide seeds, fertilizers and bear half of irrigation cost. At the harvest, both should get equal shares but *bataidar* is entitled to *panja*. Further, landowner's attempt to pass on cost of the *malguzari* tax is resisted. In some areas, where Maoist movement is strong, *maliks* find it difficult to get *bataidars* (ibid.: 17). This has further weakened landed gentry and sharpened agrarian contradictions. 'Men and Barsiwan' carnage (PUCL, 1992) by Savarna Liberation Front and 'Baran' massacre (ibid.: 24–26) by Maoist Communist Centre (MCC) were centred on wage struggle. Central Bihar plain is full of such bloody clashes where one group seeks change in existing social order, other to maintain status-quo at any cost. Government, political parties, bureaucracy, electronic and print media all have become implicated in this conflict.

Apart from introduction of Green Revolution technology and marginal developments in irrigation, government of Bihar has not taken any substantial developmental projects in primary sector. Industrial base is quite weak here. Agriculture is main source of livelihood and majority of the working population depends on cultivation. Large landowners are rare in region. Only 4 per cent households own little more than 10 acres, 90 per cent own less than 5 acres of land or are landless (ILO and A.N. Sinha Institute of Social Sciences, 1991). This data has further deteriorated over the years due to ever increasing population and deteriorated land-man ratio in the region. With the impact of Green Revolution and shift to highly profitable cultivation of wheat, etc. more and more common and wastelands have been acquired by dominant castes/classes. On the other side, land hungry poor peasants and landless labourers launched powerful struggles, under guidance of Maoist groups, to seize illegal possession of *gair mazarua* land hitherto held by *maliks*. For Dalits; traditionally denied land ownership, acquiring land ownership rights (even uneconomical) is a symbol of social prestige apart from material benefit.

Maoist groups in central Bihar are actively engaged in the seizure of surplus and *gain mazarua* lands. In 1992, landless Dalits claimed 1000 acres of surplus land in Jalpura of Patna district. Rural poor seized 616 acres of excess land and *gair mazarua* land from 28 June 1993 to 5 July 1993 in Panki block of Palamau district. MCC has seized 4500 acres in Gaya district alone; 1000 acres of land has been seized by MCC and IPF in Nawada district. In fact, monthly publications of Maoist parties are full of such instances.

Increasing pressure on land in the stagnating economy has not only accelerated rate of fragmentation of land, but also weakened landed gentry from within. Landless agricultural labourers often resort to *kam bandh,* i.e. boycott to work in *maliks* land, under guidance of Maoist groups. This strategy is so frightening due to ensuing economic hardship that *maliks* have succumbed to pressure in number of cases. Where landed gentry resorted to force, their lands remained fallow for many years. 'Cansara Carnage' and aftermath (Janwadi Mukti Marg, 1994: 23–24) is one such example. Struggles for fair wages, just shares in *bataidari,* forcefully redistribution of surplus and *gair mazarua* land, and *kam bandh* have weakened landed gentry and threatened the feudal basis of exploitation.

## Social Challenge

The substance of oppression and basis of polarization of rural society are not explicable only in economistic terms. Exercise of power crucially revolves around assertion of social status – subordination of others through a denial of self-respect and a life of dignity. Caste identities condition pattern and process of differentiation. These identities could erect contradictions within each class or forge alliances across them. What is meant is that propensity to exploit and oppress rural poor is not associated with large land holdings alone. Complex nature of rural power relations can be viewed through interaction pattern of oppressors and oppressed. Oppressors are those who trample upon dignity of labourers, deny them access to land, force them to work for low wages and subjecting them to humiliating practices. Employers having these characteristics are locally called as *zamindars* or *samants;* and their mentality may be characterized as feudal mentality or *samant vichar.* It is this *samant vichar,* which led to *'Men* and *Barsiwan* carnage' in 1992 by Savarna Liberation Front, which finally culminated into 'Baran Massacre' by MCC, where 36 *bhumihars* were killed (PUDR Report, 1992: 13–14 and 25–26). However, *samant vichar* and *rangdar* mentality is not an isolated case at *Baran.* In fact, whole central Bihar region is infected with such a worldview shared by the dominant castes/classes. Caste oppression further accentuates the condition.

Stark nature of socio-economic discrimination is reflected in very structure of village settlements. Harijan *tola* is always on outskirts, invariably to south of the main settlement. Harijan *tolas* are centre of productive activity but are marginal to society. They jokingly say that we live in South Africa, dark land south of main settlement marked for cremation.

Dalits wearing shirt or watch, living in *pucca* house, playing radio, sitting on coat in front of upper caste(s), were perceived as threat to feudal domination. Abduction, rape and sexual abuse of dalit womenfolk were legitimate ways of social interaction. Feudal norms legitimized social custom like *dola,* which make obligatory to the Dalit brides to spend their wedding night with local *malik* (Kala, Maharaj and Mukherjee, 1986: 253–58). They were subjected to humiliating treatment in the working field as well.

According to Census data, two-third of the female rural main workers in Patna, Gaya and Jehanabad work as agricultural labourers. Success of agrarian strike depends upon ability to mobilize female agricultural labour. Restoration of dignity of these womenfolk is one of the main political agenda of all Maoist parties and groups.

Before rise and development of radical movement above forms of social humiliations and feudal subjugations of Dalits were submerged within the framework of everyday relations between Dalit families and their *maliks.* But now in the areas of Maoist movement, these forms of social oppression have become an explicit issue. The resistance is a political act that questions arbitrary exercise of power by landed gentry. Even senior officials of Gaya and Jehanabad districts admitted that left wing groups have done much to force elements among *maliks* to end their sexual depredations (PUDR Report, 1992: 17). A number of *samants* have been publically humiliated and punished by Maoist groups in *Jan Adalats.* Their official monthly publications carry such reports in almost every issue. Thus, social humiliations of Dalits and *samunt vichar* have been successfully challenged by Maoist parties in their area of influence.

Miscarriage of developmental models initiated by the state, Gandhian and mainstream Left parties provided propitious ground for rise and sustenance of extra-parliamentary agrarian struggle in the state. Maoist movement revolves around basic issues for socio-economic and political emancipation of toiling masses, which is fundamental duty of democratic system. The Indian Constitution, in principle, is committed to the doctrine of socio-economic and political justice to every Indian citizen. It is basic duty of Indian State to preserve and assure *equality* of opportunity and dignity of every individual, and furthers 'participatory development'. Promotion and protection of these basic rights, especially to downtrodden section of society, assures political and social stability and peace of the country. Unless above constitutional promises are practically ensured by the Indian State, Gandhi's dream project – 'Sarvodaya and Antodaya' social order – cannot be established. However, events of world history suggest that people have changed the course of history, and through struggles created people-centred social system and people-oriented participatory democracy, where democracy for the people and not people for democracy is the order.

## Notes

1. Now a separate state called Jharkhand.
2. Land north of Ganges is known as North Bihar, plain land south of Ganges is called South Bihar and uplands in the extreme south is called *Chotanagpur.* Central Bihar consists of mostly districts of South Bihar – Patna, Gaya, Nalanda, Bhojpur, Rohtas, Bauxar, Kaimur, Jehanabad, Nawada and Aurangabad.
3. *Panja* is the share of labourers at the time of harvest. Normally labourers are given one out of every 12 bundles of paddy, but it varies from place to place.

## References

Banerjee, S. (1980). *In the Wake of Naxalbari: A History of the Naxalite Movement in India.* Calcutta: Subarnarekha.

——. (1984). *India's Simmering Revolution: The Naxalite Uprising.* New Delhi: Select Book Service Syndicate.

Bhave, Vinoba (2000). *Science and Self-Knowledge.* Varanasi: Sarva Seva Sangh.

Census of India (2001 and 2011). Registrar General and Census Commissioner, Government of India, New Delhi.

Chandra, Nirmal (1997). *Bhoomi Samasya aur Bhoodan.* New Delhi: Gandhi Peace Foundation.

Choudhary, M. (1970). *Freedom for the Masses.* Varanasi: Navachetna Prakashan.

Communist Party of India (1967). Draft for the Ideological Discussion. Central Committee, Madurai, August 18–27.

CPI (ML) Document (1986). *Report from the Flaming Fields of Bihar.* Calcutta: Prabodh Bhattacharya.

CPI (ML) Party Unity Report (1993). Committee against Repression on Peasantry in Bihar. July 9, Unpublished.

Das, A.N. (1983). *Agrarian Unrest and Socio-Economic Change in Bihar: 1900–1980.* New Delhi: Manohar Publications.

Datta, K.K. (1970). *Anti-British Plots and Movements before 1857.* Meerut: Meenakshi Prakashan.

Deo, Shankarrao (1962). *Gramdan Movement: Onward March: A Turning-Point.* Bombay: Mouj Printing Bureau.

Desai, A.R. (1961). *Rural India in Transition.* Bombay: Popular Prakashan.

Desai, A.R. (ed.) (1969). *Rural Sociology in India.* Bombay: Popular Prakashan.

——. (1986). *Agrarian Struggles in India after Independence.* Delhi: Oxford University Press.

Economic Survey (2007). Finance Department, Government of Bihar, Patna.

Gandhi, M.K. (1909). 'Ladaie Ka Arth'. *Indian Opinion*, January 23.

——. (1956). *India of My Dreams.* Ahmedabad: Navajivan Publishing House.

——. (1967). *Satyagraha in South Africa.* Varanasi: Uttar Pradesh Gandhi Smarak Nidhi.

Gangrade, K.D. (1997). 'Bhoodan-Gramdan: Revolution through Love'. *Journal of Peace and Gandhian Studies*, April-June.

Gopalan, A.K. (1968). 'Strengthen the Kisan Sabha', Presidential Address at the 19th Session of AIKS at Madurai from January 26–28, *People's Democracy*, 4(6): 5, emphasis added.

Hardiman, D. (1977). 'Essay on Gujarat', in D.A. Low (ed.), *Congress and the Raj.* London: Heinemann.

ILO and A.N. Sinha Institute of Social Sciences (1991). Empirical Study in 1981, as quoted in *Economic and Political Weekly*, XXVI(33), Bombay, August 17.

Iyengar, S. (2007). 'Bhoodan Movement as a Gandhian Approach to Resource Distribution and Development'. *Gandhi Marg*, 28(4), New Delhi: Gandhi Peace Foundation, January-March.

Janwadi Mukti Marg (1994). April.

Jha, Hetukar et al. (eds) (1985). *Social Structures and Alignments: A Study of Rural Bihar.* New Delhi: Usha Publications, also, Grierson, G.A. (ed.) (1967). *Linguistic Survey of India*, Vol. 3, Part 1. Delhi: Motilal Banarsidass.

Johnson, C. (1962). *Peasant Nationalism and Communist Power.* Stanford: Hoover Institute of Studies.

Kala, M., R.N. Maharaj and K. Mukherjee (1986). 'Peasant Unrest in Bhojpur: A Survey', in A.R. Desai (ed.), *Agrarian Struggles in India after Independence.* Delhi: Oxford University Press.

Kumar, Anand (1989). *State and Society in India: A Study of State's Agenda-Making: 1917–1977.* New Delhi: Radiant Publishers.

Mukherjee, K. and M. Kala (1978). 'Bhojpur: The Long War'. *Mainstream*, XVI(45–46), Delhi, July 8–15.

Mukherjee, K. and R.S. Yadav (1980). *Bhojpur: Naxalism in the Plains of Bihar*. New Delhi: Radhakrishna Prakashan.

Nehru, J.L. (1958). *Speeches*, Vol. 3. New Delhi: Publications Division.

NSSO (48th, 59th and 70th Round). Ministry of Statistics and Programme Implementation, Government of India, New Delhi.

Oommen, T.K. (1972). *Charisma, Stability and Change: An Analysis of Bhoodan-Gramdan Movement in India*. Delhi: Thompson Press.

——. (1985). *From Mobilisation to Institutionalisation: The Dynamics of Agrarian Movement in Twentieth Century Kerala*. Bombay: Popular Prakashan.

Prasad, Rajendra (1949). *Satyagraha in Champaran*. Ahmedabad: Navajivan Publishing House.

PUCL (1992). *Report on Massacre in Men and Barsiwan*. PUCL Bihar State Unit, Patna.

PUDR Report (1992). *Bitter Harvest*. Delhi: Harish Dhawan, August.

Rahi, R.C. (1977). 'Bhoodan Gramdan Andolan: Sambhavnaon aur Seemaon Ki Ek Kahani (mimeo)'. Sarva Seva Sangh, Varanasi.

Rawal, Vikas (2008). 'Ownership Holdings of Land in Rural India: Putting the Record Straight'. *Economic and Political Weekly*, XLIII(10), Mumbai, March 8–14.

Sengupta, Nirmal (1982a). 'Agrarian Movements in Bihar', in A.N. Das (ed.), *Agrarian Movements in India: Studies on 20th Century Bihar*. London: Frank Cass.

Sharma, A.N. (1987). 'Backwardness Trap of Bihar Agriculture', in S. Gupta and A.N. Sharma (eds). *Bihar: Stagnation or Growth*. Delhi: Spectrum Publishing House.

Singh, Satyanarayan (1969). 'Mushari and its Lessons'. *Liberation Anthology*, 2(12), October.

Sinha, Arun (1977). 'Class War, Not Atrocities against Harijans'. *Economic and Political Weekly*, XII(50), Bombay, December 10.

Sinha, B.N. (1975). 'From Naxalbari to Ekwari'. *The Searchlight*, Patna, June 11–13, emphasis added.

Sinha, L.P. (1965). *The Left Wing in India*. Patna: Bharti Bhavan.

*The Indian Nation*. Patna, 1 and 6 July 1967, also *The Searchlight*. Patna, 10 August 1967.

Thomson, Mark (1993). *Gandhi and His Ashrams*. Bombay: Popular Prakashan.

# Part 2

## The State Market and Globalization

# 3

# Globalization and the Indian Capital Market

**BHAVYA MAHESHWARI AND GANGOTRI MISHRA**

Ever since the reforms in the 1990s, capital mobility has linked the national financial markets to a more tightly inter-connected global system. Various forces have fostered the wave of capital-market development and the globalization of finance. These forces can be grouped into three categories: government policies, technological and financial innovations, and demand and supply-side factors (De la Torre, Gozzi, and Schmukler, 2007).

In most developing countries, liberalization of stock market took place during the period 1985 to 1995 when market-capitalization of all emerging markets increased by 1,007 per cent compared to an increase of 253 per cent in the case of developed markets. The share of emerging markets in the world market-capitalization increased from 4 per cent in 1985 to 11 per cent in 1995. Similarly, the trading value in these markets increased by 2,189 per cent compared to 564 per cent increase for the developed markets over the decade. As a result, the share of emerging markets in trading-volume increased by more than three times, i.e. from 2.7 per cent to 8.9 per cent in 10 years, signalling significant growth in these markets (Husain and Qayyum, 2006).

A well-functioning financial market is critical, especially for Emerging Market Economies (EMEs). India is one of the five countries classified as big emerging market economies by the World Bank. This list also includes People's Republic of China (PRC), Indonesia, Brazil, and Russia. These countries have made the critical transition from being a developing country to an emerging market. The World Bank has predicted that the output share of these five biggest emerging markets of the world will more than double from 7.8 per cent in 1992 to 16.1 per cent by 2020 (World Bank, 1997).

The economic development of a country envariability depends upon the depth and effective functioning of the capital market. A strong and healthy regulatory system is the prime requirement for the growth and efficiency of any such market. The advent of modern techniques and information technology in some vital areas of capital-market architecture like trading, payment and settlement, has given some strength and advantage to the Indian capital market. However, it still lacks the robustness required to compete effectively with the major international capital-markets.

In recent decades, globalization of finance has taken a quantum leap forward as cross-border capital flows rose from $0.5 trillion in 1980 to a peak of $11.8 trillion in 2007. But they collapsed during the financial crisis, and as of 2012, they remain more than 60 per cent below their former peak (McKinsey, 2006).

The financial crisis resulted from a confluence of leverage, risk, and deficient regulation and then globalization led to contagion, which intensified the impact. Policy-makers have begun to adjust their views on the benefits and costs of financial-sector liberalization and capital-account openness.

As per the macro-economic policy trilemma for open economies (also known as the 'inconsistent trinity proposition'), an open capital-market deprives a country's government of the ability simultaneously to target its exchange rate and to use monetary policy in pursuit of other economic objectives (Obstfeld and Taylor, 2002). Consequently, there are other negative effects of capital-market globalization which are often so large that they seem to outweigh any benefits in terms of access to more capital inflows. Financial liberalization of the capital-market has created exposure to an increased propensity to financial crisis, deflationary impact on real economic activity and reduced access to funds for small-scale producers and also other social effects in terms of loss of employment and more volatile material conditions for citizens.

## The Indian Capital Market

Although the Indian Capital Market is approximately 180 years old, it is quite young in terms of the extent of globalization and international competitiveness. The capital market is an important protagonist in the process of mobilization of finance directly from the investor. The foremost purpose of capital market is to enable allocation or re-allocation of financial resources so as to foster economic growth.

Indian capital market can be traced back to 1830 when business on corporate stocks and shares in banks and cotton-presses started in Bombay. The very first stock exchange in India, the Bombay Stock Exchange, came into existence in 1875. The stock-market have had many turbulent times in the last 180 years of their existence. It started as an independent body of stock brokers, which started doing business in the city under a banyan tree. Business was essentially confined to company owners and brokers, with very little interest displayed by the general public. Initially, the number of brokers recognized by the banks and merchants were very few (only six during, 1840–50). The year 1850 marked a rapid transformation in the history of the Indian stock market through a rapid development of commercial enterprises and the brokerage business. This resulted in an increased number of brokers (60) by 1860. The start of the American Civil War in 1860–61 further increased the number of brokers that thereafter ranged from 200 to 250. However, the end of the war resulted in a huge slump in the securities' market and the brokers continued their transactions in a street (now known as the Dalal Street). The centrally co-ordinated process of planning started in India in 1951, with importance being given to the formation of institutions and markets. The Securities Contract Regulation Act, 1956, became the parent regulation after the Indian Contract Act, 1872, a fundamental law to be followed by security markets in India. To regulate the issue of share prices, the Controller of Capital Issues Act (CCI) was passed in 1947. The 1980s witnessed an explosive growth in the Indian securities market with millions of investors suddenly discovering lucrative opportunities.

**Table 1**

*Brief History of the Indian Capital Market*

| *Date* | *Event* |
|---|---|
| 1830 | Business on corporate stock and shares in bank and cotton presses started in Bombay |
| 1875 | The Native Shares and Stock Brokers' Association was formed |
| 1956 | Securities Contracts (Regulation) Act became parent regulator |
| 1957 | Bombay Stock Exchange (BSE) granted permanent recognition |
| 1986 | Sensex: the country's first equity index launched |
| 1992 | Securities and Exchange Board of India (SEBI) Act established |
| 1993 | National Stock Exchange (NSE) was recognized as a stock exchange |
| 1995 | BSE Online Trading (BOLT) system introduced |
| 1997 | BOLT expanded nation-wide |
| 1999 | Central Depository Services Ltd. (CDSL) was set up |
| 1999 | Interest Rate Swaps (IRS)/Forward Rate Agreement (FRA) allowed |
| 2000 | Equity derivatives introduced |
| 2001 | Stock options launched |
| 2002 | Fungibility of ADR/GDR |
| 2007 | Launch of Unified Corporate Bond Reporting Platform: Indian Corporate Debt Market (ICDM) |
| 2008 | Currency derivatives introduced |
| 2009 | BSE Launches BSE Star MF – Mutual Fund trading platform |
| 2009 | Launch of clearing and settlement of Corporate Bonds |
| 2010 | Commencement of Volatility Index |
| 2010 | Commencement of Shariah Index |
| 2012 | Launch of BSE – SME Exchange Platform |
| 2013 | SENSEX becomes S&P SENSEX as BSE ties up with Standard and Poor's |

Reforms in capital markets were high on the list of priorities of policy-makers when India embarked on market-oriented reforms in the early 1990s. These efforts had several motivations: the broad idea of markets playing a dominant role in resource-allocation, an awareness of the opportunity cost that India was suffering by not being open to global capital flows, and an immediate reaction to the fixed income and equity market scandal of 1992.

The Securities and Exchange Board of India Act, 1992 (the SEBI Act), came into existence with the primary objective of protecting, developing and regulating the securities' markets. Since then, the capital markets in India have experienced tremendous progress because of the well-developed regulatory system in place. An empirical study by Goel and Gupta (2011) shows that capital-market reforms that started in the 1990s contributed to the development of the stock markets in India. This study has found significant improvement in the economy after liberalization. All indicators show an improvement in stock market activities in the post-liberalization period. Market capitalization ratio, value-traded ratio, and turnover-ratio have increased. These indicators together with decline in volatility are an evidence of stock-market development in India.

A comparison made by Chakrabarti (2010) shows the financial depth in India and other Asian countries in 2004 and 2007, respectively. In 2004, India's financial depth was among the worst among Asian countries. By 2007, it was in the median range of the Asian countries with only China and Malaysia among emerging markets being ahead. The instability in the equity markets since 2007 has shaken these figures but the message of over-all deepening remains unchanged. Looking at the extent of financial deepening during the 2004–07 period, India ranks first among major Asian countries, largely driven by the gain in the equity markets.

Even though the penetration level of the financial services sector continues to be extremely low, there needs to be a rigorous effort to adequately extract the full potential of India's savings, which stands at an impressive 34 per cent of the GDP. As of July 2011, only 1 per cent of households had invested in mutual funds and a mere 0.72 per cent, in equity shares (World Economic Forum, 2012).

The corporate bond market has remained relatively underdeveloped. This has been the result of the dominance of the banking system combined with the weaknesses in market infrastructure and the inherent complexities.

Efficient and developed financial markets can lead to increased economic growth by improving the efficiency of allocation and utilization of savings in the economy.

There is a growing body of empirical analyses, including firm and industry level studies, individual country studies and cross country comparisons that prove this strong, positive link between the functioning of the financial system and long-run economic growth. Specifically, financial systems facilitate the trading, hedging, diversifying, and pooling of risk. In addition, they better allocate resources, monitor managers and exert corporate control, mobilize savings, and facilitate the exchange of goods and services (Levine, 1997).

The pressures of financial liberalization are very high as the economic development of a country unvaryingly depends upon the depth and effective functioning of the capital market. A strong and healthy regulatory system is the prime requirement for the growth and efficiency of any capital market. The advent of modern techniques and information technology in some vital areas of capital market architecture like trading, payment and settlement, has given some strength and advantage to the Indian capital market but it still lacks the robustness to compete effectively with major international capital markets.

India's capital market lags behind those of other developed and developing markets in financial depth also. Indian exchanges are somewhat undiversified.

Equities and commodities comprise approximately 90 per cent of trading volume. Most of the other markets have a much more diversified mix, with interest rate futures, foreign exchange futures and corporate bonds accounting for a large share of exchange-trading.

The need to eliminate financial repression (McKinnon, 1973) is a powerful argument in favour of financial liberalization. Repressive policies are seen to be detrimental to financial deepening, in the context of the observed empirical relationship between financial deepening and growth. Financial repression is said to have a depressive effect on savings' rates and thereby result in capital shortages and adverse effect on growth. It is also argued that financial repression tends to selectively ration out riskier projects, irrespective of their social relevance, because interest rate ceilings imply that adequate risk premiums cannot be charged.

In terms of Financial Development (World Economic Forum, 2012), India ranks 40th among the 62 countries covered in the Report, which shows a four-spot decline from 2011. The Financial Development Index is one way of picturing the financial market developments.

Some of the findings show that among the components of this Index, India ranks poorly in terms of financial sector liberalization – 58th out of 62. There is, however, a slight improvement in financial stability in terms of which the country is ranked at 46. According to the report, it is quite clear that India's liberalization could be speeded up.

The following parameters are taken for the analysis of growth of the capital market on the eve of globalization:

- Resource mobilized from the primary market with respect to equities
- Industry-wise classification of equity raised
- Size-wise classification of equity raised
- Region-wise distribution of capital mobilized
- Sector-wise distribution of capital mobilized
- Issuance of ADRs and GDRs
- Average Annual Share Price Index (BSE and Sensex)
- Foreign investment inflows in stock market

## Objectives of the Study

- To know the industry-wise classification of equity raised
- To know the resource mobilized from the primary market with respect to equities
- To know the size-wise classification of equity raised
- To know the region-wise distribution of capital mobilized
- To know the sector-wise distribution of capital mobilized
- To know the issuance of ADRs and GDRs
- To know the Average Annual Share Price Index (BSE and Sensex)
- To know the foreign investment inflows in stock market

## Methodology

The type of research used in this study is analytical research in which facts or information available has been used and analysed to make a critical evaluation of the material.

## Period of the Study

The time-frame chosen for the study is 17 years (1997 to 2013).

## Tools Used for the Study

Simple percentage and trend percentage were applied.

## Data Source

The relevant data has been sourced from the SEBI database.

**Table 2**

*Resource Mobilized from the Primary Market With Respect to Equities*

| *At Par* | | | | *At Premium* | | | |
|---|---|---|---|---|---|---|---|
| *Year* | *Number of Companies* | *Total Amount (₹ in Crores)* | *Percentage* | *Year* | *Number of Companies* | *Total Amount (₹ in Crores)* | *Percentage* |
| 1997–98 | 608 | 3,808 | 17.80 | 1997–98 | 383 | 9,220 | 3.80 |
| 1998–99 | 942 | 5,529 | 25.85 | 1998–99 | 651 | 12,441 | 5.13 |
| 1999–2000 | 1,181 | 4,598 | 21.50 | 1999–2000 | 480 | 9,727 | 4.01 |
| 2000–01 | 697 | 3,441 | 16.09 | 2000–01 | 148 | 4,412 | 1.82 |
| 2001–02 | 64 | 271 | 1.27 | 2001–02 | 33 | 1,610 | 0.66 |
| 2002–03 | 20 | 197 | 0.92 | 2002–03 | 20 | 660 | 0.27 |
| 2003–04 | 30 | 786 | 3.67 | 2003–04 | 52 | 3,780 | 1.56 |
| 2004–05 | 84 | 818 | 3.82 | 2004–05 | 54 | 2,408 | 0.99 |
| 2005–06 | 7 | 151 | 0.71 | 2005–06 | 8 | 1,121 | 0.46 |
| 2006–07 | 6 | 143 | 0.67 | 2006–07 | 11 | 1,314 | 0.54 |
| 2007–08 | 14 | 360 | 1.68 | 2007–08 | 37 | 18,589 | 7.66 |
| 2008–09 | 6 | 420 | 1.96 | 2008–09 | 49 | 23,968 | 9.88 |
| 2009–10 | 10 | 372 | 1.74 | 2009–10 | 128 | 27,000 | 11.13 |
| 2010–11 | 2 | 12 | 0.06 | 2010–11 | 119 | 32,889 | 13.55 |
| 2011–12 | 7 | 387 | 1.81 | 2011–12 | 113 | 79,352 | 32.70 |
| 2012–13 | 5 | 96 | 0.45 | 2012–13 | 40 | 14,176 | 5.84 |
| Total | 3683 | 21,389 | 100.00 | TOTAL | 2,326 | 2,42,667 | 100.00 |

*Source:* Computed Data.

Table 2 indicates that a total of 3,683 companies hit the primary market by way of issuing equities at par and 2,326 companies placed their equities with premium during the period 1997 to 2013. From the year 1997 to 2004, nearly 90 per cent of the companies tapped the market by way of issuing equity at par and thereafter, only 10 per cent of the companies placed their equity at par in the primary market. The above data indicates that most of the companies after 2004 entered the market with premium. In the premium segment, the year 2011–12 witnessed a major portion of the amount being tapped through the primary market. Almost 60 per cent of the total amount was procured through the primary market with premium during the year 2008–2012. This indicates the trend in the market to be bullish during those periods. The large number of companies tapped the market in premium segment during the years 1997–2001, indicating that liberalization policies have shown immediate impact on stock market.

**Table 3**

*Industry-Wise Classification of Equity Raised (1997–2013)*

| *S. No.* | *Industry* | *Total Amount (₹ in Crores)* | *Percentage* |
|---|---|---|---|
| 1. | Banking | 96,936 | 28.75 |
| 2. | Cement Construction | 26,560 | 7.88 |
| 3. | Chemical | 9,340 | 2.77 |
| 4. | Electronics | 3,648 | 1.08 |
| 5. | Engineering | 5,461 | 1.62 |
| 6. | Entertainment | 4,406 | 1.31 |
| 7. | Finance | 20,961 | 6.22 |
| 8. | Food Processing | 6,035 | 1.79 |
| 9. | Healthcare | 5,908 | 1.75 |
| 10. | Information Technology | 12,990 | 3.85 |
| 11. | Paper and Pulp | 1,308 | 0.39 |
| 12. | Plastic | 1,537 | 0.46 |
| 13. | Power | 24,463 | 7.25 |
| 14. | Printing | 305 | 0.09 |
| 15. | Tele-Communication | 5,955 | 1.77 |
| 16. | Textiles | 11,269 | 3.34 |
| 17. | Others | 1,00,128 | 29.69 |
| | Total | 3,37,210 | 100.00 |

*Source:* Computed Data.

Table 3 gives the data in respect of industry-wise classification of equity raised during the period 1997 to 2013. The table reveals that the banking industry ranked 1st, the cement construction industry ranked 2nd, power industry 3rd, finance industry 4th, textile industry 5th, chemical industry 6th, food processing industry 7th, tele-communication industry ranked 8th and ranks 9 to 12 were held by healthcare, engineering, entertainment and electronics, respectively.

It is interesting to note that the textile industry continuously tapped the market from the year 1997–2013. In case of entertainment industry, large capital was procured through primary market during the year 2010–11. The tele-communication industry too witnessed a major inflow of capital procured during the period 2008–13. The contribution of other industries towards tapping capital through the market was also significant

**Table 4**

*Size-Wise Classification of Equity Raised From 1997–2013*

| S. No. | Category-Range | Total amount (₹ in Crores) | Percentage |
|---|---|---|---|
| 1. | Less than 5 Crores | 7,991 | 2.54 |
| 2. | 5–10 Crores | 8,047 | 2.56 |
| 3. | 10–50 Crores | 18,557 | 5.91 |
| 4. | 50–100 Crores | 17,871 | 5.69 |
| 5. | More than 100 Crores | 2,61,612 | 83.30 |
| | Total | 3,14,078 | 100.00 |

*Source:* Computed Data.

Table 4 indicates that approximately 83 per cent of the total amount of equity was raised by companies which issued more than 100 crores of equity in the market while approximately 6 per cent of the total amount of equity was raised by companies that issued 10–50 crores and 50–100 crores of equity. Only 2.56 per cent and 2.54 per cent of the total amount of equity was raised by companies which issued 5–10 crores and less than 5 crores of equity, respectively in the market.

**Table 5**

*Region-Wise Distribution of Capital Mobilized from 1997–2013*

| S. No. | Region | Amount | Percentage |
|---|---|---|---|
| 1. | Northern | 76,323.00 | 22.5,46,34,936 |
| 2. | Eastern | 11,732.00 | 3.46,57,15,062 |
| 3. | Western | 20,9167.00 | 61.7,89,39,843 |
| 4. | Southern | 41,294.00 | 12.1,98,53,714 |
| | Total | 33,8516.00 | 100 |

*Source:* Computed Data.

Table 5 reveals that approximately 62 per cent of the total amount of capital was mobilized from the Western region while approximately 23 per cent was mobilized from the Northern sector. Only 12.19 per cent and 3.46 per cent of the total amount of capital was mobilized from the Southern and Eastern regions, respectively.

Table 6 indicates that a total of 5237 private sector companies and 87 public sector companies have mobilized a sum of ₹ 2,41,758 crore and ₹ 72,314 crore, respectively from the primary market through equity issues, beginning 1997–98 and coming down to 2012–13. The figures for the initial years reveal that in 1998–99, 1,684 Private Sector companies and eight Public Sector companies raised a sum of ₹ 26,270 crore, and ₹ 1,362 crore respectively through equity issues; 1999–2000 saw 1,718 Private Sector and 7 Public Sector companies issues being made and a sum of ₹ 16,639 crore and ₹ 4,165 crore worth of capital respectively mobilized, whereas the figures for the year

2000–2001 reveal a total of 872 Private Sector and 10 Public Sector companies' issues involving a sum of ₹ 10,241 crore and ₹ 4,035 crore, respectively.

**Table 6**

*Sector-Wise Distribution of Capital Mobilized*

| Year | Number of Private Sector Companies | Total Amount (₹ in Crores) | Percentage | Year | Number of Public Sector Companies | Total Amount (₹ in Crores) | Percentage |
|---|---|---|---|---|---|---|---|
| 1997–98 | 0 | 0 | 0.00 | 1997–98 | 0 | 0 | 0.00 |
| 1998–99 | 1,684 | 26,270 | 10.87 | 1998–99 | 8 | 1,362 | 1.88 |
| 1999–2000 | 1,718 | 16,639 | 6.88 | 1999–2000 | 7 | 4,165 | 5.76 |
| 2000–01 | 872 | 10,241 | 4.24 | 2000–01 | 10 | 4,035 | 5.58 |
| 2001–02 | 105 | 3,852 | 1.59 | 2001–02 | 6 | 718 | 0.99 |
| 2002–03 | 57 | 5,516 | 2.28 | 2002–03 | 1 | 70 | 0.10 |
| 2003–04 | 91 | 7,617 | 3.15 | 2003–04 | 2 | 200 | 0.28 |
| 2004–05 | 148 | 5,893 | 2.44 | 2004–05 | 3 | 215 | 0.30 |
| 2005–06 | 30 | 6,601 | 2.73 | 2005–06 | 5 | 942 | 1.30 |
| 2006–07 | 18 | 1,897 | 0.78 | 2006–07 | 8 | 2,173 | 3.00 |
| 2007–08 | 39 | 4,612 | 1.91 | 2007–08 | 18 | 18,660 | 25.80 |
| 2008–09 | 55 | 17,162 | 7.10 | 2008–09 | 5 | 11,094 | 15.34 |
| 2009–10 | 131 | 20,199 | 8.36 | 2009–10 | 8 | 7,183 | 9.93 |
| 2010–11 | 122 | 31,728 | 13.12 | 2010–11 | 2 | 1,779 | 2.46 |
| 2011–12 | 120 | 67,311 | 27.84 | 2011–12 | 4 | 19,718 | 27.27 |
| 2012–13 | 47 | 16,220 | 6.71 | 2012–13 | 0 | 0 | 0.00 |
| Total | 5237 | 2,41,758 | 100.00 | Total | 87 | 72,314 | 100.00 |

*Source:* Computed Data.

Almost 60 per cent of the total capital raised by the private sector pertains to the period 2008–13 and the remaining 40 per cent of the total capital raised relates to the period 1997–2007. It is surprising to see that whereas almost 85 per cent of the total capital raised by the public sector through primary market came during the period 2007–13, only 15 per cent of the total capital was procured during the period 1997–2007. Strikingly, in the years 1997–98 and 2012–13, no Public Sector Undertakings tapped the primary market for the procurement of capital.

Table 7 shows that 24,734 $ million worth of ADR and GDR have been issued between 1996 to 2013, of which 55 per cent of the total capital falls during the period 2009–13. The maximum, 6645 $ million worth of ADR and GDR have been issued in 2011–12 and the minimum, 240 $ million worth, in 1996–97.

Table 8 reveals the Average Annual Share-Price Index BSE and Sensex, percentage of change and percentage of trend. Average Annual Share-Price Index increases from 730 in 1993 to 16,569 in 2012 but decreases to 12,366 in 2013. The percentage of trend increases from 43.84 in 1994 to 2169.73 in 2012. In the year 1995–96, the index has changed to the extent of 80 per cent over the previous year's index, showing that liberalization has proved to be a hallmark of development of the stock market.

**Table 7**
*Issuance of ADRs and GDRs*

| *Year* | *Amount of ADRs and GDRs (US $ Million)* | *Percentage* |
|---|---|---|
| 1996–97 | 240 | 0.97 |
| 1997–98 | 1,597 | 6.46 |
| 1998–99 | 2,050 | 8.29 |
| 1999–2000 | 683 | 2.76 |
| 2000–01 | 1,366 | 5.52 |
| 2001–02 | 645 | 2.61 |
| 2002–03 | 270 | 1.09 |
| 2003–04 | 768 | 3.11 |
| 2004–05 | 831 | 3.36 |
| 2005–06 | 477 | 1.93 |
| 2006–07 | 600 | 2.43 |
| 2007–08 | 459 | 1.86 |
| 2008–09 | 613 | 2.48 |
| 2009–10 | 2,552 | 10.32 |
| 2010–11 | 3,776 | 15.27 |
| 2011–12 | 6,645 | 26.87 |
| 2012–13 | 1,162 | 4.70 |
| Total | 24,734 | 100.00 |

*Source:* Computed Data.

**Table 8**
*Average Annual Share Price Index (BSE and Sensex)*

| *Year* | *Average Annual Share Price index (BSE and Sensex)* | *Percenage Change* | *Trend Percentage* |
|---|---|---|---|
| 1993–94 | 730 | — | — |
| 1994–95 | 1,050 | 43.84 | 43.84 |
| 1995–96 | 1,880 | 79.05 | 157.53 |
| 1996–97 | 2,895 | 53.99 | 296.58 |
| 1997–98 | 2,898 | 0.10 | 296.99 |
| 1998–99 | 3,974 | 37.13 | 444.38 |
| 1999–2000 | 3,288 | –17.26 | 350.41 |
| 2000–01 | 3,469 | 5.50 | 375.21 |
| 2001–02 | 3,812 | 9.89 | 422.19 |
| 2002–03 | 3,294 | –13.59 | 351.23 |
| 2003–04 | 4,658 | 41.41 | 538.08 |
| 2004–05 | 4,269 | –8.35 | 484.79 |
| 2005–06 | 3,331 | –21.97 | 356.30 |
| 2006–07 | 3,206 | –3.75 | 339.18 |
| 2007–08 | 4,492 | 40.11 | 515.34 |
| 2008–09 | 5,740 | 27.78 | 686.30 |
| 2009–10 | 8,278 | 44.22 | 1,033.97 |
| 2010–11 | 12,277 | 48.31 | 1,581.78 |
| 2011–12 | 16,569 | 34.96 | 2,169.73 |
| 2012–13 | 12,366 | –25.37 | 1,593.97 |

*Source:* Computed Data.

**Table 9**

*Showing Foreign Investment Inflows in Stock Market*

| Year | Amount of Portfolio Investment in Crores of Rupees | Percentage |
|---|---|---|
| 1995–96 | 11 | 0.003 |
| 1996–97 | 10 | 0.003 |
| 1997–98 | 748 | 0.196 |
| 1998–99 | 11,188 | 2.925 |
| 1999–2000 | 12,007 | 3.140 |
| 2000–01 | 9,192 | 2.403 |
| 2001–02 | 11,758 | 3.074 |
| 2002–03 | 6,794 | 1.776 |
| 2003–04 | -257 | -0.067 |
| 2004–05 | 13,112 | 3.428 |
| 2005–06 | 12,609 | 3.297 |
| 2006–07 | 9,639 | 2.520 |
| 2007–08 | 4,738 | 1.239 |
| 2008–09 | 52,279 | 13.670 |
| 2009–10 | 41,854 | 10.944 |
| 2010–11 | 55,307 | 14.462 |
| 2011–12 | 31,713 | 8.292 |
| 2012–13 | 1,09,741 | 28.695 |
| Total | 3,82,443 | 100.00 |

*Source:* Computed Data.

As is evident from Table 9, the Indian Stock Market inflow of foreign investment increased from 11 crores in 1995–96 to 1,09,741 crores in 2012–13. The inflow came down and reached negative figures in 2003–04 but thereafter, foreign investors have continuously invested in the Indian Capital Market. The foreign investment inflows into the country have witnessed radical changes from the year 1994 to 2013.

## Key Findings

- 3,683 companies hit the primary market by way of issuing equities at par.
- 2,326 companies placed their equities with premium during the period 1997 to 2013.
- From the year 1997 to 2004, nearly 90 per cent of the companies tapped the market by way of issuing equity at par and after the year 2004, only 10 per cent of the companies placed their equity at par in the primary market thereby indicating that after 2004 the overwhelming trend was for the companies to hit the market with premium.
- In the premium-segment, the year 2011–12 witnessed a major portion of amount tapped through the primary market.
- Almost 60 per cent of the total amount was procured through the primary market in the premium category during the years 2008–2012. This indicates that the market was in a bullish trend during this period.

- The number of companies that tapped the market in the premium segment was quite large during the years 1997–2001, indicating an immediate post-liberalization impact on the stock market.
- The banking sector is the front-runner in mobilizing capital through the primary market.
- The textile sector has been continuously tapping the market through the years 1997–2013.
- The power sector vigorously concentrated on tapping the market during the years 2008–13. In 2011–12, the sector witnessed a large chunk of capital being mobilized through the primary market.
- The sector of tele-communications too witnessed a major flow of capital during the years 2008–13.
- As far as the IT Sector is concerned, funds have been tapped from the primary market in almost all the years except 1999–2001.
- In the entertainment category, the year 2010–11 witnessed large capital being procured through the primary market.
- Apart from these major sectors, other sectors' contribution towards tapping capital through the market is also significant.
- In the size-wise classification, it is found that the companies that hit the primary market for the procurement of capital belong to the category of the more-than-100-crore size. Almost 85 per cent of the companies have so for placed their equity in the market with the capital-size of more than 100 crores.
- Companies that belong to the category of small size in terms of capital procurement are significantly less in number.
- So far, 5,237 Private Sector companies have hit the market whereas only 87 Public Sector companies tapped the market, thus revealing that Public Sector companies are reluctant to procure capital by way of approaching the primary market.
- Of the total capital raised by both the Public Sector and Private Sector, only one-fourth of the total capital has been raised by the Public Sector as compared to the procurement of capital through the Private Sector.
- Almost 60 per cent of the total capital raised by the Private Sector was during the period 2008–13 and the remaining 40 per cent was raised during the years 1997–2007.
- It is surprising to see that almost 85 per cent of the total capital raised by the Public Sector through the primary market was during the period 2007–13 and only 15 per cent of the total capital was procured during the years 1997–2007.
- It was found that in the years 1997–98 and 2012–13 none of the Public Sector Undertakings tapped the primary market for procurement of capital.
- In the region-wise analysis, the Western region takes a lead with more than 60 per cent procurement of capital through the market followed by the Northern region. The Eastern region occupies a small share in terms of procurement of capital through primary market.
- So far, $24,734 million worth of ADR/GDR has been issued. Of this, 55 per cent of the total capital falls between the years 2009–13.

- The average Annual Share Price Index rapidly rose from 730 in 1993 to 16,569 in 2012.
- In the year 1995, the index had changed to the extent of 80 per cent over the previous year's index value, showing that liberalization had proved to be a hallmark of development of the stock market.
- The years 2009–12 witnessed a significant surge in the index value of BSE.
- In 2009–10, an increase of 45 per cent was witnessed over the previous year's index-value and thereafter, in the years 2010 and 2011, an increase of 48 per cent took place over the previous year's value of index, showing that the period 2009–11 was the period of boom with respect to the Indian stock market.
- As far as the foreign investment inflows are concerned, the country witnessed a radical change over the period 1994 to 2013.

## Conclusion

The Indian Capital Market developed to a significant extent in the process of economic liberalization. It has proved to be an important aspect in the process of financing of the Indian corporate sector. Besides enabling mobilization of resources for investment directly from the investors, other major emerging functions of the Indian capital market have also been identified that is, providing liquidity for the investor, monitoring and disciplining company management, creating financial flows, attracting the institutional and retail investors (domestic as well as foreign), mediating between companies and financial warehouses, and channelizing funds for deficit fields. This, in turn, places the Indian Capital Market in the situation of having become a watch-word in the era of globalization. It is, thus, clear that globalization has acted as a driver for the development of the Indian Capital Market.

## References

Chakraborty, Indrani (2010). 'Financial Development and Economic Growth in India: An Analysis of the Post-reform Period.' *South Asia Economic Journal*, Vol. 11(2): 287–308.

De la Torre, Augusto, Juan Carlos Gozzi and Sergio L. Schmukler (2007). 'Financial Development: Maturing and Emerging Policy Issues.' *The World Bank Research Observer*, Vol. 22(1): 67–102.

Desai, Vyapak and Anil Choudhary (2011). 'Reforms in the Indian Capital Market'. Capital Markets Practice Group, Desai Associates, Legal Era, July.

Goel, Kavita and Rakesh Gupta (2011). 'Impact of Globalization on Stock Market Development in India.' *Delhi Business Review*, Vol. 12(1): 69–84.

Husain, F. and A. Qayyum (2006). 'Stock Market Liberalisations in the South Asian Region'. PIDE Working Paper No. 06.

Levine, R. (1997). Financial Development and Economic Growth: Views and Agenda. *Journal of Economic Literature*, 35(2), 688–726.

McKinnon, R. (1973). *Money and Capital in Economic Development*, The Brooking Institutions, Washington DC.

McKinsey (2006). *Accelerating India's Growth through Financial System Reform*. New York: McKinsey Global Institute.

Obstfeld, M. and Taylor, A.M. (2003). 'Globalization and Capital Markets' in *Globalization in Historical Perspective*, 121–188, University of Chicago Press.

Patnaik, Prabhat (2003). 'The Humbug of Finance', in *The Retreat to Unfreedom*. New Delhi: Tulika.

Ranciere, R., A. Tornell and F. Westermann (2008). 'Systemic Crises and Growth'. *Quarterly Journal of Economics*, 123(1): 359–406.

Rao, K.S.C., M.R. Murthy and K.V.K. Ranganathan (1999). 'Some Aspects of the Indian Stock Market in the Post-liberalisation Period'. *Journal of Indian School of Political Economy*, XI(4), October–December.

Reserve Bank of India (2009). *Handbook on Statistics of Indian Economy*. Mumbai: RBI.

*SEBI Handbook of Statistics on the Indian Securities Market* (2009).

Securities and Exchange Board of India: Annual Report (various years).

Shah, A. and S. Thomas (1997). 'Securities Markets: Towards Greater Efficiency', in K. Parikh (ed.), *India Development Report 1997*. New Delhi: Oxford University Press.

World Bank (1997). *World Development Report 1997: The State in a Changing World*. Oxford University Press. New York.

World Economic Forum (2012). The Financial Development Report 2012. Geneva, Switzerland.

# 4

# Livelihood Issues and Inequality among Dalits in the Era of Globalization

**VIRENDRA B. SHAHARE**

Many scholars have expressed concern about the consequences of globalization for the well-being of various groups, the sovereignty and identity of countries, state of disparities among peoples and the health of the environment (Hirst and Thompson, 1996) . Globalization widens the gap between the rich and the poor and increases inequalities and debt in developing countries (Atardi and Martin, 2003). The World Commission Report too has found unequal distribution of growth and disparity across nations and increasing unemployment and poverty. According to the Report, the per capita income of the 20 richest capitalist countries went up to 121 times during 1985–2001. In 16 countries, inequality was static and only in the case of nine countries had it declined. Poverty and inequality have increased post-globalization in many developing countries. This increased in many Latin American and African countries, while China and some South Asian countries improved their economic growth and social development. As far as India is concerned, where inequality persists in society, globalization has further increased the gap between the rich and the poor. Although the State, as an institution, guarantees social welfare and justice to the general population and Dalits (Scheduled Castes) in particular, globalization has not only threatened it but also made it weak. As a consequence, the State has retreated from its welfare role and shifted its responsibilities to non-state agencies. However, the conditions of the Dalits have remained sidelined in terms of education, health, political participation, employment opportunities and social justice, and this has led to a drastic attitude of militancy among them. In the present era, a small section of the population holds maximum resources and majority of Dalits are grappling with poverty. The neo-liberal economy with its ethos of liberalization, privatization and globalization, has thus further compounded the unevenness and inequality in society.

Across the world, there are communities which continue to be marginalized and are denied their rights due to their location within the society determined by their class, caste, race, ethnicity, gender and colour. In India, caste discrimination ensures that Dalits remain one of the most oppressed and exploited people. Dalits constitute 16.6 per cent of the total population of the country (Census 2011). Pursuing sustainable livelihoods can also be difficult for these groups who often do not have the appropriate education, skills or training. Their status as agricultural labourers, domestic workers, and manual scavengers directly accounts for the higher level of poverty among them. They are deprived of adequate access to the basic needs of life such as health, education, housing, food, security, employment, justice and equity. Issues of sustainable livelihood, social and political participation of these groups exist as a major problem. When Dalits are unable to support themselves in their village, they are often attracted by the promise of work in cities across India. They move to towns and cities in search of jobs, but these too are not always available, partly because they lack the qualifications. They are doubly discriminated against – first, as a worker of the unorganized sector and secondly as the member of a socially discriminated group. They face untouchability and discrimination at the workplace both by employers and fellow-workers of upper-caste communities. Governments have failed to provide livelihood rights to the Dalits. They are unable to acquire and use livelihood rights and become excluded from the mainstream of society. In spite of the Employment Guarantee Act, 2005, that provides for 100 days' employment for the people living below poverty line in rural areas and the Swarna Jayanti Shahari Rojagar Yojana in urban areas, many poor Dalits are unable to get employment and are mostly excluded and discriminated against in terms of employment opportunities and this affects their livelihood.

Globalization is uniformly anti-people and directly proportional to the degree of marginalization. Dalits being the most marginalized people in India, their movement ought to have been concerned with these policies while accepting the proven fact that globalization hits the Dalits. As capitalism has made skilful use of caste, globalization, which is essentially capitalism in the era of information and communication technology, is not going to impact it positively. Rather, in the wake of the increasing hardship of the general mass of people through declining jobs, rising inflation, teasing consumerism, reducing public services and cruel competition, caste, as a divisive instrument, comes in handy for the ruling classes to contain the people's ire. Of particular relevance to Dalits are certain implications of these policies of the free market. The privatization of the Public Sector and reduction of government jobs, through the minimalist State that globalization envisages, has directly hit the job-prospects of Dalits. Even the premature free-market ethos unleashed by these policies and so enthusiastically upheld by the high caste-bureaucracy has already impacted Dalit interests adversely. It has many negative implications in terms of exploitation of Dalit women, Dalit culture and most importantly their hopes to struggle for their own emancipation. Globalization has also resulted in reducing the staff in government departments. The impact of the globalization on Dalits can thus be assessed along several dimensions but here the study confines itself to the most predominant ones, viz., livelihood, food, education, employment, healthcare and migration.

## Inequality and Dalit Issues

Understanding the Dalits issues is a crucial factor in effective poverty reduction. Dalit issues can never be understood in any one-track logic - be it economic, social, technical, cultural or political. The livelihoods approach puts households of Dalits as its central focus. The livelihood systems are made up of very diverse elements which, taken together, constitute the physical, economic, social and cultural universe wherein the families live (Hogger, 2004). In other words, a holistic consideration of things that includes what Dalits might be vulnerable to, assets and resources that help them thrive and survive policies, and institutions that impact their livelihoods, how Dalits respond to threats and opportunities, and what sort of outcomes they aspire to. Landlessness is growing at a rapid pace among Dalits, as is evident from the fact that the proportion of all Dalit workers as agricultural labour is increasingly growing at a very fast rate as compared to the non-Dalit agricultural labourers, Nearly 70 per cent of the Dalit farmers are marginal farmers and 50 per cent of the Dalit population resides below poverty line (Census, 2001). Most of the Dalits are landless labourers and around 60 per cent of the Dalits are still illiterate. Despite decades of land reform legislation, over 86 per cent of Dalit households today are landless or near landless. This is largely because Dalits have very poor access to land and even when they are recorded as cultivators, many of them cultivate land as tenants or share-croppers and have very small area of land to operate. As with many other low caste populations, lack of access to land makes Dalits economically vulnerable; their dependence is exploited by upper and middle caste landlords. In urban areas most Dalits live in slums and they are mostly dependent on daily wage employment and working in very hazardous conditions - they are construction workers, domestic helpers, sweepers, cleaners, rickshaw-pullers, etc.

The provision of reserving 15 per cent of admission in educational institutions and jobs in government service for the Dalits has not been taken seriously. Such provisions could have made significant contribution in enhancing the status of the Dalits but effective implementation has not been done. Thus, a majority of Dalits still live in acute poverty. The better paid and dignified occupations continue to be out of reach for them through a systematic denial of rights to education, training, property rights and other livelihood resources. Literacy rate among Dalit women continues to be the lowest at 41.96 per cent (Census, 2001). Around 71 per cent of Dalit women workers are agricultural labourers. Also, about 70 per cent to 75 per cent of Dalit families are female-headed. Dalit women face various forms of violations. Their civil and political rights are violated in order to prevent them from accessing economic and social resources. Though in relative terms, there has been some improvement in their overall socio-economic condition, in absolute terms they are still what they were. The educational, economic and intellectual advancement of a few individuals from among the Dalits is not going to uproot the stigmatized identity of the entire Dalit community. The caste system is still a strong feature of Indian society and maintains the gap between the rich and the marginalized. Such division exists more in rural areas than urban areas, as identity of lower castes is easily distinguishable in rural areas. Economic upliftment of this section still remains a major challenge before the Indian state. It is a far stretch of the imagination to believe that the upper castes who are responsible for the exploitation of the Dalits, would be interested in the economic development of Dalits. The number of incidents of atrocities on the Dalits has been increasing every year. The practice of caste discrimination and untouchability still continues, especially in rural areas.

## Globalization and Livelihood of Dalits

Agriculture and allied activities support livelihoods of nearly 70 per cent of India's Dalit rural population. The land-based livelihoods of marginal Dalit farmers are increasingly becoming unsustainable, since their land has not been able to support the family's food requirements. As a result, they are forced to look at alternative means for supplementing their livelihoods. Empirical evidence shows high incidence of poverty and low human development indices where there is a concentration of Dalits. Agriculture and land-based commons are important sources of livelihood for the Dalits but land alienation and decreasing landholding size have been affecting their livelihood. Landless agricultural Dalit labourers throughout the country work for a few kilograms of rice or ₹ 15 to ₹ 35 (US$0.32 to $0.75) a day, well below the minimum wage prescribed in their state. Many Dalit labourers owe debts to their employers or other money-lenders (Human Rights Watch, 1999). Indian laws and regulations that prohibit alienation of Dalit lands, set ceilings on a single landowner's holdings, or allocate surplus government lands to SCs and STs have been largely ignored, or worse, manipulated by upper castes with the help of district administrations (Human Rights Watch, 2001).

Dalits suffer from lower access to capital assets like agricultural land and non-land assets. Lack of access to agricultural land for cultivation is a major barrier to progress among Dalits. They become economically vulnerable; their dependence is exploited by upper and middle caste landlords; their lack of political power leads to abuses by the police and politicians. From 1948 to the 1970s, 34.9 million acres were given to farmers, of which only 0.5 per cent was given to Dalits as reported by the National Campaign on Dalit Human Right (NCDHR), 2006. The NCDHR report on Caste, Race, and the World Conference against Racism (WCAR) shows that out of an estimated 30 million hectares of harvestable surplus land, only 7.5 million acres have been declared surplus, and only a small portion has been given to Dalits. Large tracts of land are being sold well below market value to multi-national corporations and the World Bank, which has resulted in the displacement of many Dalits who were living on the land (NCDHR, 2006). Shah, Meander, Thorat, Deshpande, and Baviskar (as cited in NCDHR, 2006) found that Dalits in 21 per cent of the villages surveyed were denied access to Common Property Resources (CPRs), such as lands and fishing-ponds. In 2004-2005 only one-fifth, i.e. 20 per cent, of all SC households were able to cultivate land as independent agricultural workers, whereas upper-caste households represented twice that figure. Many a time, exclusion is practiced through denial of access to agricultural land, and denial in sale and purchase or leasing of land. The Action Aid All-India Study (2000) found discriminatory treatment of SCs in access to irrigation water. In some states, restrictions were led by upper castes towards the SCs in the purchase of private agricultural land and use of public land for agricultural use. The limited access to land and capital due to the ongoing discrimination against Dalits has resulted in greater levels of poverty among this group. For example, the level of poverty was reported to be 60 per cent among agricultural labourers, a vast majority of whom are Dalits (Thorat, 2002).

Livelihoods are affected by the process of globalization. Special Economic Zones (SEZ) have been created across India to promote exports. The central government approved 237 SEZs in 19 states in 2007 (occupying 86,107 hectares) out of which 63 SEZs have already been notified. Around 23 SEZs are operational, 18 in the IT sector. Total amount of land to be acquired across India is estimated to be around 1,50,000 hectares. Reliance Industries has sought permission to build India's biggest Special Economic Zone near Mumbai comprising more than 14,000 hectares of land. Similarly, some 400 SEZ projects, amounting to 1,25,000 hectares, and offering incentives to big businesses had been approved (formally and in-principle). Some estimates show that close to 82,000 farm-worker families, mostly Dalits that are entirely dependent on these farms for their livelihoods, will be displaced. It is an amazing feature of this exclusive area where unskilled Dalits are working for their livelihood.

## Globalization and Employment of Dalits

The government implemented the reservations policy to create job opportunities for Dalits. However, the reservation system has only minimally benefitted the Dalits. This is partly because the system applies only to the government sector. Moreover, the system is reported to be flawed because many jobs are left unfilled and because of a lack of commitment on the part of a government dominated by upper-caste politicians (Artis et al., 2003). For example, most of the reservations are in low-skill, low-paying jobs. Often it is difficult for Dalits to make the transition from their traditional jobs to mainstream jobs. To allow for proportional representation of SCs, the Constitution reserves 15 per cent of seats in government jobs, state legislatures, the lower house of the Parliament, and government educational institutions. Of the total reservations for SCs in the central government, 54 per cent remain vacant. The situation is worse in other public sector jobs, with 88 per cent remaining unfilled (NCDHR, 2006). India's Constitution created formal governmental institutions (Panchayatis Raj) in an effort to foster democratic representation and control at the grassroot level. The reservation policy applies to these governing bodies, but they have been unable or unwilling to implement measures that facilitate their constitutional duties of promoting equality (Menon and Nigam, 2007).

In addition, the government supported the rural employment of the poor by various government schemes/programmes for livelihood in rural areas such as Swarnajayanti Grameen Swarozgar Yojana (SGSY) and the Sampoorna Grameen Rozgar Yojana (SGRY) to generate wage employment. The National Scheduled Castes and Scheduled Tribes Finance and Development Corporation (NSFDC) and Mahatma Gandhi National Rural Employment Guarantee Act, 2005, provides a guarantee for rural employment to households whose adult members volunteer to do unskilled manual work for not less than 100 days. In 2010, the Government of India approved the restructuring of its SGSY programme into the National Rural Livelihoods Mission (NRLM). The Government of India will invest $5.1 billion in NRLM over the next seven years in its allocation for the 12th Five Year Plan. The World Bank is committing $1 billion through its National Rural Livelihoods Project (NRLP), its largest single investment in a poverty reduction programme. It is the first national safeguard regarding the right to work (Republic of India, 2006). Meanwhile, Dalits are still forced into degrading occupations, such as manual scavenging, bonded labour, and child labour (NCDHR, 2006). Dalits who are not forced into degrading occupations are discriminated against by means of lower wages, longer periods of unemployment, and fewer opportunities for work. They have greater difficulty getting hired by others because business owners normally prefer to hire those from their own caste. Some Dalits are excluded from crop processing, residential construction, and restaurant work. Dalit agricultural labourers earn less money on an average, work less often, and are paid later than non-Dalit workers (NCDHR, 2006). A survey of 555 villages in 11 states across India was conducted by Action-Aid in 2000 wherein the study found that discrimination in labour market operates through exclusion in hiring and lower wages. The SCs faced discrimination in terms of wage payment and were denied casual employment in agriculture in 25 and 36 per cent of villages, respectively. In these villages, SC labourers received wages less than the market rate. The survey data revealed that in 47 per cent of the villages, the SCs were not allowed to sell consumer goods at the village market.

For example in the Kolleru Lake area of the West Godavari and Krishna Districts of Andhra Pradesh, nearly 60,000 Dalit families lost work opportunities in the agricultural sector when agricultural land was converted into aqua-culture ponds. Similarly, privatization of NALCO, BALCO, Singareni Collieries has affected livelihoods of millions of Dalits in the Dhanbad coal mines of Jharkhand (Divakar and Ajai, 2004). In Anugul, Orissa, the privatization of an aluminium plant, in Jharkhand and Orissa the privatization of mining lost the livelihood rights of millions of Dalits. In Dongergav village of Solapur district of Maharashtra, the employment of Dalit youths got reduced drastically. Eighty-six men and women were employed in the Public Sector and the government between 1981 till 1991. This employment has come down drastically to only nine persons from 1991 to 2004, despite increase in the number of educated capable youth among the Dalit communities (Divakar and Ajai, 2004). In Nandigram, West Bengal, 17 villagers (of whom 12 were Dalits) were shot to death in the protest against the government taking away lands for corporation chemical hubs of Salim group. The Plachimada protest over Coca Cola against the exploitation of ground water opposed the acquisition of land for the Special Economic Zones (SEZ) where majority of the marginalized faced huge crisis of water. The State, however, has not restored land-rights and titles to landless Dalits. Land given to SEZ promoters is more than 1000 hectares which obviously violates the Land Reforms Act. SEZs have not created employment for local Dalits but pushed them away because SEZs employ skilled and educated workers.

Globalization has resulted in reducing the staff in government departments. If the number of staff is reduced, it affects both the upper castes as well as Dalits. After the implementation of reservation, so many Dalits are being educated. But even as the rate of educated Dalits is increasing, the hope of getting jobs is declining. The effects of globalization are debilitating for them. When they had no education, there were government jobs, and now that they are educated, there are no government jobs. Even if there are jobs, most of them are contractual or temporary and with no security of sustenance. In fact, they are appointed for less than a year. Moreover, there is no guarantee that the same post is given to the same person. When it comes to contract basis, reservations norms are not allowed. There is lot of insecurity and the Dalits have to compromise on the jobs that they get as the jobs many a times do not suit their educational qualifications.

## Globalization and Food Security

Approximately 55 per cent of SC children are undernourished, compared to 44 per cent of children in other communities (One World South Asia, 2006). India implemented the National Programme of Nutritional Support, also known as the Mid-Day Meal Scheme (MMS), in 1995 after the Supreme Court directed the national government to create such a programme, and participation grew from 33.4 million to 105 million children between 1995 and 2004. However, the number of SC child-participants fell from 22,638,260 to 22,004,919 between 2003 and 2005. The states of Uttar Pradesh, Bihar, Andhra Pradesh Rajasthan and Tamil Nadu have been notably deficient in providing the MMS to Dalit children, because Dalit children are hesitant to enter hostile areas inhabited by higher castes. Unfortunately, higher caste members usually block Dalits from being hired as cooks and participating in the distribution of the MMS. If a Dalit was hired as a cook, non-Dalit parents sent back lunches with the children to school (Dreze and Goyal, 2003). Higher caste members were found to have the Dalit cook fired or campaigned to get the school closed (NCDHR, 2006).

The Public Distribution System (PDS) is the largest system of food distribution, and PDS shops are responsible for allocating food to the villagers. Dalits have less access to distribution centres because just 17 per cent of the shops are located in Dalit colonies and 70 per cent are in dominant caste areas, with the remaining 13 per cent being located elsewhere. Shop owners discriminate against Dalits in terms of both quantity and price (NCDHR, 2006). Food subsidies meant for the poor are often sold on the black market, and ration shop licensees bribe police officers so that complaints are not registered. For example, hundreds of complaints were filed against a distributor in Belwa, but the police did not register the complaints and the distributor was not prosecuted (Asian Legal Resource Centre).

## Globalization and Migration of Dalits

Dalits in rural areas rely on the products of the land for their livelihood, and they face many challenges for their sustainability. Every year millions of poor Dalit families migrate in search of work. They are forced to migrate due to a livelihood-collapse in the villages. These distressed migrants take a few meagre belongings and move across long distances. The children accompanying their parents are forced to drop out of school. The number of such children under the age of 14 years is estimated to be around 9 million. Being away from their village, they do not belong to the places where they go and increasingly lose acceptance in their own villages. They are disconnected from their community, culture and traditions, unable to take part in festivals, fairs, religious and social functions, which are an integral part of their lives, thus losing their sense of identity. The vulnerability of people who cross state boundaries is even greater as they find themselves increasingly at the mercy of their contractors. The family members or children left behind in villages do not know where the family has gone, or how to contact them. Dealing with emergencies, particularly back home is difficult, especially for those who go long distance. Distressed migrant Dalits find themselves with hardly any skills, assets or education. Earnings from migration are of survival level and not enough to build assets. On the contrary, medical or other personal emergencies and the unsteady nature of work often push them further into debt. Those who own a few animals have to arrange that they are cared for or just end up selling them off at low prices, thus depleting their assets. The work sites largely have no basic facilities like water, marketplace, schools, health centres, etc. Migrants are at the mercy of their employers for all their needs. Contractors retain control of labourers not only financially but also physically, forcing them to work even when they are sick or injured. If there are resident communities nearby, migrants are usually shunned by the local people, and regarded as bad elements or thieves.

## Impact of Globalization on the Education of Dalits

The free market ethos as a result of globalization has entered the educational sphere in a big way. Commercialization of education is now the established fact. Commercial institutions offering specialized education have come up in a big way from cities to small towns and rural areas. In a true spirit of globalization, many foreign universities are invading the educational sphere through hitherto unfamiliar strategic alliances with non-descript commercial agencies, of course at hefty dollar-equivalent prices. Many elite institutions like IIMs and IITs, suddenly facing fund crunch, had to resort to raising their fee and other prices manifold. They were already beyond the reach of the Dalits. As the job markets become acutely competitive, owing to a sharp decline in job opportunities, the polarization between the elite and Dalits has sharpened. Even the sphere of primary education has been miserably affected by globalization leading to expensive education. It is difficult for a village Dalit student educated in the vernacular medium to compete with his convent-educated (now an understatement!) counterpart in cities and towns. Despite several kinds of State assistance, the Dalits are plagued with an alarming rate of school drop-outs. The privatization of the Public Sector and reduction of government jobs through the minimalist State that globalization envisages, will directly hit the job-prospects of Dalits. Even the premature free market ethos unleashed by these policies and so enthusiastically upheld by the high caste bureaucracy, has already impacted Dalit interests adversely.

The illiteracy-rate for Dalit children is generally high in affected countries, compared to that of other children. Although the literacy rate among the Dalits has generally increased over the last years, the literacy gap between them and other children is still wide. Sample studies from Bangladesh indicate that around 96 per cent of the country's estimated 5.5 million Dalits are illiterate (One World Action, 2011). Apart from posing a barrier in access to education, the widespread illiteracy also results in lack of gainful employment options for Dalits (Human Rights Watch, 2007). A UNICEF report from 2006 points to the fact that the quality of education is often so low that children 'mechanically go through five years of primary education and emerge barely literate' (UNICEF, 2006).

## Globalization and Health of Dalits

Globalization has severely hit the poor and Dalits in particular. It has further increased the gap between the rich and the poor, thus affecting their health. The still-persisting discrimination and denial of healthcare is hardly recognized as a problem deserving attention. Social exclusion and discrimination of Dalits with respect to public-health facilities is of major concern. Most of them are poor and thus have less access to nutritious food. Disparity in access to resources leads to disparity in exposure to the risk of disease, leading to disparity in disease burdens. The central and state governments have considerably enhanced allocations for the provision of health, sanitation and other facilities to promote capacity building and well-being of the poor in general and Dalits in particular. But most of the Dalits live in insanitary conditions amongst open sewers and open air toilets with no access to public health and sanitation. There are no State-sponsored public-housing rights or public health rights in India. The National Family Health Surveys (IIPS, 1995, 2002, 2007) were conducted regarding the utilization of healthcare services by the scheduled communities. It was evident that the level of utilization is much lower among the Dalits as compared to the non-Dalits (Ram et al., 1998; Acharya, 2002; Kulkarni and Baraik, 2003). Poorer health status of Dalits includes higher morbidity, lower life-expectancy and higher rates of infant mortality. Inequality leads to discrimination which in turn leads to denial of resources like the physical, intellectual and emotional. A study of Dalit children and women in selected villages of Gujarat and Rajasthan found that the nature and forms of discrimination experienced by Dalit children in accessing health services are attributable to their poor health and high level of mortality (Acharya, 2010).

Inequities in the conditions of daily living are shaped by deeper social structures and processes (WHO, 2008). The inequity is systematic, produced by social norms, policies and practices that tolerate or actually promote unfair distribution of and access to power, wealth and other necessary social resources. According to Whitehead et al., 2007 health inequities arise due to social hierarchies inbuilt in the social system. The health status of individuals depends on the socio-economic factors, which in turn affects their lives and not merely on the presence or absence of any healthcare system. It is generally found that health status and access to health services is not equal among different groups divided by various socio-economic and demographic characteristics. The State healthcare system entails to provide services to all without any discrimination. However, discrimination in accessing healthcare is faced by Dalit children in many cases. The caste-based discrimination focuses directly on their health status and disadvantages they experience. In India, caste identity is a unique phenomenon which has deep-rooted linkages with access to health and health status of communities at large. Caste and social stratification in India determine health, education, employment, social, and economic outcomes (Jacob, 2009). Nayar (2007) points out that poverty, social exclusion and deprivation has a major impact on the health of Dalits. Marmot (2003) used the same logic to explain the inequities in health, as he said that the disease and suffering of disadvantaged people in all countries are a result of poverty, lack of resources; and it is social hierarchy which plays a major role in determining people's access to health and health services. Menon and Contractor (2001) point out that Dalits are not only socially discriminated against and oppressed but also face ample inequalities in the health sector as well. Poverty is an important determinant of access to healthcare services (Djurfeld and Lindberg, 1976); and most of the poor are Dalits as well as most Dalits are poor. Poverty evolves a different health culture and affects perception of illness and utilization of care. A rather national picture was generated regarding the utilization of healthcare services by the scheduled communities after the National Health and Family Surveys (IIPS, 1995, 2002, 2007) were conducted and spurt of research papers emerged. It was evident that the level of utilization is much lower among the Dalits as compared to the non-Dalits (Ram et al., 1998; Acharya, 2002; Kulkarni and Baraik, 2003).

## Conclusion

The rapid changes at the macro level that India witnessed since the early 1990s have contributed to the instability of the livelihood systems of the poorer sections, mostly the Dalits of rural households. Globalization has led to increased social exclusion of Dalits as it has resulted in denial of equal opportunities, inequity in development and inability of Dalits to participate in the basic political, economic and social functioning of the society. While the benefits of the process of globalization have largely accrued to the urban rich and the educated poor and marginalized in urban slums, the rural sector has been left behind. Further, the caste-based exclusion has also resulted in failure of access to resources, entitlements and socio-economic rights among them. The International Covenant on Civil and Political Rights (ICCPR), the International Covenant on Economic, Social and Cultural Rights (ICESCR) and laws at the central and state level, their influence in promoting the livelihood of Dalit communities in rural areas is limited. Also, the slowdown in agricultural growth and productivity, changing cropping patterns, increase in distress migration, changing consumption patterns, government policies favouring industrial houses, among others have seriously undermined the food and livelihood security of Dalit households. An integrated, multi-dimensional and holistic approach to poverty-eradication efforts at the upliftment of Dalits is crucial to preserve and enhance their livelihoods. The practice of caste-based exclusion and discrimination involves failure of access and entitlements, not only to economic rights, but also civil, cultural and political rights of the Dalits. It involves what has been described as living-mode exclusion, exclusion in political participation, social and economic opportunities. This means, in reality, the perpetuation of the traditional caste-dominated patterns of control and violence, and continued livelihood and personal insecurity on the part of the Dalits.

## References


A Study on Untouchability , Action Aid, India, 2000.

Acharya, Sanghmitra (2002). 'Health Care Utilisation in Rural North India: A Case of Nirpura, District Meerut'. CSMCHEU Project, Centre of Social Medicine and Community Health, School of Social Sciences, Jawaharlal Nehru University, New Delhi, Unpublished Report.

——. (2010). *Access 'to Health Care and Patterns of Discrimination: A Study of Dalit Children in Selected Villages of Gujarat and Rajasthan*. New Delhi: Indian Institute of Dalit Studies.

Alternate Report to the Joint 15th to 19th Periodic Report of the State Party (Republic of India), to The Committee on the Elimination of Racial Discrimination (CERD) National Campaign on Dalit Human Rights (NCDHR) India, 2006.

Artadi, E. and X. Sala-i-Martin (2003). 'The Economic Tragedy of the Twentieth Century: Growth in Africa'. *National Bureau of Economic Research Working Paper*, No. 9865, July.

Artis, E., C. Doobay and K. Lyons (2003). 'Economic, Social and Cultural Rights for Dalits in India: Case Study on Primary Education in Gujarat', Workshop on Human Rights: From Grassroots Courage to International Influence, Woodrow Wilson School of Public and International Affairs, Princeton, NJ.

Deaton, A. and J. Dreze (2009). 'Food and Nutrition in India: Facts and Interpretations'. *Economic and Political Weekly*, XLIV(7), February 14–20: 42–45.

Divakar, Paul N. and M. Ajai (2004). 'UN Bodies and the Dalits: A Historical Review of Intervention' in Thorat and Umakant (eds), *Caste, Race and Discrimination: Discourses in International Context*, Jaipur: Rawat Publications.

Djurfeldt, G. and S. Lindberg (1976). *Pills Against Poverty: A Study of the Introduction of Western Medicine in a Tamil Village*. New Delhi: Oxford and IBH Publishing Comapny.

Dreze, J. and Aparajita Goyal (2003). Future of Mid-Day Meals, *Economic and Pclitical Weekly*, Vol. 38, Issue 44, 4673–4683.

*Government of India Census*, 2011.

Guru, Gopal (2000). 'Dalits: Reflections on the Search for Inclusion', in Peter R. De Souza (ed.), *Contemporary India: Transitions*. New Delhi: Sage Publications.

Hirst, P. and G. Thompson (1996). *Globalization in Question: The International Economy and the Possibilities of Governance*. Cambridge: Polity Press.

Hogger, Ruedi (2004). 'Understanding Livelihood Systems as Complex Wholes' in *In Search of Sustainable Livelihoods: Managing Resources and Change*. Ruedi Baumgartnet and Ruedi Hogger (ed.), 94–125, New Delhi: Sage Publications.

Human Rights Watch (1999). Broken People: Caste Violence against India's 'Untouchables', available at http://www.hrw.org/reports/1999/india/india994.htm.

IDSN (2010). 'Dalit Children in India: Victims of Caste Discrimination'. Briefing Note by Navsarjan Trust (www.navsarjan.org), The Center for Human Rights and Global Justice (www.chrgj.org) and The International Dalit Solidarity Network (www.idsn.org).

International Institute of Population Sciences (1995). *National Family Health Survey (NFHS) 1992–93*, New Delhi: Institute of Population Sciences.

International Institute of Population Sciences and Macro International. *National Family Health Survey-3 (2005–06), India*. Vol. 1, Mumbai: IIPS.

Jacob, K.S. (2009). 'Caste and Inequalities in Health'. *The Hindu*, August 22 [cited December 29]: 283. Available from: http://www.thehindu.com/2009/08/22/stories/2009082255540800.htm.

Kulkarni, P.M. and V.K. Baraik (2003). 'Utilisation of Health Care Services by Scheduled Castes in India'. Working Paper No. 39, New Delhi: Indian Institute of Dalit Studies.

Marmot, M.G. (2003). Understanding Social Inequalities in Health. *Perspectives in Biology and Medicine*, Vol. 46(3): S9–S23.

Menon, N. and A. Nigam (2007). *Power and Contestation: India Since 1989*. London: Zed Book.

Menon, Sumita and Contractor, Qudsiya (2001). Dalits and Health (Paper presented at the World Conference against Racism and Xenophophobia and Related Discrimination, South Africa, Durban).

Nayar, K.R. (2007). 'Social Exclusion, Caste and Health: A Review Based on the Social Determinants Framework'. *Indian Journal of Medical Research*, 126(4): 355–63.

Paul, N. Divakar, and M. Ajai (2004). 'UN Bodies and the Dalits: A Historical Review of Intervention' in Thorat and Umakant (eds), *Caste, Race and Discrimination: Discourses in International Context*, 3–30, Jaipur: Rawat Publication.

Ram, F., K.B. Pathak and K.I. Annamma (1998). 'Utilisation of Health Care Services by the Underprivileged Section of Population in India: Results from NFHS'. *Demography India*, 30(2).

Thorat, Sukhadeo (2002). Oppression and Denial: Dalit Discrimination in the 1990s, *Economic and Political Weekly*, 39, 6, Feburary 9.

WHO (2008). Commission on Social Determinants of Health Final Report, Closing the Gap in a Generation Health Equity through Action on the Social Determinates of Health.

# Part 3

## Group Inequalities and Marginalization

# 5

# Private Unaided School, Elite Spaces and Disadvantaged Children

## *How Inclusive is the RTE Act, 2009?*

**KHUSHBU R. GUPTA**

The idea of inclusion in education has been at the core of the Education Policy of India in the wake of persistent inequality. The support to the idea of inclusion is well observed in several researches. In the field of Education, inclusion involves a process of reform and restructuring of the school as a whole, with the aim of ensuring that all pupils can have access to the whole range of educational and social opportunities offered by the school (Mittler, 2000). A large number of studies have documented the linkage between socio-religious background and educational attainment as well the quality of education (Desai, Adams and Dubey, 2009; Desai and Kulkarni, 2008; The Probe Team, 1999). Several studies have been conducted, supporting the policy of social inclusion and mitigation of social inequalities over a period of time (Young, 1971; Bowles and Gintis, 1976; Bourdieu and Passeron, 1977; Lauder, Brown and Halsey, 2009). Inclusive education is considered a progressive, democratic, and humanistic reform all over.

India is a diverse country with different levels and sources of inequality in education. Inequality is unique because it revolves around the differences among various caste-groups wherein Scheduled Castes (SCs), Scheduled Tribes (STs) are the major discriminated lot. The educational differential cannot be addressed by only expanding physical access to schools. Increased physical access to schools, in itself, will not be enough to ensure the overall development of children. This is a product of the choices made at the policy level about how to respond to the opportunities and constraints posed by diversity prevailing, such as in India. The 'quality' of schooling is the key to the widening of opportunity-set available to individuals from various sections of society.

The demand for schooling by SC and ST families has not been matched by the supply of quality education. On the contrary, the quality of education and environment in government schools has declined over the years and today not just the rich but also those with middle income prefer to send their children to private schools. Low-income parents are seen to move their children between schools in search of good education and are constrained by its availability, cost and sustainability (Kingdon, 1996; Nambissan, 2012).

It is in this backdrop that provisions under the Right of Children to Free and Compulsory Education Act, 2009 (RTE Act, 2009), have significant implications for the Indian social context. The agenda of inclusion in education by the Government of India has come to the forefront after the enactment of this Act. One of the major features of the Act is the provision of 25 per cent reservation of seats in private unaided schools for children from the disadvantaged and Economically Weaker Sections[1] (EWS) of society. The policy pronouncement calls for a pro-active role on the part of private institutions, which have so far abstained from any such social obligation, in providing education to the children of disadvangtaged and Economically Weaker Sections of society (EWS).

Considering the unique case of inequality based on the social identity of the people in the Indian context, this provision under the RTE Act has drawn a lot of attention among the stakeholders and the institutions accountable to fulfil the mandate under the Act. The success of this provision would mean how effectively it caters to the *'effective and meaningful participation'* of the EWS and the disadvantaged children. Wherein, 'effective participation' would mean that a child is an active participant in the whole learning exercise whereas 'meaningful participation' would mean that once a child enters the education system, he completes his schooling cycle. Further, inclusive education has been identified as an integral component for achieving effective and meaningful participation of the EWS and the disadvantaged children.

This paper intends to capture an account of the experiences of these children, their parents and the overall response of the school administrators with regard to the policy pronouncement in the context of the 25 per cent reservation for the EWS and the disadvantaged children under the RTE Act, 2009. It is pertinent to mention that prior to the enactment of the RTE Act 2009, the schools in Delhi were duty-bound to provide 15 per cent of the total number of seats to the children from the EWS background in lieu of the land granted to the schools on subsidized rates by the Delhi Government.[2] However, since the enactment of the RTE Act, the scope has been widened to also include the disadvantaged children under its ambit by raising the cap of reserved seats to 25 per cent.

## Methodology Adopted

The paper draws on the primary data collected through the survey of selected private unaided schools in Delhi using questionnaire and semi-structured interview as tool.

Twenty private unaided schools were randomly selected from the four zones in Delhi, viz. east, west, north and south. Five schools from the four zones were selected on random basis. This provided a geographical representation of the schools in the city-state of Delhi. Questionnaires were administered to 60 teachers from grades Nursery, KG and I. Interview was conducted with the principals of the 20 selected schools to gather insights with regard to the school policies in place for the overall integration of the EWS and the disadvantaged children. Also, semi-structured interview was conducted with 30 parents of the EWS and the disadvantaged children (selected on random basis) studying in the 20 different private schools.

Further, school's official records with regard to the admission procedures and data with regard to the children from the reserved quota were collected for the academic years 2011–12, 2012–13 and 2013–14 to map out the transition of these children in the subsequent years of schooling.

**Figure 1**

*Implementation of the Provision: Accounting for Access and Continuity in the System*

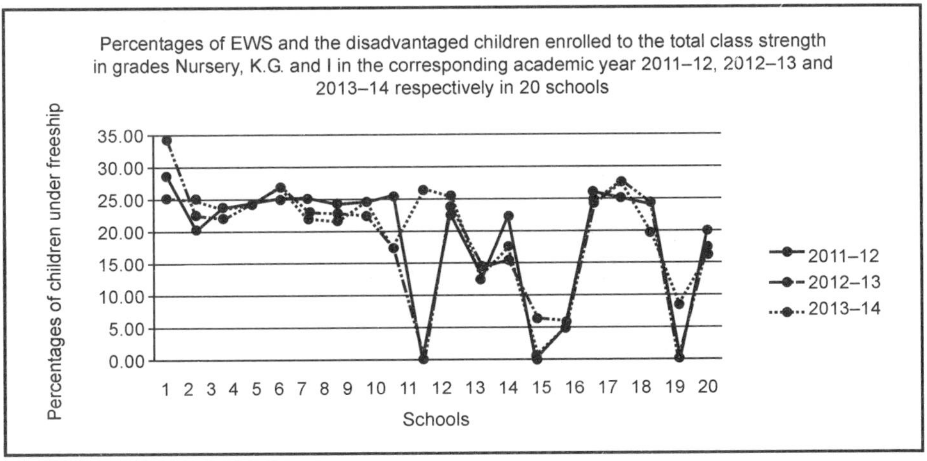


*Source:* Field Data Recorded by the Author.

The graph (Figure 1) indicates that in eight out of 20 schools even access of the requisite percentage of children has not been achieved. While on the one hand 12 schools under the Study do have the requisite percentage-representation of these children, on the other hand, there is a need to have a re-look at the adopted criteria.

Ideally, all the children who have got admission under the 25 per cent reservation should transit to the subsequent higher grades irrespective of the decrease in the total strength of the class in the following year. This is important to ensure that once a child is admitted, he or she completes primary education. While it is pertinent that 25 per cent of the total class-strength of children be maintained in the subsequent higher grades, it should not be done at the behest of maintaining the 25 per cent quota alone.

In the schools under the study, however, it was found that there are instances wherein the percentage of the children availing freeship has decreased with the decrease in the total class strength. This is indicative of the fact that some of the children have left the school, the reasons for which need to be accounted for.

Another major issue remains with regard to the implementation of the neighbourhood policy[3] under this provision of the Act. It needs to be noted that in one of the areas in south Delhi, wherein there are many private unaided schools but few children from the EWS and the disadvantaged background to cater to, these schools have got away by strictly sticking to the defined neighbourhood criteria, thus denying admission to those beyond the neighbourhood limit. Some of the schools in the study (as depicted in the graph above) had very few children availing the freeship quota. These schools have got away by manipulating the number of applicants and further stating that they did not have enough children applying for the freeship.

## Accounting for Exclusionary Processes

The provision of 25 per cent reservation in private unaided schools under the Act provides for the integration of children to *'elite spaces'* which have been beyond the reach of the EWS and the disadvantaged children so far. However, by simply adopting a norm-based provision, this Act inadvertently misses the impeding factors which lead to exclusionary processes. The provision under the Act was found to be delinked from enabling children from the disadvantaged and the EWS background to make effective and meaningful access to education.

### *Age of Children and Exclusion*

The schools are found to be taking in admissions only for Nursery/pre-school Classes and the age was restricted to 3 to 4 years. All the schools in the study rejected the applications of children over 4 years of age, the argument being that if the children are admitted at the age of 3 and 3-plus, they get enough time to prepare for primary education.

The provision under the RTE Act lays down the age criteria for entry at Grade 1 to be six years. Given this, a child entering Nursery/pre-Primary between the ages of three to four years is in tune with the laid down provision. However, considering the fact that 42 per cent of the enrolled children in elementary education are over-age,[4] restricting the age group of children between four to six years in the grade-appropriate class could lead to a further worsening of the scenario. Limiting the age criteria between 3 to 4 years is in turn excluding the children of age group of 4 to 6 years, and limiting the equality of opportunity for them.

Further, as the provision under the Act cites the age-limit to be six years, interpretation from this could be drawn that though schools can take in admissions into Nursery/pre-Primary in the age group of 3–4 years, the maximum age for admission is cited as 6 years, the entry level for this being Grade I. This, however, was not found to be the practice in any of the schools under the study. All the schools are taking admissions of children for only Nursery/pre-Primary in the age group of 3 to 4 years.

### *Admission's Notification and Exclusion*

It was also observed that it is, indeed, very difficult for these parents to get their children admitted to these schools. As cited in a study by Yagnamurthy:

> Many schools refuse admission to students from EWS, citing 'no vacancy' as the reason, some others claim to have already admitted the required number but

> are reluctant to prove it. Additionally, some schools have been very clever with the notices, announcing admissions to their institutions not in Hindi dailies, but in English ones, which most people from this section of society do not subscribe to. It is clear that private schools do not want to implement 25 per cent quota for the poor children wholeheartedly. (Ranjan, 2010 cited in Yagnamurthy, 2013)

### *Lottery System and Exclusion*

Due to the prescribed limited number of seats available under the freeship, the parents are constrained to apply in more than one school as the chances of their getting admission in one school are very low.[5] Thereafter, depending upon the draw of lots, the parents choose the available option. This has led to the maintenance of the record of children making it through the lottery-draw in multiple schools; giving the schools the leverage to manipulate the number of children who seek admission. Many of the schools in the study have been maintaining records with regard to the number of children who made it through the lottery system and not with regard to the actual number of EWS and the disadvantaged children who sought admission. The records maintained by the schools were, hence, not authentic, raising further question with regard to the existence of a single child's record in multiple schools.

### *Randomization and Exclusion*

It was observed that 19 out of the 20 schools under the study were taking admissions only under the EWS category. The common practice adopted by these private unaided schools in Delhi has been to admit children only under the EWS category, denying freeship to the disadvantaged children who fail to produce the EWS certificate. EWS certificate is the main criterion irrespective of the category of caste. Schools are not giving admission against SC/ST reservation, which is against the constitutional mandate.

### *Hidden Charges and Exclusion*

Another issue that needs to be addressed is with regard to the fees paid by the parents of these children which are usually not accounted for. The parents interviewed in the study complained of frequent expenses being incurred by them towards their child's education despite the school tuition fees being exempted for them.[6] According to some of the parents, the school usually demands some fees for activity-based participation in the school such as school concert, sports day, annual day function and others. Despite these parents not being in a position to pay towards such expenditure, they are forced by the school authorities to do so. The principal of one of the schools in the study stated:

> We have our annual function wherein each child is supposed to pay ₹ 1,000 towards their participation. These children just sit and watch their friends perform in the glittery light and show. What is the school supposed to do? We are already providing free education to these children. How do we meet the expenses for this section of the children? There are many unaccountable

> expenses; all that the government does is reimburse fees for books and stationery of these children. We do not get any school tuition fees reimbursed as the land for the school was provided under the DDA Land Grants Rule.

Interview conducted with the principals of the schools revealed that out of the 20 schools in the study, 19 schools were raising funds from the parents of the fee-paying children. Coincidently, these were the schools granted free land by the Delhi Government under the DDA Land Grant Rule. One of the schools which had not been granted land under the aforementioned provision was reimbursed for the expenses incurred towards the education of the children under freeship.

As such there are no expenses incurred by these schools towards the education of these children. The schools have been adjusting the extra expenses towards their education by hiking the fees for the fee-paying children. Hue and cry is raised by the schools with regard to providing free education to these children as the parents of the fee-paying children often complain of such increase in the fees each year. The school authorities are worried over the increase in the number of children availing the freeship a few years down the line, when beyond a certain point the fee-paying parents would refuse to pay the extra added expenditure as part of their child's school fees.

It is important to bring forth the point that this gives further leverage to the fee-paying parents to demand from the schools that it mould the rules and guidelines in their favour. It is, indeed, a matter of concern that this may prove to be fatal for the parents availing freeship *as their freeship leaves them with no voice to oppose any such rules and guidelines that go against their interest.* Further, this has a cascading effect on the treatment meted out to the children availing freeship.

### *Power Relations and Exclusion*

The difficulties in navigating power and identity in a different spatial domain are critical to understanding the exclusionary processes. The power relations that are defined within the premises of the school define the way in which the children are treated with regard to their background. During the course of the interview, one of the principals of the school under the study remarked:

> These children use abusive language and lack basic manners, their parents are least involved and do not bother about their wards, these children cannot follow basic classroom instructions and do not complete their homework. Whenever a child loses something in the classroom, they always accuse these children for having stolen their stuffs. The children are all well aware of their social and economic status and are often told by their parents not to mingle with the children under the freeship category. Some of the parents have approached us, requesting us not to allow their children to sit with the children under the reserved quota.

Hence, the successful implementation of this provision was found to be largely dependent on the way school leaders were conceptualizing the idea of meritocracy and equality of opportunity. This has a transcending effect on how teachers treat children from the EWS and disadvantaged background in the classroom-setting.

### *Exclusion in Subsequent Higher Grades*

Decreasing number of EWS and disadvantaged children in the subsequent higher grades has been observed in majority of the schools under the study. Interview conducted with parents of the children availing freeship revealed that the general practice adopted by the schools is that in the subsequent levels, where there is a lack of monitoring mechanism in place by the government agency, these schools admit fee-paying children, replacing the children under the freeship quota. This has larger implications for such provision as it only obliges private unaided schools to give *admission* and is silent on *continuation* of these children to the upper levels of grade.

### *Subservient School Culture and Exclusion*

The practice of *stereotyping these children with regard to their cultural background* shows the lack of commitment on the part of the school management. Interview with the principal of a school revealed that the cultural background of these children poses a major challenge to their overall integration. The language as medium of instruction in these schools also poses a challenge for these children. In particular, these children fail to perform well in the English language. Majority of the teachers complained that the lack of parental support hindered their meaningful participation in the classroom. Further, most of the children also face problems in peer-group interaction and this problem gets further aggravated once they learn to differentiate their own cultural background from that of their affluent counterparts.

### Concern of the School

A majority of the principals of these schools had a common concern with regard to the implications of this provision in future on their school's structure and composition. They complained of the EWS and the disadvantaged children carrying with them the values and cultures which were not in sync with their school's environment and culture. They expressed apprehensions with regard to the implications of such a policy for the future of their school. They felt that the socio-economic composition of the school would be altered in a few years down the line, when these students would transit to higher grades in large numbers.

### EWS Certificate Criteria

In order to avail admission to the unaided private schools, the parents need to submit an EWS certificate.[7] One of the important problems outlined by the parents even before getting admission is that it is very difficult to obtain an EWS certificate from the requisite authorities. The parents often find it difficult to pursue the matter with the officials for the issue of the certificates. Red-tapism further adds to their woes and in the process some even miss out on the admission deadlines.

Even if one joins a private school under EWS quota, it is no guarantee that one would be able to continue in the school even for an academic session. The EWS certificate requires renewal subject to the corresponding changes in the income levels with time. The following quote from the study by Yagnamurthy provides an understanding of the situation:

> A son of the postman who was studying in a private school was thrown out on the ground that his father's income during the year had exceeded the EWS income limit prescribed. What is perturbing is that the child was thrown out in the middle of the session. It required the intervention of the State Education Minister for the child's continuation in the school for the academic session, on humanitarian grounds. (*Times of India*, 20 July 2010, cited in Yagnamurthy, 2013)

Further, there exists a huge problem with regard to the authenticity of the EWS certificate. Majority of the principals of the schools complained of affluent parents with EWS certificates availing the facility rather than the real targetted EWS and disadvantaged children. During the course of the interview with a school principal, it was revealed that the parents availing freeship are told by the EWS certificate-issuing authorities that:

> You give us ₹ 5,000 every year for the issue and subsequent renewal of the EWS certificate and I shall give free education to your child up to grade eight in a good reputed private school.

Principals argue that there is lack of accountability when it comes to the issuance of the EWS certificates. The provision of freeship has led to the parents who are able to negotiate in getting the EWS certificate to avail the freeship rather than the real intended beneficiary.

## Accounting for the Vacancies Persisting against the Reserved Quota

According to the Directorate of Education, Delhi, many seats meant for the EWS and disadvantaged children lie vacant every year in the private unaided schools which have average performance ratings. This has been further confirmed with the news of 2,500 EWS seats going vacant each year in Delhi schools (*Times of India*, 19 March 2013). Raising this concern, the principal of one of the schools in the study remarked thus:

> While on the one hand, our school receives around 2000 applications each year and we are constrained to deny admission as our seats are limited to 25 per cent of the total at the entry level, on the other hand, there are schools where many vacancies exist and go unutilized year after year. The government has been overlooking this issue. Further, this shows that these parents choose different schools and like to opt for a better available choice.

What could be the reason that despite providing free education, these seats are lying vacant? Does this point to restraints by the schools in providing admission to these children? Have these schools not been approached at all by the parents of the EWS and the disadvantaged children?

## Conclusion

This paper looked at the issue of 'silent social exclusion' of the EWS and the disadvantaged children under the provision of 25 per cent reservation in private unaided schools in Delhi under the RTE Act, 2009, and the problems associated with its implementation. The qualitative methodology was adopted for the purpose of the study.

It is, hence, observed that it is necessary for the private unaided schools not only to admit students under EWS quota but also to retain them. This would require the schools to adopt a positive attitude, interest and awareness on the part of the parents, and regular monitoring by the government.

It is, indeed, important that the effective participation of these children is not compromised with. A shift towards meaningful participation would entail the carrying out of the concerned policy pronouncements in the true sense and spirit of their meaning. These children should not be deprived of the feeling of belonging to the class. As suggested by Hattam et al., (2009), it is about bringing the community into schools and about developing curricular and pedagogical relationships that give voice, choice, and independence to young people in the classroom.

For the effective implementation of this provision of the RTE Act, it is indeed important to build a framework of accountability on the part of the private unaided schools. Monitoring with regard to access is already in place but there are concerns with regard to the effective and meaningful participation of these children. Considering the trend of the progression of the children to the higher grades, at this stage[8] it is difficult to comment on the likelihood of the successful implementation of this provision of the Act. Further, research is required to study the overall implementation of this provision of the Act over a considerable period of time.

The findings suggest that while this Act is in place to ensure inclusion of the EWS and the disadvantaged, it is actually excluding these children. It is also observed that many schools under the study are not implementing the provision under the RTE Act, 2009, in its true spirit. Finally, the paper suggests that *the provision of 25 per cent reservation for children from the EWS and the disadvantaged background requires a framework of accountability on the part of the school to ensure that these children are not excluded.*

## Notes

1. As per the RTE Act 2009, a child belonging to a 'disadvantage group' means a child belonging to the Schedule Caste, the Scheduled Tribe, the socially and educationally Backward Class or such other group having disadvantage owing to social, cultural, economic, geographical, linguistic, gender or such other factor, as may be specified by the appropriate government, by notification whereas, a child belonging to a 'weaker section' means a child belonging to such parent or guardian whose annual income is lower than the minimum limit specified by the appropriate government, by notification.
2. The Delhi Development Authority (Disposal of Developed Nazul Land) Rules in 1981 provides for allotment of lands to educational institutions i.e. schools, colleges, and universities at concessional rates. Rule 20 stipulates that allotment of land at concessional rates may be made to a society which is registered under

the Societies Registration Act, 1860, is of a non-profit making character and is sponsored or recommended by a Department of the Delhi Government or a Ministry of the Central Government. Such allotment of land to educational institutions is made subject to certain mandatory terms and conditions. The primary purpose of such allotment of land at concessional rates is to serve a public purpose of facilitating establishment of or extending educational facilities particularly for the weaker sections of the society.

3. Existing policies and State legislation define neighbourhood in geographical terms, either as a habitation or distance within a radius of 1 km for primary and 3 km for upper primary. However, the model rules for the Right to Education Act lay down a separate definition in the case of 25 per cent quota in private unaided schools.

   Considering the underlying fact that elite schools are located in elite neighbourhoods where there may be a few children belonging to these categories residing in the school's vicinity, such schools may not admit disadvantaged children since there may not be any or not enough to fill the prescribed 25 per cent limit in that neighbourhood. On the other hand, small private unaided schools located in the underprivileged areas would have excess demand. The model rules define neighbourhood with regard to this particular provision in a wider sense (or even as zones, with children from the immediate neighbourhood getting first priority and then those from the external neighbourhood, until the quota is filled up) so that more students would be able to access the 25 per cent quota.

4. 'Overage in Grade Challenges for RTE and RMSA in India', *The Indian Journal: Journal of the Indian Economic Association*, Special Issue, December, 2011, pp. 127–34.
5. Usually the ratio of the EWS and the disadvantaged children who get admission and applied approximates around 45:2000 in many reputed private unaided schools whereas in some average-rated schools the ratio is usually around 20:800.
6. Under the RTE Act, 2009, the cost borne by private unaided schools towards the education of the EWS and the disadvantaged children is reimbursed by the state government. The reimbursed amount includes school tuition fees and allowances towards stationeries and school uniforms for these children.
7. A certificate indicating that a child belongs to such parent or guardian whose annual income is lower than the minimum limit specified by the appropriate government, by notification. The private unaided schools in Delhi accept EWS certificate issued by the Sub-District Magistrate (SDM).
8. The RTE Act came into effect in the year 2009. However, the implementation of the provision of 25 per cent reservation for the EWS and the disadvantaged children under the Act has been carried out from the year 2010 onwards and that too only in selected private unaided schools in Delhi. There were few schools in the study which had adopted this provision only from the academic session 2013–14.

## References

Bourdieu, P. and J. Passeron (1977). *Reproduction in Education, Society, and Culture.* London: Sage.

Bowles, S. and H. Gintis (1976). *Schooling in Capitalist America.* London: Routledge.

Desai, S. and V. Kulkarni (2008). 'Changing Educational Inequalities in India in the Context of Affirmative Action'. *Demography*, 45(2): 245–70.

Desai, S., C. Adams and A. Dubey (2009). 'Segmented Schooling: Inequalities in Primary Education', in S. Thorat and K. Newman (eds), *Blocked by Caste: Discrimination and Social Exclusion in Modern India.* New Delhi: Oxford University Press.

DOE (Department of Education) (2012). 'Government of NCT of Delhi: List of Schools Allotted Land'. Retrieved from http://stoic-rational.blogspot.in/2011/03/list-of-schoolswhich-wereallotted.html [accessed in New Delhi, India on 8 February 2012].

GOI (Government of India) (2005). 'Allotment of Land to Educational Institutions'. Retrieved from http://www.cag.gov.in/html/reports/civil/2005_4/chapter4.pdf [accessed in New Delhi, India on 14 November 2009].

Hattam, R. et al. (2009). 'Researching for Social Justice: Contextual, Conceptual, and Methodological Challenges'. *Discourse: Studies in the Cultural Politics of Education*, 30(3): 303–16.

Kingdon, G. (1996). 'Private Schooling in India: Size, Nature and Equity Effects'. *Economic and Political Weekly*, 31(51): 3306–14.

Lauder, H., P. Brown and A.H. Halsey (2009). 'Sociology of Education: A Critical History and Prospects for the Future'. *Oxford Review of Education*, 35(5): 569–85.

Mehta, C. Arun (2011). *Elementary Education in India: Progress towards UEE*. New Delhi, India: National University of Educational Planning and Administration.

MHRD (2010). 'Model Rules for the Right to Education Act'. Department of Education, Government of India, New Delhi.

Mittler, P. (2000). *Working towards Inclusive Education: Social Contexts.* London: David Fulton Publishers.

MoL&J (2009). 'The Right of Children to Free and Compulsory Education Act, 2009'. Government of India, New Delhi.

Nambissan, G.B. (2012). 'Private Schools for the Poor'. *Economic and Political Weekly*, 47(41): 51–58.

Ranjan, Priya (2013). 'Equity in Education: A Sociological Analysis of "Right to Education Bill"' in D. Pramila (ed.). *Eduity and Education in India: Policy, Issues and Challenges*. New Delhi: Kanishka Publisher, 277–282.

Sreekanth, Y. (2013). 'Reservation for Economically Weaker Section Children in Unaided Private Schools: Policy and Practice'. *EDUCARE: International Journal for Educational Studies*, 5(2).

The Probe Team (1999). *Public Report on Basic Education in India.* New Delhi: Oxford University Press.

Yagnamurthy, S. (2013). 'Reservation for Economically Weaker Section Children in Unaided Private Schools: Policy and Practice'. EDUCARE: International Journal for Educational Studies, 5(2).

Young, M. (ed.) (1971). *Knowledge and Control: New Directions for the Sociology of Education*. London: Collier-Macmillan.

# 6

# Cost and Pricing of Higher Education

## *Emerging Concerns for Equity and Affordability*

**BINAY KUMAR PATHAK**

With the proposal of the setting up of new IITs, IIMs, AIIMs, Agricultural and Horticulture Universities in its maiden budget, the new political dispensation at the Centre has given clear signals to continue with the ongoing policy of expansion of higher education.[1] Expansion, one of the three goals of higher education policy, has been pursued actively while the other two – equity and excellence – have received little attention as compared to the levels achieved by the first goal (Pathak, 2014). This is in unison with trends of massification of higher education and its characteristic features observed throughout the world. This trend co-exists with the trends of privatization and competition and these are influenced by some common factors such as demography, globalization, etc. (OECD, 2008 and 2009).[2]

The presence of international trends in Indian Higher Education (HE) and recent proposals for expansion of HE, indicate minimum deviation from the policy-path followed during the last 10 years which witnessed the HE sector receiving immense attention. During this period, while new IITs, IIMs and Central Universities in almost all states have been set up, the HE sector also went through scrutiny and analyses by advisory bodies starting from the National Knowledge Commission (NKC) to the Narayan Murthy Committee (NMC). The latest and most significant policy decision in this regard has been the launch of the Rashtriya Uchchatar Shiksha Abhiyan (RUSA), which is poised to weaken the University Grants Commission (Chattopadhyay, 2014).

While equity or access to HE is attempted to be addressed through expansionary or massification policies, there have also been attempts to commodify Education in general and HE in particular, manifested from the efforts to create more space for private providers of HE and allow profiteering in HE. Though private participation in HE had emerged in the colonial period itself, the recent surge in private participation in HE finds resonance with policy prescriptions.

This paper seeks to unravel these inter-connections in the light of a theoretical understanding of the processes involved. It brings forth the conceptualization of cost and pricing of HE as these are important elements for privatization. The paper examines the theoretical conceptualization of cost and pricing of HE on the anvil of peculiarities of HE as a commodity. The policy-prescriptions are then critically looked into in the light of these understandings. Thus, the paper presents a critical review of theories and practices related to cost and pricing of HE. The paper consists of five sections. This first section introduces the paper and sets the context. The second section discusses peculiarities of HE as a commodity and the HE market as observed in literature. The third section presents a review of theories to understand the cost and pricing of HE and discusses some prominent models of markets for HE. The fourth section of the paper critically analyses policy-prescriptions in the field of HE in the light of literature discussed in the previous sections. The last section brings out the approaches towards the cost and pricing of HE in theory and practice, and their implications for equity or affordability.

## HE as a Commodity and its Market

HE as a commodity is different from other commodities bought and sold in market as it has some peculiar features attached with it. These features provide the background to understand the market for HE and its cost and price. The peculiarities of HE as a commodity are as follows:

(a) *Experience-Good:* The quality of HE can only be judged by experience (Teixeria et al., 2004). This characteristic of HE may seem to be less effective for reputed institutions as their long-established reputation itself signals quality. Prospective students tend to rely on the reputation of institutions, built on the experiences of the previous batches of students to assess quality before admission. But the actual quality is judged only after admission. This particular character of HE applies to all stages of education.

(b) *Quasi-Public Good:* HE differs from other stages of education when it is looked at from the point of view of investment, as HE is characterized by simultaneous association with positive externalities and private returns. This unique feature leads it to be a 'quasi-public good' while the stages below HE may be treated as public goods (Niklasson, 1996; Chattopadhyay, 2007). On the basis of private returns being associated with HE, cost-recovery and declining public support is advocated. At the same time positive externalities associated with HE ask for public support to HE.

(c) *Absence of Production Function:* Unlike other goods, the production function is not clearly defined in the case of HE, as it lacks clear input-output relationships (Majumdar, 1983). The inputs here, the students, are the output themselves. In such a situation Higher Education Institutions (HEIs) owe their reputation to the inputs whom they charge for education.

(d) *Labour-Intensive Service:* HE, like other services, is labour intensive by nature and does not conform to capital – labour substitution – rather, capital and labour appear to be complements for HE for provision of a given quality.

### *The HE Market*

Like HE as a commodity, the market for HE is also unique in its peculiarities. Here, HEIs act as multi-product firms with degrees, passing-out students and research and innovation carried out by them as output. One of these outputs, the students, is also the input for HEIs (Majumdar, 1983; Winston, 1999). The following features characterize this market:

(a) *Quasi-Market:* The market for HE, a quasi-public good, is a quasi-market (Niklasson, 1996; Bridges and Jonathan, 2003). The term 'quasi-market' was coined to denote the organization of services on the lines of market principles as observed in the case of HE (Le Grand and Bartlett, 1993). This feature renders itself to policy interventions quite obviously as it is a policy determined feature itself.

(b) *Customer-Input Technology:* The HEIs, above the average level, seek to create a peer group which matches the quality of the institutions. This creates a unique academic ambience in which the peer teaches the peer. Peer-quality acts as an input to HEIs' production in technical terms and it cannot be bought from anyone other than its own customers (students). HEIs may have to incur a cost for this input in the form of advertisement, fee-waivers and scholarships. This input may or may not have substitutes. Its use may get adjusted to reflect its costs, available substitutes and resources (Winston, 1999; Rothschild and White, 1995).

(c) *Positional and Hierarchical:* HEIs are hierarchical and positional in nature. It starts with their unequal access to resources during the formative years, gets amplified by their reputation built upon product quality over the years and persists in competition in terms of heterogeneous goods and services and their prices (ibid., 1999; 1995). The monopolistic competition among them also emanates from their geographical location and institutional characteristics objectives and the process of institutionalization of information systems. Any institutional change through re-organization of information can be linked to a rational adjustment to a cost difference in information.

## Cost, Pricing and Models of HE

As profiteering in HE is closely associated with the cost of provision or delivery of HE and pricing of such provisions, understanding the cost, pricing and models of HE becomes indispensable. This section will take up these issues in the backdrop of the above discussion on HE as a commodity and the HE-market. These peculiarities are crucial as they restrict the application of general productivity-enhancing principles in the HE sector. As for illustration, increasing the burden of classes on a teacher or to increase the class-size may seem productivity-enhancing but considering the peculiarities of the HE sector, these can lead to compromise with research output of the faculty or deterioration in quality of HE for all students.

### *Cost of HE*

As HE is one of the labour-intensive services, the seminal work by Baumol and Bowen (1966) can be considered as the first attempt to understand the rise in cost of HE. Their study was for the labour-intensive services' sector in general but it gave rise to debates and studies to understand the cost of HE too. Their study propounded that increasing productivity in labour-intensive services sectors such as HE is not easy – as is the case in other sectors by substituting capital with labour while the wages for qualified individuals engaged in such sectors increase along with other sectors. As a result, such sectors experience rise in unit-labour costs often more than the overall economy. This phenomenon is known as 'cost disease'.[3] While Cowen (1996) expresses doubts over this phenomenon, citing that innovation in services delivery can reduce cost, Archibald and Feldman (2006) have found conforming results for this phenomenon from their studies on rising cost of HE.

The first specific attempt to explain the cost of HE was made by Howard Bowen in 1980, known as 'revenue theory of costs'. He attempted to explain the cost of HE by taking into account the peculiarities of the sector. This theory says that a HEI determines its costs by taking into consideration the revenue constraints. So, to maintain the quality of HE, a HEI has to look for more revenue when faced with rising costs. Considering Cowen's criticism of 'cost disease', Bowen includes cost-reducing technological progress which will shift the constraints downwards. The two approaches do not contradict each other over time except for two differences: (i) the latter being specific to HE and (ii) consideration of technological innovations by the latter. But the latter approach (Bowen's) suffers from an inherent contradiction which is that the HEIs can maximize either quality or revenue, not both (Archibald and Feldman, 2006).

Another model came from Massy in 1989 known as the 'autonomous cost increase model' with an implicit assumption that every university is a separate monopoly facing an inelastic demand and can raise prices at will. Massy's analysis is found lacking the explanations for very slow increase in prices, revenues and expenditures for a monopoly HEI in general and sudden changes in these variables in particular.

John Siegfried and Malcolm Getz (1991) also attempted to find explanations for the rising cost of HE also considering the peculiarities of the sector. They gave six plausible explanations, one of which is the phenomenon of cost disease. The other explanations for cost increase are: (i) change in the product-mix in favour of more expensive disciplines (ii) shortages of HE-specific inputs (iii) inflated desires for quality (iv) poor management and (v) government regulations. While the factors such as inflated desires for quality and government regulations seem to ignore the publicness associated with HE, the other explanations are general for any commodity. Thus, Siegfried and Getz appear to be not fulfilling their claim for considering HE with its peculiarities. The literature on HE financing is filled with studies treating HE as any other sector without considering the specific needs and peculiarities of the HE sector to understand the cost from supply side, which is very much linked to profiteering in HE.

## Models for HE Market

As discussed above, there are very few studies to understand HE market as it is in itself. This section presents select models for HE with attempts to explain the market with at least some of its unique features. One of the earlier attempts to understand the HE model has been by James (1978, 1986) and James and

Nueberger (1981) who assume tuition fees as pre-determined and beyond the control of individual HEIs. This unreal assumption renders the model useless. Out of various attempts, two models – one developed by Rothschild and White (1995) and the other developed by Epple et al., (1999) and Epple et al., (2001) – tend to capture the essence of the HE market. The former model recognizes the input-technology feature of HE – that is, the consumers (students) being an input – and the latter recognizes the influence of peer-effect on the overall quality of HE. A brief description of the two models to be able to understand the process of marketization of HE seems essential.

### *Pricing of Services with Consumers as Inputs*

Rothschild and White (1995) developed this model for services which are experience-goods and have consumers as inputs. They tried to understand the nuances of the HE sector in their seminal work entitled, 'The University in Marketplace: Some Insights and Some Puzzles' published in 1993. This work provided the basis for their model (1995) which is based on marginal analysis and two-sided matching theories developed by Roth, Sotomayor and Mongell in their different works.[4]

Price in this model is levied positively on a particular input (students) and cannot be charged directly. The first-order condition of equilibrium in the market requires the marginal cost of producing an additional unit of human capital to be equal to its marginal product. The convexity assumption ensures the second-order condition for the equilibrium. This model assumes students as an only output of universities. The equilibrium is characterized with discriminating product-quality and discriminating pricing at the same university. The product – quality is anyway different for different disciplines and courses at the same university. However, if it is for a given discipline or course, discriminating product-quality implies different educational technologies and pedagogy of education claiming different prices such as the cases of regular, open and online education.

The model provides the basis for competition in the HE market and explains the variations in the quality of human capital generated at the same institution due to discriminating product-quality and convexity assumptions. The discriminating-pricing indicates differentiated fee-structure, including fee-waivers and scholarships.

The model ignores some crucial market conditions, viz., resource allocation by HEIs, affordability of HE for students and capital market complexions, information asymmetries and existence of research as output; the model attempts to capture the input-technology feature of the HE market and provides a basis for further development of more precise models.

### *Education Quality Maximization Model*

This model attempts to predict the pricing behaviour of HEIs, considering students differentiated by both ability and household income, and focuses on the implications of quality maximization. The model is developed by Epple et al., (1999) and Epple et al., (2001).

At market equilibrium, households tend to maximize their alternative utilities with given qualities of HE, fee-structure and admission policies. Effective Marginal Cost (EMC) of admitting a student of a certain ability is the sum of the marginal resource-cost of educating the student and the cost of maintaining quality due to the impact of students with different abilities on peer group. The HEIs, at the same time, tend to maximize quality of HE by choosing fee and admission policies. The households choose among the affordable HEIs or no HEI.

These predictions for affordability of cost of HE is the hallmark of the model. They help in understanding the objectives and functioning of the HEIs in a peculiar kind of market in which they operate. The model also provides two important implications for the HE market: (a) diversity – to control the peer effect and (b) non-institutional financial aid – to attract better quality students with income constraints to better quality HEIs. Despite these predictions and implications, the model suffers from some valid limitations. These include ignoring students as decision-makers and information-asymmetries prevalent in the market. Nonetheless, the model is the closest to the reality of the HE market.

## HE Policy in India

The HE policy environment in India is characterized by a rising fee-structure in HE which is influenced by decline in public expenditure on HE and emergence of private providers of HE. Private providers are emerging to fill the gap between the rising demand for HE and limited supply by the public sector; privatization of HE, which implies the application of market principles in the operation and management of HE, is on the rise. In publicly funded HEIs, privatization or marketization is evident in the forms of partial privatization through fee-hikes and student-loans, and cross-subsidization of courses. The partial privatization of HE by hikes in students' fees, student-loans and other related mechanisms aims at balancing the responsiveness to demand for and supply of HE. Cross-subsidization of courses by selling the most demanded and subsidising the less demanded is also becoming popular among HEIs (CABE, 2005). Own resource generation by the hitherto publicly funded universities and the emergence of private HEIs has led to the growth of self-financing courses in these institutions. Such courses are mostly professional and technical in nature, with better job prospects. The market for higher education (HE), thus, expanded dwells on fees paid by the students. Thus, attracting students has become one of the objectives of the HEIs in the wake of increasing privatization of HE. All sorts of measures from advertising to employing agents are being taken to attract students.

### *HE Policy and Issue of Affordability*

The issue of affordability can best be understood through the policy prescriptions provided from time to time with respect to HE in India. The HE in India till the 1980s was based on recommendations of the University Education Commission (Radhakrishnan Commission), 1948–49, and the Education Commission (Kothari Commission), 1964–66. These recommendations provided the policy background to HE which is characterized by overall public support to HE, although some private providers do exist since the days of the British Raj. After the 1980s, the country witnessed a profusion of private professional education in the name of meeting the prevalent unmet demand of business and industry (Agarwal, 2006). The economic crisis towards the end of the 1980s and subsequent adoption of the New Economic Policy (NEP), characterized with liberalization, privatization and globalization in 1991 added to the impetus for the Private Sector to view higher education as a potential venture.

The issues of availability of resources and poor quality of publicly funded higher education, barring certain pockets of excellence, bind together recent policy initiatives and pronouncements in the field of higher education – from the entry of foreign education providers to engaging the corporate sector, and the recommendations of various groups and committees starting from the Ambani-Birla group to the Narayan Murthy Committee (NMC).[5] In such a favourable policy environment, the private sector has grown to cater to 59 per cent of total enrollments in higher education and is expected to contribute significantly in achieving the target of 30 per cent gross enrollment ratio by 2020–21 (GoI, 2012b).

### *Policy Prescriptions and Cost of Education*

The policy-making and financing of HE have been public 1980s. After the introduction of the NEP, the policy-making for HE started showing imprints of the NEP paradigm. The first formal imprint of policy suggesting own resource generation by HEIs comes with the CABE Committee Report of 1992.[6] The Committee recommended encouraging state universities to raise resources, allowing them to retain the self-generated resource without affecting their block grants. The second policy suggestion in this direction came from the Punnayya Committee (1992–93). The recommendations of the Committee were to provide incentives for Central universities following financial discipline, to award quality, efficiency and innovations, and disincentives for Central universities not adhering to financial discipline. The incentivization of financial discipline and disincentivization of non-adherence is still practiced by the UGC. The Punnayya Committee also initiated the trend for self-financing courses now prevalent in almost all universities barring some exceptions.

While the recommendations of CABE (1992) and the Punnayya Committee changed the landscape for financing of publicly funded HEIs, committees and commissions set up after them tend to create space for private providers of HE. The trend was initiated by the Special Subject Group on Policy Framework for Private Investment in Education set up by The Prime Minister's Council on Trade and Industry in the year 2000. The Group was convened by Mukesh Ambani and had Kumarmangalam Birla as its member. The Group specifically recommended the introduction of private universities, allowing Foreign Direct Investment in HE and limiting public funding to primary and secondary education. The recommendations seem to have been followed meticulously, characterizing Indian HE as a market.

The trend continued with the National Knowledge Commission (2006–07) and Yashpal Committee Report (2008). But the two differed on their approaches towards privatization and financing of HE. While the NKC favoured privatization and marketization and went to the extent of recommending adoption of emerging private engineering colleges by IITs, the Yashpal Committee accepted privatization as a reality with both merits and demerits and recommended the framing of guidelines to check the demerits of privatization of HE. The efforts to create space were indirect at least in the setting up of committees and commissions. Even the efforts to introduce Public-Private Partnerships (PPP) in HE have been consultative and diplomatic. But last year, the Planning Commission set up a Committee under the chairmanship of N.R. Narayana Murthy named 'Committee on Corporate Sector Participation in Higher Education'. Not only has the name of the committee signified a direct and specific approach but same was the case with the recommendations.

In the context of the economic impediments in the path of access to higher education, it is to be observed that the cost of access to education for students is on the rise in India because of two reasons: (i) hikes in fees by publicly funded institutions to meet targets of own resource generation as put forward by the Punnayya Committee (1992–93) and (ii) relatively higher fees charged by private providers to cover cost of providing education, even without profit. As has been averred earlier, in publicly funded institutions, a kind of privatization or marketization is evident through fee-hikes, student-loans and cross-subsidization of courses (GoI, 2005); again, as stated earlier, the growth of self-financing courses, mostly professional and technical in nature and having better job prospects, in publicly funded institutions coupled with the emergence of private providers have made the market for higher education relying on fees paid by the students.

## Discussion and Conclusion

The characterization of the HE sector as market is not free from debates. Leslie and Johnson (1974) examined market models starting from perfect competition to various imperfect market models to ascertain their suitability to the HE sector. They found that no existing model can explain the peculiarities of the HE sector although monopolistic competition bears closeness to explain individual firms (HEIs) to the extent of their market position and command over heterogeneous products – but the concept of market does not appear to be applicable to this sector. Chattopadhyay (2012) also denounces the application of market principles to HE on account of non-fulfilment of basic assumptions of the market and peculiarities of the HE sector. One of the arguments against the characterization of the HE sector as market, for example, is over whether or not students could be considered as customers or consumers in the first place (Sharrock, 2000: 22). Attitudes opposing marketing education believe that it is not suitable to talk about this subject and it is even 'shameful' to call students 'customers' (Holbrook, 2005: 144). Others believe that the introduction of market forces into the area of education evokes feelings of concern, even mistrust, within the world of education (Gibbs and Knapp, 2002). This opinion is supported by the idea that education is not to be marketed as this would create major social and economic problems (Sharrock, 2000). These oppositions, perhaps, lead the firms in the market for HE to claim to be 'not for profit'.

There is a lack of theoretical understanding of the HE market. This is obvious from two facts – (i) very few attempts to understand the HE sector with its own characteristics and (ii) inadequacies of the existing attempts to explain costs and pricing in this sector. The understanding of pricing behaviour in HE suggests that pricing itself is discriminatory as it negates accessibility to HE. The affordability of HE becomes dependent on the purchasing-power capacity under the market regime even if the traditional market models cannot be applied to HE in general. The models discussed in the paper imply the discriminatory nature of the market for HE. While Rothschild and White (1995) implied discriminatory prices charged and discriminatory output, Epple et al. (2001) clearly showed the impact of different pricing outcomes on accessibility and affordability. According to Epple et al. (2001), there is no problem whatsoever for those who can afford even the maximum fees charged but the real problem arises for those who cannot afford even if the HEIs are not profit maximizers.

The present scenario of Indian HE showcases trends for profiteering through privatization of HE as evidenced from recommendations of various committees and commissions discussed above. As a matter of fact, few private parties can be philanthropic in nature but the increasing privatization and the policy push for corporatization confirms the tendency of profiteering. Moreover, the 12th Five Year Plan has proposed for amendments in laws to facilitate HEIs to register as companies, thereby enabling them to shed the mask of 'not for profit organizations'. Another policy initiative to be launched from the TFYP, to be known as Rashtriya Uchchtar Shiksha Abhiyan (RUSA), vows to treat private universities and state universities at par as far as grants for development are concerned.

The emerging picture from the above discussion paints a negative association between profiteering and affordability of HE. Rising fee-structure in the publicly funded HEIs coupled with increasing marketization of HE limits the affordability of HE for the masses. The engagement of the corporate sector in higher education or marketization or privatization through fee-rise may or may not be desirable but the policies governing them should be framed with proper understanding of the higher education sector and in accordance with the goals of social equity and excellence.

Models do not capture the essence of the HE sector. They do attempt to incorporate some of the features. Policies treat HE as any other commodity. Features of HE are not taken into consideration. There is a need to develop models to capture the essence of HE. Traditional economic modelling is not sufficient for prescribing policies. Economic literature and policy, both should focus on HE peculiarities.

## Notes

1. Five new IITs (Indian Institute of Technology), five new IIMs (Indian Institute of Management), four new AIIMss (All India Institute of Medical Sciences), two Agricultural Universities and two Horticulture Universities were proposed in the Union Budget 2014–15. One Medical College in Delhi was also proposed by the Finance Minister in the Delhi Budget 2014–15.
2. Competition here refers to competition among institutions to attract faculty and students, among teachers to find positions for themselves in better institutions, among students for admission to better institutions and placement in job markets.

3. Bela Balassa (1964) and Paul Samuelson (1964) in their parallel studies have come across this phenomenon whose insights can be traced back to the works of David Ricardo in the 19th century.
4. Two-sided Matching Theories are groups of theories dealing with one-to-one, one-to-many and many-to-one demand-supply matching. Alvin E. Roth and Llyod Shapely won the Nobel Prize in Economics in 2012 for their work on these theories.
5. After the NEP, several committees, specialized groups and commissions on higher education have been set up. They include Punnayya Committee (1992–93), Ambani-Birla Special Subject Group (2000), National Knowledge Commission (2006–07), Hoda High Level Group (2008), Yashpal Committee (2008–09) and N.R. Murthy Committee (2012). Based on the recommendations of these committees, policy initiatives in the form of Acts and Bills have also been introduced or enacted.
6. Central Advisory Board on Education (CABE) Report on Gnanam Committee Report of 1992.

## References


Agarwal, Pawan (2006). 'Higher Education in India: The Need for Change'. Working Paper No. 180, Indian Council for Research on International Economic Relations (ICRIER), New Delhi.

Archibald, R.B. and D.H. Feldman (2006). 'Explaining Increases in Higher Education Costs'. Working Paper No. 42, Department of Economics, College of William and Mary, September.

——. (2007). 'Avoiding Tunnel Vision in the Study of Higher Education Costs'. Working Paper No. 53, Department of Economics, College of William and Mary, June.

Bowen, William G. and David W. Breneman (1993). 'Student Aid: Price Discount or Educational Investment'. *Brookings Review*, 11, Winter: 28–31.

Bowen, William G. and Deren Bok (1998). *The Shape of the River: Long-term Consequences of Considering Race in College and University Admissions*. Princeton: Princeton University Press.

Bridges, D. and Ruth Jonathan (2003). 'Education and the Market', in N. Blake, P. Smeyers, R. Smith and P. Sandish (eds), *The Philosophy of Education*. Oxford: Blackwell Publishers.

Chattopadhyay, Saumen (2007). 'Exploring Alternative Sources of Financing Higher Education'. *Economic and Political Weekly*, 42(7): 4251–59.

——. (2012). *Education and Economics: Disciplinary Evolution and Policy Discourse*. New Delhi: Oxford University Press.

——. (2014). 'Higher Education and the Neo-liberal Context'. Keynote Address delivered on 28 February for the Annual State Conference of the All Kerala Private College Teachers' Association held at Alappuzha, Kerala from 28 February to 2 March 2014.

Cowen, T. (1996). 'Why I Do Not Believe in the Cost Disease'. *Journal of Cultural Economics*, 20(3): 207–14.

Epple, D., R. Romano and H. Sieg (1999). 'Theory and Evidence of Competition in Higher Education'. National Science Foundation Working Paper.

——. (2001). 'Peer Effects, Financial Aid, and Selection of Students into Colleges and Universities: An Empirical Analysis'. NBER Working Paper.

Getz, Malcolm and John J. Siegfried (1991). Cost and Productivity in American Colleges and Universities In Clotfelter C., Ronald Ehrenber, Malcolm Getz and John J. Siegfried (eds) Economic Challenges in Higher Education, Chicago: University of Chicago Press.

Gibbs, P. and M. Knapp (2002), 'Marketing Higher and Further Education; An Educator's Guide to Promoting Courses, Department and Institutions'. London: Kogan Page.

Government of India (2000). *Report on a Policy Framework for Reforms in Education.* Prime Minister's Council on Trade and Industry, Government of India, viewed on 1 August 2013, http://indiaimage.nic.in/pmcouncils/reports/education/

——. (2005). *Financing of Higher and Technical Education: Report of the CABE Committee.* New Delhi: National Institute of Educational Planning and Administration, Government of India.

——. (2007). *Report to the Nation 2007.* New Delhi: National Knowledge Commission, Government of India.

——. (2008). *Report of the High Level Group on Services Sector.* New Delhi: Planning Commission, Government of India.

——. (2012a). *Committee on Corporate Sector Participation in Higher Education: Report of N.R. Narayana Murthy Committee.* New Delhi: Planning Commission, Government of India.

——. (2012b). Twelfth Five-Year Plan 2012–17 (Draft). New Delhi: Planning Commission, Government of India.

Holbrook, M. (2005). Marketing Education as Bad Medicine for Society: The Gorilla Dance', *Journal of Public Policy and Marketing*, 24(1): 134–145.

James, E. (1978). Product Mix and Cost Disaggregation: A Reinterpretation of the Economics of Higher Education, *Journal of Human Resoures*, 13: 157–186.

——. (1986). 'Cross subsidization in Higher Education: Does it Prevent Private Choice, and Public Polity?' In Levy D. (ed.) *Private Education: Studies in Choice and Public Policy*, New York: Oxford University Press.

James, E. and E. Neuberger (1981) 'The University Department as a Nonprofit Labor Cooperative', *Public Choice*, 36: 585–612.

Jongbloed, Ben (2004). 'Regulation and Competition in Higher Education', in Pedro Teixeira, Ben Jongbloed, David Dill and Alberto Amaral (eds), *Markets in Higher Education: Rhetoric or Reality?* Dordrecht: Kluwer Academic Publishers, 87–111.

Kumar, Arun (2013). *Indian Economy since Independence: Persisting Colonial Disruptions.* New Delhi: Vision Books.

Leslie, L.L. and G.P. Johnson (1974). 'The Market Model and Higher Education'. *The Journal of Higher Education*, 45(1). 1–20.

Le Grand, J. and W. Bartlett (eds) (1993). *Quasi-Markets and Social Policy.* London: Macmillan, as quoted in C. Middleton (2000). 'Models of State and Market in the Modernisation of Higher Education'. *British Journal of Sociology of Education*, 21(4), December: 537–54.

Majumdar, Tapas (1983). *Investment in Education and Social Choice.* UK: Cambridge University Press.

Mathews, E., Biju A. Chittuparamban, Sharvari Joshi and Payal Dey (2013). 'Engaging the Corporate Sector: Narayana Murthy Committee Recommendations on Higher Education'. *Economic and Political Weekly*, XLVIII(29), July 20: 41–47.

Niklasson, L. (1996). 'Quasi-market in Higher Education: A Comparative Analysis'. *Journal of Higher Education Policy and Management*, 18(1), May: 7–22.

Organisation for Economic Co-operation and Development (OECD) (2008). *Higher Education to 2030, Vol. 1: Demography.* Paris: Centre for Educational Research and Innovation.

——. (2009). *Higher Education to 2030, Vol. 2: Globalisation.* Paris: Centre for Educational Research and Innovation.

Pathak, B.K. (2014). 'Critical Look at the Narayana Murthy Recommendations on Higher Education'. *Economic and Political Weekly*, XLIX(3), January 18: 72–75.

Rothschild, M. and L.J. White (1993). 'The University in the Marketplace: Some Insights and Some Puzzles', in C.T. Clotfelter and M. Rothschild (eds), *Studies of Supply and Demand in Higher Education.* Chicago: University of Chicago Press, pp. 43–60.

——. (1995). 'The Analytics of the Pricing in Higher Education and Other Services in Which Customers are Inputs'. *Journal of Political Economy*, 103(3), June: 573–86.

Sharrock, G. (2000). Why Students are not (just) Customers (and other reflections on life after George', Journal of Higher Education Policy and Management. 22: 149–164.

Smith, Adam (2003). 'The Wealth of Nations', in Bantam Classic Edition of *An Inquiry into the Nature and Causes of the Wealth of Nations*. New York: Bantam Classic, pp. 962–65.

Teixeria, P., B. Jong Bloed, David Dill and A. Amaral (eds) (2004). *Markets in Higher Education: Rhetoric and Reality?* Dordrecht, Boston, London: Kluwer Academic Publishers.

Tilak, Jandhyala B.G. (2008). 'Transition from Higher Education as a Public Good to Higher Education as a Private Good: The Saga of Indian Experience'. *Journal of Asian Public Policy*, 1(2): 220–34.

University Grants Commission (1993). *UGC Funding of Institutions of Higher Education: Report of the Justice Dr. K. Punnayya Committee 1992–93*. New Delhi: UGC.

Winston, G.C. (1999). 'Subsidies, Hierarchy and Peers: The Awkward Economics of Higher Education'. *Journal of Economic Perspectives*, 13(1): 13–36.

# 7

# Inequalities in Participation in Higher Education in India

## *Role of Household Characteristics*

**NIVEDITA SARKAR**

Education in all its forms – and at all levels – is the single most potent instrument of social mobility and source of economic, political and cultural transformation. Education in general and higher education in particular plays a pivotal role in constructing the foundation of a knowledge-based society. Way back in 1964, the Kothari Commission (1964–66) had recognized the symbiotic relationship between education and national development. A lot of deliberation has since been generated towards the emerging concerns of higher education. The 12th Five Year Plan document of the UGC has also stated that 'the vision of higher education in India is to realize the country's human resource potential to its fullest with equity and inclusion' (UGC 12th FYP, 2011: 7).

Empirical studies on economic growth consistently maintain that there is a strong positive association between improved educational indicators and economic growth. A significant example of this are China and most of the East Asian countries, which record a striking growth in per capita income, which in turn can be (at least partially) explained by improved educational indicators (Chakrabarty, 2009). However, the current status of the education sector in India is nowhere close to that in those countries. And if we consider higher education, it is still placed on the backseat. Moreover, it is characterized by low enrollment, poor completion and high drop-out rates along with wide social and regional disparities in rates of enrollment and availability of adequate number of higher educational institutions. The low Gross Attendance Rate (GAR) at the higher education level in India at 17.6 per cent (NSS, 2007–08) is a clear testimony of the neglected position of this sector.

Now, enrollment or participation in higher education (or at any level of education) involves substantial amount of monetary investment. These investments are usually incurred in two domains – individual and societal (Majumdar,

1983). Both are essential since public investment can provide educational facilities and household investment will facilitate its optimum utilization (Tilak, 2002a). In this context, Panchamukhi (1990) points out that both these investments are inter-related and inter-dependent in such a manner that in the absence of either of them, the probability of under-allocation of resources increases. Thus it can be postulated that the level of participation in higher education is influenced by both household as well as public investment. The household/individual and the State invest in education based on certain expectations about their future returns in terms of both economic as well as non-economic benefits. While State investment is a policy decision, household investment in education is influenced by a wide range of factors (economic, social, cultural etc.). In life-cycle model of household decisions, if rates of return to education are high, a household may choose to refrain from present consumption and invest in education in order to increase earning capacity and other benefits in future. However, this is only a necessary condition - not the sufficient one. Therefore, one can conceive of a particular situation where a household may withhold educational expenditure even if the expected private rates of return - monetary and/or non-monetary - are high, due to several other economic, social and cultural constraints (Tilak, 2002a). On the basis of the available literature, on ecanargue that the social and economic factors of household investment in education play a significant role in determining the level of participation in higher education. While there are several studies in related areas which highlight the gender differences in participation in education in India, there are others which focus on the caste-factor. A direct relationship has also been established, through the literature, between household economic status and the probability of participating in higher education. It is also postulated that educational qualifications of a household-head and the parental educational background play a vital role in determining the participation in higher education.

Thus, with this background, the present paper would use the gender lens to empirically explore the levels of participation in higher education across social groups, localities and household economic status. Further, it would also attempt to find out the extent of household-characteristics responsible for determining whether or not to participate in higher education for both males and females. The paper is divided into six sections. After this Introductory Section, Section-2 documents a cursory overview of existing related literature, followed by database and methodology in Section 3. Section 4 puts forth an empirical overview of levels and patterns of participation in higher education from the 64th Round unit-level data. Section 5 presents the results of the econometric model on determinants of participation and, finally, Section 6 concludes the paper.

## Overview of Existing Literature

A huge body of existing literature on the economics of education usually views education as an investment good in the line of human capital theory. The human capital theory considers education as an investment so as to maximize lifetime wealth (Schultz, 1961; Mincer, 1974). Additional educational years generate benefits in terms of enhanced future earnings and compensate direct costs and opportunity costs associated with delayed entry into the labour market. Consequently, individuals are assumed to invest in higher education until the marginal rate of return from additional education is equal to some market rate of interest. The rate of return is calculated from the expected costs and benefits of higher education (Galper and Dunn, 1969).

However, in reality, the investment decision on the part of the individual depends on myriad factors. The study of Stafford, Lundstedt and Lynn (1984) shows that an individual's decision to participate in higher education is mainly determined by (at least) two components. The first is the economic component and the second involves both social and psychological factors. (There are always potential costs and benefits of the alternative life-choices available to an individual through higher education.) Concentrating only on economic and social factors, one can easily find out two strands of determinants affecting the demand for education: (1) income and employment expectations relevant to each level of education, and (2) the family-background characteristics of each potential student (Albert, 2000).

The literature in economics of education has given significant attention to studying the influence of household characteristics in determining the participation in higher education, along with broader macro economic aggregates. Studies dealing with importance household characteristics could be clubbed under two heads: *(a) household economic factors and (b) household social factors.*

### Household Economic Factors

Participation in higher education requires significant household investment; therefore, one can intuitively argue that the economic background of a household has a considerable impact on the participation of a student at higher educational level. The economic level of a household could be measured through earnings/income of the household and household wealth. There are some studies which have given emphasis on the economic status to examine the determinants of participation in higher education. However, in Indian context numbers of studies of these kinds are very few. One such study was conducted by Filmer and Pritchett in 1998. Taking the NFHS data, Filmer and Pritchett (1998a or b) formulated the *wealth index* for 14 major Indian states and analysed the *wealth effect* on the school enrollment across gender and social groups. (The 'wealth index' in most cases has been broadly defined on the basis of household's ownership of particular assets). The study reports a large amount of variation in the magnitude of *wealth effect* across the various states. It reveals that, the gap between the rich and the poor in terms of school enrollment is less for a state like Kerala as compared to that prevalent in Bihar or Rajasthan. In the realm of higher education similar kind of finding is corroborated by Chakrabarty (2009). The study of Chakrabarty was based on NSS 52nd round data. By analysing the state-wise unit level data of National Sample Survey, she concludes that in urban sample, the children belonging to middle income households have a 16.5 percentage points higher chance of attending a post-secondary education than those belonging to the poorest income class. Further this gap widens substantially at 43.9 percentage points when we consider the highest economic category. Several other studies on the similar aspects also highlight the similar kind of trends for different levels of education (Galper and Dunn, 1969; Stafford, Lundstedt and Lynn, 1984; Filmer and Pritchett, 1998a or b; Tilak, 2002a or b).

### *Household Social Factors*

Along with financial status of a family the educational background of parents also play a decisive role in their ward's participation in higher education. Several studies prove that having parents whose educational attainment is high increases the probability of attending higher education of their children (Kodde and Ritzen, 1988; Albert, 2000; Psacharlopoulos and Mattson, 2000; Chakrabarty, 2009). Additionally, the mother's education is more decisive than the father's in influencing the demand for higher education (see, Albert, 2000; Tilak, 2002a or b). Analysing the large household survey data (sample collected and compiled by by NCAER), Tilak (2002a or b) concluded that the higher the level of education of the head of the household, the higher will be the expenditure on education. The study further shows that in rural India it is not the most educated person in the family rather the head of the family who decides the educational expenditure. The study of Albert (2000) in Spain documents that a 'high' socio-economic status (more specifically occupational status; father is skilled or unskilled worker/employee) of the father also increases the probability of demanding higher education.

Several studies have attempted to estimate whether there is a significant difference in enrollment of children if households belong to different caste groups. Exploring the data of rural India across 14 major states, Filmer and Pritchett (1998 a or b) found out that children belonging to SC/ST households have a lower probability of getting enrolled into elementary school. This gap further widens when we look into the realm of higher education (Chanana, 1993; Hasan and Mehta, 2006; Prakash, 2007). Analysing NSS 52nd Round data (1995–96) Chakrabarty (2009), similar result for rural India were assured at. The data shows children of SC and ST background have significantly lower likelihood of going to a higher educational institution than other social groups in the rural area. Interestingly no such impact was found for the urban sample.

There is a vast amount of literature which has already highlighted that there prevails a huge gender difference in higher education in India across all states (Chanana, 2004, 2007; Prakash, 2007). However the extent and magnitude of this difference vary across states. Differential social expectation across male and female offspring and additional dowry given to a relatively more educated girl (who are usually married to spouses with higher education and better employment status) are cited as reasons for this discrimination. Though for middle and high-income families, who are belonging to urban household, the dynamics is slightly different (Chanana, 2007). The common experience tells that if a girl is having higher education, she faces a lesser amount of dowry from groom's family, as her potential earning capacity is high. The phenomenon is more prevalent for the girls who are working and belongs to urban areas.

Analysing the 52nd Round NSS data (1995–96) Chakrabarty (2009) found out that the gender differences in participation in higher education participation is more prominent among the backward castes who are residing in the rural areas. This is even larger for those who have more siblings in the household. This is also true for families belonging to the highest income/expenditure quartile, who are residing in rural areas. The results show that in rural India, probability of attending a higher education institution for an 'SC' and 'ST' (rural) female youth is significantly lower than the girls from other social group. However, no such bias was found for the male sample of rural India. Moreover, the results highlight that gender discrimination in terms of educational attainment is prevalent irrespective of geographical location and is more pervasive amongst higher income groups who are likely to subscribe to orthodox and traditional outlook. While the gender discrimination in participation in higher education is persistent in Indian context, the study of Albert (2000) on demand for higher education in Spain, shows a diametrically opposite result. She explains '*... gender has an important effect on higher education in the sense that being a man has a negative effect on the decision of attending higher education. This trend is leading more women to obtain a higher qualification than men, in order to compete in the labour market*' (Albert, 2000: 159).

There is another crucial intra-household dimension which significantly influences the availability of the resources to the potential entrant to higher education and thus the participation in higher education. Studies all over the world (Hauser and Sewell, 1985; Psacharlopoulos and Mattson, 2000) show that family size, sex and birth order have significant impact in participation in higher education. The study of Psacharoloulos and Mattson (2000) empirically proved an inverse relationship between family size and higher education participation as well as educational outcomes.

Thus, the cursory literature survey suggests that the researchers have given ample attention in finding out the significance of household characteristics in determining whether or not to participate in a specific level of education (here higher education) and spend for it.

## Database and Methodology

The present paper draws upon 64th Round NSS survey on 'Participation and Expenditure in Education', conducted in the year 2007–08. For detailed understanding we have taken the unit level data from schedule 25.2. Altogether a sample of 4,45,960 persons, 63,318 from rural households and 37,263 from urban households spread over the country, was surveyed in this round. Detailed information in educational participation and expenditure was gathered on persons belonging to the age group 5–29 years in this round. However, in case of the present analysis we have considered only those who are currently pursuing any level of higher education and belong to the age group of 18–23 years, which accounts for 1,81,43,113 individuals, 99,83,478 from rural and 81,59,635 from urban regions.

The first part of the study depicting the gender-wise differences in participation in higher education across region, social and economic category has been represented through simple descriptive statistics. While to accomplice the second part of the study, i.e. to find out the role of household characteristics in determining the participation and thus estimating their extent for both males and females separately, Binary Logistic Regression model is adopted. The following sub-section has described the econometric specification of the model.

### *Econometric Specification*

The primary objective here is to find out the role of household characteristics in determining participation in higher education. We will estimate this through binomial logistic regression model. The independent variable here is enrollment he, which is a binary variable and takes the value 1 if a person belonging to the age group of 18–23 years is currently attending any level of higher education or has higher education qualification and takes 0 otherwise. The primary objective here is to find out the role of household characteristics in determining participation in higher education and how far these factors work differently for male and female students.

The logit regression equation for the probability of attending higher education is given by the following equation:

$P(Y_i) = e^z/(1+e^z)$

where, $P(Y_i)$ = probability of participation in higher education

Thus, $[1- P(Y_i)]$ = probability of not participating in higher education

Therefore, logit of $P(Y_i)$ or log transformation of $P(Y_i)$ is the log of odds ratio or likelihood ratio that the dependent variable is 1. In symbol can be represented as:

logit $P(Y_i) = \log [P(Y_i)/1- P(Y_i)] = \ln [P(Y_i)/1- P(Y_i)] = Z$

Z is represented by the following equation:

$Z = \beta_0+\beta_1X_1+\beta_2X_2+\ldots\ldots\ldots\ldots+\beta_nX_n+ e_i$

$X_n$= the vector which includes all the independent variables included in the model snd will be elaborated in the subsequent section.

$\beta_n$= the corresponding coefficient vector of each outcome of n

$\varepsilon_i$= the difference between the predicted and observed value of Yi for the ith subject

Therefore, the coefficient vector $\beta_n$ estimates the impact of independent variables on the log of odds (logit) of attending any higher education institute vis-à-vis otherwise.

**Table 1**

*Particulars of the Variables Used in the Model*

| *Variables* | *Definition* |
|---|---|
| SC Group | Dummy variable which takes value 1 if an individual belongs to schedule caste group and 0 otherwise |
| ST Group | Dummy variable which takes value 1 if an individual belongs to schedule tribe group and 0 otherwise |
| OBC Group | Dummy variable which takes value 1 if an individual belongs to other backward caste group and 0 otherwise |
| head_primary | Dummy variable which takes value 1 if head of the household has primary education and 0 otherwise |

*Cont'd ...*

*Cont'd ...*

| | |
|---|---|
| head_secondary | Dummy variable which takes value 1 if head of the household has secondary education and 0 otherwise |
| head_hs | Dummy variable which takes value 1 if head of the household has higher-secondary education and 0 otherwise |
| head_he | Dummy variable which takes value 1 if head of the household higher education and 0 otherwise |
| sex_female | Dummy variable which takes value 1 if the individual is a female and 0 otherwise |
| female_head | Dummy variable which takes value 1 if head of the household is a female and 0 otherwise |
| HH Size | Size of household (continuous variable) |
| ln_mpce | Log of monthly per capita consumption expenditure (proxy for household income; a continuous variable) |

## Levels and Patterns of Participation at Higher Education Reflections from NSS 64th Round Data

The current section attempts to investigate the pattern of participation by males and females at different levels of higher education. NSS 64th Round data has provided information on current attendance at every educational level. Thus, by the term participation here we will mean only the current attendance. For the purpose of present study, we have divided higher education into three levels or categories, namely:

(i) diploma/certificate courses at higher education or upper level
(ii) graduation level
(iii) post-graduation and above level

For the present sub-section, we have taken those who belong to the age group of 18–23 years and currently pursuing any kind of higher education. However, we have excluded the students pursuing vocational education, and have taken only those students who are pursuing general and technical/professional education. Here, by higher education we meant any courses pursued after completing higher secondary, thus excluded those diploma/certificate courses which could be pursued after secondary level of education.

### *Gender-Wise Participation at Different Levels of Higher Education*

Gender is the most pervasive and enduring factor of inequality which exist almost everywhere, thus it is replicated in the sphere of education also. In Indian scenario, if we take the male-female distribution of participation at higher education level, approximately 57 per cent males are currently perusing any kind of higher education and the same for females is around 43 per cent. It is also evident from the data that the male-female gap narrows down sharply at the post-graduation and above level. If we take the GAR in higher education it says that while GAR of the males is 19.9 per cent, the same for the females is 15.2 per cent. The social group-wise data (Table 2) shows a more critical picture.

Now, if we take the gender-wise distribution of participation across different levels and types of higher education, it shows that male-female gap in participation is much higher for the technical education than that of general education. However, interestingly for both the streams of education the participation gap narrows down at post-graduation and above level. The reason (apart from gender stereotyping of education) might be that technical education entails much more household investment than that of general studies and households with constrained resources may decide not to invest on females for pursuing costly (technical) education. At the post-graduation level the situation improves (for both general and technical education) because those who have decided to study further have already crossed the economic and social obstacles.

**Table 2**

*GAR across Gender and Social Groups (18–23 years)*

| | *Male* | *Female* |
|---|---|---|
| ST | 9.2 | 5.7 |
| SC | 14.1 | 9.7 |
| OBC | 18.1 | 12.5 |
| Others | 29.1 | 25.2 |
| All | 19.9 | 15.2 |

Author's Calculation form NSS 64th Round Unit Level Data.

**Table 3**

*Gender-Wise Distribution of Current Attendance Across Different Levels and Types of Higher Education*

| *Levels of Current Attendance* | *General* | | *Technical* | |
|---|---|---|---|---|
| | *Male* | *Female* | *Male* | *Female* |
| Diploma/Certificate at Graduation and Upper Level | 55.6 | 44.4 | 61.0 | 39.0 |
| Graduate Level | 57.3 | 42.7 | 60.7 | 39.3 |
| Post-Graduate and Above Level | 46.8 | 53.2 | 46.4 | 53.6 |

Author's Calculation form NSS 64th Round Unit Level Data.

Table 3 gives us a glance of location-wise distribution of participation by both males and females at different levels of higher education. The data shows that male female participation gap is much higher in rural areas than that of urban region in both diploma and graduation levels. However, the situation changes at post-graduation and above level of education; gender gap narrows down in both urban and rural areas. At this level, (proportional) participation by both rural and urban females is approximately same, and even greater than males for both the cases. This table clearly reflects that the rural urban divide is much prominent and deterrent of females than their male counterpart, if we ignore post-graduation and above level, which are generally pursued by the creamy layers of the society, more so for rural regions.

Table 4 gives us an account of distribution of current attendance of students across locations, by levels and types of education. The data depicts that the females' participation is greater than their male counterpart at post graduation and above level, irrespective of types and levels of education, across rural and urban location. However, at diploma and graduate level the same produces a cluttered output. In the rural area gender gap, attendance is much higher in diploma level technical/professional courses than that of general courses. However, in urban areas, female participation is higher than males in case of diploma level technical/professional courses. Interestingly this result converses as one move up to graduation level technical professional courses.

**Table 4**

*Gender-Wise Distribution of Current Attendance Across Different Location and Levels of Higher Education*

| Levels of Current Attendance | Rural | | Urban | |
|---|---|---|---|---|
| | Male | Female | Male | Female |
| Diploma/Certificate at Graduation and Upper Level | 69.9 | 30.1 | 48.0 | 52.0 |
| Graduate Level | 61.6 | 38.4 | 54.3 | 45.7 |
| Post-Graduate and Above Level | 46.6 | 53.4 | 45.8 | 54.2 |

Author's Calculation form NSS 64th Round Unit Level Data.

**Table 5**

*Location-Wise Distribution Current Attendance of Males and Females Across Different Levels and Types of Higher Education*

| Level of Current Attendance | Rural | | | | | | Urban | | | | | |
|---|---|---|---|---|---|---|---|---|---|---|---|---|
| | General | | | Professional/ Technical | | | General | | | Professional/ Technical | | |
| | M | F | Total | M | F | Total | M | F | Total | M | F | Total |
| Diploma/Certificate at Graduation and Upper Level | 58.7 | 41.3 | 100 | 88.4 | 11.6 | 100 | 51.8 | 48.2 | 100 | 44.8 | 55.2 | 100 |
| Graduate Level | 61.7 | 38.3 | 100 | 61.5 | 38.5 | 100 | 52.6 | 47.4 | 100 | 60.5 | 39.5 | 100 |
| Post-Graduate and Above Level | 48.6 | 51.4 | 100 | 41.9 | 58.1 | 100 | 45.6 | 54.4 | 100 | 48.5 | 51.5 | 100 |

Author's Calculation form NSS 64th Round Unit Level Data.

Table 5 gives us a distribution of social group-wise participation across different levels of higher education, by both males and females. The data reveals that at diploma/certificate level, male-female participation gap is most prominent for STs and OBCs, while at graduation level the difference is lesser for OBCs and others, than that of STs and SCs. However, at post-graduation and above level a reverse result turns out. At this level, the gender inequality in participation improves almost in all social groups except SCs. For them the disparity in participation by the males and females is the highest.

Therefore, most of the tables depicted share the fact that the participation gap between males and females narrows down at post-graduate and above level. In some cases, proportion of participation by females are even better than males. This might be because of the fact that post-graduation level of study, both general and technical professional streams are pursued by those who belong to financially well-off households. Moreover, females are more rigid in opting jobs, as in Indian society they need to balance between both their home and office; therefore they choose to pursue further higher education, rather than taking up any job which is available in market after completing graduation.

**Table 6**

*Social Group-Wise Participation of Males and Females Across Different Levels of Higher Education*

| Level of Current Attendance | ST | | | SC | | | OBC | | | Others | | |
|---|---|---|---|---|---|---|---|---|---|---|---|---|
| | M | F | Total | M | F | Total | M | F | Total | M | F | Total |
| Diploma/Certificate at Graduation and Upper Level | 74.9 | 25.1 | 100 | 56.0 | 44.0 | 100 | 69.0 | 31.0 | 100 | 46.7 | 53.3 | 100 |
| Graduate Level | 58.8 | 41.2 | 100 | 61.1 | 38.9 | 100 | 58.7 | 41.3 | 100 | 55.9 | 44.1 | 100 |
| Post-Graduate and Above Level | 29.5 | 70.5 | 100 | 66.1 | 33.9 | 100 | 48.2 | 51.8 | 100 | 42.1 | 57.9 | 100 |

Author's Calculation form NSS 64th Round Unit Level Data.

## Empirical Results from Logistic Regression Model

This specific section would deal with the empirical results obtained from the econometric model specified in the previous section. The analysis has been carried out for both males and females, separately for rural and urban regions. This has been done specifically to capture the extent of influence of household characteristics in determining participation in higher education separately for males and females and to check whether there prevails any variation across rural and urban locations.

**Table 7**

*Determinants of Participation (18–23 years) in Higher Education*

| | All India | | | Male | | | Female | | |
|---|---|---|---|---|---|---|---|---|---|
| | Coeff. β | Std. Err. | P>\|z\| | Coeff. β | Std. Err. | P>\|z\| | Coeff. β | Std. Err. | P>\|z\| |
| sex_female | –0.236 | 0.001 | 0.00 | — | — | — | — | — | — |
| socialgr_st | –0.051 | 0.003 | 0.00 | –0.074 | 0.004 | 0.000 | –0.015 | 0.004 | 0.001 |
| socialgr_sc | 0.340 | 0.002 | 0.00 | 0.316 | 0.002 | 0.000 | 0.378 | 0.003 | 0.000 |
| socialgr_obc | –0.026 | 0.001 | 0.00 | 0.080 | 0.002 | 0.000 | –0.156 | 0.002 | 0.000 |
| head_primary | –0.018 | 0.002 | 0.00 | 0.031 | 0.002 | 0.000 | –0.106 | 0.003 | 0.000 |
| head_secondary | 0.229 | 0.002 | 0.00 | 0.248 | 0.002 | 0.000 | 0.173 | 0.003 | 0.000 |
| head_hs | 0.641 | 0.002 | 0.00 | 0.498 | 0.003 | 0.000 | 0.798 | 0.003 | 0.000 |
| head_he | 0.939 | 0.002 | 0.00 | 1.068 | 0.003 | 0.000 | 0.797 | 0.003 | 0.000 |
| female_head | 0.196 | 0.002 | 0.00 | 0.008 | 0.002 | 0.001 | 0.306 | 0.003 | 0.000 |
| ln_mpce | 0.653 | 0.001 | 0.00 | 0.607 | 0.001 | 0.000 | 0.728 | 0.002 | 0.000 |
| hhsize | –0.029 | 0.000 | 0.00 | –0.041 | 0.000 | 0.000 | –0.017 | 0.000 | 0.000 |
| Constant | –4.059 | 0.008 | 0.00 | –3.715 | 0.010 | 0.000 | –4.805 | 0.012 | 0.000 |
| Log likelihood | –1,11,51,756 | | | –63,56,452.4 | | | –47,69,323.5 | | |
| Pseudo R2 | 0.0683 | | | 0.0616 | | | 0.079 | | |
| Number of obs (weighted) | 1,81,43,377 | | | 1,04,29,904 | | | 77,13,473 | | |

Author's Computation from NSS 64th Round Unit Level Data.

*Note:* *** = Coefficient Significant at 1 Per cent Level ** = Coefficient Significant at 5 Per cent Level

Table 6 reports the coefficient of binary logistic regression model across gender. It is evident from the result that the household's economic status proxied by *ln*MPCE play a crucial role in determining one's probability in participating in higher education, while size of household has significant negative role. Female individuals have significantly lower chances in getting enrolled in higher education than their male counterpart, at all India level. Data also shows that STs and OBCs have significantly lower likelihood in attending higher education than others/general. However, this result does not hold true for SCs across gender. Education profile of household head acts as pivotal determinant. If the household head has higher education qualification, the student has higher odds in attending higher education. Further, if the household is headed by females, again the student has higher likelihood of getting enrolled in higher education. This result corroborates the findings of Tilak (2002a or b).

**Table 8**

*Determinants of Participation (18–23 years) in Higher Education by Sex: Rural India*

| | *All* | | | *Male* | | | *Female* | | |
|---|---|---|---|---|---|---|---|---|---|
| | *Coeff.* β | *Std. Err.* | *P>\|z\|* | *Coeff.* β | *Std. Err.* | *P>\|z\|* | *Coeff.* β | *Std. Err.* | *P>\|z\|* |
| sex_female | –0.327 | 0.001 | 0.00 | — | — | — | — | — | — |
| socialgr_st | –0.108 | 0.003 | 0.00 | –0.124 | 0.004 | 0.00 | –0.044 | 0.006 | 0.00 |
| socialgr_sc | 0.395 | 0.002 | 0.00 | 0.462 | 0.003 | 0.00 | 0.328 | 0.003 | 0.00 |
| socialgr_obc | 0.067 | 0.001 | 0.00 | 0.147 | 0.002 | 0.00 | –0.024 | 0.002 | 0.00 |
| head_primary | –0.084 | 0.002 | 0.00 | –0.101 | 0.002 | 0.00 | –0.087 | 0.003 | 0.00 |
| head_secondary | 0.204 | 0.002 | 0.00 | 0.319 | 0.002 | 0.00 | 0.038 | 0.003 | 0.00 |
| head_hs | 0.293 | 0.002 | 0.00 | 0.206 | 0.003 | 0.00 | 0.354 | 0.004 | 0.00 |
| head_he | 0.655 | 0.003 | 0.00 | 1.184 | 0.005 | 0.00 | 0.256 | 0.004 | 0.00 |
| female_head | 0.043 | 0.002 | 0.00 | –0.053 | 0.003 | 0.00 | 0.131 | 0.003 | 0.00 |
| ln_mpce | 0.612 | 0.001 | 0.00 | 0.634 | 0.002 | 0.00 | 0.574 | 0.002 | 0.00 |
| hhsize | –0.007 | 0.000 | 0.00 | –0.033 | 0.000 | 0.00 | 0.025 | 0.000 | 0.00 |
| constant | –3.910 | 0.010 | 0.00 | –4.000 | 0.014 | 0.00 | –4.048 | 0.017 | 0.00 |
| Log likelihood | –66,01,152.7 | | | –39,37,210.9 | | | –26,37,359.3 | | |
| Pseudo R2 | 0.0378 | | | 0.048 | | | 0.0,198 | | |
| Number of obs (weighted) | 99,83,464 | | | 61,01,738 | | | 38,81,726 | | |

Author's Computation from NSS 64th Round Unit Level Data.

*Note:* *** = Coefficient Significant at 1 Per cent Level ** = Coefficient Significant at 5 Per cent Level.

Tables 7 and 8 report the regression result predicting the probability of participation at more disaggregated level, separately for rural and urban regions across gender. This has been done to understand whether the geographical location changes the nature of the explanatory variable. The result shows that in rural India females have significantly lower odds in participation in higher education. It is again evident that the household's economic condition and household head's educational profile play significantly positive role in predicting the probability of one's participation in higher education. However, regarding the participation of backward caste groups in higher education, a puzzling result has come out. Data shows that in rural area only the STs (and female OBCs) are in disadvantageous position than *others*. However, this does not hold true for SCs, which is generally predicted. While the reason could not be pointed out quite conclusively, one can argue that affirmative action in the form of caste-based reservation is actually working well for SCs and OBCs in rural area. Estimates are also depicting that females have lower probability in attending higher education in rural India. Both these results reiterates the findings of Chakrabaorty (2009), where she found out that caste factor plays insignificant role in determining one's enrollment in higher education, while being females actually ensures lower probability in attending higher education. We found out similar kind of result for urban area also.

**Table 9**

*Determinants of Participation (18–23 years) in Higher Education by Sex: Urban India*

| | *All* | | | *Male* | | | *Female* | | |
|---|---|---|---|---|---|---|---|---|---|
| | *Coeff. β* | *Std. Err.* | *P>\|z\|* | *Coeff. β* | *Std. Err.* | *P>\|z\|* | *Coeff. β* | *Std. Err.* | *P>\|z\|* |
| sex_female | –0.134 | 0.002 | 0.00 | — | — | — | — | — | — |
| socialgr_st | 0.108 | 0.005 | 0.00 | 0.163 | 0.007 | 0.00 | 0.005 | 0.008 | 0.525 |
| socialgr_sc | 0.237 | 0.003 | 0.00 | 0.051 | 0.004 | 0.00 | 0.492 | 0.004 | 0.000 |
| socialgr_obc | –0.142 | 0.002 | 0.00 | 0.013 | 0.003 | 0.00 | –0.298 | 0.003 | 0.000 |
| head_primary | 0.096 | 0.003 | 0.00 | 0.291 | 0.004 | 0.00 | –0.112 | 0.005 | 0.000 |
| head_secondary | 0.283 | 0.003 | 0.00 | 0.128 | 0.004 | 0.00 | 0.421 | 0.005 | 0.000 |
| head_hs | 0.998 | 0.004 | 0.00 | 0.807 | 0.005 | 0.00 | 1.160 | 0.005 | 0.000 |
| head_he | 1.162 | 0.004 | 0.00 | 1.014 | 0.005 | 0.00 | 1.269 | 0.006 | 0.000 |
| female_head | 0.287 | 0.003 | 0.00 | 0.046 | 0.004 | 0.00 | 0.388 | 0.004 | 0.000 |
| ln_mpce | 0.444 | 0.002 | 0.00 | 0.449 | 0.003 | 0.00 | 0.464 | 0.003 | 0.000 |
| hhsize | –0.081 | 0.000 | 0.00 | –0.06 | .001 | 0.00 | –0.102 | 0.001 | 0.000 |
| constant | –2.326 | 0.014 | 0.00 | –2.39 | 0.019 | 0.00 | –2.526 | 0.021 | 0.000 |
| Log likelihood | –44,69,036.4 | | | –23,78,266.2 | | | –20,61,921.1 | | |
| Pseudo R2 | 0.0,775 | | | 0.0,571 | | | 0.111 | | |
| Number of obs (weighted) | 81,59,913 | | | 43,28,166 | | | 38,31,747 | | |

Author's Computation from NSS 64th Round Unit Level Data.

*Note:* *** = Coefficient Significant at 1 Per cent Level ** = Coefficient Significant at 5 Per cent Level

Table 9 reports the logistic regression coefficients for urban India. Like rural areas, in urban India also females have lower likelihood of getting enrolled in higher education. It is also evident from the data that students belonging to the household have head with higher secondary degree and above qualification have significantly higher odds of getting enrolled in higher education. Along with this household's economic profile also turns out as an important positive predictor. While at the outcome level we have low GER for SCs, STs and OBCs, here the study does not follow the same result. It shows that in urban area SCs and STs (also OBC males) have higher likelihood of getting enrolled in higher education than *others*. Again, apparently this result is somehow puzzling, as one can always argue that if the backward caste groups are not in disadvantageous position then what explains their lower GER at outcome level. To support the present result it can be stated that the data-set comprises only those who are age-wise and qualification-wise eligible for getting enrollment. Thus, it can be concluded that the SC/ST students who succeed to overcome the initial obstacle and cross the threshold level for getting enrolled in higher education, have lower probability of dropping out after completing 10+2 and higher chances of getting enrolled in higher education. The caste-based reservation system actually facilitates them to do so. Along with this there is a push factor in the form of status achievement which induces the socially backward students to go for higher education, as for them education is the sole factor of upward social mobility and a route out of their present situation.

## Conclusion

The present study is a attempt to investigate two important things regarding participation in higher education. Firstly, what is the pattern of participation by males and females in three levels of higher education; and secondly, what are the household level determining factors influencing one's decision to get enrolled or complete higher education; thus, to find out the critical household factors which are responsible for unequal participation by males and females in different levels and types of higher education. In line of the finding of other researches in the related field the present study reveals three important results;

(i) Household's economic condition has a crucial role to play in determining the participation in higher education. This is because of the fact that higher education entails huge amount of out-of-pocket expenditure from the part of the household.

(ii) The educational profile of the household head to which the individual belongs emerges as a significant variable. Moreover, if the student belongs to female headed household, s/he has a higher probability of attending higher education.

(iii) Once the threshold level of fulfilling eligibility criteria is achieved caste (social group) actually does not emerge as a determinant of whether or not to pursue higher education. Further, the socially backward students see this as a critical opportunity for them for upward social mobility.

It is now beyond debate that education bears a host of positive externalities which influences almost all facets of human life. Therefore, education at all levels should be viewed as a non-negotiable public good. However, in the present societal system, structure of power and dominance is such that it assigns the sources of knowledge and productive assets to the selected and privileged few and discriminate others. It is evident from the present study that gender acts as a crucial pervasive factor for inequality and affirmative action is actually facilitating socially backward groups. Therefore, this study suggests for more government intervention in the form of targetted government schemes to overcome the impediments for obtaining desirable outcomes.

## References

Albert, C. (2000). 'Higher Education Demand in Spain: The Influence of Labour Market Signals and Family Background'. *Higher Education*, 40(2): 147–62.

Belfield, C.R. (2000). *Economic Principles for Education*. UK: Edward Elgar.

Bishop, J. (1977). 'The Effect of Public Policies on the Demand for Higher Education'. *The Journal of Human Resources*, 12(3): 285–307.

Bolm, A. and M. Azam (2009). 'Progress in Participation in Tertiary Education in India from 1983 to 2004'. *Journal of Educational Planning and Administration*, 18(2): 125–67.

Chakrabarty, A. (2009). 'Determinants of Participation in Higher Education and Choice of Discipline: Evidence from Urban and Rural Indian Youth'. *South Asian Economic Journal*, 10 (2): 371–402.

Chanana, K. (2007). 'Globalisation, Higher Education and Gender: Changing Subject Choices of Indian Women'. *Economic and Political Weekly*, 42(7): 590–98.

Duchesne, I. and W. Nonneman (1998). 'The Demand for Higher Education in Belgium'. *Economics of Education Review*, 17(2): 211–18.

Filmer, D. and L. Pritchett (1998a). 'The Effect of Household Wealth on Educational Attainment Demographic and Health Survey Evidence'. Policy Research Working Paper No. 1980, The World Bank, USA.

——. (1998b). 'Educational Enrolment and Attainment in India: Household Wealth, Gender, Village and State Effects (mimeo)'. The World Bank, USA.

Galper, H. and R. Dunn (1969). 'A Short-run Demand Function for Higher Education in the United States'. *Journal of Political Economy*, 77(5): 765–77.

Hasan, R. and A. Mehta (2006). 'Under-representation of Disadvantaged Classes in Colleges: What Do the Data Tell Us?'. *Economic and Political Weekly*, 41(35): 3791–96.

Hauser, R.M. and W.H. Sewell (1985). Birth Order and Educational Attainment in Full Sibships. *American Educational Research Journal*, 22(1): 1–23.

Heller, D.E. (1997). 'Student Price Response in Higher Education'. *Journal of Higher Education*, 68(6): 624–59.

Kodde, D. and J. Ritzen (1985). 'The Demand for Education Under Capital Market Imperfections'. *European Economic Review*, 28: 347–62.

——. (1988). 'Direct and Indirect Effects of Parental Education Level on the Demand for Higher Education'. *The Journal of Human Resources*, 23(3): 356–71.

Leslie, L.L. and P.T. Brinkman (1987). 'Student Price Response in Higher Education: The Student Demand Studies'. *Journal of Higher Education*, 58(2): 181–204.

——. (1988). *The Economic Value of Higher Education*. London: Macmillan.

Majumdar, Tapas (1983). *Investment in Education and Social Choice*. Cambridge: Cambridge University Press.

Mincer, J. (1974). *Schooling, Experience and Earning*. New York: NBER Press.

National Sample Survey Organisation (NSSO) (1995–96). *Attending Educational Institutions in India: Its Nature, Level and Cost*. New Delhi: Department of Statistics, Government of India.

——. (2007–08). *Education in India: 2007–08, Participation and Expenditure*. New Delhi: Department of Statistics, Government of India.

OECD (1978). *Individual Demand for Higher Education: General Report*. Paris: OECD.

Panchamukhi, P.R. (1990). *Private Expenditure on Education in India: An Empirical Study*. Pune: Indian Institute of Education.

Prakash, V. (2007). 'Trends in Growth and Financing of Higher Education in India'. *Economic and Political Weekly*, 42(31): 49–58.

Psacharopoulos, G. and M. Woodhall (1985). *Education for Development: An Analysis of Investment Choice*. New York: Oxford University Press.

Psacharopoulos, G. and R. Mattson (2000). 'Family Size, Education Expenditure and Attainment in Poor Country'. *Journal of Educational Planning and Administration*, 15(2): 5–25.

Schultz, T. (1961). 'Investment in Human Capital'. *American Economic Review*, 51(1): 1–17.

——. (1963). *The Economic Value of Education*. New York: Columbia University Press.

Stafford, K.L., S.B. Lundstedt and A.D. Lynn (1984). 'Social and Economic Factors Affecting Participation in Higher Education'. *The Journal of Higher Education*, 55(5): 590–608.

Tilak, J.B.G. (1987). *The Economics of Inequality in Education*. New Delhi: Sage Publications.

——. (2000). 'Education Poverty in India'. NIEPA Occasional Paper No. 29, New Delhi: National Institute of Educational Planning and Administration.

——. (2001). 'Household Expenditure on Education in India'. *Business Perspectives*, 3(2): 61–86.

——. (2002). Education and Poverty, *Journal of Human Development*, 3(2): 191–207.

——. (2002a). 'Elasticity of Household Expenditure on Education in Rural India'. *South Asia Economic Journal*, 3(2): 217–26.

——. (2002b). 'Determinants of Household Expenditure on Education in Rural India'. NCAER Working Paper Series No. 88.

——. (2004). 'Public Subsidies in Education in India'. *Economic and Political Weekly*, 39(4), 24 January: 343–59.

UGC (2012). Inclusive and Quality Expansion of Higher Education, 12th Five Year Plan, New Delhi: University Grant Commission.

# 8

# Transitions in Livelihoods

## *Long-Term Study of a Slum in East Delhi*

**DEVESH VIJAY**

One of the appalling images associated with most Third World cities is that of a squalid slum huddled in the shadow of a luxury apartment or a high-rise. In 2011, the total number of slum dwellers in India exceeded 68 million (excluding millions who reside in small clusters of less than 300 persons especially in our new census towns). In the national capital itself, *jhuggie* clusters have grown from about 200 (with a population of 120) in 1951, to about 1500 (with a population of more than 3 million) by 2013, showing a jump of 28 times as against the growth of just 11 times in the city's total population in 60 years.

Besides rapid growth, another important aspect of most slums today is their internal stratification and diversity. This paper aims at throwing some light on occupational diversity and transitions in a Delhi slum (called Aradhaknagar) while charting its changing demography and social stratification across five decades.

### The Scope and Methodology of the Enquiry

Aradhaknagar is the real name of a middle-sized slum located next to the Grand Trunk Road on the border between Delhi and Ghaziabad. The slum has been visited repeatedly by me, since 1988, when I wrote a dissertation on its occupations and demography and more frequently, since 2006, when I began a post-doctoral survey on the changing income and consumption profile of the community and its interfaces with various organs of the state.[1]

Survey data on population, assets, etc. was gathered by me, in Aradhaknagar, both through household surveys and personal interviews and group discussions in 1988, 2006, 2009 and 2012. Recollections of half a dozen septuagenarians who had arrived in Aradhaknagar, in the late 1960s, were also tapped to develop a broad profile of the local economy, as it reportedly was, 50 years ago.

Still, two limitations in my data need to be noted at the outset. Firstly, my own findings relate only to one particular slum from India's capital which may be similar to some in cities like Mumbai and Bangalore but does not illustrate conditions among the poorest shanties specially in the smaller towns of India.[2] Secondly, complete precision in the understanding of every household's income and finances is not claimed here as all respondents of Aradhaknagar did not share full information on our queries and some also varied their responses during repeat surveys conducted after a short interval too.[3]

Nevertheless, a broad understanding of the occupational and class dynamics of Aradhaknagar is expected as the method of combining focus group discussions, life sketches and repeated personal interviews during fieldwork yielded considerable cross-checked information from subjects who seemed candid, on the whole, and also showed a remarkable degree of mutual knowledge emanating from close and proximate living. Errors in data collection were further minimized by using actual names wherever permitted by concerned subjects and by keeping all field notes in the Devnagari script for ready scrutiny and comment of the subjects as also by sharing the first version of this report with 40 members of the community in their language, namely, Hindi.

## Mapping Aradhaknagar

The slum of Aradhaknagar lies close to the Grand Trunk Road on the border between Delhi and Uttar Pradesh. The quadrangle of about 5.5 acres, on which this *basti* is spread, is flanked by the aforesaid highway to its north, the railway line connecting Old Delhi and Ghaziabad train stations to its south, transport godowns of Bhoora Mandi to its east and a flyover and an underpass on the west.

Surrounded by these structures, Aradhaknagar slowly turned from a grove of shrubs and *keekars* on the outskirts of the old village of Chikambarpur into a dense community of 1,694 residents by 2012. The first *jhuggies* were raised here in the early 1960s. But Aradhaknagar's growth took off in the following decade with growing immigration of labourers from villages of Uttar Pradesh and, to a lesser extent, from Bihar and Madhya Pradesh, in the wake of growing demand for manual workers in the surrounding middle class colonies such as Vivek Vihar and Surya Nagar as well as the Jhilmil and Sahibabad Industrial Complexes in its vicinity.

By 1988, when I first studied Aradhaknagar, the slum had already grown into a community of 91 families with 441 men, women and children living cheek by jowl in 90 odd *jhuggies* or *kutcha* houses made of mud, stones and thatched roofs. But, in 2012, when I returned to the slum for a detailed re-study, the jhuggies had given way to 256 semi-*pucca* dwellings (housing 292 families) and the population had swelled to 1,694 (showing a jump of about 400 per cent in 18 years). Eighty of the 91 families counted in 1988, in Aradhaknagar, were present here in 2012 too. The major Dalit castes of the region, viz. Valmikis and Jatavs, account for almost 83 per cent of Aradhaknagar's population while the rest consist of 'other backward' castes like Ahirs, Gurjars and Yadavs (10%), upper castes including Brahmins, Thakurs and Banias (6%) and a few Muslims (1%). The male-female ratio, in Aradhaknagar, has hovered around 10: 9 while the proportion of children (aged below 14) has fallen from 59 per cent to 45 per cent between 1988 and 2012, apparently due to growing acceptance of family planning over time.

## Occupational Shifts

Unlike the mega slums of Dharavi in Mumbai or, the displaced Pushta along the Yamuna, in Delhi, which have had lakhs of inhabitants and thousands of businesses spread over several kilometres, Aradhaknagar is not only small but has few manufacturing units inside it. Yet, the residents (more than 80 per cent of whom are Dalits) here also follow a wide variety of occupations including those of sweepers, scavengers and servants; hawkers, loaders and rickshaw-pullers; skilled and unskilled factory and construction workers and of several kinds of semi-skilled artisans and service-providers like tailors, cobblers, barbers, roadside-entertainers, etc.[4] The slum also has a tiny segment of professionals like teachers and semi-qualified doctors and some clerks, supervisors, etc. and a couple of lower-level party workers who act as money-lenders and brokers too.

As far as occupational shifts are concerned, two significant changes can be noted in the slum's profile since 1988. First, the small number of permanent, Grade IV employees (including sweepers, peons, gardeners, etc.) in the Public Sector has remained almost the same at 15 per cent of all workers but those employed in Private Sector malls, schools and offices as well as courier services and construction work have gone up. At the same time, it is striking that a good number of clerical or Grade III employees and even some teachers and medical practitioners and contractors are residing in the slum which has a slightly better infrastructure now and offers a cheap alternative to sky-rocketing rents in regular colonies. While in 1988 only one educated professional was seen by me in Aradhaknagar, by 2012, their number (including clerks) had risen to seven. The third noticeable change is that the proportion of earning women workers in the slum has risen conspicuously (from 30 among 90 adult women in 1988 to 224 among 408 in 2012). The biggest rise in this category has been in the number of domestic maids which were only 20 in 1988 and had gone up to 122 by 2012, partly due to greater pressure for work and income now and also because of increased demand for domestic maids in the surrounding middle class homes in which more educated women are going out to work and apparently are more open to allowing Dalit women inside their homes and kitchens.

## Occupational Strata

Before considering the changes in wages and work conditions in various jobs pursued by our subjects, we must note that the diverse occupations noted in Aradhaknagar can also be clubbed into distinct strata, mobility between which is not uncommon, yet each reflects slightly different 'life chances' or command over incomes, skills, assets and status. In this light, it may not be inappropriate to say that despite its seamless appearance, Aradhaknagar is a stratified community of the poor, the very poor and a small local elite of the 'less poor', with further gradations within each, of course.

## Entrepreneurs and Organized Workers

At the top of Aradhaknagar's social pyramid, rest about half a dozen entrepreneurs or 'multi-taskers' who constitute the tiny elite of the economically better-off or socially and politically well-connected individuals. Heads of two of these families started as skilled masons but became rich after becoming small building-contractors; another family owes its better standing to as many as three Public Sector jobs (of Class IV category) acquired by its members who together earn about ₹ 60,000 per month and also lend money on usurious rates of 5 to 15 per cent per month; four others are entrepreneurs who have combined regular jobs in the municipal corporation with several side-businesses, including those of food-catering, garbage-disposal, labour-contracts, money-lending and property investments as also regular association with a political party/leader through which they help recent immigrants obtain voter identity, ration cards, school admissions and pensions, etc. while charging commissions on the same.

Due to the amorphous nature of their operations, it is difficult to make a precise estimate of the earnings of this mobile stratum. But even if we go by their own disclosures, such families seem to fall in the minimum income bracket of ₹ 6000 per month per capita (in 2009) and own assets like cars, bikes, personal water-pumps and an additional plot or two in other working class colonies in the National Capital Region. It may also be noted that the few slum dwellers who had independent plots in villages, have mostly sold them and invested mostly in urban or sub-urban properties now. Ganesh Chand, Chaman Parcha and Ram Singh illustrate such a trend among the better-off residents of Aradhaknagar.

Political acumen and links have obviously helped in the rise of these mobile men. Yet, it would be wrong to assume that 'connections' fully explain their exceptional advancement. In their own estimation, these entrepreneurs stand above their neighbours mainly because of their intelligence and boldness; incidentally all these seven were themselves snared in poverty just two decades back and could rise mainly because of some good (or 'fortunate') decisions as well as business acumen.

The story of Chaman's rise is instructive in this context. In 1965, Chaman had left Dhantala (his ancestral village near Meerut) at the age of 15, after an argument with parents and put up in a Dalit colony of Meerut city for three years, starting on a daily wage of just ₹ 2. In 1968, he went away to Kolkata with a relative and found employment on the dock at a salary of ₹ 150 per month. But after three years, Chaman's aggressiveness landed him in a brawl and a court case, which he ultimately won, but thereafter decided to leave Kolkata and return to his native village for rest. The stagnant economy and poverty of Dhantala, however, again made him restless and, in 1973, he decided to try his luck in Delhi. The capital had a fast growing Public Sector during those days and many jobs were available in the city's Municipal Corporation for sweepers, drivers, etc. Chaman also managed to find employment as a temporary sweeper on a salary of just ₹ 105 per month, with enough time for working on other jobs such as rickshaw-pulling and hawking. In 1981, Chaman's job in the sanitation department of the Municipal Corporation of Delhi (MCD) was regularized at an enhanced salary of ₹ 450 per month. But his ambitions were higher now, and in addition to his Corporation job, Chaman also entered the business of garbage collection in upcoming colonies around Aradhaknagar. Further, he secured a sweeper's job for his wife in the same department and with his growing contacts among union leaders, he also helped his brothers and other relatives in securing more Class IV jobs in the Municipal Corporation. Years later, Chaman got his sons also placed as sweepers in the Municipality. However, the freeze brought on government recruitment, after 1991, has kept their tenures ad hoc till date.

With six members (in a family of eight adults including three daughters-in-law) drawing regular salaries, Chaman was now well-established and started investing in money-lending as well as properties around Aradhaknagar. Between 1993 and 2000, Chaman and his family also ran three stalls of juice and snacks on the adjacent Giani Border and managed to earn up to ₹ 800 a day specially from the sale of juice to drivers, etc. (who would mix it with liquor mostly). Although this roaring business came to a halt suddenly in 2000, with the take-over of the area by the Delhi Development Authority (for building a new toll-center), Chaman had by now moved up in the social ladder of Aradhaknagar. He became a senior sanitary supervisor in the MCD and is earning approximately ₹ 16,000 per month (after the implementation of the Sixth Pay Commission's recommendations in 2009). Chaman also purchased a plot of 100 sq yards (at a price of ₹ 400 per sq yard), in 2000, in the urbanized village of Banthala nearby and constructed three big rooms with adequate kitchen and bath besides amenities such as a personal bore well, washing-machine, motor-bike, etc. Beyond this, Chaman plans to invest in other properties now and is keen to get his sons settled in side businesses too.

## Public Sector Employees

Just below the entrepreneurs represented by Chaman there are, in Aradhaknagar, about a dozen families which have one or more members in Grade III and Grade IV jobs. These included, in 2012, a supervisor in the Water Department, a Lower Division Clerk in a Public Sector bank, three peons/drivers in central ministries, a head sweeper in the ordnance factory in Ghaziabad, two waiters in a three-star hotel in central Delhi and four attendants or ward-boys in major hospitals as also a gangman (line inspector) in the Indian Railways. The salaries of these superior workers of Aradhaknagar ranged between ₹ 17,000 and ₹ 25,000 per month in mid-2009.

There was a large group of sweepers, scavengers, cattle or monkey trappers, etc. who fall in the lowest Grade IV in Public Sector employment, almost exclusively manned by the Scheduled Castes. Their salaries were lower than those of the Grade III employees but secure perks, legal cover as well as union protection still make them a class apart; the envy of the mass of unprotected, unorganized workers in villages as well as cities.

But to find employment in the Public Sector even in Class IV jobs is extremely difficult. Out of a total of 292 families in 2012, in Aradhaknagar, there were 51 with one member in permanent government employment; 15 which had one permanent and another temporary government employee and thirteen which had two such privileged workers among their bread earners while one had three members in Public Sector employment. Incidentally, all these sweepers, peons, etc. had been regularized before the 1991 turnaround in public policy. It is also important to note that all Public Sector employees in Aradhaknagar belong to the Scheduled Castes of Valmikis and Jatavs only. This is understandable since the jobs available in the government for semi-literate slum dwellers are those falling in Grade IV (relating to sweepers, scavengers etc) which the upper castes as well as the OBCs are reluctant to take up.

The starting salary of a temporary sweeper in government, in 2006, was ₹ 3,500 per month and ₹ 6,000 per month if he or she was permanent (going up to ₹ 12,000 per month by the time of retirement). In 1988, when I first came to Aradhaknagar, the corresponding starting salaries of Class IV government employees had been ₹ 700 and ₹ 1,200 only; while by 2009, after the implementation of the Sixth Pay Commission recommendations, these were about ₹ 6,000 and ₹ 10,000 respectively. This suggests a rise of roughly 800 per cent in gross salaries of both temporary and permanent Public Sector employees over two decades, though the growing number of daily wagers (now increasingly engaged by the Municipal Corporation through contractors) receive ₹ 100 only for four hours of sanitation work. On the other hand, some permanent municipal employees would not report for municipal duty and their fake attendance was being marked apparently on the basis of a cut in the salary received till the introduction of stricter checks on attendance recently. (The mismanagement in the vast municipal departments was indeed the subject of several newspaper reports during the period of our study.)[5] Many of the habitual absentees from Public Sector duties were still hard-working men and women and were engaged in other jobs to supplement their salaries often.

While salaries of Grade IV employees (almost all of whom are dalits) increased eight-fold between 1988 and 2009, the whole-sale price index in the same period is said to have risen by about 400 per cent (from approximately 60 in 1988 to about 240 in mid-2009 (with base year 1993–94 being 100), thus allowing a rise of roughly 50 per cent in real incomes for this segment of workers over a period of two decades.[6] The same is amply reflected in the growth of family assets, consumer durables and consumption patterns of this second rung of the economic ladder in Aradhaknagar.

To cite an example, Geeta's family was earning ₹ 17,000 per month in June 2009 (including her own salary of ₹ 6,000, as an ad hoc sweepress in a Public Sector bank and ₹ 11,000 per month of her husband, who is a permanent Class IV employee in the Municipal Corporation). Of this total, she spent about ₹ 3,500 (or 20% of her monthly budget) on food and ₹ 7,000 (or about 40% of the same) on the education of her two children. Although such a high level of educational expenditure in Geeta's budget is on account of the fee paid for her son's expensive B.Tech course (at the G.G.S. Indraprastha University) and is rather unusual for Aradhaknagar, yet it is worth mentioning that Gita has also purchased a new bike for her son (with a bank loan) and has a neat and well-furnished house, including a fridge, a colour TV, a second-hand sofa-set, double-bed and a steel almirah besides a cycle and a music system.[7] *My surmise is that Gita's assets and hopes are not atypical of the small 'middle-class' of Class IV government employees in Aradhaknagar, or at least those in this segment who have not been hit by a major illness, accident or problems such as alcoholism.*

However, regularity and better pay is only one of the attractions of government jobs. Secure earnings and vastly relaxed working-conditions (in comparison with both self-employment and Private Sector jobs) make the Public Sector a widespread craze – whether in the middle classes or among urban or rural poor for that matter. The extent to which a slum dweller could also be relaxed with his work in the Public Sector is reflected in the career of Mr Ram Krishna Pawar. Pawar is also a Valmiki who joined the Public Sector in the early 1970s. However, his posting was as a driver in the Delhi Transport Corporation for which he had approached the General Manager of the body, through an acquaintance two days before his job interview. Once he was through his probation, Pawar joined the Congress-led workers' union which was dominating the transport sector at that time and with its backing, he not only began absenting himself from work but even thrashed up superiors (including a depot manager) when they issued notices to him for being absent or drinking on duty.

Despite such misconduct, Pawar managed to retain his job on the strength of his association with an important Congress leader of those times, although his promotions got stalled and he was repeatedly transferred from one bus depot to another. Ultimately, in 1993, Pawar took voluntary retirement. Now he has given up on heavy drinking also and is working in a courier service besides receiving his truncated pension of ₹ 2,300 per month. Interestingly, Pawar owns two houses in sub-urban villages in the National Capital Region (NCR). But he prefers to stay in Aradhaknagar because of the better position of electric supply within Delhi and also because he hopes to benefit from a possible resettlement offer for slum dwellers some day.

## Petty Entrepreneurs

As mentioned, there are almost no manufacturing units in Aradhaknagar except for one that does stitching work for a rug manufacturer and one that makes cheap ice cream. Yet, there are many small businessmen in the slum who have a very small capital and also employ one or two workers in their enterprises. Among these are some dairymen, pig and goat-rearers, a few senior sweepers who have sub-contracted their work of garbage disposal to others, caterers who arrange waiters, cooks, etc. for middle class weddings and parties, a few money-lenders, some master artisans, mechanics and musicians, etc. who have one or more apprentices working under them and one lottery-operator and a liquor-seller whose earning from the alcohol trade was reportedly in tens of thousands, till the police crackdown on his business and house in 2009.

Most of these 'businessmen' of Aradhaknagar were, however, themselves artisans or workers not long ago and their new ventures also remain highly unstable. For example, in 2006, I had a chat with Arun Kumar Parcha, an ambitious young man who was running a confectionary shop next to his house but who is also a proficient *dhol* (drum) player, an avid fan of Urdu poetry and an entertainer who beats *dhol* at parties with one or more drummers working under him. For each *dhol* performance, the group charged, in 2008, a minimum of ₹ 2,500 out of which 50 per cent was kept by Arun. Tips offered by dancing guests bring additional income for these drum players. But their work is seasonal, available for just about half the days even during the four months of maximum weddings in the city. Not surprisingly, Arun wants to diversify and dreams of starting his own computer-training institute for which he has been saving about half of his earnings every year. To fulfil his ambition, Arun initially declined offers of a driver's job in the city's Corporation arranged for by his father, and settled for the same only in 2011.

Next to the entrepreneurs and government employees, in the social-order of Aradhaknagar, is the small group of graduates or diploma-holders who are trying to move up the social ladder through educational qualifications. Although education is not a requirement for any of the better-off livelihoods discussed above, interestingly, this is a route much preferred by poor parents who dream of seeing their children finding security and respect in society, hopefully, by getting a formal-sector job *(naukri)* instead of falling back on informal work *(kaam)*.

Unfortunately, the chances of clearing school (despite official claims of support in this regard) are thin in a congested and noisy slum. The 2012 survey, done by us, shows a total of seven graduates in Aradhaknagar (most of whom obtained their degrees through the distant education mode). Further, there is only one white-collar worker (a lower division clerk) who stays in the slum and goes out for work though there are seven qualified persons who work within the slum and constitute a small but respected sub-class of three medical practitioners, two men providing home-tuitions and two Brahmins who also work as *purohits* or astrologers-cum-priests both for local residents and outsiders.

### Private Sector Workers

As mentioned earlier, there are practically no manufacturing units in Aradhaknagar. Interestingly, workers going out to work in factories or export houses are also very few (in conformity with the low employment-figures for the manufacturing sector in our economy).[8] While factory-hands in the organized sector are few in the slum, the same cannot be said for service-jobs in private banks, courier-agencies, schools, professionals' offices and upcoming malls or department-stores around Aradhaknagar. As per the 2012 data, there were 83 men and 29 women working in jobs of this nature in the slum.

To illustrate the levels of earning and family budgets of this sub-class, we may consider the case of Ramvir who has worked as a peon in two branches of the ICICI bank over the past decade. His salary has been reduced recently from ₹ 4,500 (in 2006) to ₹ 3,500, along with some curtailment of working-hours at the bank, in the wake of the economic slowdown of 2008–09. Besides his own salary, Ramvir also depends on his wife's earnings (around ₹ 1,200) who works as a domestic-maid in two houses in neighbouring colonies. In May 2009, Ramvir shared with me the list of his monthly expenses on food, clothing, medicines, entertainment, electricity, mobile phone and occasional festivals. This came to a total of approximately ₹ 4,500, of which about 60 per cent was devoted to food items alone (even when he had no addiction for smoking, drinking etc.) His household assets at the time included a colour TV and a DVD player besides some plastic furniture but no sofa, double-bed or steel almirah. Incidentally, Ramvir's is a small family as he has no child yet and his main aspiration, at the time of our conversation, was of becoming a father for which his wife was undergoing expensive treatment which had compounded the financial problems of the couple.

## Unorganized Workers

While wages and working conditions for labourers in the organized Private Sector remain poor, their position in the vast unorganized informal economy is even worse. As mentioned above, family and other connections between these two strata remain strong, yet the differences in living-standards and job security of individuals belonging to two sections are quite sharp. Indeed, it may be argued that the real 'have nots' of our cities are not so much the workers of the formal economy employed in registered factories or government departments but the vast under-class of unorganized labourers, domestic maids, hawkers, etc. who have neither unions nor legal protection in a 'free' market that pays a pittance of ₹ 100 or ₹ 150 for hard labour of 8 to 10 hours (without any leave, medical or retirement benefits) on the one hand, and thousands per day (besides perks, benefits and security of every sort) to officers and *babus* like us on the other, whether we work or not.[9]

As shown in Table 1, the total number of (paid) workers in Aradhaknagar, in 2012, was 678, of which 69 per cent were in the unorganized sector including skilled and unskilled employees of transporters, small shopkeepers, etc. as also a large chunk of self-employed men and women which could again be divided into three categories, namely *mistrees* or skilled tailors, masons, mechanics etc; semi or low-skilled barbers, cobblers, mid-wives, etc; and lastly, unskilled labourers (mazdoors), rickshaw-pullers, hawkers, etc. Another notable division within the self-employed unorganized poor is between those who own their small shops/kiosks/rickshaws/repair units and those who pay rents for the same or work on pavements, etc. for a correspondingly lower net-income.

## Domestic Maids

Amidst the mass of unorganized workers in Aradhaknagar, it is the *mazdoors* or unskilled labourers working for others that form the largest chunk. Such unskilled unorganized labourers include construction-workers *(beldars)*, loaders *(jhalliwalas)*, cleaners and helpers at depots, 'dhabas' etc. However, the biggest sub-category within this class is of 'kaamwalis' or domestic-maids who also form the largest sub-section of workers in the slum as a whole. As shown in Table 1, the number of domestic maids in Aradhaknagar, in 2012, was 122 (including 20 child maids who accompany their mothers or elder sisters to work). These women workers are mostly engaged in washing clothes and utensils or sweeping floors and, occasionally, in cooking for expanding middle class colonies all around Aradhaknagar. It may be true that the demand for maids has grown in recent decades with rising middle and upper class incomes in the wake of liberalization. Their wages are, however, still extremely low; the general rate for each job in a middle class home, in 2006, was ₹ 400 or so per month. Normally, working for six to seven hours (in one or two homes) daily, these laborious maids or *kaamwalis* managed to earn just about ₹ 1,500 to ₹ 2,000 per month with no retirement, medical or accident benefits whatsoever.

**Table 1**

*Estimated Occupations in Aradhaknagaras per Usual Principal + Subsidiary Status (Brackets Denote Women Workers)**

| *Occupations/Years* | | *1988* | | | *2012* | |
|---|---|---|---|---|---|---|
| All Workers | | 157 | | | 678 | |
| Total Population | | 441 | | | 1,694 | |
| Ratio of Workers | | 36% | | | 40% | |
| Manual Workers | 154 | | 98% | 640 | | 94% |
| Informal Sector Workers | 123 | | 78% | 471 | | 69% |
| In Manufacturing | | NA | | | 31 | |
| Employers | 03 | 1% | | 10 | | 1% |
| Self-Employed | 33 | | 21% | 127 | | 19% |
| Wage-Earners | 78 | | 50% | 389 | | 57% |
| Casual Wage-Earners | 42 | | 27% | 122 | | 18% |
| *Primary-Sector Workers* | 09 | | 6% | 06 (1) | | <1% |
| Livestock*** | | 03 | | 2 | | (1) |
| Grass Collection | | 06 | | | 04 | |
| *Semi-Skilled/Unskilled Informal Workers:* | | | | | | |
| Self-employed | | 11 | | | 92(6) | |
| Home-Based Workers | | 04 | | | 2 (2) | |
| Vendors | | 04 | | 10 | | (4) |
| Others | | 03 | | | 73 | |
| Wage-Earners | | 37 | | | 135 (122) | |
| Maids | | 20 | | | 122 (20G) | |
| Others | | 17 | | | 13 | |
| Casual Labourers | | 22 | | | 74 (17) | |
| All Semi-Skilled | 74 | 44% | | | 301 (145) 44% | |
| *Skilled Informal Workers* | | | | | | |
| Casual Masons etc | | 20 | | | 47 | |
| Wage-Earners | | 07 | | | 41 (8) | |
| Self-Employed Artisan | | 07 | | | 10 (2) | |
| Self-Employed Service | | 06 | | | 20 | |
| All Skilled | 42 | | 25% | | 118 (16) | 17% |
| *Formal Sector Workers* | 36 | | 22% | 213 | | 31% |
| Private Sector Employment | 13 | | 8% | | 101(32) | 15% |
| Grade IV Sweepers | | 08 | | | 62 (22) | |
| Grade IV Labour) | | 04 | | | 35(10) | |
| Grade III Clerks etc. | | 01 | | | 04 | |
| Public Sector Employees | 24 | | 13% | 112(29) | | 16% |
| Sweepers (R) | | 17 | | | 69 (18) | |

*Cont'd ...*

*... Cont'd*

| | | | |
|---|---|---|---|
| Sweepers (T) | | 02 | 21 (6) |
| Others in Grade IV (R) | | 02 | 04 |
| Others in Grade IV (T) | | 00 | 12 |
| Grade III Clerks etc | | 00 | 07 (5) |
| Business Persons | | 00 | 22 (1) |
| Manufacturers | | 00 | 01 |
| Professionals | | 01 | 07 (2) |
| Petty Bourgeoisie | 02 | 1% | 40 (3) 6% |
| Multi-Taskers | | 01 | 08 |
| *All Workers* | | 157 | 678 (225) |
| Total Families | | 91 | 292 |

*Notes:* Percentages are of respective grand totals of all workers in concerned columns. Semi-skilled here refers to those who are mostly described as unskilled in official parlance. F stands for number of women which are shown in bracket.

Incidentally, nearly 70 per cent of the families in Aradhaknagar manage to have two incomes largely due to the dual responsibility of home and work borne by these maids, yet the remuneration of such workers is not even half of the wages received by male workers and not even a fifth of the salaries paid to even Public Sector Grade IV employees. But there is a valuable non-cash component in the earnings of most domestic maids, as we shall soon see. It is also notable that the paltry sum brought by women workers is in fact the mainstay of several slum families as many men drain away a major portion of their earnings in drinking, gambling, etc.

## Other Labouring Groups

As stated above, Aradhaknagar has a substantial section of unskilled, unorganized workers of which domestic maids are only one part. Others in this varied section include construction workers, loaders, cleaners, etc. To illustrate the level of earnings and working conditions in such jobs, we may consider the case of Nanhku first. Nanhku worked for a transporter on the Giani border and was getting a small wage of ₹ 100 per day, in 2006, for a back-breaking job of loading and unloading trucks for 6 to 8 hours daily. Another unskilled labourer in Aradhaknagar is Puranchand who worked as an unattached construction worker or *beldar* and (till 2009, when he developed a major heart problem) sat every morning in a nearby *mandi* (mart) to be hired for the day by building contractors. Casual workers like Puran, Nanhku or Jaggu (whom I had met in 1988 but who passed away in 1998) have no source for credit or advance in case of illness, accident, etc.

## Skilled Workers

Slightly better than the unskilled labourers in economic terms are the skilled and semi-skilled workers who can again be divided into those who work for others and those who have their own petty ventures. Thus, within Aradhaknagar, Madan is a low-skilled employee who gets a monthly salary of ₹ 3,000 for manning the STD booth owned by a physically challenged neighbour.

On the other hand, Arvind 'Thakur' (a barber) and Anil (a scooter mechanic) illustrate the category of the semi-skilled self-employed whose earnings are more variable and fall anywhere in a range of ₹ 3,000 to ₹ 5,000 per month as they have greater flexibility for combining their main occupation with a part-time job (of a night-guard, a milk-supplier or a newspaper-vendor etc.).

In the category of skilled craftsmen labouring in unregistered private units, falls Shamshad who has worked for a long time in helmet-assembling units in nearby Shahdara and Seelampur, starting on a child worker's monthly salary of just ₹ 250, in 1986, and resigning (to start his own helmet-kiosk), in 2000, at a monthly wage of ₹ 1,500. Shamshad's case illustrates that though a skilled worker is also paid low in private factories, his work is in greater demand and he can afford to change employers more easily even when union support is absent in small, unregistered units.

## The Self-Employed

Apart from skilled and unskilled employees working for others, Aradhaknagar also has a few self-employed skilled artisans such as Rajender and Karan both of whom are tailors, though of different types. Rajender stitches clothes for local customers and earns anything between ₹ 4,000 and ₹ 6,000 per month depending on season. Almost all his clients are from Aradhaknagar and the rates he charged, in 2009, for a set of shirt and trousers was ₹ 170 and that for a ladies suit ₹ 60 only (less than half of the rates prevailing in middle-class colonies). A good number of independent skilled artisans in Aradhaknagar, however, are linked to the construction industry. These are masons, carpenters and welders whose wages are normally the double of those of unskilled labourers and have risen six-fold (in absolute terms) in the past two decades. Thus, in 1988, at the time of my first visits to the slum, these *mistrees* were getting a daily wage of ₹ 50 at the most; in 2006, on the other hand, the going rate was ₹ 225 which had risen to ₹ 300 by mid-2009. Considering the price rise of more than 400 per cent between 1988 and 2009, this suggests a rise of about a half in real earnings for this group also.[10]

Among the large number of self-employed persons in Aradhaknagar, there is a major section of vendors of various types. Many of them sell simple wares such as eggs, bread, *ghutka* (a mix of cracked betel nuts and cheap tobacco), *bidis*, vegetables, cold drinks etc. on small counters or mats spread next to their homes; others have more *pucca* kiosks inside or around Aradhaknagar which can also be locked when required; still others sell fruits, vegetables, bread, eggs, etc. in boxes fitted on cycles or *rehris* (four-wheeled carts) or simply on their backs, roaming in lanes and announcing their wares. The earnings of these vendors show variation depending upon the resources they are able to mobilize. But, broadly speaking, these tended to fall within the range of ₹ 100 to ₹ 300 per day, in 2006. To calculate their net earnings, however, two deductions need to be made – namely, rents (ranging from ₹ 500 to ₹ 1,000 per month) that some of the kiosk or cart users pay to their owners and *hafta* or commissions paid reportedly to beat constables (of ₹ 500 or so by the older vendors and up to ₹ 1,000 by the new ones per month) for kiosks put up on main roads.

## Pensioners and Job Seekers

Over the past decade or so, a small number of slum dwellers have started receiving monthly pensions from the state. On paper these are meant for all elders (above 65 years in age) as also widows and the physically challenged who do not have any other source of income and are registered with the local administration as Below Poverty Line (BPL) families. The actual number of recipients of this support in Aradhaknagar, however, is much smaller than those who seem eligible. Thus, in 2012, only 35 old-age pensions had been fixed in the slum even though the number of persons above 65 years was more than 90. Besides this, only one handicapped and three widows had been given this benefit although their strength is three to four times that number in Aradhaknagar. The amount given in pensions is, however, the same for all categories. In 1995, it began with a small sum of ₹ 150 per month and was raised to ₹ 1,000 by 2009.

As the Table indicates, only 10 persons in the age group of 14 to 60 years, in Aradhaknagar, described themselves as unemployed in our 2012 survey. Four of these were also physically challenged or seriously ill. Many families in the slum, in fact, have more than one earning member and some have up to four earners. This suggests that few able-bodied men and women who are willing and capable of undertaking the hard menial tasks of sweepers, labourers, etc. remain out of work in a city like Delhi. It is another matter that fair chances of finding menial work do not indicate better working conditions or wages also.[11]

## The Underclass

The last category of workers to be noted here falls in the 'grey sector' of illegal or quasi-legal jobs such as begging, child labour and criminal activities as of pick-pockets, prostitutes and *satta* (betting) or *matka* (petty lottery) operators besides some bootleggers. In 2006, a large number of girls (47 in all) were going with their mothers/elder sisters, to work as domestic helps, outside Aradhaknagar. Along with this, a number of boys (below 14 yrs) have also begun earning by selling water, coconut slices, fruits, etc. on the crossing outside the slum or, by picking rags, plastic and scrap from garbage dumps. Most of these child-workers are registered in government schools which they attend occasionally. But more commonly they can be seen working at odd jobs and earning anything between ₹ 50 and ₹ 150 per day (2006 figures). Older slum lads, on the other hand, often work as waiters at parties or weddings and get a better return of ₹ 150 per evening (besides food and alcohol), when hired. However, such work is seasonal and for most of the year these lads loiter around the *basti*. Some of them have formed small groups which have had trouble with police for alleged involvement in pick-pocketing, theft and fights. There is one family in Aradhaknagar which is forced to beg for a living.

Another career chosen by a handful of slum dwellers is that of crime. Such a tendency has reportedly grown among teenagers of late. Increasing exposure to the glamorous world of the rich but total lack of legitimate means to avail even simple comforts have evidently heightened the drift towards illegality among youngsters in the slum.

## Conclusion

There has been considerable debate, in recent years, about the exact impact of the Govt. of Indian's new economic policy or regime of economic liberalization and globalization on unorganized working in our vast informal economy. While scholars like Jan Breman have tried to show that there has been a direct correlation between economic liberalization, expansion of the informal sector, casualisation of labour and immiserization or even communalization of local communities;[12] others like Geert De Neve have established through long-term fieldwork in some communities that the process also opened up new possibilities for economic improvement and mobility;[13] most economists and statisticians have veered round to the view that the decades of 'liberalization' in India have undoubtedly seen a decline in poverty and a rise in real wages even though Public Sector employment has come down and inequalities have gone up since the mid-1990s.[14] The present study supports the latter view but also highlights the miniscule nature of economic 'improvements' experienced by the slum dwellers of Aradhaknagar after six-and-a-half decades of India's Independence and growing insecurities, congestion and alienation in their lives on other counts.

## Notes

1. I gratefully acknowledge the financial help received for the present research from the Indian Council of Social Science Research and the University Grants Commission of India for my second extended survey of Aradhaknagar in 2006 and again in 2012.
2. Most slums around Aradhaknagar (including Sunlight Colony, Sonia Camp, Rajeev Camp) have seen similar transition from *kutcha* to *pucca* housing and many more consumer durables in the past two decades.
3. I acknowledge the hard work put in by my field assistants: Rakesh Bihari and Vidya Krishnamurthy. I am also extremely grateful to all the residents of Aradhaknagar for their patient responses to our intrusive queries and especially to Virender Kumar and Rajender who helped in data collection.
4. Refer Tables IV and V for a broad classification of occupations in Aradhaknagar.
5. For instance refer Ambika Pandit, '45000 MCD Employees Fake?', *Times of India*, June 30, 2009, p. 1.
6. Refer *Statistical Outline of India*, Tata Information Services, 2012 and 'Current Statistics', *Economic and Political Weekly*, 2009 (July numbers).
7. Refer snaps.
8. For national data on employees in the manufacturing sector, refer *Statistical Outline of India*, op. cit.
9. For a major work on the problems and predicament of informal/unorganized sector workers refer Jan Breman, *The Laboring Poor in India: Patterns of Exploitation, Subordination, and Exclusion*, Oxford University Press, Oxford, 2002.
10. Refer 'Current Statistics' shown by all issues of the *Economic and Political Weekly* besides the *Statistical Outline of India* and also Arjun Sengupta et al., 'India's Common People: Who Are They, How Many Are They and How Do They Live?', *Economic and Political Weekly*, March 15, 2008.

11. For similar evidence refer Margaret Antony and G. Maheshwaran, op. cit., 2001 and Arup Mitra, 'Rural Migrants and Labour Segmentation', *Economic and Political Weekly*, January 12, 2002.
12. Jan Breman, *The Making and Unmaking of an Industrial Working Class: Sliding Down the Labour Hierarchy in Ahmedabad, India*, Oxford University Press, New Delhi, 2004.
13. G.D. Neve, *The Everyday Politics of Labour*, Social Science Press, New Delhi, 2005.
14. Refer Arjun Sengupta et al., op. cit. and R.H. Dholakia, 'Liberalisation in Gujarat: Review of Recent Experience', *Economic and Political Weekly*, Vol. 35, No. 19, 2006.

# Part 4

## Environment: The Regional Context

# 9

# A Losing Battle with Development and Human Indifference

## *A Case of Gomti River in Lucknow*

**ARCHANA PANDEY**

Rivers are defined as an incredible part of our civilization, as one of the oldest witnesses to the changes taking place from the ancient times to the modern. Civilizations have come up around rivers as they are not only a perennial source of supplying water but also one of the important reasons for the existence and sustainability of towns. This journey of civilizations from the stage of a hunting-gathering economy to settlers converted to the management of domestication of animals and cultivation of food crops is what led to the possibility of the existence of towns. Rivers are even worshipped in many civilizations as goddesses which, in due course of time, came to be personified. Rivers, credited in scriptures as a lifeline for human beings, are now facing a threat from the very same humans. The main objective of this paper is to study the indifference shown towards the river by us in the name of development and beautification, in the context of *Gomti river – symbol of Ganga-Jamuni tehzeeb in Lucknow city*. This symbol is losing its identity in the name of development and unplanned city layout as it leads to uncontrolled diversions of the *nullahs* into the river, mismanagement of the sewage treatment plants etc. The present BJP government has initiated several steps for the purification of the river Ganges but it is also true that till the time river Gomti is cleaned, Ganges cannot be purified completely, because Gomti travels 715 kms and, unfortunately, collects garbage and waste materials and then merges into the river Ganga.

In short, the credit for this loss goes to us for the indifference which we have shown to these rivers, usually in the name of science, technology, growth etc. But in this process of development, we forget that indirectly we are contributing to the decline of our civilization. This problem is more or less common to all rivers. But here the special focus is on river Gomti. When we stand at the banks of this river and imagine that our forefathers once stood at the same place, it gives us a feeling of being linked to the past and we feel proud, and so it becomes our responsibility to ensure that our future generations feel the same. This we can do by protecting these rivers. In other words, it can also be said that the protection of rivers is a matter of necessity, not of choice.

## Gomti

Gomti is a tributary of river Ganges. It is not mountain-fed. At some places it is recharged by underground water sources and at some it recharges natural water-sources. It has 22 tributaries and Sai is the major among them. The total drainage area of Gomti is 30,437 sq kms, whereas the drainage area of Sai is 12,900 sq kms, approximately 43 per cent of the total catchment area of Gomti Basin. There are 15 towns located in its catchment area but the most prominent among them are Lucknow, Lakhimpur Kheri, Sultanpur and Jaunpur located on the banks of the Gomti. It originates from a natural lake, Gomat Taal (earlier known as Fulhaar Jheel), near Madho Tanda in Pilibhit. Origin of the river is in the form of the fragmented lake. At a few places it is a chain of fragmented lakes. Its formation consists mainly of Sand, Silt, Clay and occasional Kankar bands (Dutta and Srivastava et al., 2011: 100). It extends up to 900 kms and meets the Ganges river near Saidpur, Kaithi in Ghazipur (Kumar and Verma et al., 2013: 337). Twenty kms from its origin, the very small river Gaihaaee meets it. The river is a thin stream until it reaches Mohammad Kheri (about 100 kms from its origin), a tehsil of Lakhimpur Kheri district, where it is joined by some tributaries. Here, the river is well-defined. Later, other tributaries join this river and the major one, as stated earlier, is the Sai River which joins near Jaunpur. The river cuts Jaunpur city into two equal halves. It becomes wider in Jaunpur. There are rivers that contribute to its flow; the two tributaries Choha and Andhra Choha are completely dry. They used to get water from land and there are many places where water seeps from the underground aquifer. However, due to bad management, most of these critical sources have been destroyed. At the Sangam of Gomti and Ganges, the famous Markandey Mahadeo temple is situated. After 240 kms, the Gomti enters Lucknow, through which it meanders for about 12 km. At the entrance point, water is lifted from the city's water supply (www.lucknow4u.com/gomti.htm).

## Lifeline to Graveyard

Rivers are the major supply of water for the sustainability of towns. That is why they are referred to as a lifeline. But now the definitions are changed; river Gomti is mentioned as a graveyard of some species, for it is nothing more than a neglected river. It has become the victim of development and human indifference in the city. Several causes are responsible for turning this river from a lifeline into a graveyard. After looking into these reasons, it becomes clear that human activities play more or less a dominant role in polluting this river. Some of the reasons are explained as follows:

## Unplanned Layout of the City

Planning of a city plays a substantial role for the protection of rivers. Apart from unplanned diversions of the *nullahs*, mismanagement of the Sewage Treatment Plant (STP) and, most important, the blunder of constructing colonies like the Gomti Nagar Colony (which was once a dumping ground for waste coming out of Sewage Treatment Plant), many other reasons too are responsible for the conversion of this natural lifeline of the city into the stinking *nullah* that it has become. As the Gomti is a major source of drinking water for over 32 lakh people, its survival is at risk because the place where the waste out of the STP has to be dumped has now been constructed as a residential area. The farm of 600 acres is now popularly known as Gomti Nagar. The disposal of the waste coming out of the STP came up, indeed, as a major problem. Secondly, the old Lucknow was built on a high-level area, but the new Lucknow is located in a low-level area that is not much above the water level. During the rainy season this creates lots of problems. Gomti too faces the adverse impact of this unplanned layout of the city. It is being said that over the years, the water source feeding the river has shrunk, thus, reducing the flow in the river. Experts are of the opinion that its flow has been reduced to one-third of what it was originally. The major problem Gomti is facing is, indeed, of sewage disposal.

## Sewage Disposal in the River

Sewage discharge directly into the river is a major problem and if it is tackled, around 80 per cent of the problem can be solved. The domestic sewage releasing into the river from over 26 drains is a curse for Gomti. In the present times, the discharge from these drains is more than 500 MLD. The release of the sewage in its raw form is not environmentally safe. It should be treated in the STP before being released into the river. These raw sewages are transported to these treatment plants through a network of pipes and characterized as pumping stations. These networks of pipes are gravity-fed according to their higher and lower levels. On the other hand, there are sewage treatment plants with limited capacity – for example, the *Daultaganj Sewage Treatment Plant* – where 42 MLD is treated, whereas total waste water generated is approximately 356 MLD. The rest of the 314 MLD is being directly discharged into the river without treatment. There is another *Bharwara STP (Asia's largest STP in Chinhat, Lucknow)*, which might be helpful to a certain extent. There is an increase of effluent discharge in the river every year by more than 50 MLD. Large number of drains are already diverted to the Kukrail *nullah* and Ghaziuddin Haider Canal and these in turn are connected to the Gwari Gaon Pumping Station and then they are sent to Bharwara STP where sewage is gushed through the pipe into a chamber which would make the river free of sewage discharge. There are channels and reactors from which this sewage is moved and they remove the larger and finer impurities respectively. Then the remaining water is diverted downstream of Gomti (near Indira canal) about 2 kms off the plant with the help of pipes. The sewage is subsequently dried and converted into manure. Methane gas produced in the process will be stored in a chamber for production of power through dual fuel-generators (*TOI*, 2013: 4). This will work as a backup for the plant which is expected to consume around 1.5 mw of power daily. Moreover, the chambers and digesters would require specific bacteria which would break the organic matter.

Theoretically, this seems to be the solution to all problems but practically these STPs have brought no significant change. This mega project was thought to be the boon for river Gomti but it has made no remarkable improvement in the water-quality of the river. Waste water treated at Bharwara STP is disposed into the river. Instead, it can be disposed into the Indira Canal for Irrigation. Jal Nigam officials said that after the diversion of certain drains into the STP, the quantity of the water also decreased in the river, leading to increase in the concentration of the pollutants. One reason for this problem can be the mismanagement of these plants. Efforts are made for the revival of this dying river but so far no satisfactory results have come up. Earlier, sewage from the rising main used to be discharged into a 1.25 x 30 m. brick-channel leading to a 600 acre sewage farm. But as has already been mentioned, this sewage farm has been converted into a housing colony, that is the Gomti Nagar Colony. In the absence of any facility for disposal, the sewage is discharged directly into the river, thereby increasing the problem of pollution, as now the sewage is discharged upstream of the Gomati Barrage. Gomti Nagar is a blunder of the planners of the city.

Recently, since November 2013, efforts were made to divert the drains to the STP at Bharwara. Jal Nigam says that out of the 26 drains carrying sewage content into the river, 24 have been tapped (leaving two still untapped) and diverted towards the STPs at Daultaganj and Bharwara. But there is a problem in the diversion of two drains (the Pata Nullah and near Lakshman Jhula Maidan). In Pata Nullah the retaining wall got damaged permanently as the result of which sewage is getting mixed with the drain-water and flowing into the river. There is a problem also at the Gomti Sewage Pumping Station, as most pumps of this station are in a dilapidated condition and not able to pump the sewage effluents efficiently. News of the crumbling of the Ghasiyari Mandi culvert is also there and this is polluting the drain beneath. This machinery needs regular maintenance. It has been usually observed that whenever there is a blockage in sewers, they are broken and connected to the nearby *nullahs*, further aggravating the practice of disposal of solid waste into the drainage system.

Efforts made to prevent the flow of waste from *nullahs* directly into the river by constructing a retaining wall fail – because of the deposited silt in *nullahs*, the water overflows the wall and directly pours into the river. Water, after coming out from the treatment plant, has Dissolved Oxygen 3.20, and the Biological Oxygen Demand (BOD) is 9.30 milligram/litre and bacteria is 1,34,800. This shows that the water after treatment too is seriously unsafe and poisonous. At Majhighat, Gomti enters Lucknow – and BOD is measured as 2.98 mg/litre. At Kudia Ghatit is 4mg/litre and at Nishatganj it is 6.5mg/litre; upstream barrage it is 7.79 mg/litre. At downstream of Gomti after Bharwara STP, BOD is maximum 9.30 mg/litre (Sinha, 2014: 16).

## Encroachment of River Banks Reduces Forest Cover and Destroys Underground Aquifers

As mentioned above, Gomti is not a mountain-fed river. It depends on various natural-water sources for its survival. But because of encroachments (in the form of slums, cultivation by farmers etc. around the river) and deforestation around the banks of the river, underground and other natural-water sources fail to survive. Thus ultimately, their contribution in the free flow of supply of water to Gomti is not possible. In order to recharge river Gomti, it is important to undertake plantation around the banks which will allow the rain water to go deep inside the river sources and further prevent encroachments, and will also kill poisonous pollutants of the river. NBRI senior scientist Dr U.N. Rai says planting of trees is very important for the healthy growth of the river. STPs are important for removal of sewage disposal but it is very difficult to remove metals deposited in the river bed as poisonous pollutants. Dense forest cover around the river not only provides life to it but also prevents encroachments and reduces deposition of garbage around it. When roots of trees reach deep into it, the river water absorbs pollutants.

NBRI has developed a 'Constructed Wet Land' concept. It helps in removing metals from the river without using chemicals. The river has chemicals like phosphorus, nitrogen, chromium, cadmium, iron, lead, copper and other metals which make it poisonous. For its treatment, a temporary water reservoir is made with the help of some plant-species like *Pipataj, Sirpus, Narkul, Kumudani*, etc. They clean the water by absorbing these poisonous metals (Sinha, July 2014).

Other reasons for depleting underground water sources are irrigation of fields through underground water source, water being misused by industries and in construction work. From Pilibhit to Sitapur, farmers encroach river beds for seven-eight months for cultivation. In Uttar Pradesh, 70 per cent of irrigation is done by underground waters and only 30 per cent by canals. Dr J.S. Samra, CEO of National Rainfed Area Authority, Planning Commission, New Delhi, says that investment in underground water protection is very less in comparison to that in canal irrigation. To maintain the availability of underground water, which usually goes down in summer, Fulhaar Jheel was connected to the Sarda Canal through a minor canal. Later, release of water was stopped from the Sarda canal by officials because the maximum use of water was by farmers for cultivation. This is all happening because of the water crisis and the drain was diverted to the lake, and large volume of sewerage started flowing into the river. Many natural ponds, lakes and other recharge areas have been occupied. This has led to severe reduction in water. He further suggests alternative ways of irrigation such as Drip Irrigation and the Sprinkler System, and advises the sowing of seeds which demand less amounts of water (ibid., 16).

Dam's construction is another way of encroachment. It deposits silt in river which not only reduces water-holding capacity but also reduces the depth of the river at several places and even changes its geographical features. Dr Venkatesh Dutta, Assistant Professor of Environmental Science, Babasahab Bhimrao Ambedkar University, Lucknow, also advises separation of the Gomti river from *nullahs*. Encroachments around the bank result in the reduction of forest cover from 14 per cent to 5 per cent, river-flow is reduced to 60 per cent, and 35 kms of river-bank area is converted to fields, whereas 55 kms' area has no water (ibid., 15).

A study was conducted by the Geological Survey of India to ascertain the level of pollution and it revealed that two marine species are also found in the river – Solariella, Hemicypris arorai; these species are endemic to coastal waters that ordinarily have high levels of alkalinity (ph values of 8.2 to 9.1), indicating high levels of pollution. High ph value is due to the use of fertilizers in nearby fields. Thus, encroachments by farmers in nearby areas are, as indicated earlier, affecting it adversely and the reduced forest cover has adversely affected the flow of water in the river. In the Gomati basin, majority of forests are open and less dense. A figure shows that forest cover has declined from an average of 9.01 per cent to 4.10 per cent. Because of deforestation, the water sources of Gomati are drying up.

## Gomati Barrage (Another Problem for Gomati)

The Gomti Barrage was constructed in 1980 near Ballu Adda, to maintain adequate level of water in the upstream area of the Gaughat. From Gaughat to Ballu Adda, Gomti river is 12 km in length but it looks like a huge pond. The gates of the barrage constructed over the Gomti river restrict the natural flow of water. Between Kudia Ghat and Gomti Barrage, 20 open drains discharge large volumes of sewage directly into the Gomti. Because of the barrage-construction, the gates are closed and this does not allow the sewage to flow downstream, as the water gets stagnated and thus increases the level of pollution at a particular place, thereby affecting the aquatic life of the river because of a fall in Dissolved Oxygen. In May 2011, locals claimed that around 50 quintals of fish perished in Kathina river – a major tributary of Gomti.

## Disposal of Industrial Effluent into the River

There are 15 towns on the banks of the Gomti river, with Lucknow, Lakhimpur Kheri, Sitapur, Hardoi, Barabanki being some of the prominent ones. They contribute almost 90 per cent of industrial wastes in the Gomti. Sugar factories and distilleries of Lakhimpur Kheri (that has three sugar factories and one distillery), Sitapur (paper mill), Hardoi (yeast and milk-processing factory), Barabanki (meat-processing unit) are mainly responsible for draining industrial pollutants. During the rainy season, pollutants from these factories drain into the river. The effluents from these industries pouring into the river are very dangerous (ibid., 8).

From Sitapur to Jaunpur, it is facing the problem of discharge of untreated effluents from industrial areas. It is worst polluted in mid-segment and lower-stream as major urban towns are located on its banks. Downstream of Sitapur, due to the sudden discharge from sugar factories, there have been several cases of fish-kill in Sarayan river (a tributary of Gomti). The standard value of Dissolved Oxygen should be 6.0 mg/litre – at Gaughat, where the Gomti enters into the city-area, the DO level varied from 7 to 12.5 mg/litre from

January to April. This shows that the Dissolved Oxygen level at Gaughat has always been higher than the standard value because it is only after the river enters into the city that it gets polluted along the 14 km stretch in the city – the level of pollution increases as drains discharge effluents into the river. And as this level increases, the level of Dissolved Oxygen decreases in the river, and thus it becomes dangerous for aquatic life. With a decrease in the variety of fish and aquatic plants, there is a drastic drop in the river's bio-diversity, thereby further depleting the river's powers of self-purification. The result is a major drop in the population of fresh-water turtles (Environmental Monitoring and Assessment, Lohani et al., 2008: 253). Moreover, around 347 feet of water-level should be maintained for supplying water in the old city area. In summers, it is difficult to maintain this level, which is done at the cost of this aquatic life. Gomti was a source of livelihood for various peoples like fisherman but now they have to buy fish imported from Andhra Pradesh. The Gomti Action Plan was formulated in the year 1993 for three major districts – Lucknow, Jaunpur and Sultanpur but it was started finally in Lucknow in 1995. Work is still going on, yet so far no satisfactory result has come out.

## Climatic Reasons

Several natural climatic reasons are responsible for the problems in the river – for example, regular flooding during the monsoon leads to several problems when it recedes, especially due to drying potholes and pits because of which diseases like malaria and dengue occur. In the past, there were large ponds that received storm water and helped manage the problem of water-logging in the city, but in the present scenario these ponds, *nullahs* and embankments have been encroached upon, thus causing floods by restricting the flow of the drains.

## People's Indifference

People being indifferent towards these issues, and towards the river is also one of the important reasons for its pollution. At several places, the river is converted into a dumping ground (Laxmipur village, Shahjahanpur district). Officials, even being aware of such things, did not take action. Rivers are considered as holy places, several pilgrims visit these places, and they too have a role in polluting it as they throw flowers, garlands, etc. into it. Dumping of articles used in rituals has converted this river into drain at some places. Human beings have changed the surroundings of the river, transforming it into a tourism centre with hydroelectric generators, quarrying of minerals, and other such activities.

## Efforts for a Cleaner Gomti

Several efforts were made by the earlier government, but the result is in front of us – the poisonous Gomti. The present government – BJP – too is making a claim for a cleaner Gomti and Ganges. Not only the government but also the people should participate in purification of rivers. Active participation of people not only helps in cleaning the river but it gives a new life to the river.

The waste poured into the river is the result of human activities. Some of the very toxic waste dumped into the river is polythene. The receding waters of the river reveal the amount of polythene that is dumped into Gomti. The polythene reaches the sole sewage treatment plant at Daulatganj. As a result of this, the plant is often choked and unable to process the wastes. Meanwhile, untreated water continues to flow into the river, causing the depletion of the aquatic environment as well as marine life. Polythene pollution is widespread and affects the ecosystem. It obstructs drains, natural water bodies and landfills. Plastic causes serious damage to the environment and the only way is to reduce its use and production. The major chemicals that go into the making of plastic are highly toxic and pose a serious threat to living beings of all species. Besides hitting the ecosystem which is already fragile, these chemicals can cause an array of maladies ranging from birth defects to cancer. Plastic dumped into rivers, streams and sea contaminates water, soil, marine life and also the air. Choked drains are excellent breeding grounds for mosquitoes besides causing flooding during the monsoon. Since plastic does not undergo bacterial decomposition, land-filling using plastic means preserving the poison forever (*Bulletin of Environmental Contamination and Toxicology*, Agarwal et al., 2007: 118).

Thus, it is of utmost importance for the localities to stop throwing polythenes and packets in the river so as to maintain its purity. There are several examples of people's efforts in regenerating rivers in Rajasthan like Ruparel river of Alwar district, Bhagadi river in the Aravalli Range, Sabi river, etc. The Thames river of London, once the lifeline of the city, was declared dead in 1950, but later on with the efforts of government and the people, planning and management, it again revived and is now flourishing.

Now efforts are also being made to plant trees around Gomti, for example in Naimisharan around 80,000 trees have been planted. Several *rath yatras* have been organized to create awareness among people and several organizations are contributing for the purification of river Gomti.

## Conclusion

Rivers in India are facing multiple problems of severe pollution, over extraction, deforestation in catchment areas, encroachment, dams and barrages which cut off the connectivity of the river with its associated ecosystems. Gomti river is under assault at various points of its journey as it meanders through the 900 km stretch of rich alluvial plains of Uttar Pradesh. From industrial effluents to domestic discharge, the river becomes more of a dumping ground of the 15 smaller and bigger towns, including Lakhimpur Kheri, Sitapur, Lucknow, Sultanpur and Jaunpur, in its catchment area. The barrage should be constructed such that the extra water and sewage flows over the gates of the barrage regularly so that the decline in water quality is negligible. The river collects large amounts of human and industrial pollutants as it flows through the highly populous areas (18 million approximately) of Uttar Pradesh. STP has caused a change but not a significant one. Mismanagement and unawareness among people is also one of the important reasons for this condition of Gomti.

## References

Agarwal, R., R. Kumar and J.R. Behari (2007). 'Mercury and Lead Content in Fish Species from the River Gomti, Lucknow, India, as Bio-markers of Contamination'. *Bulletin of Environmental Contamination and Toxicology*, 78(2), February: 118–22.

Dutta, Venkatesh (2014). 'Pradushan Se Mukti Ko Banay Nadi Mein Pravah'. *Dainik Jagran*, July 5.

Dutta, Venkatesh, Ravindra Kumar Srivastava, M. Yunus, Shamshad Ahmed, Vinayak Vandan Pathak, Alok Rai and Nupoor Prasad (2011). 'Restoration Plan of Gomati River with Designated Best Use Classification of Surface Water Quality Based on River Expedition, Monitoring and Quality'. *Earth Science India*, 4(3): 80–104.

Government of Uttar Pradesh (2006). 'City Development Plan Lucknow'. www.npakmakdoom.com.

——. (2006a). 'A Civil Society Initiative to Restore the Sanctity and Beauty of River Gomti'. www.gomtifoundation.webs.com.

Jain, Akanchha, Tabish Ahmad Abdullah, Khurram Ashraf and Zeba Nisar (2011). 'A Conceptual Approach for Development of Kukrail Nullah, Lucknow'. *Institute Town Planners India Journal*, July– September: 67–72.

Kumar, Dhananjay, Anjali Verma, Namita Dhusia and Nandkishore More (2013). 'Water Quality Assessment of River Gomti in Lucknow'. *Universal Journal of Environmental Research and Technology*, 3(3): 337–44. www.environmentaljournal.org

Lohani, Minaxi B., Amarika Singh, D.C. Rupainwar and D.N. Dhar (2008). 'Seasonal Variations of Heavy Metal Contamination in River Gomti of Lucknow City Region'. *Environmental Monitoring and Assessment*, 147(1–3): 253–63.

Singh, Rajesh Kumar (2007). 'Barrage Effect: Gomti a Graveyard for Fish'. *Hindustan Times*, January 18.

——. (2007a). 'Where Gomti Turns a Carrier of Muck'. *Times of India*, January 11.

Sinha, Ruma (2014). 'Neharon Se Zyada Bhugarb Jal Ko Nivesh Ki Darkar'. *Dainik Jagran*, July 23.

visitlucknow. 'Gomti River in Lucknow–Information and Photos, Images, Pictures of River Gomti in Lucknow'. www.google.com

# 10

# Governing the Forest Resources

## *A Case Study of Uttarakhand*

**RUKMANI**

Since time immemorial the relationship between tribal communities and forests has been characterized by co-existence and these communities were considered integral to the survival and sustainability of the ecological system. But in the era of consumerism, the rate at which the natural resources like forests are depleting is as never before. Being everyone's property, forests have become no one's property.

The forest policies and programmes define the nature of forest use and management as well as the property regime within which the resource is held. The policies specify the right to property and ownership vis-à-vis the resource. For instance, the early Acts of 1878 and 1894 illustrate the process through which a certain regime of property in forests gave way to a different type of regime, i.e. State Ownership. Further policies and Acts are also a reflection of the State's response to socio-economic conditions and are primarily guided by concerns as perceived by the State.

Recent years have witnessed an increasing focus on people's participation in the policy discourse at the national and the international level. Even at the level of local institutions, voluntary agencies and NGOs, emphasis has been given to participation by local communities. The introduction of Joint Forest Management (JFM) and the central government order in the 1990s, directing state governments to encourage the involvement of village communities in the regeneration of degraded forest land, showed a major shift from State regulation to people's participation in forest management. However, it is important to carefully observe and interpret the claims of the legislation and its limitations. The Acts and policies need to be 'eagre' to know whether these legislations have achieved their objectives of people's participation, efficiency, accountability, etc. as claimed.

In this paper, an attempt is being made to 'eagre' the impact of the process of decentralization on forest resources and the interaction patterns between the institutions created at the third tier of government. The argument which has been defended here is that different types of property rights over resources allocated in different societies powerfully affect how resources will be used and how benefits will be distributed. In this study, the underlying argument is that it is the institutions, not the population or market forces, that form the significant explanation of resource conservation or degradation.

This paper is divided into four sections. First is about the governance of natural resources. This section explains different models followed by various national governments to govern the natural resources. The second Section is about the field area and local institutions, the third Section describes the case-studies and in the last Section, analysis of the case-studies has been done.

## Section 1: Governance of Natural Resources

Issues in natural resource management are complex and encompass various dimensions of development such as social, economic and environmental. As human civilization progressed, man started altering the natural environment in the pursuit of creating an economic, social and cultural environment of his own choice which slowly resulted in the depletion of natural resources and degradation of environment. Hence, the governance challenge regarding the utilization of natural resource is to balance the need for development with the demands and aspirations of the differentiated social structure, future generations and the environment.

The condition of natural resources like forests has deteriorated in recent times. In the era of consumerism, the rate at which the forests are depleting is as never before. Being everyone's property, forests have become no one's property. As it becomes difficult to exclude anyone from deriving the benefits of forests through physical barriers like fencing, unlimited consumption of forest products by everyone leads to a net reduction in the benefits available for the next generation or indeed the next individual. The cost of protecting and managing the forests is very high; therefore, like any other Common Property Resource (CPR), forests are facing the challenges of overuse, non-cooperation, free riders, low productivity and rent dissipation.

The centralized regulation of the resources by a sovereign or Central government has been suggested as a solution by policy-makers and scholars such as Hardin, Gordon, Olson, etc. in their respective models of governing CPRs to resolve the problems of over-usage and non-cooperation. Till the 1970s, the world witnessed a great amount of confidence also in the centralized State but the centralized regulation of resources did not prove hugely successful or even satisfactory in overcoming the challenges of CPR. Centralization is considered as insensitive to the local problems and conditions which require attention. The management of natural resources by the central governments fails to include the local-level knowledge, needs and aspirations, for the level of participation by the local communities in central regulation is very low.

By the late 20th century, most developing nations witnessed reforms, through which power was transferred from the central authority to lower levels, transforming the local institutional infrastructure. In recent years, we have seen a considerable restructuring of the institutional arrangements governing the management of natural resources like water and forests with the aim of attaining democratization. According to the study conducted by the World Bank in 1999, more than 80 per cent of all developing countries and countries with economies in transition are experimenting with some form of decentralization[1] in managing common property resources so that they can balance the need for economic growth as well as sustainable development and achieve the objective of efficiency, equity and democracy by bringing the government closer to people, increasing local participation and government accountability. The important argument for decentralization in the forestry sector is to include the historically excluded local people in access to forest resources as well as in the decision-making process.

The trends of decentralization have a profound impact even on the forests – and this is profoundly local on the one hand and truly global[2] on the other. In fact, decentralized governance has become a crucial issue in sustainable forest management because the quality of governance determines the fate of forest resources in all aspects – economic, social and ecological.

National governments often assert the importance of establishing autonomous local decision-making institutions for the management of natural resources within their local jurisdiction. Yet, specific laws governing these resources, and forests in particular, limit this decision-making to playing, at best, a supportive role to the central government's authority (Larson, 2005). In other words, authority is rarely transferred to representative and accountable local institutions. The study of the local institutions of the Joint Forest Management managing the forest resources in the state of Jharkhand encourages us to ask the question as to whether – and to what extent – the process of decentralization has actually taken place in the State.

## Section 2: The Field

Forests in India are jointly managed by the Federal and state governments, but the state governments have the primary responsibility for implementation. States are expected to decentralize the responsibility and certain rights to the third-tier levels of government. The third-tier of government relationships is left mainly to the states. The National Forest Policy encourages partnerships with local communities for securing forest raw material supplies.

Uttarakhand is the 27th state of India, divided into two regions of Kumaon and Garhwal, with a total of 13 districts. It covers an area of 51,125 sq kms, of which 92.57 per cent is hilly. Forests constitute a significant portion of Uttarakhand. Around 12.60 per cent of the hilly region is cultivated and 64 per cent is forested (India State of Forest Report, 2009). Forests are a source of livelihood for rural hilly residents and provide resources such as fodder, fuel, green manure, and construction timber.

Forests in Uttarakhand are managed by different administrative agencies, with three different categories of forest land:

- Forests under the Forest Department.
- Panchayati or Community Forests under Van Panchayats i.e. the Forest Councils (hereafter VPs).
- Forests controlled by the Revenue Department.

Of the total forest area, two-third is under the jurisdiction of the Forest Department and only 4,000 sq km (12%) is managed by VPs or the forest councils and the rest comes under the jurisdiction of the Revenue Department (Mukherjee, 2004). (For details see Table 1). This study is confined to two institutions governing Panchayati or Community Forests, i.e. VPs and Village Forests' Joint Management Committees.

**Table 1**

*Statistics of Van Panchayats' Area in Uttarakhand*

| *District* | *Area (Sq Km)* | *Forests Area (Sq Km)* | | | | |
|---|---|---|---|---|---|---|
| | | *Under Forest Department (1)* | *Civil Soyam under Revenue Department (2)* | *Under Van Panchayat (3)* | *Under Private/Other agencies (4)* | *Total Forest Area (1+2+3+4)* |
| Almora | 3,139 | 785.195 | 848.558 | 698.531 | 29.557 | 2,361.841 |
| Bageshwar | 2,246 | 690.333 | 23.021 | 387.829 | 0.43 | 1,101.596 |
| Pithoragarh | 7,090 | 751.966 | 417.480 | 870.537 | 13.003 | 2,052.986 |
| Champawat | 1,766 | 735.379 | 275.480 | 312.328 | 0.188 | 1,323.375 |
| Nainital | 4,251 | 2,574.452 | 111.892 | 280.678 | 15.338 | 2,982.360 |
| Udham Singh Nagar | 2,542 | 938.370 | 0.000 | 0.000 | 0.000 | 938.370 |
| Garhwal | 5,329 | 2,327.024 | 983.675 | 528.140 | 12.103 | 3,850.942 |
| Rudraprayag | 1,984 | 1,277.783 | 318.854 | 207.016 | 0.000 | 1,803.653 |
| Chamoli | 8,030 | 2,817.198 | 447.174 | 1,883.552 | 9.924 | 5,061.002 |
| Tehri | 3,642 | 2,315.175 | 768.665 | 131.80 | 0.000 | 3,215.640 |
| Uttarkashi | 8,016 | 6,954.914 | 231.889 | 72.645 | 0.000 | 7,216.641 |
| Dehradun | 3,088 | 1,522.708 | 342.016 | 72.586 | 76.991 | 2,018.301 |
| Haridwar | 2,360 | 724.307 | 0.000 | 0.000 | 0.000 | 724.307 |
| Total | 53,483 | 24,414.804 | 4,768.704 | 5,449.642 | 157.517 | 34,651.014 |

*Source:* Forest Department, Almora.

## Van Panchayats (VPs)

There are total 12,089 VPs in Uttarakhand. The VPs in Uttarakhand were created in 1931 as the result of a protest by the local people against the British colonial State when between 1911 and 1917 it transferred more than 3000 sq km of forest area to Imperial Forest Department through an act of decentralization (Agrawal, 2005; Kumar, 2006).

The VPs are elected bodies that come under the jurisdiction of the Revenue Department. The villagers vote to elect between five and nine council members and the council leader. Elections to the VPs are held under the supervision of the Forest Council Inspector who is an employee of the Revenue Department. The VPs select guards, fine rule-breakers, manage finances and maintain records of their meetings, accounts and local rule-infractions. The VPs have the ability to harvest firewood for commercial purposes and their access to markets for timber is mediated by the Forest Department (Mukherjee, 2004; Kumar, 2006).

## Joint Forest Management Committees (JFMCs)

There are 1,434 JFMCs in Uttarakhand which stands second to Madhya Pradesh. These committees were formed under Joint Forest Management (JFM)

Programme, 1990, through the guidelines of the Ministry of Environment and Forests which remain the basis for the JFM Programme. The JFMCs in the region were introduced in 1997 as an outcome of the conditionality of the World Bank's $65m loan given to the Uttar Pradesh Forestry Project for the period of 1998–2002. The Uttarakhand Government has continued with the same legacy. JFMCs are generally registered under the Forest Department. The committees formed under JFM are not legal bodies and they turn into legal bodies only when they are registered under the Societies Act or the Co-operatives Acts. Therefore, the legal status of JFMC differs from state to state. The JFMCs are expected to protect their forests from grazing, encroachments, poaching, fire and timber smugglers but they are not delegated any authority to enforce such protection. Only after the successful protection for a minimum of five to 10 years, the JFMCs gain entitlement to 25–100 per cent benefits of its produce. The Forest Department has the power to cancel the JFM agreement if a JFMC is considered to have violated any of its terms and conditions.

There are spearhead teams in the JFMCs to communicate with and develop micro-plans for the selected villages. These teams consist of one Assistant Conservator Forest (ACF), one Ranger or Deputy Ranger, one Forester or Forest Guard, and two NGO members as 'social motivators' (Upadhayay, 2003; Kumar, 2006; Mukherjee, 2004).

## Section 3: The Case Studies

In order to get a true picture of the current functioning of VPs, a primary survey was conducted. A total of four VPs (Satyun, Bajethi, Chauda Falyati and Ranman) were selected from two developmental blocks, namely Takula and Lamgara, of district Almora on the basis of stratified random sampling. The main criterion for selection of VPs was the implementation of the JFM programmeme and its impact. The district of Almora can be classified into four divisions which manage and protect the forests of the area. These four divisions are: Forest Department, Almora, Civil Soyam Forests, Almora, Land Conservation, Ranikhet and Land Conservation, Ramnagar.

The developmental blocks selected here for the survey belong to the division of Forest Department, Almora and Civil Soyam Forests, Almora. The rationale behind choosing these particular divisions and blocks representing them was the forest-land area covered by them. The area covered by Van Panchayats under the Forest Department, Almora, is 26,756.230 ha. and the area covered by Van Panchayats under the Civil Soyam Forests, Almora, is 21,887.625 ha. which is much more than the area covered by the other two divisions (Table 2).

The developmental block Takula representing the Forest Department, Almora, in this study covers the area of 5710.08 ha. As Panchayati Forests which is much less than the blocks of Dwarahat and Chaukhutiya (which are also part of Forest Department, Almora) but the area of forest land on which the programmeme of JFM has been implemented in this block is 1199.10 ha. which is maximum among all the blocks under the Forest Department.

**Table 2**
*Block-Wise Statistics of Van Panchayats*

| *Sl. No.* | *Division* | *Development Block* | *No. of Van Panchayat* | *Area Covered by Van Panchayats* | *Area under JFM (Ha)* |
|---|---|---|---|---|---|
| 1. | Almora Forest Department | Hawalbagh | 237 | 5,151.30 | 570.57 |
| 2. | Almora Forest Department | Takula | 155 | 5,747.16 | 1,199.10 |
| 3. | Almora Forest Department | Dwarahat | 218 | 6,239.04 | 787.64 |
| 4. | Civil Soyam Forest | Chakhutia | 187 | 9,978.60 | 1,171.25 |
| | Total | | 797 | 27,116.097 | 3,728.56 |
| 5. | Civil Soyam Forest | Lamgara | 183 | 7,025.09 | 2,672.37 |
| 6. | Civil Soyam Forest | Bhaisiachanna | 103 | 4,537.53 | 444.11 |
| 7. | Civil Soyam Forest | Dhauladevi | 244 | 10,325.01 | 1,439.88 |
| | Total | | 530 | 21,887.625 | 4,556.355 |
| 8. | Land Conservation, Ranikhet | Syaldey | 197 | 5,373.03 | 626.44 |
| 9. | Land Conservation, Ranikhet | Bhikiyasan | 180 | 3,470.54 | 885.87 |
| 10. | Land Conservation, Ranikhet | Tarikhet | 247 | 5,262.90 | 1,241.34 |
| | | | 624 | 14,106.465 | 2,753.646 |
| 11. | Land Conservation, Ramnagar | Salt | 248 | 7,102.75 | 1,021.05 |
| | Total | | 2199 | 70,212.9322 | 12,059.611 |

*Source:* Forest Department, Almora.

Similarly, the developmental block Lamgara representing the Civil Soyam Forests, Almora, in this study covers the area of 7025.09 ha. As Panchayati Forests which is much less than the Dhauladevi Block (which is part of Civil Soyam Forests, Almora) but the area of forest land on which the programmeme of JFM has been implemented in this block is 2672.37 ha., which is maximum among all the blocks under Civil Soyam Forests, Almora.

The Van Panchayats were selected through stratified random sampling from the population of Van Panchayats in the identified blocks. The main criterion for sample selection was the implementation of the JFM programme and its impact. Therefore, out of four, two were Van Panchayats where JFM was implemented and two, where JFM was not implemented, and these were selected for the study.

The Van Panchayats selected were Satyun and Bajethi from Lamgara block and Falyati and Ranman from Takula block. Satyun and Falyati were the Van Panchayats where the JFM programme was implemented and in Bajethi and Ranman, it was not implemented (Table 3).

## Section 4: Analysis

The field study showed that the characteristics of the resource, the size, initial quality and the contiguity of the Protected Forest and the size of the User Group – influence the success and failure of the collective resource management. A large resource faces less pressure of population but then it also becomes difficult to guard effectively for the small user group.

**Table 3**

*Description of Selected Case Studies of Van Panchayats*

| Van Panchayats | Satyun | Bajethi | Falyati | Ranman |
|---|---|---|---|---|
| Block | Lamgara | Lamgar | Takula | Takula |
| Year of Establishment | 1932 | 1975 | 1967 | 2003 |
| Area of Van Panchayat (Ha) | 145 | 80.20 | 55.200 | 1.394 |
| JFM duration in village | 1999–2003 | Not implemented | 1999–2003 | Not implemented |
| Area under JFM (Ha) | 28 | — | 30 | — |
| Expenditure under JFM | 09.50 Lakh | — | 14 Lakh | — |
| Activities under JFM | 20 Ha Protection; 10 Ha Grazing area development; 25,000 plants raised | — | 30 Ha Protection; 25 Ha Grazing area development; 70,000 plants raised | — |
| Last elections held in VP | 2009 | 2007 | 2007 | 2007 |
| Social Composition of Households | 205 (00 Brahmins; 170 Thakurs; 35 SC/STs) | 45 (18 Brahmins; 22 Thakurs; 05 SC/STs) | 85 (00 Brahmins; 70 Thakurs; 15 SC/STs) | 66 (16 Brahmins; 50 Thakurs; 00 SC/STs) |
| Composition of EC of VP | 09 (6 M; 3 F) (7 Thakur; 2 SC/ST) | 09 (7 M; 2 F) (4 Brahmin; 2 Thakur; 3 SC/ST) | 09 (6 M; 3 F) (2 Brahmin; 7 Thakur) | 09 (7 M; 2 F) (7 Thakur; 2 SC/ST) |
| Gender of Sarpanch | Male | Male | Male | Male |
| Total Women Members in EC | 03 | 02 | 03 | 02 |

*Source:* Field Survey.

The field study confirms Ostrom's (1990) views that there is a relationship between the size of a user group and the resources, and the percentage of success and failure of collective action. However, it departs from her argument that as the size of the user group increases, the possibilities of failure of collective action also increase.

Based on the analysis of four VPs in two development blocks, the study confirms the argument of Arun Agrawal that resources with a larger user group are more successfully managed. The reason for this relates to the protection of forests from unauthorized users and uses. According to him, a group which is large enough is better able to raise more resources and expand greater monitoring and enforcement efforts (Agrawal, 2000 and 2005).

A second important insight of the Field Study is that despite the fact that women are more dependent on forests and are the direct beneficiaries of resources from forests, their presence in these local institutions has been negligible. The study of four VPs (Satyun, Bajethi, Falyati and Ranman) and the data (Table 4), provided by the Forest Department, Almora reveals that women's participation in formal structures of governance has remained a mere illusion. It was also found that all the women members have not contested voluntarily. They are frequently persuaded to contest elections because the seats are reserved for women and because their male relative such as husband, brother, father, etc. wanted to retain political power and status within the family. In many cases, women members are treated as mere proxies or surrogates for their husbands.

**Table 4**

*Number of Van Panchayats headed by Woman*

| *Sl. No.* | *Block* | *Total Van Panchayats* | *Van Panchayats headed by Woman* | *Average* |
|---|---|---|---|---|
| 1. | Bhaisiachanna | 103 | 09 | 0.08 |
| 2. | Bhikiyasan | 182 | 16 | 0.08 |
| 3. | Chaukhutia | 187 | 12 | 0.06 |
| 4. | Dhauladevi | 244 | 30 | 0.12 |
| 5. | Dwarahat | 218 | 20 | 0.09 |
| 6. | Hawalbagh | 237 | 26 | 0.10 |
| 7. | Lamgara | 183 | 15 | 0.08 |
| 8. | Salt | 247 | 17 | 0.06 |
| 9. | Syaldey | 197 | 07 | 0.03 |
| 10. | Takula | 155 | 16 | 0.10 |
| 11. | Tarikhet | 247 | 38 | 0.15 |

*Source:* Forest Department, Almora.

It was also observed in the field that the greater involvement of women in institutions like VPs can increase the effectiveness of these institutions of governance. This is because women are more dependent on forests; they spend a large amount of time in forests in comparison to men as they collected firewood, fodder and other non-timber forest products. As compared to men, women possess more knowledge about the particularities of forests such as which forest product should be extracted and when, whether or not the forest should be open periodically; which products should be promoted in planting efforts, etc.

Another reason for the increase in the effectiveness of the institution with the increase in the presence of women is that women, when inducted into the executive committee, are more likely to follow rules themselves and be able to persuade other village women to act in accordance to the rules. Women are likely to be more motivated to actively participate in protection activities by forming a patrol group or will be more vigilant while working in the fields, when involved in the management body.

The third significant observation of the field study is that the emergence of co-operative behaviour is very difficult in a socio-economic structure where heterogeneous agents are present. Divergence of interest is likely to emerge when socially and economically heterogeneous groups are sharing CPRs, since their interests in resource management may significantly differ from one another's. Economic inequality or social heterogeneity among the members of a resource-using group might be associated with different degrees of access to, and control over, the local commons due to dominance of one group over another.

The fourth observation of the field study was that over time, the control of bureaucracy over the use of resources has increased. In the case of VPs, the communities earlier had the freedom to use the resources according to their needs on the condition that they use the resources in a sustainable manner. But in the present scenario, to use any forest produce, need requires the prior approval of a bureaucrat. The Uttranchal Panchayati Forest Rules (UPFR) of 2001 and 2005 both provide sensible control of bureaucrats over the functioning of VPs. For instance – Rule 51 of the UPFR of 2005 states that the members of the Legislative Assembly, Adhyaksh Zila Panchayat, and Sarpanch of the village Panchayat shall be entitled to inspect any Van Panchayat and its forests within the area they represent.

If one evaluates the pattern of interaction, it is observable that although decentralization is called a bottom-up approach, in the case of institutions like VPs it is very much the top-down approach. Villagers have to look to the officials of the district administration for approval of each and every move. Even the Micro Plans – which are the basic plans for the management of the Panchayati forest – are formulated with consensus of the villagers, but require consultation with the Forest Department. The EC has been provided with the power to formulate by-laws for managing the Panchayati forests but those laws can be implemented only when the consent of DM has been taken. Any cheque of an amount of over ₹ 500 has to be countersigned by the Secretary of the Forest Department. VPs are largely dependent upon government grants and funds – whatever the eagre amount is available, it is managed under the overall control of the Van Vikas Adhikari.

## Conclusion

In short, it can be said that the rate at which forests' products are being consumed and deforestation is taking place due to concretization, industrialization, modernization, etc, it is high time to think of the mechanisms to save our ecological system in a sustainable manner – the implications of neglect are, indeed, alarming. Though it is often asserted by the central government that the process of policy-formulation in the forest sector has moved away from the domain of bureaucracy and experts to consultations with many stakeholders from the public and private sectors and civil society to formulate a method by which damage to the ecology can be prevented and a new forest-friendly social system can be framed. In reality it is to be observed that at the grassroot level the domain of bureaucracy has rather increased. Gradually, policy changes have expanded the role of local institutions in terms of functional areas. Communities are increasingly involved in forest protection and the implementation of forestry schemes at the local level. The need to strengthen capacities of local institutions remains. It can be said that the process of decentralization still has to cover a long journey to achieve its goal. A lot of changes are required in the rules to move firmly and completely accomplish its object. The approach also requires institutions to strive for the right balance of effectiveness, efficiency, equity and sustainability. The changes in the policy process require problem-oriented forest-policy research. Issues which require greater attention are strengthening of community forestry management and resource mobilization.

## Notes

1. Decentralization is defined as the process in which power is transferred from the Central government to lower levels in the political, administrative and territorial hierarchy (Crook and Manor, 1998). Decentralization takes place in two forms – either as administrative decentralization in which power is transferred to the lower-level authorities who are upwardly accountable or as political/democratic decentralization in which power is transferred to the local representatives or to the downwardly accountable actors
2. Forest resources are considered of global importance because any kind of damage to forest eco-systems has an effect on every aspect of the world in the form of climate change, scarcity of water and the loss of biodiversity.

## References

Agrawal, Arun (2000). 'Small is Beautiful, but is Larger Better? Forest Management Institutions in the Kumaon Himalaya, India', in Clark C. Gibson, Margaret A. McKean and Elinor Ostrom (eds), *People and Forests: Communities, Institutions and Governance*. Cambridge, London, England: The MIT Press, pp. 57–85.

——. (2005). *Environmentality: Technologies of Government and the Making of Subjects*. New Delhi: Oxford University Press.

Government of India (2009). 'India State of Forest Report 2009', Ministry of Environment and Forest, New Delhi.

Kumar, Ashok (2006). 'Van Panchayats in Uttaranchal', in Niraja Gopal Jayal, Amit Prakash and Pradeep K. Sharma (eds), *Local Governance in India: Decentralization and Beyond*. New Delhi: Oxford University Press, pp. 47–96.

Larson, A.M. (2005). Democratic Decentralization in the Forestry Sector: Lessons Learned from Africa, *Asia and Latin America. The Politics of Decentralization: Forests*, People and Power, 32–62.

Mukherjee, P. (2004). 'Community Rights and Statutory Laws: Politics of Forest Use in Uttarakhand Himalayas'. *Journal of Legal Pluralism*, 55: 161–72.

Ostrom, E. (1990). *Governing the Commons: The Evolution of Institutions for Collective Actmon*. Cambridge: Cambridge University Press.

Upadhayay, Sanjay (2003). 'JFM in India: Some Legal Concerns'. *Economic and Political Weekly*, 38(5), August 30: 3629–31.

# 11

# Emerging Environmental Security Threats to the Maritime Security in the Indian Ocean Region

## *Challenges and Responses*

**PRAGYA PANDEY**

### Objective

The central theme of the paper would be to scrutinize the environmental threats to the maritime security environment in the Indian Ocean region and, further, it would enumerate initiatives the countries of the region have taken and institutional mechanisms they have evolved to deal with these challenges.

### The Indian Ocean

The Indian Ocean is going to hog the limelight in the coming century, with huge economic and human resource potential. Geographically, with an area of 68.56 sq km i.e. around 20 per cent of the earth's surface, Indian Ocean is the third largest water body on the earth, washing the shores of the Indian sub-continent and the continents of Australia and Africa. One-third of the world population lives in the region, including most of the Third World countries (Dowdy and Troad, 1983).

The ocean is closed by land-rim on three sides, with maritime access only through seven established gateways or choke-points. These are Malacca, Sunda, Lombok, Hormutz Straits, Suez Canal, Bab-el-Mandeb, and The Cape of Good Hope (Ministry of Defence (Navy), 2009). Approximately two-third of the world's oil shipment and one-third of the bulk cargo passes through the Indian Ocean. Around 40 per cent of the sea-borne crude oil passes through the Hormutz at the one end and 50 per cent of the world's merchant-fleet capacity via Strait of Malacca at the other end, making the Indian Ocean home to the busiest sea-lanes of the world (Kaplan, 2010). Given the peculiarities of the region, the issue of peace and security of the region has become an acute concern not just among littorals but among certain extra-regional powers as well. For centuries before the

Atlantic gained prominence, Indian Ocean was the main theatre of global activity and earliest long distance navigation, facilitated by Hindus, Chinese, Muslims traders for exchange of silk and porcelain, spices, gems, pearls, cotton, incense, horses, gold, ivory and slaves (Bateman and Bergin, 2001). Naval powers emerged in the 10th and 11th centuries, to secure influence and access to this mammoth maritime commerce and its important trade routes. This included the Buddhist kingdom of Sri Vijaya in Sumatra and the Hindu Chola Tamil kingdom of south India. The Chinese, the Ottomans, the Persians and the Mughals also developed naval forces (DeSilva-Ranasinghe, 2010). European navigators reached it in the 15th century in search of new markets, particularly after the Voyage of Portuguese explorer Vasco de Gama in 1497, followed by the Dutch, the French and the British. However, after World War II, the expansion of nationalist sentiments precipitated the process of decolonization, as the British forces withdrew from 'east of Suez' in the early 1970s. With the Anglo-American Accord of 1966, US, entered the scene as a major power (Raghavan, 1996). Throughout the Cold War, the Indian Ocean remained the principle theatre of super-power rivalry. Again, in the post-Cold War period, various countries are vying for influence in this geo-strategic, geo-economically significant Ocean.

## Changing Dimension of Maritime Security in the Post-Cold War Period

Traditionally, the concept of security very often in the context of international relations has been referred to as national security. However, in the post-Cold War era, a new wave of thinking has emerged which, unlike the conventional approach, has tended to identify 'security' as an all-encompassing concept. The focus has shifted to other areas like freedom from economic exploitation, energy-security, clean and safe food and water. This debate on the meaning of security is the reflection of new conditions of global politics engendered by escalating globalization (Muller, 2006).

Safer shipping in the Indian Ocean is vulnerable to various threats that range from those induced by human activity to natural hazards like cyclones (Bateman, 2002). More than 60 oil tankers pass through the ocean daily which is expected to go up to 200 in a decade or so. While such optimism is a welcome sign, the SLOCs are being threatened from several directions. Any disruption of sea-traffic through these choke-points would have a catastrophic impact well beyond the Indian Ocean for the international economy as a whole (Sakhuja, 2001).

'Maritime security' has a different meaning for different people. UNCLOS defines it as 'peaceful use of sea' and 'peaceful purpose' (Rehman, 2009: 31–32). The Indian Maritime Doctrine 2004 defines maritime security in terms of protecting our vulnerability from actions of the enemy (Ministry of Defence (Navy), 2009). Of late, however, the nature of threat to the maritime peace and security has assumed a new dimension. Earlier, the threats were due to the acts of the state actors, the disputes used to involve the recognized sovereign independent countries. Today, we have come to live in an era characterized by the rise of sinister non-traditional threats which have redefined security responses the world over and the more earnest issues at hand are from non state actors. Safer shipping in Indian Ocean is vulnerable to various such threats that range from piracy, maritime terrorism, climate change, natural disasters, smuggling of persons, drug trafficking, gun-running and other forms of trans-national crime –they are trans-national in scope; they arise at very short notice and are transmitted rapidly as a result of globalization and the communication revolution. National solutions are often inadequate, and thus regional and multilateral cooperation is essential; and finally, the object of security is no longer the state but people, their survival, well-being and dignity.

Scholars like Barry Buzan talked about the applicability of comprehensive and co-operative security to the realm of maritime security (Tan and Boutin, 2001). The CSCAP memorandum, 'Guidelines for Regional Maritime Co-operation', explicitly 'adopts a comprehensive approach to regional security', stating that 'issues of ocean management are closely inter-related and need to be considered as a whole,' and that 'a comprehensive concept of regional maritime security requires a multi-disciplinary approach, necessitating co-operation and co-ordination among all interested bodies and activities' (Rehman, 2009: 43). The Indian Ocean Region is also faced with such major menaces.

## Emerging Environmental Security Threats in the Indian Ocean

In the aftermath of the Cold War, there is a growing recognition that 'security' should be understood as a contested concept. The discourse of 'environmental security' has emerged as a significant departure from the conventional theoretical approaches to national security, as a result of a growing number of ecological problems such as global warming, resource depletion and trans-boundary pollution. The proponents of environmental security argue that since environmental degradation is often trans-boundary, and diverse sections of humanity are unevenly threatened by the forces of environmental degradation in an increasingly inter-dependent but highly asymmetrical world, it cannot be adequately tackled by traditional analyses (Chaturvedi, 1998).

The strategic significance of the India Ocean is well-established. Yet, the environmental challenges facing it – and the rim countries – often receive less attention. Environmental issues can significantly affect the region's economic activities and environmental stability. While the natural environment in the Indian Ocean is faced with a plethora of threats, some of the critical challenges which need to be addressed are like the threat to ocean resources, climate change, bio-security, and marine pollution, impact on fisheries, etc. The various environmental threats to maritime security can be discussed as following.

## Threat to Natural Resources of the Ocean

The Indian Ocean possesses a range of valuable natural resources, including sea minerals, coral reefs, etc. Coral reefs are under the threat of depletion due to global climate change, direct human pressures, and inadequate governance and awareness. The destruction of coral reefs and coastal eco-system also impact the tourism industry, fisheries, livelihoods of coastal communities, etc. in the rim countries. The Indian Ocean contains a great abundance of wealth of economically valuable mineral resources and energy resources. The littorals contain more than two-third oil reserves, 35 per cent of the world's gas reserves and 60 per cent of uranium, 40 per cent of gold and 80 per cent of diamond deposits, and large variety of other mineral substances, iron ore, tin, bauxite, gold, diamond, manganese, uranium, and chromium (Dowdy and Troad, 1983). In recent years, technology has had an even greater impact on the exploitation of mineral resources. Indeed, the Massachusetts-based Woods Hole Oceanographic Institution now has a vehicle that can access depths of up to 11 kms (Michel et al., 2012). Utilization of these resources needs to be done collaboratively by the rim countries as over-exploitation of these can have a detrimental impact on the marine environment.

## Marine Pollution

The Indian Ocean region is also vulnerable to high levels of pollution caused by ocean-dumping, waste-disposal and oil-spills as a significant amount of international trade takes place in the region's waters. The wastes pose threats to the survival of marine organisms and consequently, to the marine eco-system, on which millions of livelihoods depend. In addition, being bordered by fast-growing economies, there is a high possibility of more industrial waste being disposed of into the ocean. Eutrophication of near-shore environments due to pollution from land-based sources and their run-off has impacted economic activities such as fisheries, tourism and also affected fragile eco-systems (Wickramasinghe, 2011).

With a high density of maritime traffic in the Malacca Strait, accidents have taken place on a regular basis. Regional governments are concerned that a major oil-spill and subsequent pollution could seriously disrupt or even close the strait. Little attention is being paid to the environmental dimension of piracy, though it is not directly connected with it. Pirates attacking a ship often put the crew in life-rafts and boats, and the ship is then left adrift. These vessels can result in collision or grounding, leading to environmental and navigational hazards. In September 1992, the *MV Ocean Blessing,* a container-vessel and a'rogue ship, collided with the super tanker *MV Nagasaki Spirit,* resulting in a major spillage and fire (Sakhuja, 2001: 696). The coastal waters of the Yellow and East China seas already suffer from heavy contamination caused by dangerous cargo pollutants, from the fast-growing industrial activities of the coastal States, and illegal dumping at sea (Lee, 2010).

## Nuclear Waste

Pressures aimed at maximizing energy security have contributed to increased global demand for nuclear power, notwithstanding the Fukushima catastrophe in Japan. This has led to a potential increase in environmental insecurity due to the requirement of the safe disposal of large volumes of nuclear-waste materials. These impacts, in turn, raise a host of security questions linked to nuclear safety, uranium trade-flows, storage of nuclear waste and safety of SLOCs. Africa has the dubious distinction of being the first choice for the dumping of its European nuclear wastes. Many containers of nuclear and toxic waste were dumped during the past decades on Somalian beaches. Given Somalia's strategic location, such illegal or unauthorized movements of nuclear waste have potentially very significant implications not only for the human security of the Somalian population, but for the Indian Ocean's environment, the Indian Ocean routes along which such flows take place, as well as the lethal prospects of the potential terrorist use of such nuclear materials. IORA has the potential of playing a very important role as a pressure group, regionally and in international forums, to try and eradicate the smuggling of radio-active materials in the region and to prevent dumping into the ocean (Rumley, 2013).

## Natural Disasters

Today, more than 40 per cent of the world's population lives within 100 km of the coast. Natural calamities like the 2004 Tsunami remind us that nature can pose mammoth challenges that directly affect people living close to the coast. According to the Asia Pacific Disaster Report 2010, countries in Asia and the Pacific are four times more likely to be affected by a natural cataclysm than those in Africa, and 25 times more vulnerable than Europe or North America. It is a fact that almost 80 per cent of the human fatalities in natural disasters of the last decade have been in Asia. The death, devastation, and destruction caused by natural calamities, whether within our own country or beyond, require to be alleviated. There are more than 150 collisions at sea on an yearly basis due to poor visibility, non-serviceability of radars, hull-failure, boiler-explosions and human errors. The natural perils of ocean transportation - such as cyclones - are common in the eastern Indian Ocean and adjoining seas (Khurana, 2004: 41).

## Climate Change and Global Warming

Added to the challenges of natural disasters is the effect of global warming. Global warming is a non-traditional security issue that could result in the melting of the polar ice and other ice bodies, ultimately raising the mean sea-level. This could not only be appalling for low-lying areas and island nations, but due to the mass exodus which would follow, it could also trigger a demographic upset and a resource-crunch in the neighbouring regions (Verma, 2010).

The Indian Ocean region is highly vulnerable to the impacts of climate change (Wickramasinghe, 2011). It has been estimated that the Indian Ocean States were responsible for emitting more than approximately 100 million metric tons of carbon in 2006 - and four States in the region rank among the world's top emitters: Qatar, Kuwait, UAE, Bahrain and Australia. The cloud made of pollutants hovering over the Ocean, contributes to climate change, threatening biological species as well as human health, and triggering acid rains which destroy the forests. In particular, climate change is likely to lead to an increase in the magnitude and frequency of regional humanitarian crises that will, in turn, exacerbate border security questions due to the emergence of 'climate refugees' and possible associated changes in migration patterns. In addition, rising sea-levels due to climate change are likely to have a major impacton the prospects of some Indian Ocean States' existence - as could be the case with Maldives and other low-lying coastal areas around the region which are the major centres of populations, and which could disappear under the rising Ocean waters and trigger climatic migrations (Rumley, 2013).

## Bio-security

Marine bio-security refers to the protection of marine environments from non-indigenous species, and this has direct implications for bio-diversity in the marine ecological systems in the Indian Ocean. It has been found that Invasive Alien Species (IAS) are becoming a significant threat to marine bio-diversity, where ballast-water is viewed as a major cause of their proliferation. However, comprehensive studies on bio-security are rarely to be found in the case of the Indian Ocean. Bio-security requires the co-operation of a range of actors including scientists, policy-makers, law-enforcement officials etc. (Wickramasinghe, 2011).

Deep-sea bio-diversity is still a relatively emerging area of scientific study. In the oceans as a whole, 10 million species exist. Marine life arguably offers just as much, if not more, economic value as compared to the mineral resources. Species living around hydro-thermal vents, sustain life in a hostile environment of extreme temperatures and chemical energy. Microbial and prokaryote gene in the oceans, particularly in the deep-sea, enzymes from these species are also being used for a variety of DNA-related products and technologies, including finger-printing technology, and have substantially contributed to pharmaceutical research and products. In the Indian Ocean, a peptide called Dolastatin-10 isolated from sea-hare has served as an anti-tumour agent in clinical trials to treat breast and liver cancers, solid tumours, and leukaemia. Some marine organisms absorb carbon during photosynthesis, which helps to regulate the climate; others also assimilate waste-materials that pollute the ocean (Michel et al., 2012). Discharge of waste-water from ships, mining poly-metallic nodules or massive sulphides can endanger marine organisms. When these ships eject sea-water after extracting its mineral content, the waste frequently contains trace metals, which interferes with the penetration of light through the top layer of sea water and reduces photosynthesis in surface layers. Temperature differences in the discharged and surrounding sea water also threaten life dwelling in the top layers of the ocean (ibid.).

One thing many of the Indian Ocean islands have in common is high levels of endemic species – they contain many species that have evolved in isolation from the mainland and occur nowhere else on Earth. Some of the major endangered species are like land-crabs and endangered Abbott's booby left of Christmas Island, Livingstone's Flying Kox of Comoros, tigers, elephants, rhinos, orangutans of Sumatra, lemurs of Madagascar and various others. Major threat to these species comes from the widespread deforestation on these islands – Sumatra lost a large percentage of its forests, with the centre of Madagascar having been almost entirely deforested. Seychelles's coral reef system is threatened by the coral bleaching and climate change combined with predation by feral cats and rats and mice.

## Environmental Degradation and Impact on Fisheries

Rising rates of pollution increasingly threaten Indian Ocean fisheries. Coastal fisheries are particularly vulnerable to agricultural run-off, sewage, and construction. Deepwater fishing practices such as bottom trawling have also seriously damaged the eco-systems of continental shelves and slopes by levelling the sea-bed, kicking up clouds of sediment, destroying coral, and generating huge amounts of by catch (ibid.). In the Indian Ocean, stocks of southern blue-fin tuna are classified as 'depleted', the FAO's worst category. Several other species in the Indian Ocean – for example, emperor, Indian mackerel and big-eye tuna – range from being fully exploited to over-exploited. Most of the States in the regions are increasingly unable to meet the growing demand within their own national jurisdictions. A critical regional holistic evaluation of fisheries-resource exploitation policies is essential in order to ensure a sustainable future for the Indian Ocean (Rumley, 2013).

The East Indian Ocean is home to 45 per cent of the world's fishers and brings in catches of 8 per cent of the world's total fish production and contributes to a larger percentage of littoral States' GDP. Australia is unique among the countries in the Indian Ocean region in that it has developed strict management controls and limits the exploitation of its fish stocks, resulting in a healthy fisheries industry (Michel et al., 2012). A global shortage of fish is projected in the future. The FAO reports that 47 per cent of global fish stocks are already fully exploited, while another 18 per cent are over-exploited. Technological advances have considerably increased commercial fisheries catches and deep-water fisheries. GPS and radar allow ships to venture into the open ocean and target lucrative fishing grounds with precision. Degradation of coastal estuaries, mangroves, lagoons, coral reefs, and kelp forests has destroyed the habitats of many species that support artisanal and commercial fisheries. In addition, oil fires and weapons debris have polluted the ocean in this conflict-prone region, further degrading its fisheries. The Indian Ocean possesses some of the few remaining underexploited fish stocks in the world, making it likely that it will come under enormous pressure in the future as the next frontier of the global fisheries market (Rumley, 2013).

The depletion of the Indian Ocean fish stocks could have serious implications for regional and global food security. One recent study has projected that the world's fisheries will collapse by 2048 if catch-rates continue unabated. Current global food-insecurity affects more than 33 States, 19 of which are located in the Indian Ocean Region. Faced with so many obstacles, it is little wonder that protracted crises can become a self-perpetuating vicious cycle. Consequently, the international community and individual States have been developing appropriate food-security strategies.

## Response Mechanisms: Limitations and Road Ahead

In the post-Cold War period, with disasters like the 2004 tsunami, subsequent other threats to shipping and sea-borne trade have forced a reappraisal of what we mean by maritime security. It is recognized that it is a government's first responsibility to provide for the security and well-being of its citizens. The concept of maritime security has now expanded since the threats of concern are veiled and perhaps even 'unthinkable'. Nations have to talk about and agree on issues such as the principles of the law of the sea, the prevention of marine pollution, the conservation of fish stocks, the safety and security of shipping, and the delimitation of maritime boundaries. The countries located on the rim of the Indian Ocean must bear in mind that they are affected not only by the economic significance of this ocean, but also the environmental challenges facing it. In implementing policies on these issues, nations have to take into account the interests and rights of their neighbours, as well as those of other countries.

The UN Convention on the Law of the Sea is relevant to the issues regarding Ocean Sciences and Environment. The important features of the Convention include navigational rights, territorial sea-limits, economic jurisdiction, legal status of resources on the sea-bed beyond the limits of national jurisdiction, passage of ships through narrow straits, conservation and management of living marine resources, protection of the marine environment, a marine research regime and most importantly, a binding procedure for settlement of disputes between States. Collaboration among the States in our region is the key to make the Convention operate effectively (United Nationas, Division for Ocean Affairs and Law of the Sea, 1982).

To enable ecologically sustainable and socially just development and management of Indian Ocean fisheries, it requires a paradigm shift in the perceptions and policies of major stakeholders. A central policy challenge is to identify a collective regional interest for fisheries and, accordingly, the development of integrated management policies that link ecology and society and that incorporate individuals, communities, agencies, States and regimes into a holistic co-operative endeavour.

Various safeguard procedures have been put in place by the governments of the islands of the Indian Ocean Region to protect the marine life – for instance, trapping and relocation of animals before clearing any sites on the island. Many organizations active in the field of conservation are working with local partners in Sumatra to protect the remaining natural habitat. In recent years, there has been an increase in protected areas and the development and implementation of conservation strategies for many of the endangered and endemic species. In 2013 the Republic of Maldives pledged to become the first nation where the entire country and its Exclusive Economic Zone will be a UNESCO Biosphere Reserve. These are sites established by countries to promote sustainable development based on the efforts of the local community and science. The Seychelles has been recognized as a bio-diversity hotspot by Conservation International and has high levels of endemic species as the islands have been isolated for billions of years. The Seychelles became the first country in the world to protect 50 per cent of its land, fulfilling its obligations under the Convention on Biological Diversity to ensure conservation of the islands' bio-diversity.

Natural disaster is yet another perennial challenge to the States in the Indian Ocean Region which needs a comprehensive and co-operative framework for it to be dealt with both in terms of prevention of such disasters as well as humanitarian operations during the time of disasters. The 2004 tsunami was a powerful reminder of the littoral States' shared vulnerabilities in the realm of human security, and it has given rise to a concrete co-operative scheme for the Indian Ocean Tsunami Warning and Mitigation System.

Failure to address these issues on a co-operative basis fundamentally inhibits the development of a stable maritime security environment in the region. When the environmental challenges are regional in nature, national level policies and strategies of individual countries alone are insufficient. Future actions have to take cognizance of the fact that environmental challenges are inherently inter-related and complex, caused by complex man-made and natural factors. There needs to be regional level co-operation to deal with the environmental challenges which are common to all Indian Ocean rim countries. Therefore, the formulation of regional policies and strategies has to be supported with comprehensive research which brings in actors from all relevant disciplines, from the entire region. The Indian Ocean Rim Association (IORA) has a role to play here and should take up this issue as a priority in its future deliberations (Thapa, 2011). Naval forces of various countries should come together and join hands with the maritime agencies working in the region for humanitarian assistance and disaster relief, in mitigating and adapting to the detrimental effects of these challenges, and finding ways of protecting the maritime assets.

## Conclusion

Successful ocean governance therefore requires greater inter-State and inter-agency consultation and co-operation, and improvement in linking national initiatives to local action. Achieving this overall goal requires either the enhancement of existing regional institutions or the creation of a new regional body. Problems such as land degradation, water, fisheries, climate change, nuclear waste, environmental refugees and urban explosion and deterioration, if not addressed, will lead to increases in human conflict and, ultimately, wide-scale disease, poverty and death. In the 21st century, the region has witnessed sweeping changes and considerable turbulence. India being a major maritime power in the Indian Ocean Region, has the expertise and interests to co-operate with the other regional navies to deal with these emerging environmental challenges in the region. India has made major strides in its role, as the largest democracy and an emerging economy. India's role as a responsible player towards promoting peace and stability and development has been recognized in the region and the international arena. India has interests in harnessing the resources for the development and just progress of it people. Dealing with environmental security, these threats must be taken as a 'global security challenge' and the goal of sustainable growth must be looked at as the global public good which cannot be achieved by any one organization or country of the region, and therefore co-operation is necessary to develop a co-ordinated and focused approach to deal with the challenges.

## References

Bateman, Sam (2002). 'Freedom of Navigation and Indian Ocean Security: A Geopolitical Analysis', Journal of Indian Ocean Studies, 10(3): 355–374.

Bateman, Sam (2010). 'Capacity Building for Maritime Security Co-operation: What are We Talking About?'. Papers in Australian Maritime Affairs No. 30, Sea Power Centre, pp. 5–21, http://www.navy.gov.au/sites/default/files/documents/ piama30.pdf

Bateman, Sam and Anthony Bergin (2001). 'New Challenges for Maritime Security in the Indian Ocean: An Australian Perspective'. *Journal of Indian Ocean Region*, 7(1): 117–25, http://ro.uow.edu.au/cgi/viewcontent.cgi?article=1528&context=lawpapers

Bradford, John F. (2008). 'Shifting the Tides against Piracy in Southeast Asian Waters'. *Asian Survey*, 48(3), May/June: 473–91.

Braun, Dieter (1972). 'The Indian Ocean in Afro-Asian Perspective'. *The World Today*, 28(6), June.

Chaturvedi, Sanjay (1998). 'Common Security? Geo-politics, Development, South Asia and the Indian Ocean'. *Third World Quarterly*, 19(4): 701–24.

DeSilva-Ranasinghe, Sergei (2010). 'Dominating the Waves'. September, http://www.himalmag.com/component/content/article/275-dominating-the-waves.html

Dowdy, William L. (1985). *The Indian Ocean: Perspectives on a Strategic Arena*. Durham: Duke University Press.

Dowday, William L. and Troad, Russel B. (1983). 'Indian Ocean an Emerging Geostrategic Region', *International Journal*, 38(3), *Ocean Politics Summer*, 432–458.

Ghosh, P.K. (2004). 'Maritime Security Challenges in South Asia and the Indian Ocean: Response Strategies'. A paper prepared for the Center for Strategic and International Studies – American-Pacific Sealanes Security Institute Conference on Maritime Security in Asia, Honolulu, Hawaii, January 18–20, pp. 1–13, http://www.youscribe.com/catalogue/presentations/maritime-security-challenges-in-south-asia-and-indian-ocean-359296 http://www.un.org/depts/los/conventionagreements/texts/unclos/unclos_e.pdf

Indian Ocean Islands, http://www.arkive.org/habitats/islands/indian-ocean-islands/?gclid=coqkkqv4mbwcfyju4godzwsacq

Kaplan, Robert D. (2010). *Monsoon: The Indian Ocean and the Future of American Power*. New York: Random House Trade Paperbacks.

Khurana, G.S. (2004). 'Maritime Security in The Indian Ocean: Convergence Plus Cooperation Equals Resonance', *Strategic Analysis*, 28(3), Jul-Sep. 2004, Institute of Defence Studies and Analyses, 411-426.

Lee, Cordner (2010). 'Rethinking Maritime Security in the Indian Ocean Region', Journal of the Indian Ocean Region, 6, 67–85.

Michel, David, Halae Fuller, Lindsay Dolan, Russell Sticklor and Rupert Herbert-Burns (2012). *Indian Ocean Rising: Maritime Security and Policy Challenges*. Washington: Stimson.

Muller, Harold (2006). 'Security Co-operation', in Carlsneas Walter, Resse Thomas and Beth A. Simons (eds), *Handbook of International Relations*. New Delhi: Sage Publications, p. 369.

National Geographic, Freshwater Threats, http://environment.nationalgeographic.com/environment/habitats/freshwater-threats/

Prakash, Reva (2010). 'Ocean and Us'. National Maritime Foundation, June 9, pp. 1–5, http://maritimeindia.org/sites/all/files/pdf/commentarybyrevaprakash09jun10.pdf

Raghavan, Sudha (1996). *The Indian Ocean Power Politics: Attitudes of Southeast Asian and South Pacific Countries*. New Delhi: Lancers Books.

Rehman, Chris (2009). *Concepts of Maritime Security: A Strategic Perspective on Alternative Visions for Good Order and Security at Sea, with Policy Implications for New Zealand*. New Zealand: The Centre for Strategic Studies, p. 8, http://www.victoria.ac.nz/css/docs/discussion_papers/dp07-09.pdf.

Rumley, Dennis (ed.) (2013). 'The Indian Ocean Region: Security, Stability and Sustainability in the 21st Century'. Task Force on Indian Ocean Security, Australia India Institute, pp. 1–132, http://www.aii.unimelb.edu.au/sites/default/ files/iotf_0.pdf

Sakhuja, Vijay (2001). 'Indian Ocean and Sea-lanes of Communications'. *Strategic Analysis*, XXV(5): 689–702.

Tan, Andrew T.H. and J.D. Kenneth Boutin (eds) (2001). *Non-traditional Security Issues in Southeast Asia*. Singapore: Institute of Defence and Strategic Studies, p. 581.

Thapa, Manish (2011). 'Non-Traditional Security Co-operation Framework: A Step towards Regionalism in South Asia'. *GCST New Voices Series*, Global Consortium on Security Transformation (GCST), No. 15, May, pp. 1–20, http://www.securitytransformation.org/gc_publications.php.

Wickramasinghe, Kanchana (2011). 'Environmental Challenges in the Indian Ocean Region: Half of the World's Trade Travels through it, but are We Protecting it?'. January 9, 6: 57 pm, http://www.island.lk/index.php?page_cat=article-details&page=article-details&code_title=15486.

# Part 5

## Urbanization, Migration and Informal Sector

# 12

# Urbanization and Slum Dwellers

## *A Study of NGOs in Delhi's Slum*

**SUJEET KUMAR**

In an era of urbanization, there is an obvious influx of population in urban areas in order to have better employment opportunities and social security for better living conditions. This huge influx of population is creating demographic, environmental, economic, socio-spatial and institutional challenges for cities especially in developing countries. The developing world is urbanizing at an unprecedented rate due to natural growth and more due to rural-urban migration and refugees of war and natural disasters (World Bank, 2006). During the period of 2001–2010, the urban population in developing countries has increased to 5.2 per cent from 40.1 per cent and it is projected to reach 50.25 per cent by 2020 (UN-HABITAT, 2006).

The rural-urban migration has intensified the formation and growth of slums in metropolitan cities and several studies have been done to understand this migration and its pattern. Virtually, these studies contributed that migration has resulted due to factors such as better livelihood – opportunities and attraction of urban economics – characterized as pull factors. Increased agricultural productivity resulting in labour surplus as well as cross-border conflict worked as a push factor for this migration. In most developing countries, the rapid growth of urban economics, including informal economics, especially in poorer cities, has generated significant livelihood opportunities for the urban poor. While better economic prospects with urban growth have reduced overall absolute poverty, and urban dwellers are better off than rural residents, the proportion of urban population below locally defined poverty lines is increasing. In the period 1993-2002, the global poor population (household-consumption per-capita less than US$1 a day) fell by 150 million in rural areas, but rose by 50 million in urban areas (ibid.). In 2002, almost half the world's urban poor lived in South Asia. In Latin America, the majority of the poor has lived in urban areas since 1990s (ibid.). This unprecedented rate of urbanization in developing countries, created challenges for cities in providing better infrastructure and other civic amenities. The urban poor had to cope up with the sky-rocketing prices of housing and food, and in this process was also witnessed the emergence of a large number of slums. In 2006, World Bank estimated that 32 per cent of the urban population was living in slums, where there is a lack of basic services including health, education and livelihood. However, international development agencies started looking at these areas in the late 20th century and in the early 21st century; developing countries like India came up with slum-upgradation plans, e.g. Rajiv Awas Yojna (RAY) and Jawaharlal Nehru National Urban Renewal Mission (JNNURM). Government agencies as well as international development institutions like the World Bank (WB) and United Nations (UN) have started considering Non-Governmental Organizations (NGOs) as a medium of change due to their participatory and grassroot approach since the late 20th century. In India, 22.4 per cent people live in the slums, the percentage of slum dwellers being higher in metropolitan cities like Mumbai and Delhi.[1]

In this study, the researcher used qualitative evidence to uncover the strategies developed by slum-dwellers and the role of NGOs in providing assistance to them. A central focus of this study is not only to identify the roles of NGOs, but also to trace the path of development through several perspectives. The qualitative evidence draws on interviews, focused group discussions (FGDs) and observations carried out in two different slums and NGOs working with them.

Section II discusses the social and political context of the study and the methodology. Section III presents the qualitative evidence of the conflict of the image of development and the NGOs' role within two slums. Section IV brings out the conclusions.

## Methodology

We have seen how urbanization has led to the formation of slums globally and how a discourse is underway with the aim of developing a better upgradation plan. On the other hand, there are several debates, some going around, defining and collecting data of slums and slum dwellers. However, the larger debate centralized in this paper is to locate the role of NGOs in addressing the challenges faced by slum dwellers. Two major questions emerge. First, what are the existing challenges of slum dwellers for them to have a decent life? And second, how the NGOs intervene in addressing these challenges? There may be several sub-sections of these two questions, such as 'what are the most frequent areas where NGOs are engaged', 'what is the slum-dwellers' perception about NGOs?', 'how do NGOs impact the slum-dwellers' potential?' Any investigation that involves these questions requires fieldwork and methodology for collection and analysis of data.

As discussed earlier, the number of slums in developing countries is increasing unprecedentedly. A review of literature makes itapparent that enormous number of studies have been conducted with a view to understand the factors leading to migration, the rate of migration, nature of migration and so on (UN-HABITAT, 2006).[2] However, very few studies have been conducted about the role of NGOs in slums, specially in looking into the slum dwellers' political and social dynamics of coping up with these challenges. The Census categorized slums into three categories – Notified (i.e. notified by the State or the Union Territory administration by any Act including a Slum Act), Recognized (i.e. slums may not be identified by any Act but recognized by the State, Union Territories, local government, Housing and Slum Boards) and Identified (i.e. compact area of at least 300 population or 60–70 households of poorly-built congested tenements, unhygienic environment and lacking in proper sanitary and drinking water facilities).[3] The National Sample Survey Organization (NSSO), however, comes with a different definition of slums. It particularly considers a slum to comprise at least 20 households.[4] Hence, there is a debate at the definitional level of slums in India because for the designing of any concrete, effective development policies or plan, the first need is to estimate the numbers in terms of population (2013). However, this study did not go into the debate of defining slums and enumeration of data. Rather, it looked into the challenges and studied the mechanisms to cope with the problems. Hence, the selection of slums for this study was based along two dimensions – the proximity of the residents' state of origin and the age of the settlement (Jha, Rao and Woolcock, 2007). Furthermore, I selected two slums in Jehangirpuri in Northern Delhi to investigate emerging questions – these were K Block (denoted as Slum A) and the slum near Metro Apartment (denoted as Slum B). Most of the residents in the first slum were from nearby Uttar Pradesh, Bihar and Rajasthan and it is an old slum settled for more than 30 years. In contrast, in the second one, a newly-settled slum, the residents came mostly from Bengal and they used to change their site after five-six years.

Consequently, in order to collect data, there was a need to look into the feasibility of the availability of the slum dwellers, NGOs' staffs and others such as political leaders and Pradhans. Additionally, time and financial constraints were also important to be taken into consideration. The method of data collection could be qualitative or quantitative or both. However, each method has its own merits and demerits. On the other hand, it was not feasible for the researcher to adopt both methods due to constraints of time. There is enough data available to study demographic trends, rates of urbanization and patterns of migration (Misra and Misra, 1989), but information about strategies for survival and coping up by these poor and powerless slum dwellers is still limited.[5] Comparatively speaking, qualitative study has its approaches to shed light on issues pertaining to history, context and process (Rao and Woolcock, 2003). In this study, the researcher aimed to have a greater understanding of social and political mechanisms underpinning ways and means to manage problems collectively and in relation to NGOs' assistance programmes. Therefore, to investigate these issues, preferably qualitative method have been adopted for this research. Furthermore, the selection of NGOs was based upon their presence in the slums and nature of their work. However, it was very difficult to identify visible evidence of interventions by all those NGOs. Slum dwellers also asserted that a number of NGOs' staffs come in these slums on a regular basis to know about the problems of the slums and some of them ask for a small amount of money to get their work done regarding issues such as ration card, birth certificate and so on. It has been observed that slum dwellers are anxious of these visiting NGOs' staffs because they do not provide any kind of solution to them, nor did they visit the slums again. Therefore, to understand the role of NGOs in slums, two NGOs, on the basis of their presence with slum dwellers as well as initiatives in the slums were selected, i.e. 'Prayas' and'Bharat Swabhiman Trust' (BST).

During the field study, it was frequently observed that the interaction with slum dwellers at any particular or working time is very difficult because most of them are engaged in daily wage labour or are domestic workers. One factor in this regard was also the fact that they frequently change their employer; still another was their trust-deficit with outsiders. The NGOs' staffs did not come to the slums every day. They used to visit these slums on either weekly or monthly basis. On the other hand, the study was not aimed to look into the NGOs' internal organizational structure and the study of particular projects. The aim, rather, was to get acquainted with their interventions and see how the challenges of the slum dwellers could be met.

The researcher worked in the field on this study as a social work trainee over a period of one year, two days a week. There were several field discussions (Focussed Group Discussions – FGD) and interviews of slum dwellers, community leaders, government staff and staff of NGOs working in these slums. The research interviews and FGDs covered a wide variety of issues ranging from household to social engagements. Some of the FGDs were conducted, combining slum dwellers and NGOs' staff. However, there was a central focus put up to address specific questions regarding the role of NGOs and slum dwellers' conception of their image. The data were later transcribed and arranged primarily in order to investigate demographic and economic challenges.

### *Literature and Context: Urbanization and Slum Dwellers*

Understanding the level of urbanization or its scale in developing countries is a challenging task due to differences in defining 'urban' as well as lack of reliable data (Ooi and Phua, 2007). 'Urban' has multivariate characteristics, which includes a similar sense of cities and towns. Furthermore, the definition of 'urban' differs from country to country.

Urbanization has become ineluctable in the 21st century. However, the discussion shifted in terms of the ways to see the challenges emanating from urbanization. Foremost, the formation of slums in developing countries is a much talked about issue in the global academic discourse in order to attain certain parameters. For performance on a scale of development strengthens a country's performance in the international community as well as it assists in getting financial assistance from global development agencies like the World Bank.

There is enough quantitative evidence to reveal the level of urbanization at the global level. In 2003, the UNDP and UNHABITAT exploration showed that one-sixth of the population lives in slums worldwide, out of which 60 per cent alone are in Asia. On the other hand, 50 per cent of the total population lives in urban areas and it is expected to be 70 per cent by 2050. As per 2011 Census of India, 15 per cent of the population is living in slums. If we categorically observe the rural, urban and slum percentages, it is 72 per cent, 27 per cent and 15 per cent, respectively, as per the 2011 census, which shows that 60 per cent of the urban population are living in slums. On the other hand, there is an estimation of exponential growth of about 2.2 per cent annually in developing countries due to natural progress as well as rural-urban migration compared to that in developed countries of 0.49 per cent only (World Bank, 2013). Therefore, the data reflects that there is a direct relationship between urbanization and the formation of slums. An increasing number of slums in developing countries, including India, demands for a better academic engagement with slums and interventions related to slum-upgradation on the one hand, and on the other, there is a need to look into the role of NGOs' intervention, whose emergence has been seen as a failure of the State in addressing issues adequately at the grass-roots. In the following discussion, there is a reflection on the challenges in slums and the approach of NGOs to deal with it.

Urbanization and increasing number of slums is posing several challenges for the urban people, especially those who are economically challenged. Development agencies like the World Bank, United Nations and local development and academic institutions are regularly evaluating the conditions of life in cities and in slums. The latest global report prepared by UN-HABITAT (2009) identifies five present and future global urban challenges, namely demographic, environmental, economic, socio-spatial and institutional – and argues that the 21st century urban development planning requires better understanding of these challenges. In this Paper, we are primarily looking into how do demographic and economic challenges affect the life of slum-dwellers and what current interventions by NGOs are going on to mitigate these challenges.

As has been pointed out earlier, one-sixth of the world population is living in slums and 60 per cent of the slum population is from the Asian region. The prominent reason is that of rapid urbanization, with people heading towards cities for better employment opportunities, and this has also resulted in shrinking of huge populations in a fixed territory. This demographic trend created principal challenges associated with frequent inability to provide adequate infrastructure, institutional support and public services and, most critically, to generate sufficient revenues to fund these needs, and the same has been discussed a few years back by the World Bank (2003). Additionally, a recent recession created enormous problems for urban cities in terms of economic challenges. It led to (i) shrinking of economic growth, leading to less funding for urban development (ii) higher level of unemployment (iii) increase in poverty levels due to unemployment and food price hike, which created greater income inequalities and subsequent increase in political and social instabilities (UN-HABITAT, 2009). Somehow, these are larger challenges for the urban areas, but when we place these challenges in slums, which have been in vulnerable situations for a long time, we find major problems like inadequate civic amenities and basic requirement of survival. The Census of India defines slums as 'residential areas where dwellings are unfit for human habitation' because they are dilapidated, cramped, poorly ventilated, or unclean, or 'any combination of these factors which are detrimental to safety and health'.[6] The UN-HABITAT (2007) Report has a similar view pertaining to the vulnerability of slums. However, it described the challenges in seven categories, which are (i) Inadequate and often unstable income (ii) Poor quality, hazardous, overcrowded, and often insecure housing (iii) Inadequate, unstable or risky asset-base (iv) Inadequate public infrastructure (v) Limited or no safety-nets (vi) Inadequate protection of rights through the operation of law (vii) Voicelessness and powerlessness within non-responsive political systems and bureaucratic structures.

These challenges are not only forcing slum dwellers to have indecent lives, but also restrain them from growing to their potential and capability. The literacy rate, though, is 77.7 per cent (as per Census, 2011) but still lags behind the urban average. On the other hand, this education does not make them fit to get a government job or regular employment. Both men and women are largely engaged in daily wage labour and very few have regular employment through the year.[7] This kind of indicator is fair enough to look into the challenges of slums and devise an inclusive and participatory framework for their transformation. The Government of India has clearly defined the idea of 'Making India Slum Free' in the 11th Plan and UPA (United Progressive Alliance) also launched its flagship scheme Rajiv Awas Yojna (RAY) in the 12th Five Year Plan (2012–17). However, Kundu (2013) argues that before the full implementation of this programme, the government does not have an adequate framework for identifying non-tenable slums and legitimate households. Furthermore, Kamath (2012) commented about the recent approach of addressing the challenges of slums. She questioned the basic framework of RAY and JNNURM, which are aimed at making India 'Slum Free' through an integrated approach to slum-redevelopment that combines housing, infrastructure and land-titling. Despite several challenges at the policy level and sustainability of such a re-developed framework, she concludes '... NGOs/entrepreneurs play an influential role in identifying beneficiaries and engaging in negotiations over affordable housing policy. Where factions within slums have contested this role, the practice of giving NGOs key roles in 'speaking for' slum communities has created conflicts'.[8] Similarly, several housing projects were initiated in Mumbai for slum dwellers in order to make the city 'slum free'. Nijman (2008) has also commented on the slum housing project in a Mumbai slum in collaboration with local state bodies and Private Sector, and made it a valuable step towards slum upgradation and enhancing the living conditions of the poor. However, he added that the Private Sector, urban land and finance markets will not deliver a large-scale solution to the challenge of slums.

There are ample empirical research studies showing housing to be a major challenge in slums. Some projects have been initiated and completed in cities like Mumbai, Bengaluru and Ahmedabad in collaboration with the private sector and NGOs. Ultimately, the process of upgradation and increase of slum population is a big threat for developing countries like India to attain the status of being 'slum free'. The central debate revolves around NGOs in addressing challenges of slums around the developing world. Tembo (2002), in his empirical study of two small cities in Africa, explored the contrast of the need of the people and intervention by NGOs. He reflected that a very basic premise of NGOs is the collective voice and community's participation in framing the development agenda, which has frequently not been followed, thereby resulting in the failure of specific projects. On the other hand, Mosse's (2005) argument regarding the success of projects explored was that projects run by NGOs work under the pressure of funding agencies and their accountability was ensured towards funding agencies, and not to recipients.

On an average, living conditions in slums are challenging and the degree of these challenges is unchanged after several policy formulations as well as the inclusive and decentralized approach of development. In the late 20th century, international development agencies showed their interests in NGOs due to the character of their volunteers and claim of grassroot gardeners. An NGO was first used in 1945 by United Nations primarily with the aim of registering all kinds of private bodies independent from the control of government (Willetts, 2002). Later on, NGOs acquired wider legitimacy due to their transparent, accountable and non-bureaucratic approach, especially after the 1990s (ibid.). It geared the growth of NGOs worldwide. However, its basic nature got blurred with the passage of time and most of these NGOs, taking shape into an institution, started recruiting professionalized people and started following bureaucratic processes in functioning. Thus, this NGOization[9] started being seen critically among scholars, but there is a lack of literature available on critical evaluation of interventions carried out by NGOs among the poor, by independent agencies and research scholars, especially in the case of slum dwellers. Therefore, we are going to locate the role of NGOs in two slums of Delhi to have an abstract idea of NGOs' interventions and conflict between different shades of constructing development.

## Findings and Discussions

According to the established paradigmatic position in the 20th century, images that form of development and help identify the challenges NGOs assist to transform those in the field through the process of interaction, a collective voice and participatory approach. Therefore, a multiple understanding of these images is implied through this qualitative Study. The contrasts of these images are seen as critical and constructivist in order to address the felt challenges of slum dwellers. The felt challenges of slum dwellers have been seen as food security (ration card), employment, and demand of bribes by the police, false electricity bills, supply of drinking-water, sanitation, education and legal entitlement to their lands.

Investigating into the people's effort to live in these slums or considering people as 'striving to make a living' (Long, 1997; cited in Tembo, 2003) is a major consideration in seeking an NGOs' assistance-mechanism or role here.

The data demonstrates that slum dwellers are in need to have a livelihood arrangement because an absence of this leads to several consequences, i.e. failure to send children to school, failure to have regular food and buy household necessities, failure to procure household assets, frequent sickness, etc. The NGOs are well informed about this and they even claim that all this leads slum dwellers into poverty. On the other hand, the informed government, through several development agencies and NGOs, too is not able to work on these issues. It has been seen that the ration card (on which slum-dwellers depend for their food requirement) of a large number of slum-dwellers is cancelled without any intimation and they do not have their say in all these activities. However, the problem of such kind of irregularities is more frequent in the first slum rather than the second one. On the other hand, it has been seen that people from higher castes and those comparatively well off are less vulnerable to this kind of problems. The slum, though, largely comprises the poor and powerless and they need to seek assistance on these issues from the NGOs. However, accepting these challenges and admitting inability, they suffer due to malfunctioning of government officials. However, they add up that they are unable to do that because their organization is engaged in providing education and training to rag-pickers, which children in slums used to earn money to fulfil their families' need. The situations are more vulnerable as it appears in several reports. Here is an excerpt from one of the rag-picker respondents: (age 12 years) '... I want to study in a school but my parents do not have money to arrange even for food. Therefore, I am engaged in this. There are many of my age, who are doing this work'.[10] In this essence, the children in these slums are lacking opportunity of inclusive development. Another respondent, Manjula, opines: 'My ration card has been cancelled and I have been wandering from office to office, yet my card has not been reactivated.'[11] Such cases were prevalent in these slums and people have no any assistance from these organizations. Leaders did use to visit the slums and mobilize the slum dwellers but on the basis of caste and religion.[12]

Moreover, very few of the children living in slums complete their high school. Their parents also accept it and express their inability in sending them to a school. However, there are a number of girls in these slums, who completed their high school. In contrast, the situation in terms of education and livelihood is comparatively worse in Slum-B. Another organization found working in these slums was Bhalaswa Lokshakti Manch (BLM) based on local funding and stressing upon bringing the slum dwellers together for their rights but it is hostile to the big organization which used to take its ground report to publish their reports and the organization also did focus as per the orders of big organization.[13] Also, the nature of the intervention by BLM seemed very conflicting. They used to curse slum dwellers for their states of mind and lacked in considering the worth and dignity of slum dwellers. The BST is, however, engaged in providing computer education in Slum-A at night. Slum dwellers are very positive about this step, but they also do not forget to add that this organization is very much on the way to politicizing on the basis of caste reservation; lower caste slum dwellers are much against it. In Slum-B, the challenges are more vulnerable and the NGOs' interventions are dubious. The NGOs are not interested in this slum because most of the issues are related to law and order as well as their origin that is put under the scanner on account of their being Bangladeshi migrants.[14] This slum is settled on government land, but local leaders used to charge for space as well as electricity. On the other hand, police also asks for bribe due to their Bengali origin, new settlements and little interaction with local leaders. All these factors resulted in the fact that NGOs are disinterested in working in Slum-B even on a single issue. They even do not want to start any awareness and information-dissemination programme because they do not want to go against local leaders and the police.

It was found that the NGOs were largely engaged in service-delivery programmes and had been working in line with their funding agencies. Rajani, working as a Self-Help Group's co-ordinator in the slums questioned the intention of her organization and also complained about her salary, which is far less than that of a daily wage labourer's income. She said, 'The organization is just running. The head of the organization is not bothered about the progress of the slums. The focus is just on running the project'.[15] Similarly, slum dwellers were not happy with the working of BST because BST was engaged in creating nationalism and aimed at promoting the Hindu agenda among the slum dwellers. It was also working to mobilize slum-dwellers against caste reservation. In principle, both these organizations have their reach amongst the slum-dwellers and have the potential to change their lives but it was rarely to be seen that they elicited the participation of slum-dwellers in order to devise inclusive initiatives for grassroot change.

## Conclusion

This paper reflects upon NGOs' interventions in the Jehangirpuri slums of Northern Delhi and argues that the new paradigm poses several challenges to urban development schemes, which do not have a pragmatic participatory framework on the one hand. On the other hand, NGOs' presence in these slums is depoliticizing slum dwellers and weakening their potential to collectively raise a voice for their rights, and asking the State to be accountable to citizens. Furthermore, the political parties are using these slums as a garrison of vote and they attempt to mobilize slum dwellers at the time of election through key members of the slums. Slum dwellers frankly assert their view about the game of vote-bank politics played by political leaders. They also claimed that money and muscle power are prevalent and people are used to chosing money over going into the fight and debate in the slums at the time of elections. On the other hand, NGOs' appearance as service-providers and their collaboration with government agencies was experienced by slum dwellers. NGOs are engaged in executing their projects in fulfilling the requirements of funding agencies and some of them are even earning from the slum dwellers.

Finally, urbanization in Delhi does not appear to be providing the poor with a greater voice in order to fulfil their legitimate demands in the largest democracy of the world. Political leaders are only visible during elections and

NGOs' interventions are aimed at running their projects rather than focusing on the felt needs of slum dwellers. In this process, slum dwellers have become objects of social experiment rather than subjects in this democratic discourse. The situation in newly-settled slums is worse than that in long-settled slums. New settled slums are 'Big Adda' for collecting money because the degree of legitimization is comparatively less and the slum dwellers are not friendly with the police and local leaders and State administration due to the barrier of language. Additionally, NGOs are less interested in working on these issues. No specific evidence of such ignorance has been found, but some on the NGOs' staff admitted the threat of the State with regard to delinking of running projects and cancellation of allotted spaces to run several projects by the government because these organizations were given spaces on subsidized rentals. Therefore, the study stresses upon the demand for strong and vibrant NGOs, seen as representative of civil society in the present era, and which can challenge the State rather than legitimize the State's way of functioning. Consequently, the approach to civil society in which NGOs are portrayed on the basis of the nature of their participation, with a recognition of the voluntary and collective voice, needs to be restored – otherwise this way of functioning may be seen as being a colonization of slums by these NGOs. Further, this excessive NGOization will lead to a weakening of peoples' collective voices asking the State to be responsible, for this will be a group of professional people posing as an agency with doors closed for natural participation. NGOs were actually seen by the State as the representatives of people from the grassroots, that led to inclusion of the ideas of NGOs in policies like RAY and JNNURM but the reality has come to be far removed from that notion.

Finally, this paper does not come to any specific theorization of NGOs' interventions but has focused to show the picture of challenges faced by slum dwellers, which further need to be examined for inclusive and grassroot development. Additionally, the paper also comes to the conclusion that mechanisms for ensuring relevant participation need to be devised with the aim of bringing about inclusive development and also to shift focus on grassroot structural challenges rather than planning superficially.

## Notes

1. See Primary Census Abstract on Slum 2011, http://www.censusindia.gov.in/2011-documents/slum-26-09-13.pdf, accessed on 20 December 2013.
2. See the World Bank, http://siteresources.worldbank.org/introspects/resources/334934-1327948020811/8401693-1355753354515/concept_note_gmr2013.pdf, accessed on 30 December 2013.
3. See Primary Census Abstract for Slum 2011, http://www.censusindia.gov.in/2011-documents/slum-26-09-13.pdf, accessed on 20 December 2013.
4. See *The Times of India*, http://timesofindia.indiatimes.com/india/census-nsso-differ-on-slum-population-figures/articleshow/28415537.cms, accessed on 25 December 2013.

5. The idea of Research Method comes from a Paper written by Jha, Rao and Woolcock in 2005 titled 'Governance in the Gullies'. Research Method is devised in a way to study the role of NGOs and challenges of slum dwellers. Therefore, the method of qualitative study has been used to locate central dynamics and NGOs' assistance.
6. See Census of India 2011, censusindia.gov.in/2011-documents/on_slums-2011final.ppt, accessed on 28 December 2013.
7. *The Hindu*, http://www.thehindu.com/news/national/slum-population-up-from-52-million-to-65-million/article5187166.ece, accessed on 23 December 2013.
8. This is the outcome of the study based on a case study of housing projects in two slums of Bengaluru, which is a critical analysis of affordable housing schemes through a re-developed framework of RAY and JNNURM. But, she poses major challenges about the information-gap as well as misinformation regarding legal rights of land-title at the housing place.
9. NGOization refers to a process by which civic actors from social movements in particular but also from smaller community groups are drawn to incorporate and perform as NGOs. There are several forces which shaped NGOization and she explored these forces in details. However, economic and institutional factors are primary.
10. Interview took place at Secondary Co-education School on the main road (Metro-Jahangirpuri) in March 2012.
11. Interview during fieldwork in K-Block during 2011–2012.
12. This conclusion is based after attending several meetings of slum dwellers and political leaders during the MCD (Municipal Corporation of Delhi) election in 2011–2012.
13. The conclusion is based on the researcher's interview with the slum dwellers as well as organizations' staff during 2011–2012.
14. This is based on observation as well as interviews with slum dwellers living in Slum-B during 2011–2012.
15. Interview with a woman working with 'Prayas' for years but it appears that she also got frustrated with it and she is doubtful about the goal of the organization.

## References

Doshi, S. (2013). 'The Politics of the Evicted: Redevelopment, Subjectivity and Difference in Mumbai's Slum Frontier'. *Antipode*, 45(45): 844–65.

Jha, S., V. Rao and M. Woolcock (2007). 'Governance in the Gullies: Democratic Responsiveness and Leadership in Delhi's Slums'. *World Development*, 35(2): 230–46.

Kamath, L. (2012). 'New Policy Paradigms and Actual Practices in Slum-Housing: The Case of Housing Projects in Bengaluru'. *Economic and Political Weekly*, XLVII(47–48): 76–86.

Kundu, A. (2013). 'Making Indian Cities Slum-Free: Visions and Operations'. *Economic and Political Weekly*, XLVIII(17).

Lang, S. (2013). *NGOs, Civil Society and Public Sphere.* New York: Cambridge University Press.

Lewis, D. and N. Kanji (2009). *Non-Governmental Organizations and Development.* New York: Routledge.

Lisa, P. (1979). 'Housing Policy in Developing Countries: Two Puzzles'. *World Development*, 7(11): 1017–22.

Misra, R.P. and K. Misra (eds) (1999). *Million Cities of India (Vol. 1–2)*, New Delhi: Sustainable Development Foundation.

Mitlin, D., S. Hickey and A. Bebbington (2007). 'Reclaiming Development? NGOs and the Challenge of Alternatives'. *World Development*, 35(10): 1699–720.

Mosse, David (2005). *Cultivating Development: An Ethnography of Aid, Policy and Practice.* London: Pluto Press.

Nijman, J. (2008). 'Against the Odds: Slum Rehabilitation in Neo-liberal Mumbai'. *Cities*, 25(2): 73–85.

Ooi, G.L. and K.H. Phua (2007). 'Urbanization and Slum Formation'. *Journal of Urban Health: Bulletin of the New York Academy of Medicine*, 84(1): 27–34.

O'Hare, G. and D. Abbott (1998). 'A Review of Slum-housing Policies in Mumbai'. *Cities*, 15(4): 269–83.

Planning Commission (Government of India) (2013). Twelfth Five Year Plan (2012–2017): Social Sectors, Vol. III. New Delhi: Sage Publications India Pvt. Ltd.

Pugh, C. (2000). 'Squatter Settlements: Their Sustainability, Architectural Contributions, and Socio-economic Roles'. *Cities*, 17(5): 325–37.

Rao, V. and M. Woolcock (2003). Integrating Qualitative and Quantitative Approaches in Programme Evaluation, in Bourguignon FranCois and Luiz A. Pereira Da Silva (eds) *The Impact of Economic Policies on Poverty and Income Distribution: Evaluation Techniques and Tools*, 165–190, Washington, DC: World Bank.

Sean, F. (2014). 'The Political Economy of Slums: Theory and Evidence from Sub Saharan Africa'. *World Development*, 54: 191–203.

Tembo, F. (2003). *Participation, Negotiation and Poverty: Encouraging the Power of Images.* London: Ashgate.

UN-HABITAT (2003). *The Challenges of Slums: Global Report on Human Settlements.* London: Earthscan.

——. (2006). *The State of the World's Cities Report 2006/2007.* London: Earthscan.

——. (2009). *Planning Sustainable Cities: Global Report on Human Settlements.* London: Earthscan.

Willets, P. (2002). 'What is a Non-governmental Organization?'. Output from the Research Project on Civil Society Networks in Global Governance, http://staff.city.au/cs-ntwks-art.htm, accessed on 30 March 2014.

World Bank (2003). *Sustainable Development in a Dynamic World: Transforming Institutions, Growth and Quality of Life*, Washington, DC: World Bank.

World Bank (2006). *World Development Report 2006*, New York: Oxford University Press.

World Bank (2013). *Global Monitoring Report: Rural-Urban Dynamics and the Millenium Development Goals*, Washington, DC: World Bank.

# 13

# Decision of Migration

## *A Case Sudy of Students from Bihar Enrolled in University of Delhi*

**SUMIT KUMAR**

### Understanding Inter-State Migration for Higher Education

Migration is a form of mobility in which people change their residential location across defined administrative boundaries for a variety of reasons, which may be involuntary or voluntary, or a mixture of both (Srivastava, 2012). The place from where someone migrates is characterized as 'source' and the place where he/she reaches after migration is the 'destination' and the person who migrates is called a 'migrant'. The duration of migration can be either permanent or semi-permanent or temporal in nature (Premi, 1990). Census of India (2001) defines migration on the basis of both birth-place and place of last residence. It defines migrants by place of birth as those who are enumerated at a village/town that is other than their place of birth at the time of Census. On the other hand, someone is considered as migrant by place of last residence, if the place in which he/she is enumerated during the Census is other than his place of immediate last residence. National Sample Survey Organization (NSSO), a wing of the Ministry of Planning and Programme Implementation, defines migration on the basis of place of last residence only. A person whose last Usual Place of Residence (UPR) is different from the present place of enumeration is considered as a migrant and UPR of a person is defined as a place (village/town) where a person had stayed continuously for a period of six months or more (NSSO, 2007–08).

### Types of Migration

Migration can mainly be classified on the basis of geographical boundaries and also on the basis of the purpose of migration.

### Types of Migration on the Basis of Geographical Boundaries

Migration on the basis of geographical boundaries is broadly classified into external migration and internal migration. External migration refers to migration beyond the national boundaries and is also known as international migration whereas internal migration refers to migration within the national boundaries. External or international migration is further classified into immigration and emigration. The process of moving into a new country is termed as immigration and such a person is better known as an immigrant. On the other hand, the process of moving out of the home country to another country is emigration and such a person is known as an emigrant.

Internal migration is further classified into inter-state migration and intra-state migration. Intra-state migration involves change in residence within the boundaries of a state whereas inter-state migration involves a change of residence beyond a state's boundaries but within the national borders (Dang, 2005). Internal migrants in the world are four times as many as there are international/external migrants (UNDP, 2009: 22). Inter-state migration is generally long-distance migration compared to the short distance of intra-state migrations (Bhagat, 2009). Therefore, inter-state migrants are comparatively large in numbers as compared to intra-state migrants.

### Types of Migration on the Basis of Purpose of Migration

Migration is caused by several reasons: in search of employment, in search of *better* employment, business, to *take up* employment/better employment, transfer of service/contract, proximity of place of work, marriage, movement of parents/earning member, studies – and other reasons (64th Round NSSO, 2007–08). Census of India (2001) categorizes reasons of migration as work/employment, business, education, marriage, moved after birth, moved with household and others. Thus, migration can be categorized into several types on the basis of its purposes.

### Migration for Studies/Education

Migration for studies/education is one of the prominent reasons behind migration of young people. Going by the Census of India 2001, 3 per cent of the total migrants account for this reason while the 64th Round NSSO, 2007–08 suggests that 23.8 per cent of the total migrants who migrated for up to 9 years belong to this very category.

Migration for education is classified on the basis of geographical boundaries and also on the basis of levels of education.

On the basis of levels of education, migration for studies/education can be broadly classified as migration for school education and migration for college/higher education. Migration for higher education can further be classified as migration for non-professional courses and migration for professional courses, on the basis of the nature of courses. Migration for higher education can be categorized as external migration for higher education and internal migration. Internal migration for higher education can be further categorized into inter-state migration for higher education and intra-state migration for higher education on the basis of geographical boundaries of states.

Therefore, overlapping of types of migration (on the basis of education and geographical boundaries) will lead to inter-state and intra-state migration for professional/non-professional higher education. Inter-state migration for higher education, a major thrust-area of this paper, is one of the streams of migration.

## Review of Literature

Migration, especially labour migration, has been dealt with widely in various disciplines (Economics, Geography, Sociology, etc.). Migration for higher education has also been a major thrust area of many researches but in just the context of international migration. Very limited literature is available on inter-state migration for higher education (Kumar, 2014). Therefore, in order to satisfy the objectives of this study, literature available on migration or international migration or mobility for higher education has been borrowed. Borrowed literatures in the context of the nature of decision-making and stages/levels of decision for higher education have been sequentially discussed below.

## Decision of Migration

The decision of migration (individual migration) is debatable as it is considered variously by scholars as an individual decision or household decision or mixed decision. An attempt has been made to make some sense of this debate through the literature discussed below.

## Migration as an Individual Decision

The micro-level model of neo-classic equilibrium perspective of migration which is also known as the Human Capital Theory of Migration (Todaro, 1969), coined by Sjaadstad in 1962, considers a migrant as an individual rational actor whose decision for migration is spearheaded by a 'cost-benefit calculation'. Assuming free choice and full access to information, the migrant is expected to go where he or she can be the most productive or can earn the highest wages. The cost-benefit analysis will be done by involving expected income/wage rather than real income/wage (Massey et al., 1993). Human capital endowments, skills, age, marital status, gender, occupation and labour-market status along with preferences and expectations strongly determine who will and will not migrate.

## Migration as a Household Decision

The New Economics of Migration (NEM) theory had proposed 'migration as a household or family decision'. It is based on the assumption of mutual inter-dependence as opposed to individual independence of neo-classic equilibrium perspective of migration (Stark, 1991). It suggests that migration decisions are not made by isolated individual actors but by families or households (Massey et al., 1993) in order to minimize their income-risks through sending the most suitable member to earn outside (Stark and Levhari, 1982). Remittances are an indicator of maximization of household income and can be considered as a household decision. Gubhaju and De Jong (2005) have found in their study on migrants of South Africa that migration is mostly an individual decision and household decisions play a very insignificant role in the context of non-married migrants. In case of married individuals, both individual and household decisions play a determing role.

They also find that the argument of migration to 'reduce household risk' is more applicable for intentions of a longer time horizon migration of married men and women, at least in South Africa.

## Migration as Mixed Decision

Authors such as Mincer (1978) and Hoddinott (1994) have taken migration as a dependent variable in their models to find determinants of migration, and suggested that an individual's decision to migrate depends not only on his/her utility function but also on the family's utility function. Therefore, the decision to migrate is an outcome of both the individual's and household's utility function (Hoddinot, 1994). According to Hoddinott (1994), the level of remittances gets influenced by a parent's ability to reward good behaviour through the promise of bequests. In poor countries, migration is financed mostly by contributions from the resources of other family members. Thus, the migrant compensates for this investment by remitting to his/her household or family members.

The above-mentioned literature indicates that an individual's decision of migration is either driven by 'maximization of his/her own income/wage' or by 'maximization of family's income/wage' or by 'minimization of family-risk' or 'maximization of income of self and household/family both'. Therefore, profit of individual or household or individual and family are the impetus behind the decision to migrate.

Besides the nature of migration, this paper also explores the stages of decisions of migration. Therefore, related literature has been reviewed and discussed below.

## Stages/Levels of Decisions of Migration

As in the case of the nature of decision of migration, the issue of the stages of decision of migration is also debatable because scholars have variously suggested two or three or four stages of the decision of migration. Those stages are as discussed below:

The intentions to move and subsequent actual moving behaviour have been considered as two stages of the decision of migration (Duncan and Newman, 1976).

Rossi (1955, 1980) had proposed three stages of migration using data for relocations of residents in the metropolitan area of Philadelphia. Those stages were – the desire to move, the concrete intention and the actual move. Brown and Moore (1970) had considered search for a new dwelling caused by stress at the place of residence as the first phase of their three-stage model of migration.

The second phase comprises a search-process for housing and other opportunities that lead to a decision either in favour of or against relocation, and the third phase is the act of moving. Speare et al., (1975) had also suggested three stages of decision on migration. Initially, people develop a desire to move mostly due to dissatisfaction followed by whether or not to move (a stage in which they weigh the costs and benefits of various alternative locations and decide) and at the last stage they actually move.

Beside these three-stage models, there is 'The Psychological Rubicon Model' which suggests four levels of decision-making on migration: the first is the pre-decisional phase or motivational phase where desire or wish to move takes birth and preferences also get selected on the basis of desirability and feasibility. The second stage is the pre-actional phase encompassing planning on 'when', 'where' and 'how' to migrate. The third stage is the actional phase where migration gets realized through determined and persistent pursuit of goal. In the final stage one starts living in the destination place (Heckhausen, 1991).

Therefore, initially, the idea or desire to migrate takes its root due to various dissatisfactions and reasons and then gets followed by actualization of that idea or desire in real world on the basis of available resources which lead to actual migration and change in address.

## Rationale of the Study

Inter-state migration for higher education has been considered as migration for higher education for the purposes of this paper, which is a new attempt, especially, in the Indian context. The demand to understand it comprehensively is increasing as the demand for understanding 'internal brain-drain' is increasing (Sapra, 2013; Chandrashekhar and Sharma, 2014) as the result of aiming for a 'knowledge-based economy' by the nation (National Knowledge Commission, 2006). Keeping this in view, the present study aims to understand two of its contexts – the nature of migration and stages of migration through considering migration for higher education as a decision. Bihar has been considered as a source while Delhi University (DU) has been considered as destination for such migration. Keeping the rationale in consideration, objectives were drafted for conducting this study and they are as given below.

## Objectives of the Study

- To identify the nature of the decision for migration of students from Bihar enrolled in DU
- To identify the stages of the decision for migration of students from Bihar enrolled in DU

On the basis of objectives, research questions were drafted. They are:

## Research Questions

- What is the nature of the decision for migration of students from Bihar enrolled in DU?

- What are the stages of the decision for migration of students from Bihar enrolled in DU?

## Methodology

### *Research Approach*

Out of three approaches (Qualitative Approach, Quantitative Approach and Mixed Method Approach) of researches, the Mixed Method Approach has been employed for this study due to the flexibility it gives, specially in the context of data collection. Data has been collected at two levels for this study. Descriptions of the nature of questions and involved methods to decode given answers have been given below:

**Table 1**

*Levels of Data Collection, Nature of the Questionnaire, Methods and Sample Size*

| *Levels of Data Collection* | *Nature of the Questionnaire* | *Methods* | *Sample-size* |
|---|---|---|---|
| Pre-Questionnaire Survey | Unstructured | Content analysis | 20 |
| Questionnaire Survey | Semi-structured | Ranking (Ordinal Scale) | 100 |

*Source:* Field Survey.

### *Research Design*

This study is an exploratory case study due to its objective to deal with widely untouched areas of migration, that is nature and stages of decision of migration for higher education from Bihar to DU.

### *Universe of the Study*

All students from Bihar enrolled in non-professional undergraduate courses, in regular mode, offered by University of Delhi, are universe of this study. Further, lack of data regarding total number of such data has converted it into an infinite universe.

### *Sample*

As shown in the Table 1, 20 students were surveyed for pre-questionnaire survey and 100 students were surveyed for questionnaire survey. Students were identified through snowball-sampling technique for this study without being replicated. Even those 20 students were not selected for questionnaire survey. This study has restricted itself to limited number of students belonging to clientele due to the time and resource constraints.

### *Data-collection*

The study is based on primary data collected through questionnaire survey. Questions of the questionnaire have been formed on the basis of pre-questionnaire survey of migrant students belonging to the same clientele. Pre-questionnaire survey had open-ended questions and on the basis of given responses, close-ended or structured questionnaire has been drafted.

## Findings of the Study

### *Decision of Migration for Higher Education*

On the basis of available data, this paper proposes a multi-layered model for decision of migration for higher education and those stages are: decision to migrate, selection of destination, selection of university, selection of college and selection of course. The multi-layered model of migration for higher education has been mentioned and discussed below.

**Figure 1**

*A Graph Showing Level of Decisions of Migration for Higher Education*

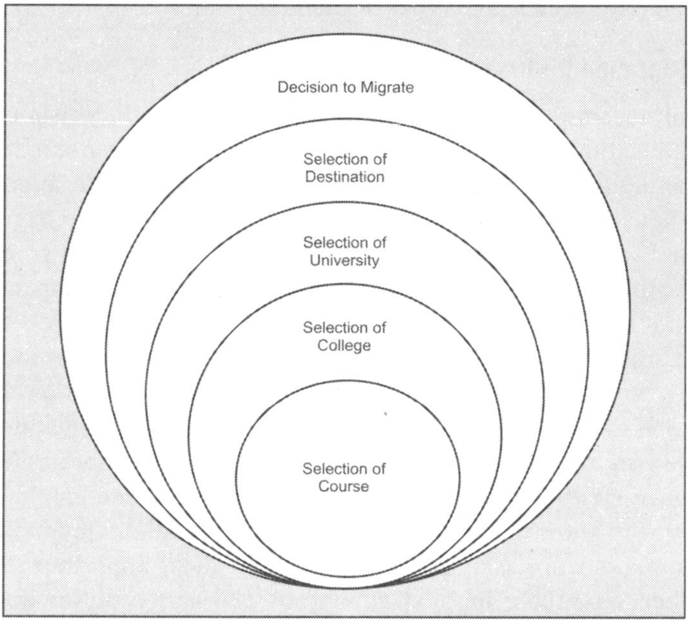


The graph (Figure 1) suggests that there are five levels at which decisions have to be taken in the context of migration for higher education.

Decision to migrate refers to decision on whether to migrate or not to migrate. Dissatisfaction at the source state in the context of the available status of higher education leads to migration. A positive decision to migrate leads the way for next levels of migration for higher education. Some students had given priority to university irrespective of its location whereas some had given priority to college or course. Therefore, sequences of levels of decisions after the decision to migrate has not been proposed as it has been found very subjective in nature.

Selection of destination refers to selection of a location where universities offering desired courses or having desired colleges are located. Sometimes, people do make comparisons between several destinations while at other times they go for one destination place only. In that case, comparison between universities or institutions located in that place gets done. Universities located in the desired destination get selected on the basis of resources, information and availability of colleges and courses. Sometimes, students move to a university or institution irrespective of its location or without any comparison with any other university or institution. In the case of this study, 78 per cent of total respondents had applied only to DU, while 28 per cent had applied to other universities also located either in Delhi NCR or Bihar or elsewhere. Besides university, decisions are also taken for the selection of college and courses. Marks secured in the last exam (either of +2 exam or qualifying test) is also responsible for selection of university, college and courses. One among all colleges of DU get selected by migrant students due to their own choices, expenditure, marks secured in last exam, reputation of colleges etc. Students choose a course based on their preferences, choices, career options, etc.

## Nature of Migration for Higher Education

As noted earlier, there is a dearth of literature dealing with decision to migrate for higher education. The available literature on migration *per se* is substantive. The general understanding points to the fact that decision to migrate can be individual, household or a mixed decision. The findings obtained from review of literature are helpful in conceptualizing the nature of decision to migrate for higher education. The knowledge captured was utilized to develop indicators in order to fulfil the objectives of the study.

Self, parents, siblings, relatives and others have been identified as individual/s influencing the decision of inter state migration for higher education. Self is the indicator for individual decision whereas parents, siblings and relatives are components of a household decision. 'Others' refer to other than the above-mentioned motivators and have been included in the chart with the motivation to know someone other than these individuals mentioned above.

Respondents were asked to tick against the most important individual/s having influence on their decision to migrate. Thereafter, on the basis of their frequency in total ranking chart, ranking for each individual/s has been done. Table 2 consists of ranking of individual/s in the context of decision to migrate from Bihar to DU for higher education.

Table suggests that students themselves have maximum influence followed by parents on their decision to migrate. Parents fund educational expenditure (as described earlier) despite it. They were overpowered by 'self' (i.e. students themselves) in this regard. Relatives have a better say in the decision to migrate as compared to siblings. No one was found under the 'others' category. The Table suggests that in the case of 54 per cent of respondents, self (indicator of individual decision), while in 46 per cent cases parents, siblings and relatives (indicators of household decision) have taken decision to migrate for higher education. Therefore, it can be easily said that the migration for higher education, in the context of students migrated from Bihar to DU, is a mixed decision rather an individual or household one because altogether self, parents, relatives and siblings are components of a mixed decision.

**Table 2**

*Ranking of Individual(s) and Decision of Migration*

| *Individual/s* | *Frequencies* | *Ranks* |
|---|---|---|
| Self | 54 | 1 |
| Parents | 36 | 2 |
| Siblings | 3 | 4 |
| Relatives | 7 | 3 |
| Others | 0 | 5 |

*Source:* Field Survey.

## Conclusion

The decision of migration to DU from Bihar for higher education is multi-layered and those layers are – decision to migrate, selection of destination, selection of university, selection of college and selection of course. Decision to migrate makes way for other steps. But since the decisions are found to be very subjective, any sequence of layers has not been suggested. The decision of migration for higher education (in the context of migration from Bihar to DU) is neither an individual nor a household decision but it is actually a mixed decision. In some cases, an individual is seen to have taken it while in other cases the household components (parents, siblings and relatives) do so. Decisions taken by individuals themselves have outshined household components with respect to taking decision of migration for higher education.

## References


Bauer, T. and K. Zimmerman (1998). 'Causes of International Migration: A Survey', in P. Gorter, P. Nijkamp and J. Root (eds), *Crossing Borders: Regional and Urban Perspectives on International Migration*. Aldershot: Ashgate, pp. 95–127.

Bhagat, Ram B. (2009). 'Internal Migration in India: Are the Underclass More Mobile?'. Paper presented in the 26th IUSSP General Population Conference held in Marrakech, Morocco, 27 September–2 October.

Brown, L.A. and E.G. Moore (1970). the Intra-urban Migration Process: A Perspective, Geografiska Annaler. Series B, *Human Geography*, 52(1), 1–13.

Census of India (2001). 'Migration Data'. Ministry of Home Affairs, Government of India, New Delhi.

——. (2001a). 'Population Data'. Ministry of Home Affairs, Government of India, New Delhi.

Chandrashekhar, S. and A. Sharma (2014). *Internal Migration for Education and Employment among Youth in India*. Mumbai: Indira Gandhi Institute of Development Research, January.

Dang, N.A. (2005). *Internal Migration. Opportunities and Challenges for the Renovations and Development in Vietnam*. Hanoi: Gioi Publisher.

De Haas, Hein (2008). 'Migration and Development: A Theoretical Perspective'. International Migration Institute Working Paper No. 9, University of Oxford.

Duncan, G.J. and S.J. Newman (1976). Expected and Actual Residential Mobility. Journal of the American Institute of Planners, 42(2), 174–186.

Fang, Y. (2006). Residential Satisfaction, Moving Inentionand Moving Behaviours: A Study of redevelopmentNeighbourhood in Inner-city Beijing. *Housing Studies*, 21(5), 671–694.

GOI (2006). National Knowledge Commission: Report to the Nation 2006–2009, New Delhi.

Gubhaju, B. and Gordon F. De Jong (2005). 'Individual versus Household Migration Decision Rules: Gender Differences in Intentions to Migrate in South Africa'. Population Research Institute, Pennsylvania State University, Pennsylvania.

Ghuntla, Tejas P. et al. (2012). 'A Study of Socio-Economic and Parental Educational Background of First-year Medical Students of Medical College, Bhavanagar'. *IRJP*, 3(9): 253.

Heckhausen, H. (1991). *Motivation and Action*, New York: Springer.

Hoddinott, J. (1994). 'A Model of Migration and Remittances applied to Western Kenya'. *Oxford Economic Papers*, 459–476.

Kumar, S. (2014). 'Inter-State Migration for Higher Education: A Case Study of Students from Bihar Enrolled in University of Delhi'.

Kley, S. (2010). 'Explaining the Stages of Migration within a Life-Course Framework'. *European Sociological Review*, 27(4): 469–86.

Massey, Douglass S. et al. (1993). 'Theories of International Migration: A Review and Appraisal'. *Population and Development Review*, 19(3): 431–66.

Mincer, J. (1978). 'Family Migration Decisions'. *Journal of Political Economy*, 86(5), 749–773.

National Sample Survey Office (2007–08). 'Migration in India, Report No. 533'. NSSO 64th Round, Ministry of Programme Implementation, Government of India.

Pathak, K.N. (2012). 'Education in Bihar: Retrospect and Prospect'. *Journal of Social and Economic Studies*, 22(1), January-June.

Premi, M.K. (1990). Issues in the Field of Population for the 1990s. State of Natural and Human Resources (2 Vols. Set), 34.

Rossi, P.H. (1955), Why Families Move: A Study in the Social Psychology of Urban Residential Mobility. Glencoe, IL: Free Press.

Sjaastad, Larry (1962). 'The Cost and Returns of Human Migration'. *Journal of Political Economy*, 49(1): 104–15.

Sapra, R. (2013). 'Higher Education and Cross-State Migration'. Rutgers University, November 18.

Speare, A. Jr., S. Goldstein, and W.H. Frey (eds) (1975). *Residential Mobility, Migration and Metropolitan Change*, Mass: Ballinger Publishing Company.

Srivastava, R. (2012). 'Internal Migration in India: An Overview of its Features, Trends and Policy Challenges'. Workshop Compendium, Vol. 2: Workshop Papers, National Workshop on Internal Migration and Human Development in India, ICSSR, New Delhi, December 6–7.

Stark, O. (1991). *The Migration of Labour*. Cambridge: Basil Blackwell.

Stark, O. and D. Levhari (1982). 'On Migration and Risks in LDCs'. *Economic Development and Cultural Change*, 31(1): 191–96.

Todaro, Michael P. (1969). 'A Model of Labour Migration and Urban Unemployment in Less Developed Countries'. *American Economic Review*, 59: 138–48.

UNDP (2009). *Human Development Report 2009, Overcoming Barriers: Human Mobility and Development*, New York, USA: UNDP.

Yin, Robert K. (2012). *Applications of Case Study Research*. New Delhi: Sage Publications.

# Part 6

## Public Policies and Institutional Change

# 14

# Dimensions of Urban Female Educational Status and its Linkages in Eastern Uttar Pradesh

**AKRAM HANNAN**

The concept of literacy rate which varies from country to country, generally refers to the minimum level of literacy skills. Indian Census considers a person as literate if he/she can both read and write in any language. A person who, with age above six years, can read, write and understand any language is literate (Census of India, 2011). The analysis of literacy patterns and trends therein is of immense significance for population geographer. Literacy is an effective instrument for social and economic development and national integration. It is considered as an important social indicator, because people with higher levels of literacy tend to have healthier lifestyle, less disease and generally a better quality of life (Siddiqui and Hannan, 2011). Literacy is one of the basic determinants of socio-economic development attained by a human group. Literacy and education are like oxygen for human being in contemporary technology driven world and knowledge economy (Siddiqui et al., 2011). Most of the studies on educational status have been attempted with reference to literacy rate in general and by sex and residence in particular (Siddiqui et al., 2008, 2005; Chandna, 2009 and Hannan, 2014).

Education is known to have vital and important link with the achievement of income and health security. A number of recent studies also provide ample evidence of the mutual analytical and empirical linkages between human resources and poverty in India (Tilak, 1989; Krishnan, 1996; Rao, 1985). Improvement in educational performance, especially of women, is closely related to health and fertility behaviour. Female literacy and workforce participation are important determinants of variations in child mortality (Kishor,

1994). Education is important in overall development of human kind. It is a key factor for the rapid development within the country. Education which is the base of all development and advancement of civilization, aims at the evolution of a better man and development of mind (Sharma, 2003). Education cultures the individual and helps him in his needs all over the world. Its implications are rich and varied. It deals with ever growing man in the ever growing society. Different philosophers, politicians, statesmen and educationists have defined education according to their own point of view and circumstances (Bano, 2005).

Female's education and health have an impact on improvements in gender equality, gender relations and women's empowerment. The spread of education among the poorer groups and women has a significant influence on participation in the democratic processes and in influencing the priorities of development in accordance with the principles of sustainable development and local needs. Education impacts directly on virtually all dimensions of deprivation (physical, social, economic, political and psychological) enumerated by UP Development Report (2010), and Siddiqui and Kaushik (2013) highlighted the development of educational level and its relation with some independent variables of socio-economic development and employment. With this background, an attempt is made in this paper to analyse the spatial distribution of urban female education and the problems, and suggest the effective measures to minimize the problems in Eastern Uttar Pradesh. In view of the relevant literature in this study, an attempt has been made to analyse the district level variations in the attainment of urban female educationand linkages with the variables of educational facilities and socio-economic development in study area. Finally, this study suggests some suitable measures which can help to accomplish almost hundred per cent attainments in urban female education.

## Objectives

The present study is attempted under three points. The first point discusses trends of urban females' educational status in Eastern Uttar Pradesh. The second examines the district-level distribution of urban female education during 2001, and third explains the factors which influence urban females educational status in the study area.

## Study Area

Eastern Uttar Pradesh is popularly known as 'Purvanchal' and is most vulnerable part of the state because of its various and multi-faceted agro-ecological situations, characterized by frequent flood and drought. Due to largest highly fertile plain of the Ganga region, it has a high population density and dominance of agriculture as its economic activity. Eastern Uttar Pradesh (EUP) lies between the latitudes of 24°10′ and 25°21′ N, and longitudes of 82°10′ and 84°40′ E, covering an area of 85,298.79 km$^2$ (29.10% of the state). EUP consists of 27 districts (Figure 1). It has a maximum population density of 935 persons km$^2$ (2011 census) against 324 persons km$^2$ in the country. The northern boundary of EUP runs along the Himalayas touching Nepal and is also well defined by river Ghaghara. The eastern boundary is bordered by the state of Bihar, southern by Madhya Pradesh and south-eastern by Chhattisgarh and Jharkhand (Hannan and Siddiqui, 2012).

## Data and Methods

The present study is entirely based on secondary data collected from different published and unpublished sources. Apart from the demographic data obtained from the Census of India, the relevant non-demographic data have also been obtained from publications of the State Planning Institute of Uttar Pradesh, Lucknow, and the Ministry of Human Affairs, Government of India, New Delhi. The spatial pattern of female population by literacy rate and educational status separately of the female population have been examined to below primary education, primary, middle, high school and intermediate, technical and non-technical education and graduate and above education. Besides these, books, articles and journals are also used to give final shape to the present work. Cartographic techniques and GIS-Arc View (Version, 3.2a) programme have been adopted to represent the distribution of urban female educational status among the districts of the region and for easy understanding of data with the help of choropleth method. Correlation techniques were applied to test the linear relationship between urban female educational status and selected explanatory variables.

## Trends of Literacy Rate in Eastern Uttar Pradesh (1971–2011)

Trends of literacy rate (1971–2011) in country (India), Uttar Pradesh, Eastern Uttar Pradesh (EUP) for persons, male and female are depicted in Table 1. Between 1971 and 2011, during a span of 40 years, literacy rate has gone up by 39.54 per cent points, from 34.50 in 1971 to 74.04 in 2011. Though from 1971 to 1981, general literacy rate increased by 9.10 per cent points, during the period from 1981 to 1991, it has increased by about 8.60 per cent points and from 1991 to 2001, a marginal increase of 12.60 per cent points, during 2001 to 2011, it has recorded 9.24 per cent points. The increase in literacy rate has been due to rapid increase in the number of educational institutions and many government schemes like National Literacy Mission (NLM) and Sarva Shiksha Abhiyan (SSA). The Education Guarantee Scheme is another central scheme which has the objective of setting up educational centres, called Vidya Kendra in educationally unserved areas where there are at least 30 children in the 6 to 11 years of age group. The teachers in these centres are appointed on a contract basis by the panchayats, and the community is expected to find the space for the centre. The Mid-Day Meal is an incentive scheme under which each child, in a recognized primary school, with minimum certified attendance, has been (till September 2004) provided a ratio of three kilos of cereal per month.

**Table 1**

*Trends of Literacy Rate in Eastern Uttar Pradesh, 1971–2011 (in %)*

| Census Years | India | | | Uttar Pradesh | | | Eastern Uttar Pradesh | | |
|---|---|---|---|---|---|---|---|---|---|
| | P | M | F | P | M | F | P | M | F |
| 1971 | 34.50 | 46.00 | 22.00 | 25.40 | 36.70 | 12.50 | 19.05 | 29.44 | 7.93 |
| 1981 | 43.60 | 56.40 | 29.80 | 33.30 | 47.40 | 17.20 | 24.40 | 37.31 | 10.71 |
| 1991 | 52.20 | 64.10 | 39.30 | 41.60 | 55.70 | 25.30 | 30.50 | 43.42 | 16.51 |
| 2001 | 64.80 | 75.30 | 53.70 | 56.30 | 68.80 | 42.20 | 54.64 | 68.60 | 39.13 |
| 2011 | 74.04 | 82.14 | 65.46 | 69.72 | 79.24 | 59.26 | 67.40 | 78.11 | 56.23 |

*Source:* Census of India, 1971–2011, P: Persons; M: Males; F: Females.

*Note:* (i)Literacy rate for 1971 Census relates to population aged five years and above. The rate for the 1981, 1991, 2001 and 2011 Census relate to population aged seven years and above.
(ii)The 1981 literacy rate exclude Assam where Census could not be conducted and the 1991 literacy rate exclude Jammu and Kashmir where Census could not be conducted due to disturbed conditions.
(iii)The 2001 Census, literacy rate exclude entire Kachh district, Morvi, Maliya-Miyana and Wankanertalukas of Rajkot district, Jodiyatalluka of Jamnagar district of Gujarat state and entire Kinnaur district of Himachal Pradesh where population enumerate of census of India, 2001, could not be conducted due to natural calamities.

However, since September 2004, cooked meals are being proved to the school-going children and provision has been made for cooking and sundry expenses (UP Development Report, 2010). The female literacy rate is still low in comparison with male population. Country's half of the female population is still illiterate even after so many years since 1971. During the last four decades, population of the country has been increasing at an exponential growth rate of more than 2 per cent per annum. While the expanded educational facilities pushed up the number of literates in the country, it has not been able to keep pace with the increasing population. Number of illiterates has simultaneously increased, though it is declining due to reduced population growth rate. The pace of education growth geared up in successive years and by the end of 2001, the total crude literacy level was 55.30 per cent, whereas it was 64.13 per cent for males and 45.84 per cent for females.

Table 1 shows that a slight improvement in literacy rate over the previous decade was observed. It was 34.50 per cent in the country, 25.40 per cent in UP and 19.05 per cent in EUP. Over 1981 and 1991 decades, literacy rate has shown a substantial improvement. In Eastern Uttar Pradesh, it was 24.40 per cent in 1981 and 30.50 per cent in 1991. The increase during the period was 6.1 per cent points corresponding country level figures for 1981 and 1991 were 43.60 and 52.20 per cent, respectively, and the state figures were 33.30 per cent and 41.60 per cent, respectively. In 2001, 64.80 per cent literacy rate was recorded in India, 56.30 per cent in Uttar Pradesh and 54.64 per cent in EUP. The literacy rate during 1991–2001 were found to be an increase of 12.60, 14.70 and 13.14 per cent points, respectively, in India, UP and EUP. India has recorded literacy rate of 65.38 per cent wherein of male, it was 75.30 per cent and of female 53.70

per cent in 2001. Also in 2011, 74.04 per cent literacy rate was observed in India, 69.72 per cent in Uttar Pradesh and 67.40 per cent in EUP.

The literacy rate by sex as shown in the Table 1 depicts that in 1971 male literacy rate was 46.00 per cent in the country, 36.70 per cent in the state and 29.44 per cent in E.U.P. In 1981, India (56.40%), UP (47.40%) and EUP (37.31%) recorded low male literacy rate. At the national level, male literacy rate of population aged 7 and above has improved from 64.10 per cent in 1991 to 75.30 per cent in 2001 and 82.14 per cent in 2011. In 2001 at the state and region levels, male literacy rate has changed from 55.70 per cent to 43.42 per cent and 55.70 per cent to 68.80 per cent which showed sharp increase of 13.1 per cent and 25.18 per cent points, respectively, over the decade. Also in 2011, at the state and region level, male literacy rate has stood at 79.24 per cent and 78.11 per cent. Almost same trends of female literacy rate were observed during 40 years as shown in Table 1. In 1971, female literacy rate was 7.93 per cent in EUP which was less than state average (12.50%) and national average (22.00%). In 1981, it increased to 29.80 per cent in India, 17.20 per cent in UP and 10.71 per cent in EUP same pattern of growth was reported in 1991, 2001 and 2011.

**Table 2**

*Trends of Urban Females Educational Level in EUP, 1971–2001 (in %)*

| *Census Years* | *Below Primary* | *Primary* | *Middle* | *High School and Intermediate* | *Technical and N-Technical* | *Graduate and Above* |
|---|---|---|---|---|---|---|
| 1971 | 42.09 | 25.69 | 13.73 | 14.95 | 0.08 | 3.46 |
| 1981 | 34.10 | 27.16 | 14.09 | 18.24 | 0.09 | 6.32 |
| 1991 | 30.85 | 24.28 | 17.38 | 21.12 | 0.37 | 6.00 |
| 2001 | 22.87 | 23.57 | 16.53 | 25.78 | 0.14 | 11.11 |

*Source:* 1.Census of India, 1971, Series 21 Uttar Pradesh Part II C (ii) Social and Cultural Tables I, A, B, C II, C III A, B, C, IV, CV, CVI and F Series Tables.
2.Census of India 1981, Series 22, Uttar Pradesh Part IV A. Social and Cultural Tables.
3.Census of India 1991 Series 25, Uttar Pradesh Part-IV A-C Series Socio Cultural Tables Vol. 1, Ministry of Human Affairs, Govt. of India, UP Publications.
4.Census of India, 2001, Series 1, and Paper I and II, Part III, General Economic Tables, Series 22, Registrar General, New Delhi.

## Trends of Urban Female Educational Status, 1971–2001

Urban female population by educational level is presented in Table 2. In 1971, below primary education, it was 42.09 per cent, primary education was at 25.69 per cent, middle education at 13.73 per cent, high school and intermediate education at 14.95 per cent, technical and non-technical education at 0.08 per cent and graduate and above education at 3.46 per cent. In 1981, below primary education was 34.10 per cent, primary education was 27.16 per cent, middle education was 14.09 per cent, high school and intermediate education was 18.24 per cent, technical and non-technical education was 0.09 per cent and graduate above education was 6.32 per cent. In 1991, below primary education, it was 30.85 per cent, primary education was 24.28 per cent, middle education was 17.38 per cent, high school and intermediate education was 21.12 per cent, technical and non-technical education was 0.37 per cent and graduate and above education was 6 per cent. In 2001, below primary education was 22.87 per cent, primary education was 23.57 per cent, middle education was 16.53 per cent, high school and intermediate education was 25.78 per cent, technical and non-technical education was 0.14 per cent and graduate above education was 11.11 per cent.

## Urban Female Educational Status, 2001

### *Total Literacy Rate*

According to 2001 Census, female literacy rate varied from the highest in Allahabad district (63.09%) to lowest in Shrawasti district 38.29% with an average of 51. 71% in EUP. The seven districts of high female literacy rate in 2001 are Allahabad 63.09%, Sonbhadra 61.92%, Basti 60.16%, Sultanpur 59.75%, Gorakhpur 58.83%, Faizabad 56.75% and Gonda 55.47%. They form one region north-west to include Gorakhpur, Sonbhadra and Allahabad. The medium level of female literacy rate is observed in 12 districts of Pratapgarh (54.75%), Varanasi (53.99%), Chandauli (53.88%), Ambedkar Nagar (53.66%), Jaunpur (53.26%), Ghazipur (53.18%), Deoria (53.01%), Azamgarh (51.40%), Mau (49.67%), Mirzapur (49.59%), Ballia (49.23%) and Bahraich (48.98%). It is found one region to include Bahraich district. Districts with low levels of female literacy rate are Kushinagar (48.44%), Maharajganj (48.27%), Siddharthnagar (46.43%), Balrampur (44.93%), Sant Kabir Nagar (44.74%), Sant Ravidas Nagar (44.14%), Kaushambi (40.23%) and Shrawasti (38.29%). They form one region to north-west and north-east to include Allahabad and Sant Ravidas Nagar district.

As per 2001 Census, the district level analysis of female literates (without any educational level) of age 7-plus revealed a gain of 2.39 per cent points in Eastern Uttar Pradesh. Table 3 presents the districts which recorded the highest gain of 3.24 per cent point. The district-wise distribution of literate (without educational level) education is arranged into three categories: high, medium and low grades. The high percentages districts are Mau (4.76%), Allahabad (4.46%), Azamgarh (4.18%), Varanasi (3.87%), Ambedkar Nagar (3.72%), Balrampur (3.71%), Shrawasti (3.25%) and Sant Ravidas Nagar (3.25%). The districts of medium grade of female literacy (without educational level) are Siddharthnagar (3.23%), Jaunpur (3.17%), Ballia (3.11%), Bahraich (2.77%), Kaushambi (2.61%), Ghazipur (2.57%), Kushinagar (2.55%), Gonda (2.48%), Basti (2.43%) and Deoria (2.39%). There are nine districts in the low rate of literacy (without educational level): Mirzapur (2.16%), Pratapgarh (2.17%), Maharajganj (2.11%), Chandauli (2.01%), Sultanpur (1.93%), Gorakhpur (1.89%), Sant Kabir Nagar (1.54%), Faizabad (1.46%) and Sonbhadra (1.27%).

The Census of Uttar Pradesh, 2001, presented the percentage of female literates (below primary level) by districts. The percentage distribution of female literates (below primary level) has been arranged with the help of mean and standard deviation into three grades of high (23.67%), medium (19.89 to 23.67%) and low (below 19.89%). Table 3 shows that nine districts fall in high grade, namely Mau (29.37%), Siddharthnagar (27.24%), Sant Kabir Nagar

(27.08%), Sant Ravidas Nagar (26.74%), Kaushambi (25.66%), Azamgarh (25.43%), Shrawasti (25.19%), Ambedkar Nagar (24.97%) and Maharajganj (24.24%). The districts falling under medium grade of female literates (below primary level) are in Balrampur (22.74%), Kushinagar (22.52%), Jaunpur (21.69%), Ghazipur (21.60%), Mirzapur (21.45%), Chandauli (20.77%), Pratapgarh (20.57%) and Bahraich (20.03%). There are 10 districts in the low rate of literates (below primary level). They are Varanasi (19.83%), Deoria (19.57%), Sonbhadra (19.29%), Sultanpur (19.04%), Gonda (18.89%), Ballia (18.68%), Faizabad (18.60%), Gorakhpur (16.76%), Basti (16.21%) and Allahabad (13.90%).

### *Primary Education*

In respect with female's primary education in 2001, percentage has decreased to 0.71 per cent over the previous Census. The decrease was caused by the frequent changes in the definitions. However, the percentage distribution of primary education among the districts of Eastern Uttar Pradesh is uneven as the districtwise percentage distribution of primary education is arranged into three grades of 26.95 per cent and above (high), (medium 23.83 to 26.95%) and below 23.83 (low). The under high percentage districts are Ambedkar Nagar (32.97%), Sant Kabir Nagar (30.88%), Mau (29.55%), Shrawasti (29.54%), Sant Ravidas Nagar (28.83%) and Azamgarh (27.57%). They form an identifiable region in the central part of the study area to include Sant Ravidas Nagar and Shrawasti. Fourteen districts lie under medium rate of female primary education and they form three regions: north-east, south and include the Bahraich district of Eastern Uttar Pradesh (EUP). They are Pratapgarh (26.80%), Siddharthnagar (26.62%), Kaushambi (26.51%), Ghazipur (25.89%), Maharajganj (25.76%), Jaunpur (25.60%), Ballia (25.05%), Mirzapur (25.04%), Balrampur (24.66%), Sonbhadra (24.39%), Bahraich (24.37%), Kushinagar (24.22%), Sultanpur (24.18%) and Faizabad (23.97%). Under low level of females primary education they are Gonda (23.75%), Chandauli (23.61%), Varanasi (22.29%), Deoria (22.27%), Basti (21.21%), Gorakhpur (20.84%) and Allahabad (19.25%), in (Table 2b). They form three regions north-east, north-west and south-west to include Allahabad.

### *Middle Education*

The districts having high percentage are Chandauli (19.46%), Shrawasti (19.23%), Kaushambi (18.57%), Ballia (18.48%), Ghazipur (18.07%), Pratapgarh (18.04%), Deoria (17.88%), Maharajganj (17.86%), Sultanpur (17.75%) and Mirzapur (17.72%). They form two regions west and stretching to include Maharajganj and Shrawasti. Two identifiable regions south-west and one contigous to include Sonbhadra of relatively medium grade for Sonbhadra (17.59%), Kushinagar (17.45%), Jaunpur (17.35%), Faizabad (17.09%), Basti (16.94%), Balrampur (16.84%), Bahraich (16.81%), Gorakhpur (16.74%), Sant Kabir Nagar (16.57%), Sant Ravidas Nagar (16.49%) and Gonda (16.46%). The other region of the low grade comprises the districts of Siddharthnagar

(15.92%), Allahabad (15.69%), Varanasi (15.69%), Ambedkar Nagar (15.16%), Azamgarh (15.11%) and Mau (13.43%).

**Table 3**
*District-Wise distribution of Urban Females by Educational Status (in %) in EUP, 2001*

| Districts | Total Literacy Rate | Literate Without Education Level | Below Primary | Primary | Middle | High School and Intermediate | Technical and Non-Technical | Graduate and Above |
|---|---|---|---|---|---|---|---|---|
| Bahraich | 48.98 | 2.77 | 20.03 | 24.37 | 16.81 | 25.44 | 0.02 | 10.56 |
| Shrawasti | 38.29 | 3.25 | 25.18 | 29.54 | 19.23 | 18.80 | 0.00 | 3.93 |
| Gonda | 55.47 | 2.48 | 18.88 | 23.75 | 16.46 | 26.30 | 0.18 | 11.94 |
| Balrampur | 44.93 | 3.71 | 22.73 | 24.66 | 16.84 | 23.17 | 0.02 | 8.87 |
| Siddharthnagar | 46.43 | 3.23 | 27.24 | 26.62 | 15.92 | 20.94 | 0.05 | 5.94 |
| Basti | 60.16 | 2.43 | 16.22 | 21.21 | 16.94 | 29.47 | 0.08 | 13.67 |
| Sant Kabir Nagar | 44.74 | 1.54 | 27.08 | 30.88 | 16.57 | 19.07 | 0.02 | 4.84 |
| Maharajganj | 48.27 | 2.11 | 24.23 | 25.76 | 17.86 | 24.33 | 0.02 | 5.68 |
| Gorakhpur | 58.83 | 1.89 | 16.75 | 20.84 | 16.74 | 28.93 | 0.21 | 14.58 |
| Deoria | 53.01 | 2.39 | 19.59 | 22.27 | 17.88 | 28.77 | 0.03 | 9.07 |
| Kushinagar | 48.44 | 2.55 | 22.52 | 24.22 | 17.45 | 26.20 | 0.06 | 6.99 |
| Faizabad | 56.75 | 1.46 | 18.59 | 23.97 | 17.09 | 26.41 | 0.14 | 12.33 |
| Ambedkar Nagar | 53.66 | 3.72 | 24.97 | 32.97 | 15.16 | 17.38 | 0.13 | 5.66 |
| Sultanpur | 59.75 | 1.93 | 19.04 | 24.18 | 17.75 | 24.68 | 0.19 | 12.19 |
| Azamgarh | 51.40 | 4.18 | 25.43 | 27.57 | 15.11 | 20.16 | 0.07 | 7.41 |
| Mau | 49.67 | 4.76 | 29.37 | 29.55 | 13.43 | 17.27 | 0.84 | 4.73 |
| Ballia | 49.23 | 3.11 | 18.68 | 25.05 | 18.48 | 27.46 | 0.04 | 7.18 |
| Pratapgarh | 54.75 | 2.17 | 20.57 | 26.80 | 18.04 | 23.69 | 0.17 | 8.55 |
| Jaunpur | 53.26 | 3.17 | 21.69 | 25.60 | 17.35 | 23.52 | 0.04 | 8.62 |
| Ghazipur | 53.18 | 2.57 | 21.60 | 25.89 | 18.07 | 23.58 | 0.05 | 8.24 |
| Allahabad | 63.09 | 4.46 | 13.90 | 19.25 | 15.69 | 30.41 | 0.07 | 16.20 |
| Kaushambi | 40.23 | 2.61 | 25.66 | 26.51 | 18.57 | 22.60 | 0.12 | 3.91 |
| Varanasi | 53.99 | 3.87 | 19.83 | 22.29 | 15.69 | 25.60 | 0.12 | 12.60 |
| Chandauli | 53.88 | 2.01 | 20.77 | 23.61 | 19.46 | 26.18 | 0.09 | 7.87 |
| Sant Ravidas Nagar | 44.14 | 3.25 | 26.74 | 28.83 | 16.49 | 19.59 | 0.06 | 5.04 |
| Mirzapur | 49.59 | 2.16 | 21.45 | 25.04 | 17.72 | 24.48 | 0.14 | 8.99 |
| Sonbhadra | 61.92 | 1.27 | 19.29 | 24.39 | 17.59 | 26.32 | 0.21 | 10.92 |
| Eastern U.P. | 54.55 | 3.13 | 19.71 | 23.57 | 16.53 | 25.79 | 0.14 | 11.13 |

*Source:* Census of India, 2001, Series 1, and Paper I and II, Part III, General Economic Tables, Series 22, Registrar General, New Delhi.

### *High School and Intermediate Education*

The graded distribution of secondary (high school) and senior secondary (intermediate) level of education varies considerably across the districts from 17.27 per cent in Mau to 30.41 per cent in Allahabad. The district-wise distribution of high school and intermediate education is arranged into three categories of high, medium and low grades. The under high percentages districts are Allahabad (30.41%), Basti (29.47%), Gorakhpur (28.93%), Deoria (28.77%), Ballia

(27.46%), Faizabad (26.41%), Sonbhadra (26.32%), Gonda (26.30%), Kushinagar (26.20%) and Chandauli (26.18%). They form three regions north-west, north-east and south-east to include Allahabad. The under medium percentage districts are Varanasi (25.60%), Bahraich (25.44%), Sultanpur (24.68%), Mirzapur (24.48%), Maharajganj (24.33%), Pratapgarh (23.69%), Ghazipur (23.58%), Jaunpur (23.52%), Balrampur (23.17%) and Kaushambi (22.60%). They form continuous region to include Maharajganj, Bahraich and Balrampur. The overall distribution shows that low percentage districts are Siddharthnagar (20.94%), Azamgarh (20.16%), Sant Ravidas Nagar (19.59%), Sant Kabir Nagar (19.07%), Shrawasti (18.80%), Ambedkar Nagar (17.38%) and Mau (17.27%) is found stretching to include Sant Ravidas Nagar and Shrawasti districts.

### *Technical and Non-Technical Education*

The percentage share of female population is very small in technical and non-technical education and high percentage districts are Mau (0.84%), Gorakhpur (0.21%) and Sonbhadra (0.21%). They are found in one region of north-east to include Sonbhadra district. The under medium percentage districts of female technical and non-technical education are Sultanpur (0.19%), Gonda (0.18%), Pratapgarh (0.17%), Mirzapur (0.14%), Faizabad (0.14%), Ambedkar Nagar (0.13%), Kaushambi (0.12%), Varanasi (0.12%), Chandauli (0.09%), Basti (0.08%), Azamgarh (0.07%), Allahabad (0.07%), Kushinagar (0.06%), Sant Ravidas Nagar (0.06%), Siddharthnagar (0.05%), Ghazipur (0.05%), Jaunpur (0.04%) and Ballia (0.04%). They are a big continuous region. Six districts lie under low percentage of technical and non-technical education are Deoria (0.03%), Maharajganj (0.02%), Bahraich (0.02%), Sant Kabir Nagar (0.02%), Balrampur (0.02%) and Shrawasti (0.00%). It makes one region north-west to include Maharajganj, Deoria and Sant Kabir Nagar.

### *Graduate and Above Education*

Graduate education shows the districtwise distribution of females at graduate and above education. It varies from with a maximum of 16.20 per cent and minimum of 3.91 per cent in Kaushambi for the study region (Table 3). They are categorized into high, medium and low grades. The high percentages districts are Allahabad (16.20%), Gorakhpur (14.58%), Basti (13.67%), Varanasi (12.60%), Faizabad (12.33%), Sultanpur (12.19%), Gonda (11.94%), Sonbhadra (10.92%) and Bahraich (10.56%).They form one region north-west to include Sonbhadra, Varanasi, Allahabad and Gorakhpur. The districts in medium grade of graduate and above of female education are Deoria (9.07%), Mirzapur (8.99%), Balrampur (8.87%), Jaunpur (8.62%), Pratapgarh (8.55%), Ghazipur (8.24%), Chandauli (7.87%), Azamgarh (7.41%) and Ballia (7.18%). Nine districts lie under low percentage of female graduate and above education. These are Kushinagar (6.99%), Siddharthnagar (5.94%), Maharajganj (5.68%), Ambedkar Nagar (5.66%), Sant Ravidas Nagar (5.04%), Sant Kabir Nagar (4.84%), Mau (4.73%), Shrawasti (3.93%) and Kaushambi (3.91%). It makes one region to include Mau, Shrawasti, Sant Ravidas Nagar and Kaushambi.

## Relationship between Urban Female Educational Status and Other Selected Independent Variables

In the present investigation for causal analysis of the urban female educational status, a list has been prepared for 30 different independent variables (Table 4) that influence the educational status of urban female population in the 27 districts of the study area (EUP). In this regard, a correlation is computed as shown in Table 4, between urban female educational status and the independent variables and tested, with the assumption that linear relationships existed in all the cases (Siddiqui and Hannan, 2011).

The primary level of urban female education ($Y_1$) has direct negative relationship with number of student per teacher in senior basic school ($X_5$) and negative significant relationship with number of Industrial areas per lakh population ($X_{19}$) at 1 per cent significant level. Table shows that along with these two variables, numbers of industrial areas per lakh population also turn out to have a significant inverse relationship with primary education ($Y_1$) at 1 per cent significant level. This relationship suggests that urban areas generally have lower proportion of number of student per teacher in senior basic school in primary educational status and urban areas have higher percentage of female population educated up to higher education level. For middle education, variables have been found to be significantly positively and negatively related. They are junior basic school per lakh population ($X_1$), positively related at 5 per cent level, also percentage of rural population ($X_{21}$) positively correlated at 1 per cent level, percentage of female population in primary occupations ($X_{28}$), positively related at 1 per cent level and negatively correlated at 1 per cent level with percentage of urban population ($X_{22}$), female secondary worker ($X_{29}$) negatively correlation at 1 per cent level.

Significant association occurs between high school and intermediate levels of female education ($Y_3$), one independent variable is positively correlated at 1 per cent significance level with female tertiary occupation ($X_{30}$). Technical and non-technical education is positively correlated with female literacy rate ($X_9$) at 1 per cent level; female primary occupation ($X_{28}$) at 1 per cent level negative correlated and positively correlated with percentage of female secondary occupations ($X_{29}$) at 5 per cent level.

The variables which have positive correlation at 1 per cent level and well above the confidence limit, with the graduate and above education ($Y_5$) are $X_5$ (Number of studentsper teacher in senior basic schools), $X_{19}$ (Number of industrial area per lakh population), $X_{20}$ (Number of industrial Establishments per lakh population), $X_{22}$ (Percentage of urban population), $X_{30}$ (Percentage of female workers in tertiary occupations), Besides, one variable which are found to have negative correlations is $X_{21}$ (percentage of rural population) related with the graduate and above level of female education ($Y_5$) and are significant at 1 per cent level. This analysis leads to a broad conclusion that number of percentage of urban population, population density and female workers in primary, secondary and tertiary occupations are the chief variates which influence the percentage distribution of female graduate and above levels of female education in Eastern Uttar Pradesh.

## Table 4

*Results of Correlation (r) Between Urban Females Educational Status and Other Variables, in Eastern Uttar Pradesh, 2001*

| | *Independent Variables* | *Primary $Y_1$* | *Middle $Y_2$* | *High School and Intermediate $Y_3$* | *Technical and Non-Technical $Y_4$* | *Graduate and Above $Y_5$* |
|---|---|---|---|---|---|---|
| $X_1$ | Junior Basic Schools per 100, 000 Population | 0.024 | 0.526** | −0.014 | −0.061 | −0.164 |
| $X_2$ | Senior Basic Schools per 100, 000 Population | −0.116 | 0.344 | 0.123 | 0.113 | −0.007 |
| $X_3$ | Higher Secondary Schools per 100, 000 Population | −0.161 | −0.021 | 0.171 | 0.147 | 0.154 |
| $X_4$ | Number of Students per Teacher in Junior Basic School | −0.354 | 0.293 | 0.291 | −0.042 | 0.107 |
| $X_5$ | Number of Students per Teacher in Senior Basic School | −0.421* | −0.172 | 0.322 | 0.216 | 0.452* |
| $X_6$ | Number of Students per Teacher in Higher Secondary School | 0.133 | 0.118 | −0.123 | −0.137 | −0.088 |
| $X_7$ | Total Literacy Rate | −0.076 | −0.233 | 0.08 | 0.354 | 0.164 |
| $X_8$ | Male Literacy Rate | −0.132 | −0.204 | 0.143 | 0.303 | 0.186 |
| $X_9$ | Female Literacy Rate | −0.124 | −0.301 | 0.138 | 0.401* | 0.273 |
| $X_{10}$ | Difference in Literacy rates of Male and Female | 0.033 | 0.334 | 0.053 | −0.172 | −0.266 |
| $X_{11}$ | Number of Allopathic Hospitals/Dispensaries per 100, 000 Population | −0.141 | 0.273 | 0.121 | 0.031 | −0.16 |
| $X_{12}$ | Number of Beds in Allopathic Hospitals/Dispensaries per 100, 000 Population | −0.348 | −0.068 | 0.373 | 0.251 | 0.371 |
| $X_{13}$ | Number of Ayurvedic/Unani/Homeopathic Hospitals/Dispensaries per 100, 000 population | −0.077 | 0.181 | 0.18 | 0.14 | −0.053 |
| $X_{14}$ | Number of Beds in Ayurvedic/Unani/Homeopathic Hosptals/Dispensaries/100, 000 Population | −0.348 | −0.068 | 0.373 | 0.251 | 0.371 |
| $X_{15}$ | Number of Primary Healthcare Centres per 100, 000 Population | −0.253 | 0.189 | 0.366 | 0.229 | 0.2 |
| $X_{16}$ | Percentage of Net Sown Area to the Total Reported Area | 0.127 | −0.309 | −0.149 | −0.077 | −0.14 |
| $X_{17}$ | Intensity of Cropping | 0.331 | 0.03 | −0.204 | 0.002 | −0.261 |
| $X_{18}$ | Production of Foodgrains per Person (in kg) | 0.28 | 0.182 | −0.216 | −0.23 | −0.297 |
| $X_{19}$ | Number of Industrial Areas per 100, 000 Population | −0.398* | −0.201 | 0.345 | −0.055 | 0.442* |
| $X_{20}$ | Number of Industrial Establishments per 100, 000 Population | −0.289 | −0.01 | 0.291 | 0.13 | .415* |
| $X_{21}$ | Percentage of Rural Population | 0.364 | 0.402* | −0.248 | −0.314 | -.463* |
| $X_{22}$ | Percentage of Urban Population | −0.364 | −0.402* | 0.248 | 0.314 | .463* |
| $X_{23}$ | Percentage of Scheduled Caste and Scheduled Tribes to Total Population | 0.13 | 0.138 | −0.075 | 0.226 | −0.099 |
| $X_{24}$ | Percentage of Population Growth | 0.00 | 0.064 | −0.023 | 0.19 | −0.1 |

*Cont'd...*

*...Cont'd*

| | | | | | | |
|---|---|---|---|---|---|---|
| $X_{25}$ | Number of Student/Teracher Ratio at defferent Education Level | −0.052 | −0.032 | 0.051 | 0.045 | −0.146 |
| $X_{26}$ | Sex Ratio (Female per 1000 Males) | 0.088 | −0.05 | −0.073 | 0.242 | −0.252 |
| $X_{27}$ | Total Female Work Participation Rate | 0.187 | 0.102 | −0.227 | −0.042 | −0.268 |
| $X_{28}$ | Percentage of Female Population Workers in Primary Occupations | 0.087 | 0.400* | 0.033 | −0.458* | −0.181 |
| $X_{29}$ | Percentage of Female Population Workers in Secondary Occupations | 0.051 | −0.397* | −0.152 | 0.560** | 0.073 |
| $X_{30}$ | Percentage of Female Population Workers in Tertiary Occupations | −0.37 | −0.002 | 0.393* | 0.172 | 0.457* |

* Significant at 1 per cent level. ** Significant at 5 per cent level.

## Conclusion and Suggestions

Urban female population by educational level has been presented from 1971.The below primary education was 42.09 per cent; primary education was 25.69 per cent, middle education was 13.73 per cent, high school and intermediate education is 14.95 per cent, technical and non-technical education was 0.08 per cent and graduate and above education was 3.46 per cent. In 1981, below primary education was observed to be 34.10 per cent, primary education to 27.16 per cent, middle education was 14.09 per cent, high school and intermediate education was 18.24 per cent, technical and non-technical education 0.09 per cent and graduate above education was 6.32 per cent. In 1991 below primary education was investigated to be 30.85 per cent, primary education was 24.28 per cent, middle education was 17.38 per cent, high school and intermediate education was 21.12 per cent, technical and non-technical education was 0.37 per cent and graduate and above education was 6.00 per cent. In 2001, below primary education was observed to be 22.87 per cent, primary education was 23.57 per cent, middle education was 16.53 per cent, high school and intermediate education was 25.78 per cent, technical and non-technical education was 0.14 per cent and graduate above education was 11.11 per cent.

The regional patterns of female educational status are quite notable. In 2001 and with primary education tended to increase from central part of the region. In the central to north-east, low proportion of middle education, high school and intermediate education, technical and non-technical and graduate and above education is observed; but it tended to increase south-east, south-west, northern, southern part in EUP. The primary level of urban female education ($Y_1$) has direct negative relationship with number of students per teacher in senior basic school ($X_5$) and negative significant relationship with number of Industrial areas per lakh population ($X_{19}$) at 1 per cent significant level. The Table shows that along with these two variables, numbers of industrial areas per lakh population also turn out to have a significant inverse relationship with primary education ($Y_1$) at 1 per cent significant level. This relationship suggests that urban areas generally have lower proportion of number of student per teacher in senior basic school in primary educational status and urban areas have higher percentage of female population educated up to higher education level.

For middle education, variables have been found to be significantly positively and negatively correlated. They are junior basic schools per lakh population ($X_1$), positively related at 5 per cent significant level, also percentage of rural population ($X_{21}$), positively correlated at 1 per cent significant, percentage of female primary occupations ($X_{28}$), positively significant correlation at 1 per cent level and percentage of female secondary occupation ($X_{29}$) negatively correlation related at 1 per cent level, percentage of urban population negatively correlated at 1 per cent level.

Significant association occurs between high school and intermediate levels of female education ($Y_3$), one independent variable is positively correlated at 1 per cent significance level with female tertiary occupations. Technical and non-technical education is positively correlated with female literacy rate ($X_9$) at 1 per cent significant level, female primary occupation ($X_{28}$) at 1 per cent level negative correlated and percentage of female tertiary occupation ($X_{29}$) at 5 per cent level positively correlation.

The variables which have positive correlation at 5 per cent and 1 per cent level and well above the confidence limit, with the graduate and above education ($Y_5$) are $X_5$ (Number of studentsper teacher in senior basic schools), $X_{19}$ (Number of industrial areas per lakh population), $X_{20}$ (Number of industrial Establishments per lakh population), $X_{22}$ (Percentage of rural population), $X_{21}$ (Percentage of rural population), $X_{29}$ (Percentage of female in secondary occupations) they are positively correlated at 1 per cent significant level, Besides, one variables which are found to have negative correlations is $X_{21}$ (percentage of rural population) related with the graduate and above level of female education ($Y_5$) and are significant at 1 per cent level. This analysis leads to a broad conclusion that number of percentage of urban population, population density and females in primary, secondary and tertiary occupations are the chief variates which influence the percentage distribution of female graduate and above levels of female education in Eastern Uttar Pradesh.

- Special attention must be paid to the training of educational planners, administrators and heads of institutions and moreover more women should be incorporated in planning.
- Women's must be motivated to seek higher qualifications and skills and, on the other, facilities to be provided for them to do so.
- The poor infrastructure and social services will not get the benefit of trained and educated youth, unless disparities are reduced and determined measures are taken to promote diversification and dispersal on education opportunities.
- Educated women should be encouraged to form co-operative societies to be controlled and run exclusively by them.
- An important factor hindering the higher education of females is lack of colleges in or near by the city. Hence, steps should be taken to establish colleges to provide educational opportunities of females close to their residence.

- There is a need to specifically focus on increasing the educational status of female population. More schools for girls should be set up. A sincere effort needs to be done to enhance the overall educational status of female population in particular.
- Induction of female teachers in schools and provision for hostel facilities would go a long way in increasing the female educational institutes. Drop-out rates are also one of the pertinent problems affecting education system. There is a need to deal them seriously and intensively.

## References


Bano, S. (2005). 'Regional Dimensions of Female Education and Structure of Employment in Bihar'. Department of Geography, Aligarh Muslim University, Aligarh, Uttar Pradesh, India (Unpublished M.Phil. Dissertation).

Census of India (2011). Primary Census Abstract, Utter Pradesh, India: Directorate of Census Operation, Series 10, Government of India, New Delhi.

Chandna, R.C. (2009). 'Literacy in Punjab and Haryana-2001 Map Series-II'. *Punjab Geographer*, 5: 15–20.

Hannan, A. (2014). 'Spatial Dimensions of Female Educational Status and Work Participation Rate in Eastern Uttar Pradesh'. Department of Geography, Aligarh Muslim University, Aligarh, Uttar Pradesh, India (Unpublished Ph.D. Thesis).

Hannan, A. and F.A. Siddiqui (2012). 'Regional Trend and Pattern of Female Work Participation Rate in Eastern Uttar Pradesh'. *Indian Journal of Social Development*, 12(2): 246.

Kishore, Sunita (1994). 'Gender Differentials in Child Mortality: A Review of the Evidence', in Monica Dasgupta, T.N. Krishnan and Lincon Cheu's (eds) *Women's Health in India: Risk and Vulnerability,* New Delhi: Oxford University Press.

Krishnan, T.N. (1996). 'Health Poverty and Labour', in Indian Journal of Labour Economics, 39(1), Jan.-March.

Rao, N.J.U. (1985). *Female in a Developing Society*. New Delhi: Ashish Publishing House, p. 47.

Sharma, Dinesh (2003). 'Management of Education in India Need for a Fresh Look', *Yojana*, 47(2): 12–13.

Siddiqui, F.A. (2008). 'The Pattern of Educational Status in Western Uttar Pradesh (India) and its Linkages'. *Malaysian Journal of Tropical Geography*, 39(1 and 2): 13–24.

Siddiqui, F.A. and A. Hannan (2011). 'Trend and Pattern of Literacy Rate in Eastern Uttar Pradesh'. *The Geographer*, 58(1): 16–25.

Siddiqui, F.A. and K. Kaushik (2013). 'Primary Education Facilities and Attainment Interactions in Mathura District (U.P.), India'. *Asian Profile*, 41(6): 534.

Siddiqui, F.A. and S. Yadav (2010). 'Female Education and Fertility Differentials in Koil Tehsil, Aligarh: A Village Level Study'. *The Geographer*, 56(2): 7–13.

Siddiqui, F.A. et al. (2005). 'Dimension of Educational Development and its Correlation in Western Uttar Pradesh'. *Indian Journal of Regional Science*, 37(1).

Siddiqui, F.A., N. Hussain and A. Hannan (2011). 'Literacy and Work Participation among Muslims in Uttar Pradesh (India)'. *Journal of Geography and Regional Planning*, 4(6): 305–25.

Tilak, J.B.G. (1989). 'Education and its Relation to Economic Growth, Poverty and Income Distribution, *World Bank Comparative Studies, Research Paper No. 3,* The Wold Bank.

U.P. Development Report (2010). *Planning Commission Government of India*. Vol. 2, New Delhi.

# 15

# Gender Disparity in Literacy in India

## *Reflections from Census Data*

**HEMANT KUMAR VARSHNEY**

Education is a prerequisite for the development of a society. The importance of education in economic growth (Shultz, 1961) and human development (Sen, 1985) has been widely recognized by all sections of the society and in all types of economies. An essential feature of Human Resource Development (HRD) is to have equity in terms of accessibility to the facilities of education irrespective of sex, caste, region, etc. In fact, equity in education is not purely an educational issue as it cuts across the entire social and political fabric of a nation.

Literacy and education are reasonably good indicators of development in a society. Growth and diffusion of literacy is generally linked with culture, attitude, infrastructure facilities, level of urbanization and economic condition of parents. Being in the lower rungs of the socio-cultural and economic ladder, a negative relationship between female literacy and their population is expected. Literacy is an important component-both as an input and outcome of the development process. It plays a crucial role in the overall development of an individual enabling him/her to comprehend his/her social, political and cultural environment better and to respond to it in a better way.

Though literacy measures the most basic level of educational attainment in any society and may not have all the advantages of education, yet literacy rate is a fairly reliable indicator of educational development. The importance of literacy has well been recognized for the successful implementation of various social and economic programmes. As such, thrust on spread of literacy has been an important component in all development programmes since Independence. Adult literacy continued to receive special attention since 1978 when administrative and technical structures were established and voluntary agencies got involved in large numbers. The National Policy on Education (NPE, 1986) envisaged that adult education would be a means for reducing economic, social and gender disparities. As a result of these and other new policy thrusts, the literacy rates have improved gradually despite tremendous increase in population. There has been a monotonic increase of 7 to 8 percentage points in each of the decades.

Although the growth in educational facilities has been somewhat satisfactory, yet the rate of improvement in literacy has not been sufficient to reduce the disparity in male-female literacy. It is often argued that, despite planned and concentrated efforts, both gender and regional disparities could be seen as a part of wider regional imbalances that existed as a result of India's varied socio-cultural and historical past. In India, the education of girls has historically lagged behind that of boys (Agrawal and Aggarwal, 1994; Sengupta and Guha, 2002; Bandopadhyay and Subrahmaniam, 2010; Das and Mukherjee, 2008). Hussain (2010) found that, on an average, gender disparity is lower across educational levels in southern states and disparity decreases with the rise in socio-economic characteristics.

In the light of this, the paper aims to analyse the trends in gaps in male-female literacy rates (as obtained through Census of India, 1991, 2001 and 2011), both at national and state levels. It tries to focus on the level of literacy rather than educational attainment. In our population census, a person aged 7 years and above, who can read and write with understanding in any language is treated as a literate. Though gap in male-female literacy is perhaps the most popular method to describe gender disparity, a mere gender gap or absolute difference in literacy in percentages can be a misleading indicator, since it would be necessarily small when literacy rates are low (or high). The study of disparity indices avoids this problem. As a result, a number of equality/disparity indices have been suggested by scholars for the purpose of measuring the disparity.[1] Varshney (2002) used three different coefficient/indices, as suggested by Naik[2] (1971), Tilak[3] (1983) and Kundu and Rao[4] (1986), observed that though the values of indices differ, the relative ranking of the states in terms of gender disparity remains almost identical. Hence, in the present paper, state level disparity has been analysed by using the index of Tilak (1983), which is based on literacy rates for male, female and persons.

The paper is divided into four Sections. After introducing the subject matter in the first Section, the gender disparity in literacy at (a) all India level, and (b) at the state level has been analysed in Sections two and three respectively. In particular, the state-level analysis provides five distinct profiles, viz., (i) Literacy map of India; (ii) Decadal difference in literacy; (iii) Literacy Development Index; (iv) Gaps in male-female literacy; and (v) Analysis of disparity indices. Then the concluding observations follow in Section four.

## Gender Disparity at All India Level

India had a population[5] of 361.1 million, with a literacy rate of a mere 18.33 per cent at the time of Independence from colonial rule. Currently, as per the data of 2011 Census, its population was 1210.2 million with a literacy rate of 73 per cent. The most important contributor for the growth of literacy is the expansion of elementary education. The Compulsory Elementary Education Act under Right to Education (RTE) Act (2009), the 'District Primary Education Programme (DPEP) (1994) and the "Education for All" movement called 'Sarva Shiksha Abhiyan' (SSA) (2001) are instrumental for this progress.

The Census of India adopts a very liberal definition of literacy. As mentioned earlier, any persons aged 7 years and above, who can both read and write with understanding in any language is termed as literate. It is not necessary for a person to have received any formal education or passed any minimum educational standard for being treated as literate.

Table 1 provides an overview of progress of literacy rates by sex at all India level since 1951. It is observed that though significant improvement in literacy rates have been achieved during the last few decades, the literacy rate for the country as a whole in 2011 for persons, males and females is still 73.0 per cent, 80.9 per cent and 64.6 per cent respectively. Thus, about one-fourth of the total population and nearly one-third of the females in the country are still illiterate. During the last decade, it has recorded an increase of 8.2 percentage points – from 64.8 in 2001 to 73.0 in 2011. The increase in literacy rates of males and females during the same period are of the order of 5.6 and 10.9 percentages points, respectively. Thus, during 2001–2011, the growth in literacy rates for both male and female have been slowed down significantly as compared to the earlier decades. However, the improvement in literacy rates in the country are needed not only to be sustained but also requires a stimulus, particularly in the case of females.

**Table 1**

*Gender Disparity in Literacy in India (1951–2011)*

| *Year* | *Literacy Rates* | | | *Decadal Change* | | | *CAGR in Literacy Rates (%)* | | | *Gap in M/F Lit. Rate* | *Disparity Indices* | | |
|---|---|---|---|---|---|---|---|---|---|---|---|---|---|
| | *P* | *M* | *F* | *P* | *M* | *F* | *P* | *M* | *F* | | *D (N)* | *D (T)* | *D (KR)* |
| *1* | *2* | *3* | *4* | *5* | *6* | *7* | *8* | *9* | *10* | *11* | *12* | *13* | *14* |
| 1951 | 18.33 | 27.2 | 8.86 | | | | — | — | — | 18.3 | 67.38 | 99.84 | 53.02 |
| 1961 | 28.30 | 40.40 | 15.4 | 9.97 | 13.24 | 6.49 | 4.44 | 4.05 | 5.65 | 25.1 | 42.00 | 88.52 | 48.36 |
| 1971 | 34.45 | 46 | 22 | 6.15 | 5.56 | 6.62 | 1.99 | 1.3 | 3.65 | 24 | 52.20 | 69.81 | 38.34 |
| 1981 | 43.57 | 56.4 | 29.8 | 9.12 | 10.42 | 7.79 | 2.38 | 2.06 | 3.08 | 26.6 | 47.32 | 61.1 | 35.13 |
| 1991 | 52.21 | 64.1 | 39.3 | 8.64 | 7.75 | 9.53 | 1.82 | 1.3 | 2.82 | 24.8 | 38.73 | 47.58 | 28.57 |
| 2001 | 64.8 | 75.3 | 53.7 | 12.59 | 11.17 | 14.41 | 2.18 | 1.62 | 3.17 | 21.6 | 28.60 | 33.18 | 21.62 |
| 2011 | 73.0 | 80.9 | 64.6 | 8.20 | 5.60 | 10.90 | 1.20 | 0.72 | 1.87 | 16.3 | 20.14 | 22.33 | 15.34 |

*Note:* P = Persons; M = Male; F = Female.

D(N) = Disparity Index by Naik (1971)
D(T) = Disparity Index by Tilak (1983)
D(KR) = Disparity Index by Kundu and Rao (1986)

*Source:* (i) Census of India, 2001, Series I (India), Provisional Population Totals, Paper I of 2001
(ii) Primary Census Abstract (India), 2011.

The data provided in Table 1 reveal that, since Independence, female literacy improved at a faster rate than the male literacy. Though, initially the decadal difference in male literacy was higher than that of female literacy, it is the female literacy since 1981 that is increasing more. A comparison between male and female literacy shows that throughout the period, compounded annual growth rate (CAGR) in literacy among females is significantly higher than males. During 2001–11, the annual rate of growth in literacy rates for females is 1.87 per cent as against 0.72 per cent for males. This has resulted in considerable decline in the male-female gaps (Figure 1).

**Figure 1**
*Literacy Rates in India, 1951–2011*

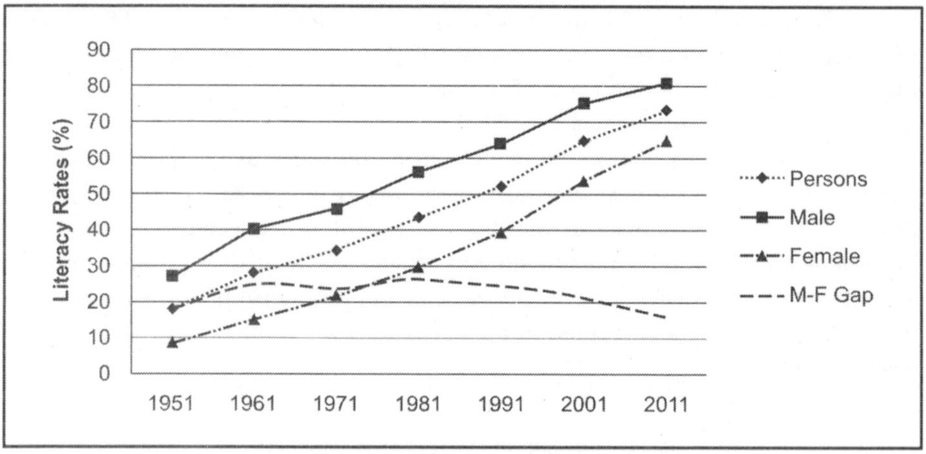


An analysis of gap in male-female literacy rates highlights that the gap which was 18.3 percentage points in 1951, increased to 26.6 in 1981. The increase in gap was more because of social and cultural ethos which gives more importance to males than females. However, due to attitudinal change and awareness generation programmes, the gap has been uniformly declining since 1981. After a marginal reduction in 1991, this gap reduced to 21.7 percentage points in 2001 and further to 16.3 percentage points in 2011.

The disparity indices, however, suggest that there has been a continuous decline in the gender disparity over the years. The decline is bound to be slow initially, as a result of the continuing past legacy of a large number of adult illiterate women.

Despite the disparity that exists between male and female literacy, the two themselves are highly correlated ($r = 0.98$), indicating a close spatial co-variation of the two rates, despite differences in absolute value levels. It is observed that a rise in the levels of literacy is accompanied by reduction in gender disparity, in general. The empirical evidence further supplements the result. The correlation between the literacy rates and disparity indices by Naik, Tilak and Kundu and Rao are respectively (-) 0.92, (-) 0.99 and (-) 0.99, which indicates that there exists a very high negative correlation between the two.

## Gender Disparity at State Level

### *Literacy Map of India*

A quick look at the literacy map of India shows wide variations in the literacy rates in different states/UTs of the country. Table 2 presents the state level data on literacy by sex for the last three Census years i.e. for 1991, 2001 and 2011. It is observed that though literacy rates improved for both the sexes over the period under study, everywhere male literacy is higher than female literacy. In 2011, 24 states/UTs were above the national average in literacy. Kerala, with literacy rate of 94 per cent, holds the first rank in the country, followed by Lakshadweep (91.8%) and Mizoram (91.3%). On the other hand, Bihar with a literacy rate of 61.8 per cent ranks last in the country preceded by Arunachal Pradesh (65.4%) and Rajasthan (66.1%).

**Table 2**

*Literacy Rates in India by States/UTs, 1991, 2001 and 2011*

| S. No. | States/UTs | 1991 | | | 2001 | | | 2011 | | |
|---|---|---|---|---|---|---|---|---|---|---|
| | | Persons | Males | Females | Persons | Males | Females | Persons | Males | Females |
| 1 | 2 | 3 | 4 | 5 | 6 | 7 | 8 | 9 | 10 | 11 |
| 1. | Andhra Pr. | 44.09 | 55.13 | 32.72 | 60.5 | 70.3 | 50.4 | 67.0 | 74.9 | 59.1 |
| 2. | Arunachal Pr. | 41.59 | 51.45 | 29.69 | 54.3 | 63.8 | 43.5 | 65.4 | 72.6 | 57.7 |
| 3. | Assam | 52.89 | 61.87 | 43.03 | 63.3 | 71.3 | 54.6 | 72.2 | 77.8 | 66.3 |
| 4. | Bihar | 37.49 | 51.37 | 21.99 | 47.0 | 59.7 | 33.1 | 61.8 | 71.2 | 51.5 |
| 5. | Chhattisgarh | 42.91 | 58.07 | 27.52 | 64.7 | 77.4 | 51.9 | 70.3 | 80.3 | 60.2 |
| 6. | Goa | 75.51 | 83.64 | 67.09 | 82.0 | 88.4 | 75.4 | 88.7 | 92.6 | 84.7 |
| 7. | Gujarat | 61.57 | 73.39 | 48.92 | 69.1 | 79.7 | 57.8 | 78.0 | 85.8 | 69.7 |
| 8. | Haryana | 55.85 | 69.10 | 40.47 | 67.9 | 78.5 | 55.7 | 75.6 | 84.1 | 65.9 |
| 9. | Himachal. Pr. | 63.94 | 75.41 | 52.26 | 76.5 | 85.3 | 67.4 | 82.8 | 89.5 | 75.9 |
| 10. | Jammu and Kashmir | N.A | NA | NA | 55.5 | 66.6 | 43.0 | 67.2 | 76.8 | 56.4 |
| 11. | Jharkhand | 41.39 | 55.80 | 25.52 | 53.6 | 67.3 | 38.9 | 66.4 | 76.8 | 55.4 |
| 12. | Karnataka | 56.04 | 67.26 | 44.34 | 66.6 | 76.1 | 56.9 | 75.4 | 82.5 | 68.1 |
| 13. | Kerala | 89.81 | 93.62 | 86.17 | 90.9 | 94.2 | 87.7 | 94.0 | 96.1 | 92.1 |
| 14. | Madhya Pr. | 44.67 | 58.54 | 29.35 | 63.7 | 76.1 | 50.3 | 69.3 | 78.7 | 59.2 |
| 15. | Maharashtra | 64.87 | 76.56 | 52.32 | 76.9 | 86.0 | 67.0 | 82.3 | 88.4 | 75.9 |
| 16. | Manipur | 59.89 | 71.63 | 47.60 | 70.5 | 80.3 | 60.5 | 79.2 | 86.1 | 72.4 |
| 17. | Meghalaya | 49.10 | 53.12 | 44.85 | 62.6 | 65.4 | 59.6 | 74.4 | 76.0 | 72.9 |
| 18. | Mizoram | 82.27 | 85.61 | 78.60 | 88.8 | 90.7 | 86.7 | 91.3 | 93.3 | 89.3 |
| 19. | Nagaland | 61.65 | 67.62 | 54.75 | 66.6 | 71.2 | 61.5 | 79.6 | 82.8 | 76.1 |
| 20. | Orissa | 49.09 | 63.09 | 34.68 | 63.1 | 75.3 | 50.5 | 72.9 | 81.6 | 64.0 |
| 21. | Punjab | 58.51 | 65.66 | 50.41 | 69.7 | 75.2 | 63.4 | 75.8 | 80.4 | 70.7 |
| 22. | Rajasthan | 38.55 | 54.99 | 20.44 | 60.4 | 75.7 | 43.9 | 66.1 | 79.2 | 52.1 |
| 23. | Sikkim | 56.94 | 65.70. | 46.76 | 68.8 | 76.0 | 60.4 | 81.4 | 86.6 | 75.6 |
| 24. | Tamil Nadu | 62.66 | 73.75 | 51.33 | 73.5 | 82.4 | 64.4 | 80.1 | 86.8 | 73.4 |

*Cont'd...*

*...Cont'd*

| | | | | | | | | | |
|---|---|---|---|---|---|---|---|---|---|
| 25. Tripura | 60.44 | 70.58 | 49.65 | 73.2 | 81.0 | 64.9 | 87.2 | 91.5 | 82.7 |
| 26. Uttar Pradesh | 40.71 | 54.82 | 24.37 | 56.3 | 68.8 | 42.2 | 67.7 | 77.3 | 57.2 |
| 27. Uttarakhand | 57.75 | 72.79 | 41.63 | 71.6 | 83.3 | 59.6 | 78.8 | 87.4 | 70.0 |
| 28. West Bengal | 57.70 | 67.81 | 46.56 | 68.6 | 77.0 | 59.6 | 76.3 | 81.7 | 70.5 |
| 29. A&N Island | 73.02 | 78.99 | 65.46 | 81.3 | 86.3 | 75.2 | 86.6 | 90.3 | 82.4 |
| 30. Chandigarh | 77.81 | 82.04 | 72.34 | 81.9 | 86.1 | 76.5 | 86.0 | 90.0 | 81.2 |
| 31. D&N Haveli | 40.71 | 53.56 | 26.98 | 57.6 | 71.2 | 40.2 | 76.2 | 85.2 | 64.3 |
| 32. Daman and Diu | 71.20 | 82.66 | 59.40 | 78.2 | 86.8 | 65.6 | 87.1 | 91.5 | 79.5 |
| 33. Delhi | 75.29 | 82.01 | 66.99 | 81.7 | 87.3 | 74.7 | 86.2 | 90.9 | 80.8 |
| 34. Lakshadweep | 81.78 | 90.18 | 72.89 | 86.7 | 92.5 | 80.5 | 91.8 | 95.6 | 87.9 |
| 35. Pondicherry | 74.74 | 83.68 | 65.63 | 81.2 | 88.6 | 73.9 | 85.8 | 91.3 | 80.7 |
| India | 52.21 | 64.13 | 39.29 | 64.8 | 75.3 | 53.7 | 73.0 | 80.9 | 64.6 |

*Source:* Same as in Table 1.

Barring a few exceptions, the status of states/UTs in relation to above/below national average – both for male and female literacy – has remained more or less the same in the two decades. A ranking of states, according to literacy levels, reveals that while there were 23 states above the national average in 1991 (no Census was held in Jammu and Kashmir in 1991), the number decreased to 22 in 2001 and increased to 23 in 2011. It is significant to note that Kerala, Mizoram and Lakshadweep, have managed to occupy the first three ranks since 1991.

In 1991, the number of states/UTs with less than 50 per cent literacy was 11 which reduced to one (Bihar 47%) in 2001 and by 2001, all states/UTs have achieved at least 50 per cent literacy. The number of states/UTs having 75 per cent or more literacy in 1991 was 7; this increased to 12 in 2001 and further to 22 in 2011.

All states/UTs had achieved more than 50 per cent male literacy by 1991. 14 states/UTs had more than 75 per cent male literacy in 1991; this increased to 25 in 2001 and in 2011, only three states, viz. Andhra Pradesh, Arunachal Pradesh and Bihar had male literacy less than 75 per cent.

In 1991, 15 states/UTs had less than 50 per cent female literacy; this number reduced to 7 in 2001 and in 2011, all states/UTs had achieved more than 50 per cent female literacy. While there were only two states with more than 75 per cent female literacy in 1991, the number increased to 6 in 2001 and to 14 in 2011.

### *Decadal Difference in Literacy*

Table 3 presents the decadal difference in the literacy rates over the period 1991–2001 and 2001–11. All the states/UTs without exception have shown increase in literacy rates during these periods; the rates being higher for females throughout the country. During 1991–2001, the literacy rates in India increased by 13.3 percentage points. The states/UTs where literacy increased by more than 15 percentage points during this period are Rajasthan (22.48),

**Table 3**

*Decadal Difference in Literacy Rates and Male-Female Gaps, 1991–2001 and 2001–11*

| S. No. | States/UTs | Decadal Difference in Literacy Rates | | | | | | Gap in M/F Literacy Rates | | |
|---|---|---|---|---|---|---|---|---|---|---|
| | | 1991–2001 | | | 2001–2011 | | | | | |
| | | P | M | F | P | M | F | 1991 | 2001 | 2011 |
| 1 | 2 | 3 | 4 | 5 | 6 | 7 | 8 | 9 | 10 | 11 |
| 1. | Andhra Pradesh | 17.02 | 15.72 | 18.45 | 6.50 | 4.60 | 8.70 | 22.41 | 19.68 | 15.8 |
| 2. | Arunachal Pradesh | 13.15 | 12.62 | 14.55 | 11.10 | 8.80 | 14.20 | 21.46 | 19.83 | 14.9 |
| 3. | Assam | 11.39 | 10.06 | 13.00 | 8.90 | 6.50 | 11.70 | 18.84 | 15.90 | 11.5 |
| 4. | Bihar | 10.04 | 8.95 | 11.58 | 14.80 | 11.50 | 18.40 | 29.38 | 26.75 | 19.7 |
| 5. | Chhattisgarh | 22.27 | 19.79 | 24.88 | 5.60 | 2.90 | 8.30 | 30.55 | 25.46 | 20.1 |
| 6. | Goa | 6.81 | 5.24 | 8.42 | 6.70 | 4.20 | 9.30 | 16.35 | 13.37 | 7.9 |
| 7. | Gujarat | 8.40 | 7.11 | 9.68 | 8.90 | 6.10 | 11.90 | 24.47 | 21.90 | 16.1 |
| 8. | Haryana | 12.74 | 10.15 | 15.84 | 7.70 | 5.60 | 10.20 | 28.63 | 22.94 | 18.2 |
| 9. | Himachal Pradesh | 13.19 | 10.61 | 15.82 | 6.30 | 4.20 | 8.50 | 23.15 | 17.94 | 13.6 |
| 10. | Jammu and Kashmir | N.A | NA | NA | 11.70 | 10.20 | 13.40 | NA | 23.93 | 20.4 |
| 11. | Jharkhand | 12.74 | 12.14 | 13.86 | 12.80 | 9.50 | 16.50 | 30.28 | 28.56 | 21.4 |
| 12. | Karnataka | 11.00 | 9.03 | 13.11 | 8.80 | 6.40 | 11.20 | 22.92 | 18.84 | 14.4 |
| 13. | Kerala | 1.11 | 0.58 | 1.69 | 3.10 | 1.90 | 4.40 | 7.45 | 6.34 | 4 |
| 14. | Madhya Pradesh | 19.44 | 18.26 | 20.93 | 5.60 | 2.60 | 8.90 | 29.19 | 26.52 | 19.5 |
| 15. | Maharashtra | 12.40 | 9.71 | 15.19 | 5.40 | 2.40 | 8.90 | 24.24 | 18.76 | 12.5 |
| 16. | Manipur | 8.98 | 6.24 | 12.10 | 8.70 | 5.80 | 11.90 | 24.03 | 18.17 | 13.7 |
| 17. | Meghalaya | 14.21 | 13.02 | 15.56 | 11.80 | 10.60 | 13.30 | 8.27 | 5.73 | 3.1 |
| 18. | Mizoram | 6.22 | 5.08 | 7.53 | 2.50 | 2.60 | 2.60 | 7.01 | 4.56 | 4 |
| 19. | Nagaland | 5.46 | 4.15 | 7.17 | 13.00 | 11.60 | 14.60 | 12.87 | 9.85 | 6.7 |
| 20. | Orissa | 14.52 | 12.86 | 16.29 | 9.80 | 6.30 | 13.50 | 28.41 | 24.98 | 17.6 |
| 21. | Punjab | 11.44 | 9.97 | 13.14 | 6.10 | 5.20 | 7.30 | 15.25 | 12.08 | 9.7 |
| 22. | Rajasthan | 22.48 | 21.47 | 23.90 | 5.70 | 3.50 | 8.20 | 34.55 | 32.12 | 27.1 |
| 23. | Sikkim | 12.74 | 11.03 | 14.70 | 12.60 | 10.60 | 15.20 | 18.94 | 15.27 | 11 |
| 24. | Tamilnadu | 10.81 | 8.58 | 13.22 | 6.60 | 4.40 | 9.00 | 22.42 | 17.78 | 13.4 |
| 25. | Tripura | 13.22 | 10.89 | 15.76 | 14.00 | 10.50 | 17.80 | 20.93 | 16.06 | 8.8 |
| 26. | Uttar Pradesh | 16.65 | 15.41 | 18.61 | 11.40 | 8.50 | 15.00 | 30.45 | 27.25 | 20.1 |
| 27. | Uttarakhand | 14.53 | 11.22 | 18.63 | 7.20 | 4.10 | 10.40 | 31.16 | 23.75 | 17.4 |
| 28. | West Bengal | 11.52 | 9.77 | 13.66 | 7.70 | 4.70 | 10.90 | 21.25 | 17.36 | 11.2 |
| 29. | A&N Island | 8.16 | 7.08 | 9.83 | 5.30 | 4.00 | 7.20 | 13.53 | 10.78 | 7.9 |
| 30. | Chandigarh | 3.95 | 3.61 | 4.13 | 4.10 | 3.90 | 4.70 | 9.70 | 9.00 | 8.8 |
| 31. | D&N Haveli | 19.32 | 19.76 | 16.01 | 18.60 | 14.00 | 24.10 | 26.58 | 30.33 | 20.9 |
| 32. | Daman and Diu | 9.89 | 5.74 | 10.97 | 8.90 | 4.70 | 13.90 | 23.26 | 18.03 | 12 |
| 33. | Delhi | 6.53 | 5.36 | 8.01 | 4.50 | 3.60 | 6.10 | 15.02 | 12.37 | 10.1 |
| 34. | Lakshadweep | 5.74 | 2.97 | 8.67 | 5.10 | 3.10 | 7.40 | 17.29 | 11.59 | 7.7 |
| 35. | Pondicherry | 6.75 | 5.21 | 8.50 | 4.60 | 2.70 | 6.80 | 18.05 | 14.76 | 10.6 |
| | India | 13.29 | 11.83 | 15.00 | 8.20 | 5.60 | 10.90 | 24.85 | 21.68 | 16.3 |

*Source:* Computed from Table 2.

Chhattisgarh (22.27), Madhya Pradesh (19.44), Dadra and Nagar Haveli (19.33), Andhra Pradesh (17.02) and Uttar Pradesh (16.55). Among the states/UTs, which had literacy rates below 50 per cent in 1991, Bihar has registered a minimum increase of 10.04 percentage points, moving from 37.49 per cent to 47.53 per cent and it was the only state where literacy rates was less than 50 per cent in 2001. During 2001–11, the literacy in India increased by 8.2 percentage points. The states/UTs with visible increment were Dadra and Nagar Haveli (18.6%), Bihar (14.8%), Tripura (14%), Nagaland (13%), and Jharkhand (12.8%).

During 1991–2001, male literacy in India increased by 11.8 percentage points. The highest visible improvement in male literacy during this period is for Rajasthan, where it has moved forward by 21.47 percentage points, followed by Chhattisgarh, Dadra and Nagar Haveli, Madhya Pradesh, Andhra Pradesh and Uttar Pradesh, which registered an improvement of 19.79, 19.76, 18.26, 15.72, and 15.40 percentage points, respectively. However, during the decade 2001–11, the male literacy increased by just 5.6 percentage points. States/UTs with more than 10 per cent increase in literacy rates during this period are Dadra and Nagar Haveli, Nagaland, Bihar, Meghalaya, Sikkim, Tripura and Jammu and Kashmir.

In the case of females, literacy rates at national level increased by 15 percentage points during 1991–2001 and by 10.9 percentage points during 2001–11. The States of Chhattisgarh, Rajasthan and Madhya Pradesh were among the top performers during 1991–2001 where female literacy increased by 24.9 per cent, 23.9 per cent and 20.9 per cent, respectively. During 2001–11, the outperforming states/UTs were Dadra and Nagar Haveli, Bihar, Tripura and Jharkhand where female literacy rates advanced by 24.1 per cent, 18.4 per cent, 17.8 per cent and 16.5 per cent respectively.

Thus, the states/UTs where both male and female literacy advanced by more than 15 per cent points during 1991–2001 were Rajasthan, Chhattisgarh, Dadra and Nagar Haveli, Madhya Pradesh, Andhra Pradesh and Uttar Pradesh. Both male and female literacy increased by more than 10 per cent points during 2001–11 in the states/UTs of Dadra and Nagar Haveli, Nagaland, Bihar, Meghalaya, Sikkim, Tripura and Jammu and Kashmir.

In the case of female literacy, Chhattisgarh occupies the first place, recording a creditable increase of 24.87 percentage points during 1991–2001, closely followed by Rajasthan with an upward movement of 23.90 per cent points. The other states/UTs reporting significant improvement in the female literacy are Madhya Pradesh (20.93), Uttarakhand (18.63), Uttar Pradesh (18.61), Orissa (16.29), and Dadra and Nagar Haveli (16.01). As in the case of males, and, for the same reasons, Kerala has shown the least increase in both male and female literacy rates, these being 0.58 per cent and 1.69 per cent respectively. The reason might be that the state has already reached the saturation point and had broad base-year figures. The female literacy rates increased at faster rate than male literacy rates in all the states/UTs except Dadra and Nagar Haveli during the decade under review.

From the above analysis, it appears that during the reference period, the states with low literacy rates like Bihar, Jharkhand, Rajasthan, etc. have performed well as compared to the states with high literacy rates like Kerala. However, the states like Bihar have not reached the level in 2011 that Kerala had achieved in 1991 and these states are still about 20 years behind the developed states. The reason for less decadal growth in states like Kerala is that after achieving a respectable level of literacy, these states are concentrating on other aspects of education like quality and universalization of education.

### *Literacy Development Index*

From the above analysis, a heterogeneous increase in literacy is being observed across the states in the country. As mentioned earlier, a simple difference in the literacy rates between a particular period of time does not include the development aspect and also if the simple method of measuring the growth rate, viz., $(R_1-R_0/R_0)*100$ is considered, some of the least developed states may even register high growth rate than the most of the developed states. In order to get rid of this problem of measurement, the UNDP methodology of Range Equalization (UNDP, 1990)[6] has been used to develop Literacy Development Index for the states/UTs and presented in Table 4. However, the ranking of states/UTs according to Literacy Development Index and literacy rates is just the same for the three points of time; meaning thereby that the relative literacy levels have not improved over time.

**Table 4**

*Literacy Development Index for 1991, 2001 and 2011*

| S. No. | State/UT | Persons | | | Male | | Female | | |
|---|---|---|---|---|---|---|---|---|---|
| | | 1991 | 2001 | 2011 | 2001 | 2011 | 1991 | 2001 | 2011 |
| 1. | A&N Island | 8 | 7 | 7 | 8 | 9 | 8 | 6 | 6 |
| 2. | Andhra Pradesh | 27 | 28 | 31 | 29 | 33 | 26 | 27 | 29 |
| 3. | Arunachal Pradesh | 29 | 33 | 34 | 34 | 34 | 27 | 30 | 30 |
| 4. | Assam | 23 | 25 | 26 | 26 | 28 | 22 | 24 | 23 |
| 5. | Bihar | 34 | 35 | 35 | 35 | 35 | 33 | 35 | 35 |
| 6. | Chandigarh | 4 | 5 | 9 | 9 | 10 | 4 | 4 | 7 |
| 7. | Chhattisgarh | 28 | 23 | 27 | 18 | 25 | 29 | 25 | 27 |
| 8. | D&N Haveli | 32 | 30 | 20 | 28 | 18 | 30 | 33 | 25 |
| 9. | Daman and Diu | 9 | 9 | 6 | 7 | 6 | 9 | 11 | 10 |
| 10. | Delhi | 6 | 6 | 8 | 6 | 8 | 6 | 7 | 8 |
| 11. | Goa | 5 | 4 | 4 | 5 | 4 | 5 | 5 | 4 |
| 12. | Gujarat | 14 | 17 | 18 | 16 | 17 | 16 | 21 | 21 |
| 13. | Haryana | 22 | 20 | 22 | 17 | 19 | 24 | 23 | 24 |
| 14. | Himachal Pradesh | 11 | 11 | 11 | 11 | 11 | 12 | 9 | 12 |
| 15. | Jammu and Kashmir | | 32 | 30 | 32 | 30 | | 31 | 32 |

*Cont'd...*

*...Cont'd*

| | | | | | | | | |
|---|---|---|---|---|---|---|---|---|
| 16. Jharkhand | 30 | 34 | 32 | 31 | 31 | 31 | 34 | 33 |
| 17. Karnataka | 21 | 21 | 23 | 20 | 21 | 21 | 22 | 22 |
| 18. Kerala | 1 | 1 | 1 | 1 | 1 | 1 | 1 | 1 |
| 19. Lakshadweep | 3 | 3 | 2 | 2 | 2 | 3 | 3 | 3 |
| 20. Madhya Pradesh | 26 | 24 | 28 | 21 | 27 | 28 | 28 | 28 |
| 21. Maharashtra | 10 | 10 | 12 | 10 | 12 | 11 | 10 | 13 |
| 22. Manipur | 16 | 15 | 16 | 15 | 16 | 17 | 16 | 17 |
| 23. Meghalaya | 24 | 27 | 24 | 33 | 32 | 20 | 18 | 16 |
| 24. Mizoram | 2 | 2 | 3 | 3 | 3 | 2 | 2 | 2 |
| 25. Nagaland | 13 | 22 | 15 | 27 | 20 | 10 | 15 | 11 |
| 26. Orissa | 25 | 26 | 25 | 24 | 23 | 25 | 26 | 26 |
| 27. Pondicherry | 7 | 8 | 10 | 4 | 7 | 7 | 8 | 9 |
| 28. Punjab | 17 | 16 | 21 | 25 | 24 | 14 | 14 | 18 |
| 29. Rajasthan | 33 | 29 | 33 | 23 | 26 | 34 | 29 | 34 |
| 30. Sikkim | 20 | 18 | 13 | 22 | 15 | 18 | 17 | 14 |
| 31. Tamil Nadu | 12 | 12 | 14 | 13 | 14 | 13 | 13 | 15 |
| 32. Tripura | 15 | 13 | 5 | 14 | 5 | 15 | 12 | 5 |
| 33. Uttar Pradesh | 31 | 31 | 29 | 30 | 29 | 32 | 32 | 31 |
| 34. Uttaranchal | 18 | 14 | 17 | 12 | 13 | 23 | 19 | 20 |
| 35. West Bengal | 19 | 19 | 19 | 19 | 22 | 19 | 20 | 19 |

*Source:* Computed from Table 2.

## Gap in Male-Female Literacy Rates

Most states in India, including Kerala, have more literate males than literate females, but the gap between male and female literacy varies widely across the country. The data highlight that the sates with low literacy rates show higher gap between male and female literacy rates.

The gaps in male-female literacy rates at three points of time, viz., at 1991, 2001 and 2011 have been provided in Table 2. It is significant to note that the gap in male-female literacy is inversely proportional to the literacy level of the state/UT. The minimum gap in male-female literacy rates in the country has been observed for Mizoram (4.56 percentage points), followed by Meghalaya (gap of 5.73 percentage points) and Kerala (gap of 6.34 percentage points). It is important that in the case of Meghalaya, although the combined literacy rate of the state is below the national average, the gap in male-female literacy rates is very small. On the other hand, Bihar, Jharkhand, Madhya Pradesh, Rajasthan, and Uttar Pradesh, where literacy level is on the lower side of the scale, have shown much higher gap in male-female literacy.

Out of the 13 states/UTs, whose literacy rates are below the current national average of 65.38 per cent, nine also occupy the first nine positions in the male-female gaps in literacy rates. Rajasthan, however, continues to occupy the unceremonious top position in male-female gap in literacy rates. The other eight states/UTs in this group are Dadra and Nagar Haveli (30.32), Jharkhand (28.57), Uttar Pradesh (27.25), Bihar (26.75), Madhya Pradesh (26.52), Chhattisgarh (25.46), Orissa (24.98) and Jammu and Kashmir (23.93).

### *Analysis of Disparity Indices*

As mentioned earlier, literacy is inversely related to disparity. Table 5 provides the gender disparity indices in literacy by states/UTs in 1991, 2001 and 2011. The Disparity Index at all India level has reduced by about 15 percentage points during 1991–2001 and further by more than 10 percentage points during 2001–11. It is observed that during 1991–2001, the states/UTs where disparity has been reduced by more than 20 percentage points are: Bihar, Chhattisgarh, Jharkhand, Madhya Pradesh, Rajasthan, Uttar Pradesh and Uttarakhand. The states of Chhattisgarh, Rajasthan and Uttar Pradesh have remarkably reduced the disparity by more than 25 percentage points. The states/UTs where disparity reduced by more than 10 percentage points during 2001–11 were: Andhra Pradesh, Bihar, Gujarat, Jammu and Kashmir, Jharkhand, Madhya Pradesh, Orissa, Tripura, Uttar Pradesh, Uttarakhand, West Bengal and Dadra and Nagar Haveli.

**Table 5**

*Tilak's Gender Disparity Index in Literacy Rates, 1991, 2001 and 2011*

| *S. No.* | *States/UTs* | *Disparity Index* | | |
|---|---|---|---|---|
| | | *1991* | *2001* | *2011* |
| *1* | *2* | *6* | *7* | *8* |
| 1. | Andhra Pradesh | 50.83 | 32.20 | 23.58 |
| 2. | Arunachal Pradesh | 52.32 | 36.23 | 22.78 |
| 3. | Assam | 35.62 | 24.74 | 15.93 |
| 4. | Bihar | 78.37 | 56.28 | 31.88 |
| 5. | Chhattisgarh | 71.20 | 39.06 | 28.59 |
| 6. | Goa | 21.92 | 16.24 | 8.91 |
| 7. | Gujarat | 39.74 | 31.30 | 20.64 |
| 8. | Haryana | 51.26 | 33.45 | 24.07 |
| 9. | Himachal Pradesh | 36.21 | 23.46 | 16.43 |
| 10. | Jammu and Kashmir | NA | 43.94 | 30.36 |
| 11. | Jharkhand | 73.16 | 52.76 | 32.23 |
| 12. | Karnataka | 40.90 | 28.10 | 19.10 |
| 13. | Kerala | 8.30 | 6.97 | 4.26 |
| 14. | Madhya Pradesh | 65.35 | 41.37 | 28.14 |
| 15. | Maharashtra | 37.37 | 24.28 | 15.19 |
| 16. | Manipur | 40.12 | 26.38 | 17.30 |
| 17. | Meghalaya | 16.84 | 9.05 | 4.17 |
| 18. | Mizoram | 8.52 | 5.15 | 4.38 |
| 19. | Nagaland | 20.88 | 14.68 | 8.42 |

*Cont'd...*

*...Cont'd*

| | | | |
|---|---|---|---|
| 20. Orissa | 57.87 | 39.27 | 24.14 |
| 21. Punjab | 26.06 | 17.27 | 12.80 |
| 22. Rajasthan | 89.62 | 52.63 | 41.00 |
| 23. Sikkim | 33.26 | 21.91 | 13.51 |
| 24. Tamil Nadu | 35.78 | 24.20 | 15.73 |
| 25. Tripura | 34.63 | 21.80 | 10.09 |
| 26. Uttar Pradesh | 74.80 | 47.51 | 29.69 |
| 27. Uttarakhandl | 53.96 | 32.86 | 22.08 |
| 28. West Bengal | 36.83 | 25.08 | 14.68 |
| 29. A&N Island | 18.53 | 13.28 | 9.12 |
| 30. Chandigarh | 12.47 | 11.01 | 10.23 |
| 31. D&N Haveli | 65.29 | 50.52 | 27.43 |
| 32. Daman and Diu | 32.67 | 22.23 | 13.78 |
| 33. Delhi | 19.95 | 15.12 | 11.72 |
| 34. Lakshadweep | 21.14 | 13.24 | 8.39 |
| 35. Pondicherry | 24.15 | 18.11 | 12.35 |
| India | 47.61 | 33.1 | 22.33 |

*Source:* Computed from Table 2.

From the above analysis, it is observed that by 2011, Andaman and Nicobar Islands, Lakshadweep, Goa, Kerala, Meghalaya, Mizoram, Nagaland and Tripura have achieved more than 90 per cent equality, while Maharashtra, Chandigarh, Daman and Diu and Delhi have achieved 85 per cent equality.

It is worth mentioning that with the spread of literacy, the disparity has come down, but, barring the states of Andhra Pradesh and Uttarakhand, the status of states in respect to above and below the national average remains almost identical as can be seen from Table 6.

It is clear that disparity is more where literacy level is low. This is in accordance with the earlier observation and we find that gender disparity is inversely correlated to literacy in a state. This fact appears to derive partial empirical validation by the values of correlation coefficients (being –0.83) observed between the literacy rates in states/UTs and the disparity index in 2011.

**Table 6**

*Disparity Levels by Tilak's Disparity Index, 1991, 2001 and 2011*

| *Level of Disparity* | *1991* | *2001* | *2011* |
|---|---|---|---|
| More than the National Average | Andhra Pradesh, Arunachal Pradesh, Bihar, Chhattisgarh, Haryana, Jharkhand, Madhya Pradesh, Orissa, Rajasthan, Uttar Pradesh, Uttarakhand, Dadra and Nagar Haveli | Arunachal Pradesh, Bihar, Chhattisgarh, Haryana, Jharkhand, Madhya Pradesh, Orissa, Rajasthan, Uttar Pradesh, Dadra and Nagar Haveli | Andhra Pradesh, Arunachal Pradesh, Bihar, Chhattisgarh, Haryana, Jammu and Kashmir, Jharkhand, Madhya Pradesh, Orissa, Rajasthan, Uttar Pradesh, Dadra and Nagar Haveli |

*Cont'd...*

*...Cont'd*

| | | | |
|---|---|---|---|
| *National Average* | | | |
| *D (T)* | *47.61* | *33.10* | *22.31* |
| Below National Average | Assam, Goa, Gujarat, Himachal Pradesh, Karnataka, Kerala, Maharashtra, Manipur, Meghalaya, Mizoram, Nagaland, Punjab, Sikkim, Tamil Nadu, Tripura, Wet Bengal, Andaman and Nicobar Islands, Chandigarh, Daman and Diu, Delhi, Lakshadweep, Pondicherry | Andhra Pradesh, Assam, Goa, Gujarat, Himachal Pradesh, Karnataka, Kerala, Maharashtra, Manipur, Meghalaya, Mizoram, Nagaland, Punjab, Sikkim, Tamil Nadu, Tripura, Uttarakhand, West Bengal, Andaman and Nicobar Islands, Chandigarh, Daman and Diu, Delhi, Lakshadweep, Pondicherry | Assam, Goa, Gujarat, Himachal Pradesh, Karnataka, Kerala, Maharashtra, Manipur, Meghalaya, Mizoram, Nagaland, Punjab, Sikkim, Tamil Nadu, Tripura, Uttarakhand, Wet Bengal, Andaman and Nicobar Islands, Chandigarh, Daman and Diu, Delhi, Lakshadweep, Pondicherry |

*Source:* Computed from Table 5.

## Conclusions

It is a matter of great concern that even with a liberal definition of literacy; India has 73 per cent literate population and only 64.6 per cent literate females. Historically, a variety of factors have been found to be responsible for poor female literacy rate, viz., gender based inequality, social discrimination and economic exploitation, occupation of girl child in domestic chores, low enrollment of girls in schools, low retention rate and high drop-out rate, etc. Programmes like National Literacy Mission, initiated in 1988, for imparting functional literacy has been instrumental for increasing female literacy in the country.

From the discussions in the preceding paragraphs, it is clear that there has been a significant improvement in the literacy levels of both males and females with latter having an edge, which helped in reducing the gap and disparity in male-female literacy. The fruits of this major achievement are bound to have positive bearing on our society. In this respect, performance of Chhattisgarh, Rajasthan and Madhya Pradesh during 1991–2001, and Dadra and Nagar Haveli, Bihar and Tripura during 2001–11, stand out for their remarkable progress in literacy rates. However, Literacy Development Index highlights that this development has not changed the relative ranks of the states/UTs on literacy map of India.

It is a matter of concern that despite noticeable improvement in female literacy, the states/UTs of Arunachal Pradesh, Bihar, Chhattisgarh, Haryana, Jammu and Kashmir, Jharkhand, Madhya Pradesh, Orissa, Rajasthan, Uttar Pradesh, Uttarakhand and Dadra and Nagar Haveli did not make any progress towards the reduction of gender disparity and, considering disparity index by Tilak as yardstick for comparison; these have continued to show more disparity than the national average. Bihar, Rajasthan and Jharkhand remain the three states with highest disparity. On the other hand, the states/UTs of Chandigarh, Tripura,

A&N Islands, Goa, Nagaland, Lakshadweep, Kerala, Meghalaya and Mizoram have achieved more than 90 per cent equality in terms of male-female literacy.

It seems that disparity in literacy is linked to the socio-cultural and economic background of the region. Most of the states/UTs with higher disparity are from the north India and are part of erstwhile BIMARU (Bihar, Madhya Pradesh, Rajasthan, Uttar Pradesh) states.

It tends to derive the fact that improvement in literacy contributed significantly in narrowing down the disparity. Also, the disparity is more in the states/UTs where literacy level is low i.e. gender disparity is inversely correlated to the literacy level. Hence, any programme aimed at removing disparity should focus its attention on literacy development missions.

It is observed that states/UTs with low literacy rates have, in general, achieved more decadal increase in literacy rates as compared to the states/UTs with higher literacy rates. This may be attributed to two factors: (i) government intervention in comparatively backward States/UTs, and (ii) states/UTs with higher literacy rates might be working on educational development and quality of education.

The analysis of data suggests that in the Indian society, the increase in male literacy is followed by increase in female literacy which results in decrease in gender disparity in literacy. Hence, to reduce gender disparity, a holistic approach needs to be adopted; focus on female alone may not result in desired results.

## Notes

1. A number of indices have been proposed by various researchers to define and describe the equality/disparity. While some of them relied on simple differential measure of the two rates (popularly known as gap in male-female literacy), others have used ratio of the two rates (ratio measure) and a combination of differential-ratio measure. Census of India frequently makes use of the male-female gap in literacy. Athreya and Chunkath (1996), Bose (1996) and Chanana (1996) have also used differential measure extensively in their studies on literacy. Datt (1996), Ram and Annamma (1997), Mehta (1996), Grover (1996) and D'Souza (1990) have preferred to use ratio measure in their studies on literacy. Tilak (1983) has chosen to use the differential-ratio measure. It is important to note that the first two are based on literacy rates of males and females only; the third one is based on literacy rates of males, females and total population.
2. Disparity Index by Naik (1971): If $R_1$ and $R_2$ represent the literacy rates for males and females respectively, then

   $D(N) = \{1-(R_2/R_1)\}*100$

   The index is zero when perfect equality, positive value indicates disparity against females and negative value indicates disparity against males.
3. Disparity Index by Tilak (1983): If $R_1$, $R_2$ and R represent the literacy rates for males, females and combined population, then

   $D(T) = \{(R_1-R_2)/R\}*100$

   The index is zero when perfect equality, positive value indicates disparity against females and negative value indicates disparity against males.

4. Disparity Index by Kundu and Rao (1986): If $R_1$ and $R_2$ represent the literacy rates for males and females respectively, then

   $D (KR) = \log (R_1/R_2) + \log \{(200-R_1)/(200-R_2)\}$

   The index is zero when perfect equality, positive value indicates disparity against females and negative value indicates disparity against males. This index is a modification to the index by Sopher (1974) by using 200 in place of 100.
5. The limitations of Census data for various Censuses are applicable.
6. Using Range Equalisation Methodology by UNDP, Literacy Development Index (LDI) = (Actual – Minimum)/(Maximum – Minimum)

## References


Agrawal, S.P. and J.C. Aggarwal (1994). *Third Historical Survey of Educational Development in India: Select Dimensions, 1990–92*. New Delhi: Concept Publishing Company.

Athreya, V.B. and S.R. Chunkath (1996). *Literacy and Empowerment*. New Delhi: Sage Publications.

Bandopadhyay, M. and R. Subrahmaniam (2010). 'Gender Equity in Education: A Study of Trends and Factors'. *Research Monograph No. 18*, National University of Educational Planning and Administration, New Delhi.

Bose, Ashish (1996). *India's Basic Demographic Statistics*. Delhi: B.R. Corporation.

Chanana, Karuna (1996). 'Gender Inequality in Primary Schooling in India: The Human Rights Prospective'. *Journal of Educational Planning and Administration*, 10(8): 361–81.

Das, S. and D. Mukherjee (2008). 'Role of Parental Education in Schooling and Child Labour Decision: Urban India in the Last Decade'. *Social Indicators Research*, 89(2): 305–22.

Datt, Ruddar (1996). 'Inequalities in Educational Development with Special Reference to Literacy Status and School Education'. *Journal of Educational Planning and Administration*, X(3).

Grover, R.P. (1996). *Education for All*. New Delhi: The Associate Publishers.

Hassan, R. and A. Mehta (2006). 'Under-representation of Disadvantaged Classes in Colleges: What Do the Data Tell Us?'. *Economic and Political Weekly*, XLI(35): 3791–96.

Hussain, Zakir (2010). 'Gender Disparities in Completing School Education in India: Analyzing Regional Variations', *Munich Personal RePEc Archive (MPRA)*, Paper No. 25748, posted on 11 October 2010, Online at http://mpra.ub.uni-muenchen.de /25748/

Kundu, A. and Jagan M. Rao (1986). 'Inequalities in Educational Development: Issues in Measurement, Changing Structure and its Socio-economic Correlates with Special Reference to India', in Moonis Raza (ed.), *Educational Planning: A Long Term Perspective*. New Delhi: NIEPA.

Mehta, A.C. (1996). *Education for All in India: Myth and Reality*, New Delhi: Krishna Publishers.

Ministry of Human Resource Development (1986). National Policy on Education (NPE), Government of India.

——. (1994). District Primary Education Programme, Government of India.

——. (2001). Sarva Shiksha Abhiyan, Government of India.

——. (2009). Right to Education (RTE) Act, Government of India.

Naik, J.P. (1971). 'Education of the SCs and STs in 1965–66'. *Occasional Monograph Nos. 5–6*, ICSSR, New Delhi.

Raza, Moonis and Yash Aggarwal (1984). 'Higher Education in India: The Regional Dimensions'. *NIEPA Occasional Paper No. 7*, NIEPA, New Delhi.

Registrar General of India (2001). Census of India, Series–1 (India), Provisional Population Totals, Paper 1 of 2001, New Delhi.

——. (2011). Census of India, Primary Census Abstract (India), New Delhi.

Sen, A. (1985). *Commodities and Capabilities*, Oxford: Oxford University Press.

Sengupta, P. and J. Guha (2002). 'Enrolment, Dropout and Grade Completion of Girl Children in West Bengal'. *Economic and Political Weekly*, 37(17): 1621–37.

Shultz, T.W. (1961). 'Investment in Human Capital'. *The American Economic Review*, 51(1): 1–17.

Sopher, D.E. (1974). 'A Measure of Disparity'. *The Professional Geographer*, 26(4): 389–92.

Tilak, J.B.G. (1983). 'Inequality in Education by Sex in India'. *Indian Journal of Industrial Relations*, 18(3): 375–95.

United National Development Programme (1990). Technical Note: 1.

Varshney, Hemant Kumar (2002). Inter-state Gender Disparity in Literacy Rates: A Look at Census Data (1991 and 2001). *Journal of Educational Planning and Administration*, XVI(4), 537–49.

# 16

# Benefit Incidence Analysis of Public Spending on Education in India

**ANUNEETA MITRA**

Education as the pivotal factor of development had moved to prominence in the 1960s with the pioneering studies of T.W. Schultz and G.S. Becker. However, the germination of this idea dates back to the times of Adam Smith and the early classical economists. Consequently, not only public expenditure but subsidy too emerged as an important instrument of investment.

The rationale for providing subsidy is established on the grounds of equity and efficiency. Governments are often required to subsidize services that the market will not provide – or provides insufficiently. Pure public goods, where the marginal cost of additional consumptionis zero, usually call for full State-financing. Typically, the market would under-provide suchgoods, and a government subsidy would be justified on the grounds of efficiency (Demery, 2000). Subsidies might also be justified because of failures in related markets, such as subsidies on Education arising from credit-market failure. Left to themselves, markets would under-provide such services, resulting in sub-optimal resource allocations. Governments are, therefore, called upon to subsidize some services for reasons of efficiency. But equity is another fundamentalrationale for government subsidies. The fact that the poor are disadvantaged in gaining access to important services which would help them escape poverty suggests that the State should seek to target the provision of these services to such groups. This paper makes an attempt to outline an approach to assess whether the poor actually benefit from State-subsidies on services where equity concerns are paramount.

Benefit Incidence Analysis (BIA) is a tool used to assess how government-subsidy affects the distribution of welfare in the population. In other words, BIA evaluates the distribution of government-subsidies among different groups in the population. BIA is centred on assessing whether or not public spending is progressive – that is, whether or not it improves the distribution of welfare, proxied by household income or expenditure (Manasan, Cuenca and Ruiz, 2008).

This tool named BIA, thus, stands capable of addressing a long-standing concern in Economics, which is – how to measure the benefits of publicly-provided goods to individuals in society. For market-based goods and services, the prices paid by individual consumers can be taken as reflecting underlying values, so that combining prices and quantities yields measures of welfare that can be compared across individuals and over time. But unlike market-based goods, it is difficult to use prices as the basis for valuing publicly-provided goods. First, many such goods and services are pure public goods, which can be considered as freely-provided goods benefiting communities as a whole. But even when government-spending subsidizes the provision of private goods (such as health and educational services, and many infrastructure-services), their supply is usually rationed, so that it is no longer valid to use the price paid (if any) as a measure of the underlying value of the good in question to the individual consumer. Most of the recent literature has been concerned with this fundamental problem (van de Walle and Nead, 1995). The 'benefit incidence' approach, also called the classic or the non-behavioural approach, was pioneered by twin World Bank studies by Selowsky (1979) for Colombia and Meerman (1979) for Malaysia. The main goal of Benefit Incidence Analysis is to identify as to who benefits from public spending and by how much.

This paper is divided into four Sections. Section one talks about the previous researches; Section two focuses on the methodology adopted; Section three engages in discussing and analysing the benefit-incidence of public subsidy received by the various income groups across the various levels of education (the difference across various states in terms of benefits received bythe various income groups also being looked into); and Section four concludes the paper even as it throwslight on policy implications.

## Benefit Incidence Analysis: Related Literature

Literature has it that earlier, the distributional aspect of public-spending on education could be measured by using estimation techniques, which stem from the work of Aaron and McGuire (1970) who had set out the basic principles to be followed in assessing how public expenditures benefit individuals. They argued that a rationed, publicly-provided good or service should be evaluated at the individual's own valuation of the good (his or her demand). Such prices would vary from individual to individual. But the difficulties inherent in estimating these valuations (reviewed in de Wulf, 1975 and also by Cornes, 1995) led to less demanding approaches, in which publicly-provided goods and services are valued at the marginal cost (Brennan, 1976). Since then, the (welfarist) literature has been characterized by two broad approaches. The first emphasizes the need to measure individual preferences for the goods in question, based on refinements of the Aaron and McGuire methodology. These analyses are well-founded in micro-economic theory, but are data-demanding, requiring, for example, knowledge of the underlying demand-functions of individuals or households. The second approach is that of Benefit Incidence Analysis, which combines the cost of providing public services with information on their use in order to generate distributions of the benefit of government-spending. This has become an established approach in developing countries since the path-breaking work by Meerman (1979) on Malaysia and Selowsky (1979) on Colombia.

To some extent, the most interesting part of benefit-incidence is what happens within the lowest 30 per cent of the income-distribution, especially to the bottom 10 or 20 per cent of the households, as these results shed light on benefit-incidence in the poorest households (Seldon and Wasylenko, 1992).

Jallade (1974) and Selowsky (1979) looked into the distribution of public expenditure in education in Columbia and found that re-distribution was progressive only at the primary-level of education. With respect to methodology, Jallade divided quintile based on household income – which was criticized and improved upon by Selowsky by making the divisions based on household per-capita income.

Meerman's (1979) benefit-analysis based on Malaysia revealed that the total benefits based on use of services have a pro-rich distribution, but less so than the benefits assigned in proportion to income. Other specific expenditures are assigned to households in proportion to their income. The study has normalized total benefits or divided total benefit per household by a constant (average household income). Thus, the distribution of benefits is on a total basis rather than as a percentage of income. Meerman finds that out-of-pocket costs, such as uniforms, shoes, lunch, transportation, books and supplies, amount to 13 per cent of household income in the first Income Quintile and 11 per cent of household income in the second Income Quintile. Meerman also examines the benefits across races within Malaysia.

Dasgupta and Tilak (1983) came out with an empirical study to assess the pattern of distribution, by Quintile Income Groups, of education at the Elementary, Secondary and Higher Education levels in West Godavari District, Andhra Pradesh, India, in 1977–78. The purpose was to see if the distribution of education is egalitarian in nature. Household income and household per-capita income has been used to divide Quintile Income Groups. The results show that Primary Education is clearly equitable, Secondary Education is fairly equitable and Higher Education is amonotonically increasing function of income. While the pattern is more or less the same in rural and urban areas, there exist striking rural-urban disparities at every quintile and at every level ofeducation, i.e. the educational and enrollment rates are higher in urban areas than in rural areas. Further, there seems relatively less unequal distribution of educational facilities in urban areasas compared to rural areas. Public financing of Education on the whole was found to be egalitarian. In this study, it has been pointed out that quintile-division based on household per-capita income is a better measure as compared to division based on household-income, as the former reflects the standard of living.

The World Bank (1986), in its study, used Lorenz curves to study the Cumulative Public Educational Expenditure appropriated by various socio-economic groups across seven different regions, namely, Anglophone Africa, Francophone Africa, Asia, Latin America, the Middle East and Africa, the Developing Countries and the Developed Countries. It was seen that the most egalitarian distribution was in the developed countries; in Asia it was seen that 34 per cent of educational expenditure is appropriated by rural workers, 38 per cent by manual workers and 28 per cent by white-collared workers.

Manasan, Cuenca and Ruiz (2008) had conducted a study of Benefit-Incidence of Public Spendingon Education in Philippines. Using the household income, the population was divided into deciles. The study assesses the targetting of government subsidies with reference to the graphical representation of the distribution of benefits, i.e. the Concentration Curve or the Benefit Concentration Curve. Suits Index has also been used to determine progressivity/regressivity of public-spending at the various levels. Total government spending on Education is found to be progressive in absolute terms as indicated by the negative sign of the Suits Index. However, while government spending on Elementary and Secondary Education in 1998 is progressive in absolute terms (with the Suits Index being negative in both cases), government spending on college education and TVET is regressive in absolute terms (with theSuits Index being positive in both cases).

Lopez-Acevedo and Salinas (2000) showcased the results of benefit incidence of public spending across various deciles (based on householdincome), by levels of education and by various regions (i.e. North, South and Central). Education subsidies by levels of schooling for 1994 and 1996 have also been compared. This comparison revealed that the subsidy at the primary level had increased from 1994 through 1996. Such increment was slightly higher for the bottom-income deciles as compared to the top deciles. In contrast, subsidies decreased from 1994 to 1996 for the lower secondary level. Such reduction had a higher impact on deciles 6 through 9. For the upper secondary education level, per capita subsidies decreased on an average by 200,000 thousand pesos for students in deciles 7 through 9. Finally, the tertiary level also experienced a reduction of approximately 1,000,000 thousand pesos in decile 9. However, it was seen that across different school categories, public spending on education per capita had become more egalitarian. Some of the most interesting results are: (i) at the national level, the poorest income groups receive the bulk of primary education subsidy (federal plus State expenditures), while at higher-levels of education they receive progressively smaller subsidies. (ii) The government's pattern of educational expenditure changes across regions. That is, in the northern region, primary education is near the equality line and regressive forother levels of instruction. In the central region, primary schooling lies above the equality line while lower secondary is very close to it. Upper secondary and tertiary instruction benefits the richest income deciles. In the southern region, basic education is very progressive, upper secondary is at the equality line and the Tertiary Education level lies below the 45-degree line. In Mexico City, the cumulative distribution at all levels of education, except for primary, is far below the 45-degree line. An important observation made in the study is that enrollment rates for the educational levels beyond primary and probable lower secondary levels decrease dramatically, particularly for the extremely poor, thus resulting in an increase in the educational gap between the poor and the non-poor. Given that coverage at the primary level and the first years of lower secondary is already sizable and that demographic pressure is decreasing, the population of this group is virtually stagnated and will start to shrink at the beginning of the next century. This in turn frees some public resources, which can eventually be used to increase coverage at the upper secondary level.

Meesook (1984), using the 1978 National Socio-Economic Survey, estimated the government subsidies per student in Indonesia. This was eventually applied to the estimated numbers of public students to obtain the shares of government subsidies going to different household groups. It was concluded that the present distribution of government subsidies in education was skewed toward the rich, especially in urban areas, because the rich are more likely to use the highers levels of service where the subsidies per student are greater. According to the study, 51 per cent of the subsidy goes to the poorest, 40 per cent, 27 per cent to the middle 30 per cent and 22 per cent to the upper 30 per cent in the level of primary education. Conversely, for the University level, 83 per cent went to the upper 30 per cent and 7 per cent to the poorest 40 per cent.

Demery (2000) has said that for the calculation of unit-subsidy, which is the first step in the process of calculating Benefit Incidence Analysis, the recent practice has been to confine the analysis to recurrent spending, thus avoiding the difficulties encountered in estimating the flow of services/benefits from capital expenditures. But when capital budgets are large, they can have a profound effect on the benefit-incidence of public spending. It is important for the analyst to keep in mind that unit-subsidies are flow variables, being defined for a finite time-period, usually an year. The flow of services from capital spending should be defined for the same period.

Alderman, Behrman, Khan, Ross, and Sabot et al. (1991) adopted a behavioural approach to measure the benefits of public education with household and school level data for rural Pakistan in the year 1989. Benefits from schooling-investments were measured in terms of incremental gains in lifetime earnings. Other benefits accruing to the students, to members of their households, or to society as a whole were not taken into account. The chapter's main findings are that the rates of return to primary-level schooling investments are generally high across all groups and that targeting disadvantaged groups does not entail a significant trade-off in terms of efficiency. The study does not specifically calculate the willingness to pay for various levels of schooling in terms of quantity and quality, but it does provide information on what households should rationally be willing to pay at a minimum, assuming that parents are perfectly informed and altruistic. Alderman and others have had access to an unusually detailed data-set. In practice, data-constraints still often prevent such a data-intensive methodology.

Sabir (2003), in his paper, tried to evaluate the effectiveness of government education spending in Pakistan to the poor people using Benefit Incidence Analysis. Major findings are that government subsidies directed towards primary education are pro-poor in all the four provinces of Pakistan. However, government subsidies directed towards higher education favour the ones who are better off. Improving targetting to the poor involves not only re-arranging the subsidy, but also addressing the constraints that prevent the poor from accessing these services.

Canagarajah and Ye (2001) in their paper analyse the equity and efficiency of public spending on education in Ghana. Given the regional disparity in public-resource distribution, the purpose of the study is to evaluate how public-education spending benefits the poor compared to the non-poor. The Benefit Incidence Analysis for public expenditures in 1998 shows the share of subsidies captured by population-groups of different income-levels and locations, compared with 1989 and 1992 data. Between 1992 and 1998, the benefit incidence of public primary school subsidies for the poor population (bottom two quintiles) had either declined or stabilized, but for the richest quintile, it has increased. At the higher education level, the encouraging trend is that the share of secondary and tertiary education subsidies for the poorest of the poor (lowestquintile) has been increasing, although they are under-subsidised as compared to other income groups.

Peter Lanjouw et al., (2001) assessed Benefit Incidence Analysis (BIA) on education spending in Indonesia using the 1998 Census data. The study found that public spending on Primary Education was pro-poor; benefits of spending on junior secondary school accrued to the middle consumption quintile; for senior secondary education, benefits were distributed regressively. It was observed that the total transfer to the richest quintile was more than triple that to households in the poorest quintile.

Davoodi, Tiongson and Asawanuchit (2003) did cross-country BIA on education spending, covering 56 nations from 1960–2000. The study made the following findings: (i) overall spending on Education was on average pro-rich; (ii) spending on primary education was on average pro-poor and progressive; and (iii) spending on secondary and tertiary Education primarily benefits the non-poor, with a strong evidence of middle-class capture.

Post studying the above relevant literature, the gaps that emerged are that with respect to the Indian context, very few empirical evidences of Benefit Incidence Analysis on a state-wise basis are available. Thus the present study has, by using the NSSO 64th Round data, made a modest attempt to measure the Benefit Incidence of public subsidy received by various income-groups across the various levels of education. An attempt has also been made to see the difference across various states in terms of benefits received by the various income groups.

## Methodology and Database

The research is empirical, based on secondary data sources. Benefit Incidence Analysis will be estimated by using data from the National Sample Survey Organization (NSSO) database '*Participation and Expenditure in Education*' (unit-level records) for the 64th Round pertaining to the year 2007–08.

### Major Variables Used for Analysis

*Total Expenditure:* Total Expenditure (Revenue Account) has been used from Analysis of Budgeted Expenditure. The actual figures have been used, which have been converted into the 2004–2005 constant price.

*Enrollment:* Enrollment figures for the purpose of calculating per-capita growth rate have been taken from the selected Educational Statistics of various years from 1990–91 to 2009–10. Enrollment figures for Benefit Incidence Analysis (BIA) have been taken from NSS 64th Round. Enrollment figures for the same cover government, local bodies and public-aided institutes.

1. *Elementary Level Enrollment:* This consists of enrollment figures from Classes 1 to 8.
2. *Secondary-level Enrollment:* This consists of enrollment figures from Classes 9 to 12.
3. *Higher-level Enrollment:* In the present study, Higher Education implies any Graduation, Post-Graduation courses and courses above these levels which come under general (not technical) education and Degree and Diploma Course at the level of Graduation/Post Graduation.

*Family Income:* Since the NSS data does not provide figures on family income, Monthly Per-Capita Consumption Expenditure (MPCE)[1] has been used as a proxy for income. MPCE has been used for five equal quintile divisions with Quintile One being the lowest.

*Scholarship:* This has been computed by adding 'Annual Amount Waived' Item 17 and 'AnnualAmount Received' Stipend, Item 20 of Block 5, Schedule 25.2 of NSS 64th Round.

*Cost Recovery:* This variable has been computed by adding the following variables: 'tuition fee'; 'examination fee' and 'other fees and payments'. These variables are given in Block 6, Item 3, 4 and 5, Schedule 25.2 of NSS 64th Round.

*Subsidy:* Total Expenditure – Cost Recovery

Suits Index/Concentration Co-efficient-

Area of $A[1/N\sum_{i=1}^{N-1} ci + 1/NCn], Cn = 1$ ..................... (1)

Suits Index = 2A ..................... (2)

Where N is the number of equal divisions (quintile), Cn is the cumulative frequency of subsidydistribution quintile-wise.

### Steps Involved in Calculation of Benefit Incidence Analysis

*Step 1:* Total Expenditure (Revenue Account), actual 2007–08 figures have been taken from Analysis of Budgeted Expenditure. From this, 'Scholarships' (Revenue Account) of the three levels of education have respectively been deducted.

*Step 2:* Total Expenditure, net, of scholarship from Analysis of Budgeted Expenditure has been divided by total enrollment state-wise to get per capita total expenditure values, which have been assumed to remain constant across all quintile groups.

*Step 3:* To the above obtained per capita expenditure, scholarship/stipend and cost recovery figures computed from NSS quintile-wise have been adjusted for to arrive at the quintile-wise subsidy (Table in the Appendix Section).

*Step 4:* Based on a welfare-indicator such as household expenditure expressed in per capita terms, households have been arranged from the poorest to the richest. They are then aggregated into sub-groups (quintiles) to get an idea whether public spending is well targetted to the poorest portions of the population. The grouping has been done across households. For example, dividing total monthly expenditure by household-size, we first compute MPCE (Monthly Per CapitaConsumption Expenditure). Now, this newly computed variable i.e. MPCE is used for makingquintile divisions by dividing into five equal groups. Where quintile 1 is >390, Quintile 2=390–500,Quintile 3=500–609, Quintile 4=609–801, Quintile 5=<801 (all figures in ₹).

*Step 5:* Distribution of benefits by multiplying the average benefit calculated previously by the number of users of the service in each income or consumption group.

The last four steps can now be illustrated by some simple algebra as applied to the case ofeducation-spending. Total benefits from government spending on 'all' education (i.e. thecombined elementary, secondary and higher spending) accrued to group *j* is estimated as

$$\sum_{i=1}^{3} E_{ij} \frac{S_{ij}}{E_i} \qquad (3) \text{ Where j=1, 2,3,4,5}$$

Where *Xj* is the benefit incidence in local currency accrued to income or consumption group *j*from (net) government-spending on level *i* (Elementary, Secondary, or Higher Education) for corresponding consumption Group j denoted as *Sij* i.e. it measures the subsidy for a particular Quintile Group for a particular level of education, also measured in local currency; *Eij* represents number of students enrolled in Level *i* from Group *j* where each group is a quintile; and $Si\, j/E_t$ is the unit cost of providing education at Level i. Groups are typically ordered from lowest to highest with respect to the classifying variable. If desired, the groups in the middle of the distribution can be aggregated to define a 'middle class'.

$$x_j = \sum_{i=1}^{3} \left(\frac{E_{ij}}{E_i}\right) \times \left(\frac{S_{ij}}{S_i}\right) = \sum_{i=1}^{3} e_{ij}\, s_{ij} \qquad (4) \text{ where j=1,2,3,4,5}$$

By dividing both sides of expression (3) by total (net) government education spending, S, one obtains the share of benefits accrued to Quintile *j* from total government-spending on Education:

Where $x_j$ = Xj/S; eij is the jth quintile share of total students enrolled at Primary, Secondary and Tertiarylevel; $s_i j$ is the share of government subsidy for a given level in the total spending on education.

## Benefit Incidence Analysis: Measuring the Distribution of Subsidy

This Section makes an attempt to focus on the disaggregation of the distribution of subsidy state-wise, with an all-India figure, across the three levels of education (elementary, secondary, higher), over the five quintile groups. By combining the subsidy to the public education system quintile-wise (given in the Appendix

Table) with the educational attainment available by MPCE Quintile[2], we can roughly arrive at the benefit estimates of government spending on education. The results of this exercise as per education-levels are presented in Table 1.

**Table 1**

*Percentage of Subsidy Received by MPCE Class at Various Educational Levels*

| *States/MPCE Class* | *Elementary* | *Secondary* | *Higher* |
|---|---|---|---|
| *Andhra Pradesh* | | | |
| Quintile 1 | 33.21% | 10.06% | 2.14% |
| Quintile 2 | 33.11% | 33.65% | 8.66% |
| Quintile 3 | 26.66% | 37.47% | 17.55% |
| Quintile 4 | 6.81% | 13.12% | 33.43% |
| Quintile 5 | 0.22% | 5.70% | 38.21% |
| *Assam* | | | |
| Quintile 1 | 21.15% | 1.13% | 0.39% |
| Quintile 2 | 25.02% | 17.81% | 6.98% |
| Quintile 3 | 32.12% | 29.84% | 20.39% |
| Quintile 4 | 17.97% | 34.42% | 40.85% |
| Quintile 5 | 3.74% | 16.81% | 31.40% |
| *Bihar* | | | |
| Quintile 1 | 49.47% | 23.39% | 0.30% |
| Quintile 2 | 39.21% | 36.10% | 6.57% |
| Quintile 3 | 9.82% | 28.43% | 36.74% |
| Quintile 4 | 1.46% | 8.04% | 19.43% |
| Quintile 5 | 0.04% | 4.05% | 36.95% |
| *Gujarat* | | | |
| Quintile 1 | 15.26% | 2.24% | 0.23% |
| Quintile 2 | 33.21% | 10.83% | 0.39% |
| Quintile 3 | 25.17% | 13.31% | 1.67% |
| Quintile 4 | 21.47% | 30.92% | 10.46% |
| Quintile 5 | 4.89% | 42.69% | 87.25% |
| *Haryana* | | | |
| Quintile 1 | 17.13% | 1.41% | 0.28% |
| Quintile 2 | 31.76% | 10.12% | 1.19% |
| Quintile 3 | 33.40% | 31.17% | 0.64% |
| Quintile 4 | 14.88% | 25.66% | 14.73% |
| Quintile 5 | 2.83% | 31.64% | 83.15% |
| *Karnataka* | | | |
| Quintile 1 | 41.26% | 19.49% | 7.16% |
| Quintile 2 | 34.11% | 24.96% | 6.74% |
| Quintile 3 | 14.89% | 21.24% | 10.32% |
| Quintile 4 | 8.81% | 24.73% | 33.94% |
| Quintile 5 | 0.94% | 9.58% | 41.84% |

*Cont'd...*

...Cont'd

| | | | |
|---|---|---|---|
| *Kerala* | | | |
| Quintile 1 | 7.25% | 1.32% | 0.05% |
| Quintile 2 | 17.45% | 3.00% | 4.34% |
| Quintile 3 | 29.03% | 24.04% | 1.16% |
| Quintile 4 | 29.41% | 31.13% | 23.25% |
| Quintile 5 | 16.86% | 40.51% | 71.20% |
| *Madhya Pradesh* | | | |
| Quintile 1 | 76.67% | 48.85% | 4.63% |
| Quintile 2 | 14.77% | 21.72% | 3.23% |
| Quintile 3 | 7.09% | 15.86% | 12.50% |
| Quintile 4 | 1.39% | 10.41% | 14.00% |
| Quintile 5 | 0.08% | 3.16% | 65.65% |
| *Maharashtra* | | | |
| Quintile 1 | 34.11% | 11.23% | 1.20% |
| Quintile 2 | 27.99% | 19.26% | 3.71% |
| Quintile 3 | 17.93% | 17.27% | 5.76% |
| Quintile 4 | 14.09% | 29.16% | 44.81% |
| Quintile 5 | 5.88% | 23.08% | 44.51% |
| *Orissa* | | | |
| Quintile 1 | 85.07% | 50.43% | 7.09% |
| Quintile 2 | 9.77% | 26.88% | 15.75% |
| Quintile 3 | 4.72% | 19.48% | 36.74% |
| Quintile 4 | 0.37% | 1.99% | 9.84% |
| Quintile 5 | 0.08% | 1.22% | 30.58% |
| *Punjab* | | | |
| Quintile 1 | 15.19% | 0.83% | 0.64% |
| Quintile 2 | 22.82% | 3.63% | 0.30% |
| Quintile 3 | 34.18% | 8.92% | 6.22% |
| Quintile 4 | 26.57% | 31.38% | 32.20% |
| Quintile 5 | 1.23% | 55.24% | 60.65% |
| *Rajasthan* | | | |
| Quintile 1 | 29.61% | 5.91% | 0.09% |
| Quintile 2 | 40.83% | 24.46% | 20.41% |
| Quintile 3 | 21.44% | 27.32% | 12.36% |
| Quintile 4 | 7.41% | 27.74% | 35.25% |
| Quintile 5 | 0.72% | 14.57% | 31.88% |
| *Tamil Nadu* | | | |
| Quintile 1 | 9.25% | 2.93% | 0.51% |
| Quintile 2 | 31.34% | 15.87% | 1.45% |
| Quintile 3 | 37.68% | 29.14% | 9.45% |
| Quintile 4 | 19.72% | 36.60% | 50.13% |
| Quintile 5 | 2.00% | 15.47% | 38.46% |

*Cont'd...*

...*Cont'd*

| | | | |
|---|---|---|---|
| *Uttar Pradesh* | | | |
| Quintile 1 | 53.29% | 22.07% | 7.44% |
| Quintile 2 | 32.08% | 30.18% | 17.22% |
| Quintile 3 | 12.95% | 29.78% | 30.59% |
| Quintile 4 | 1.66% | 13.88% | 17.50% |
| Quintile 5 | 0.02% | 4.09% | 27.26% |
| *West Bengal* | | | |
| Quintile 1 | 55.62% | 12.19% | 1.28% |
| Quintile 2 | 23.41% | 21.86% | 2.99% |
| Quintile 3 | 14.86% | 24.21% | 9.13% |
| Quintile 4 | 5.33% | 23.91% | 32.78% |
| Quintile 5 | 0.78% | 17.84% | 53.81% |
| *All India* | | | |
| Quintile 1 | 41% | 11% | 1% |
| Quintile 2 | 29% | 18% | 3% |
| Quintile 3 | 18% | 22% | 9% |
| Quintile 4 | 9% | 27% | 22% |
| Quintile 5 | 2% | 22% | 65% |

*Source:* Author's Self-Computation from NSSO 64th Round Unit-level Data.

Table 1 gives information of the inter-state disparities and an all-India estimation of percentage distribution of public subsidy by various quintile groups for the three levels of education. Distribution of public subsidy for elementary-level of education is pro-poor at the all-India level and across the States. At the all-India level, it is seen that 41 per cent of the benefits are distributed in favour of the poorest quintile and 2 per cent in favour of the richest quintile.

However, it is seen that in the state of Kerala, the distribution of subsidy for elementary level is almost equally divided among the various quintile groups. This fact throws positive light on the quality of public elementary schools as children from the higher-income groups are also sent to schools which are run by the government. The participation with respect to enrollment in Kerala across all five quintile groups is spread out almost uniformly which can be seen from the quintile-wise enrollment table given in the Appendix. In all the remaining 14 states, the distribution of subsidy for the elementary level is highly skewed in favour of quintile group–1 vis-à-vis the richestquintile. This revelation throws light on the fact that the rich lack confidence in the quality of public institutions and prefer private schools instead. The finding is consistent with the Sujatha and Geetha 2011 study where the lack of preference by the higher-income families to send their children to government schools has been found dominant. Thus, it can be seen that the distribution of subsidy at the Elementary-level is pro-poor i.e. it is progressive in nature.

On assessing the distribution of subsidy at the secondary level of education in a similar manner, it is seen that on an all-India level, 11 per cent of the subsidy distribution accrues to quintile 1 and 22 per cent to quintile 5. In the states of

Maharashtra and West Bengal, the distribution of subsidy has been more or less equal among all quintile groups. In Orissa, Bihar and Madhya Pradesh the distribution of subsidy is progressive with higher levels of subsidy accruing to the lower income groups. This can be seen from the Table on distribution of subsidy (quintile-wise) in the Appendix Section. The even distribution of enrollments across the quintile groups may imply that the quality of secondary government schools in these states is good and, above everything, the subsidy distribution encourages enrollment from the lower income quintiles.

But it is clear from Table 1 that in the states of Assam, Gujarat, Karnataka, Haryana, Kerala, Punjab and Rajasthan the distribution of subsidy has been skewed in favour of quintile 5, revealing less participation captured by enrollment from the lower quintile groups – which arises as a disturbing fact. The above finding with respect to Gujarat is consistent with the findings of Shah and Agarwal, 2008 which stated that despite relatively adequate funding in Gujarat, the intermediate level of schooling has performed poorly, the weakest link identified having been the failure to vocationalize secondary education, which has culminated in drop-outs, especially from the lower-income groups.

An interesting aspect that surfaced is that the states of Kerala and Punjab, despite disbursing high levels of subsidy, have low enrollments from lower quintile groups (Mitra, 2013). Zachariah et al., (2008) cited the declining birth rate in Kerala as a reason for its drop in enrollment. The study also pointed out the declining proportion of revenue expenditure on education as a percentage of the state's total budget and the State Domestic Product. In the case of Punjab, since its cost-recovery rate is relatively high as compared to other states, this may be cited as one of the problems discouraging enrollment from the poorer sections. Gill et al., (2008), in their study mentioned that despite having higher per capita income as compared to the rest of the country, Punjab is yet to translate it into high human development. Both Punjab and Haryana, despite being prosperous agriculturally, have not allocated a high share of resources towards education, even during the 1990s (Sujatha and Rani, 2011). These reasons together may be held responsible for the above-mentioned scenario inthe respective States.

On looking at the distribution of subsidy for the higher level of education, it is seen that at the all India level, the distribution of subsidy is regressive, with 1 per cent of subsidy-benefits accruing to the poorest and 65 per cent to the richest quintile group. Glaring inequalities in subsidy distribution are seen in the state of Gujarat with 87 per cent of the benefits accruing to quintile 5 and 0.23 per cent accruing to quintile 1. Inching close is the state of Haryana, with 83 per cent subsidies benefitting quintile 5 and 0.28 per cent benefitting quintile 1. It is seen that in the states of Karnataka, Orissa and Uttar Pradesh the distribution is relatively less unequal. Like in the case of Orissa where 7 per cent of the benefits accrue to quintile 1 and 31 per cent to quintile 5. A striking commonality that one can draw in the case of Orissa, and it being well-positioned with respect to relatively equal distribution of subsidy amongthe quintile groups both at the secondary and higher level of Education, is its low level of cost-recovery which is least both in the case of Secondary as well as Higher Education (Mitra, 2013).

Another way of assessing the distribution of government subsidies across the various quintile groups is graphically, by using Concentration Curves. A Concentration Curve is generated by plotting the Cumulative Distribution of Frequency of Benefits of Public Spending on the y axis against the Cumulative Distribution of Population sorted by MPCE on the x axis. The progressivity and regressivity of the subsidy distribution can be inferred by comparing the 45 degree line of perfect equality with the Concentration Curve. If the Concentration Curve lies above the 45 degree line, it would imply a progressive distribution, indicating that the poorest 20 per cent of the population receives more than 20 per cent of the subsidy, and similarly a Concentration Curve below the 45 degree line would imply a regressive distribution which would mean that the poorest 20 per cent ofpopulation is receiving less than 20 per cent of the subsidy. Suits-Index or Concentration-coefficient is a summary measure of Benefit Incidence; if the Suits-Index is positive, it implies regressive distribution of benefits. Conversely, if it is negative, it implies that distribution is progressive. It should also be emphasized that Suits-Index is sensitive only to the relative magnitude of subsidies across quintile groups and not to the absolute amounts.

**Figure 1**

*Concentration Curves of India*

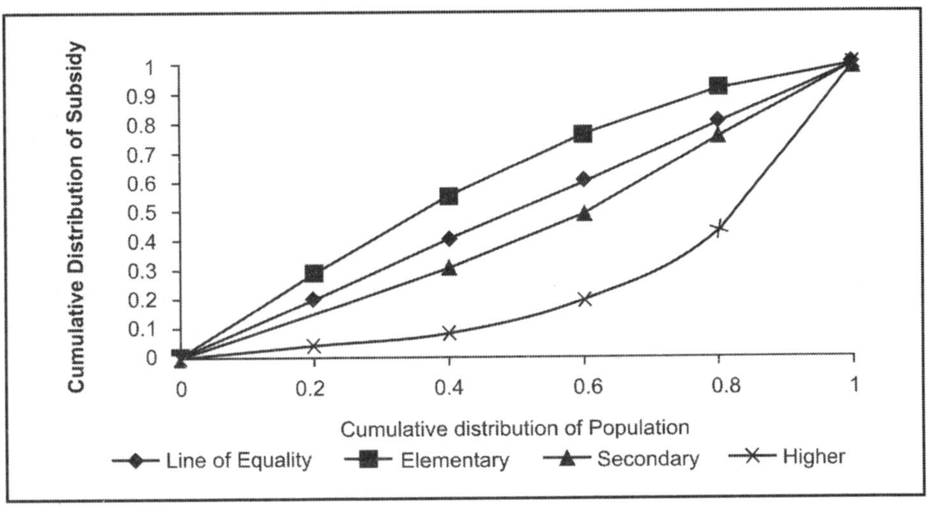


*Source:* Self-computation by the author, based on Table 1.

In Figure 1, Concentration Curves above the line of equality imply progressive subsidy-distribution and below the line of equality reveals that the subsidy-distribution is regressive. Thus on the basis of this explanation, subsidy-distribution for elementary and secondary levels are progressive, and regressive for higher levels of education on an all-India level. Table 2 gives the summary measure of Concentration Curve – both state-wise and at an all-India level.

**Table 2**
*Suits Index*

| | *Elementary* | *Secondary* | *Higher* |
|---|---|---|---|
| Andhra Pradesh | -0.57 | -0.32 | 0.19 |
| Assam | -0.37 | -0.01 | 0.18 |
| Bihar | -0.75 | -0.47 | 0.14 |
| Gujarat | -0.33 | 0.20 | 0.54 |
| Haryana | -0.38 | 0.10 | 0.52 |
| Karnataka | -0.62 | -0.28 | 0.19 |
| Kerala | -0.08 | 0.23 | 0.44 |
| Madhya Pradesh | -0.87 | -0.61 | 0.33 |
| Maharashtra | -0.48 | -0.07 | 0.31 |
| Orissa | -0.92 | -0.69 | -0.04 |
| Punjab | -0.30 | 0.35 | 0.41 |
| Rajasthan | -0.56 | -0.12 | 0.11 |
| Tamil Nadu | -0.30 | -0.02 | 0.30 |
| Uttar Pradesh | -0.75 | -0.41 | -0.04 |
| West Bengal | -0.71 | -0.15 | 0.34 |
| All India | -0.20 | 0.23 | 0.53 |

*Source:* Self-computation by the author, based on the formula given in Equations 1 and 2.

As can be seen from Table 2, it becomes clear that in the case of elementary level of education for an all-India basis, the distribution of subsidy is progressive - with a negative Suits-Index. All the 15 states also reflect a progressive distribution of subsidy, as can be seen from the negative sign. For the secondary level, the all India figure with a positive Suits-Index implies a regressive distribution of subsidy. A state-wise assessment for the same reveals a progressive distribution in the states of West Bengal, Uttar Pradesh, Tamil Nadu, Rajasthan, Orissa, Maharashtra, Madhya Pradesh, Karnataka, Bihar, Assam, Andhra Pradesh - and for the remaining states, it is regressive. For the higher level of education, the distribution of subsidy is regressive if we see the all India level with a positive Suits-Index. However, a state-wise analysis reveals that in all states except in the states of Orissa and Uttar Pradesh, the distribution of subsidy benefits remains progressive. This finding is in sync with the study by Muzammil (2008) which mentioned that education in Uttar Pradesh is highly subsidized by the government, which is because of the special programmes for different categories of people, which gives rise to enhanced expenditure by the government. The study points out that Uttar Pradesh has the largest Higher Education Sector in the country.

## Conclusion and Policy Implications

Assessing the distribution of subsidy across the three levels of education, State-wise and over quintile groups, it is seen that the distribution is pro-poor at the elementary level. It is seen that in the states of Gujarat, Haryana, Kerala the distribution of subsidy is not skewed towards the poorer sections unlike in the other states but rather equally distributed across all the quintile groups, implying faith in the quality of public elementary schools. In the case of the secondary level, the distribution was quite varied, with the distribution being skewed in favour of the richest quintile in Assam, Gujarat, Haryana, Kerala and Punjab. In Orissa, the distribution was pro-poor and it was also seen that the cost-recovery for the secondary level of education was the least. The distribution of subsidy for the higher level of education is pro-rich, with high levels of inequality seen in the state of Gujarat, followed by Haryana. Relatively equal distribution has been seen in the state of Orissa which has a relatively low cost recovery. From the Suits-Index it becomes clear that on an all India level the distribution of subsidy is progressive only for the elementary level of education and regressive for both secondary and higher levels. However, a state-wise assessment shows that the distribution of subsidy is progressive for the elementary level across all the states, regressive in the states of Punjab, Gujarat, Kerala and Karnataka for the secondary level and for the higher level, the distribution was progressive only in the states of Orissa and Uttar Pradesh.

With information gathered from the above Section, it comes across clearly that though subsidy is regressive at the higher levels of education, this should not serve as the premise to reduce subsidy at this level; the reason for the same being lack of participation from the poorer quintile groups which will dwindle further if the subsidy levels get squeezed. Public funding in higher education should be encouraged rather than being replaced by private funding to ensure increased enrollment from the lower income groups. Moreover, alternative strategies like differentiated fee structure could help the funding of higher education to become sustainable.

## Notes

1. $\text{MPCE} = \dfrac{\textit{Total Monthly Consumption Expenditure}}{\textit{Household Size}}$
2. Quintile 1 = poorest, Quintile 2 = poor, Quintile 3 = middle, Quintile 4 = upper middle, Quintile 5 = rich.

## References

Aaron, H. and Martin C. McGuire (1970). 'Public Goods and Income Distribution'. *Econometrica*, 38(6): 907–20.

Alderman, H. et al. (1991). 'Who Goes to School in Rural Pakistan?'. International Food Policy Research Institute, Washington, D.C.: Williams College, Williamstown, Mass.

Brennan, G. (1976). 'The Distributional Implications of Public Goods'. *Econometrica*, 44(2): 391–99.

Canagarajah, S. and Xiao Ye (2001). 'Public Health and Education Spending in Ghana 1992–98: Issues of Equity and Efficiency'. *Working Paper Series 2579*, Washington, D.C.: The World Bank.

Cornes, R. (1995). 'Measuring the Distributional Impact of Public Goods', in D. Van de Walle and K. Nead (eds), *Public Spending and the Poor: Theory and Evidence*. Baltimore: The Johns Hopkins University Press.

Dasgupta, A.K. and J.B.G. Tilak (1983). 'Distribution of Education among Income Groups: An Empirical Analysis'. *Economic and Political Weekly*, 18(33): 1442–47.

Davoodi, R.H., R.E. Tiongson and S.S. Asawanuchit (2003). 'How Useful are Benefit Incidence Analyses of Public Education and Health Spending?'. *IMF Working Paper* WP/03/227, Washington, D.C.: IMF.

de Wulf, Luc (1975). 'Fiscal Incidence Studies in Developing Countries'. *IMF Staff Papers*, 22: 61–131.

Demery, L. (2000). *Benefit Incidence: A Practioner's Guide*. Poverty and Social Development Group, Africa Region, The World Bank.

Gill, S.S. et al. (2008). 'Financing of Secondary Education in Punjab: Sources, Patterns and Emerging Issues in Secondary Education', in J.B.G. Tilak (eds), *Financing of Secondary Education in India*. New Delhi: NUEPA.

Government of India, Ministry of Statistics (2007–08). *National Sample Survey Organisation* (Socio-Economic Survey, 64th Round, Schedule 25.2, Participation and Expenditure in Education).

Jallade, J.P. (1974). 'Public Expenditure in Education and Income Distribution in Columbia'. *Staff Occasional Paper*, The World Bank.

Lanjouw, P. et al. (2001). 'Poverty, Education and Health in Indonesia: Who Benefits from Public Spending?'. *Policy Research Publication No. 2739*, The World Bank.

Lopez-Acevedo, G. and A. Salinas (2000). *The Distribution of Mexico's Public Spending on Education*. Washington, D.C.: The World Bank.

Manasan, R.G., J.S. Cuenca and E.C.V. Ruiz (2008). 'Benefit Incidence of Public Spending on Education in the Philippines'. *Discussion Paper Series No. 2008–08*, Philippines Institute for Development Studies.

Meerman, J. (1979). *Public Expenditures in Malaysia: Who Benefits and Why?* New York: Oxford University Press.

Meesook, O.A. (1984). 'Financing and Equity in the Social Sectors in Indonesia: Some Policy Questions'. *Staff Working Paper No. 703*, Washington, D.C.: The World Bank.

Ministry of Human Resource Development, Analysis of Budgeted Expenditure (various years). New Delhi: Government of India, Department of Education.

——. Selected Educational Statistics (various years). New Delhi: Government of India, Department of Education.

Mitra, A. (2013). 'Benefit Incidence Analysis of Public Spending in India in a Regional Perspective'. Unpublished M.Phil. Thesis, New Delhi: NUEPA.

Muzammil, M. (2008). 'Uttar Pradesh: Financing of Secondary Education, Grants-in-Aid Policies and Practices in Secondary Education', in J.B.G. Tilak (ed.), *Financing of Secondary Education in India*. New Delhi: NUEPA.

Sabir, M. (2003). Benefit Incidence Analysis of Public Spending on Education.

Selden, Thomas M. and Michael J. Wasylenko (1992). 'Benefit Incidence Analysis in Developing Countries'. *Policy Research Working Papers No. 1015*, Washington, D.C.: The World Bank, November.

Selowsky, M. (1979). *Who Benefits from Government Expenditure?* New York: Oxford University Press.

Shah, K.R. and S. Agarwal (2008). 'Financing of Secondary Education in Gujarat'. *Journal of Educational Planning and Administration*, 17(3): 299–330.

Sujatha, K. and P.G. Rani (2011). *Development of Secondary Education in India*. New Delhi: National University of Educational Planning and Administration.

The World Bank (1986). *Financing Education in Developing Countries*. Washington, D.C., U.S.A.

van de Walle, Dominique and Kimberly Nead (1995). *Public Spending and the Poor: Theory and Evidence*. Baltimore: The Johns Hopkins University Press.

Zachariah, George et al. (2008). 'Kerala: Grants in Aid Policies and Practices in Secondary Education', in J.B.G. Tilak (eds), *Financing of Secondary Education in India*. New Delhi: NUEPA.

## Appendix

*Enrollment – Quintile-Wise/State-Wise/Level of Education-Wise*

| | | *Quintile 1* | *Quintile 2* | *Quintile 3* | *Quintile 4* | *Quintile 5* |
|---|---|---|---|---|---|---|
| Punjab | Elementary | 0.03 | 4,08,629 | 5,19,300 | 4,86,355 | 4,85,836 |
| | Secondary | 39,680 | 82,575 | 1,31,045 | 2,47,487 | 3,49,675 |
| | Higher | 5,703 | 3,836 | 17,973 | 50,742 | 1,01,674 |
| Haryana | Elementary | 3,90,693 | 5,31,890 | 5,51,528 | 3,79,638 | 2,64,501 |
| | Secondary | 45,141 | 1,25,494 | 2,19,437 | 2,03,455 | 2,45,822 |
| | Higher | 8,776 | 17,620 | 12,818 | 63,955 | 1,66,154 |
| Rajasthan | Elementary | 19,72,916 | 23,22,253 | 16,89,882 | 10,28,596 | 3,76,467 |
| | Secondary | 1,86,996 | 3,86,585 | 4,05,699 | 4,10,872 | 3,23,545 |
| | Higher | 8,390 | 64,549 | 59,647 | 1,25,562 | 2,23,301 |
| Uttar Pradesh | Elementary | 1,03,17,388 | 80,36,889 | 52,26,229 | 19,57,445 | 7,67,508 |
| | Secondary | 12,77,731 | 14,96,768 | 15,31,319 | 10,68,135 | 7,82,991 |
| | Higher | 2,14,299 | 2,97,133 | 4,14,151 | 5,00,735 | 6,01,393 |
| Bihar | Elementary | 53,79,011 | 47,93,076 | 24,01,031 | 9,52,876 | 1,65,212 |
| | Secondary | 4,64,765 | 5,92,383 | 5,34,018 | 2,88,035 | 2,41,403 |
| | Higher | 8,064 | 37,647 | 89,124 | 64,700 | 89,877 |
| | Elementary | 8,70,311 | 9,56,715 | 10,80,918 | 8,16,529 | 3,83,070 |
| Assam | Secondary | 52,721 | 2,08,550 | 2,70,815 | 2,93,431 | 2,06,485 |
| | Higher | 6,526 | 25,715 | 45,442 | 67,592 | 58,757 |
| West Bengal | Elementary | 46,04,294 | 29,97,208 | 24,03,199 | 14,67,907 | 6,59,492 |
| | Secondary | 4,11,596 | 5,52,010 | 5,81,318 | 5,81,063 | 5,18,920 |
| | Higher | 36,479 | 58,168 | 1,01,465 | 1,95,425 | 2,84,762 |
| Orissa | Elementary | 31,11,714 | 10,69,136 | 7,47,519 | 2,11,215 | 1,26,234 |
| | Secondary | 4,14,578 | 3,05,266 | 2,64,211 | 86,571 | 1,04,308 |
| | Higher | 24,598 | 35,158 | 54,177 | 28,136 | 58,967 |
| Madhya Pradesh | Elementary | 52,82,988 | 23,49,978 | 16,45,769 | 7,55,008 | 2,37,910 |
| | Secondary | 5,82,092 | 3,81,621 | 3,44,020 | 2,77,029 | 2,06,442 |
| | Higher | 43,563 | 38,255 | 74,951 | 1,00,888 | 2,20,875 |
| Gujarat | Elementary | 12,20,179 | 18,15,526 | 15,97,377 | 15,11,658 | 8,91,995 |
| | Secondary | 1,26,297 | 2,80,717 | 3,12,743 | 4,87,480 | 6,04,791 |
| | Higher | 13,308 | 17,730 | 38,841 | 90,864 | 3,02,216 |
| Maharashtra | Elementary | 32,64,365 | 29,57,110 | 23,77,749 | 21,61,333 | 14,97,144 |
| | Secondary | 7,09,685 | 9,33,451 | 8,86,679 | 11,64,721 | 10,70,355 |
| | Higher | 55,222 | 94,399 | 1,30,223 | 3,55,183 | 6,51,833 |
| AP | Elementary | 21,40,745 | 21,36,042 | 19,55,072 | 10,16,930 | 2,78,087 |
| | Secondary | 3,77,770 | 6,98,062 | 7,46,263 | 4,56,798 | 2,90,265 |
| | Higher | 40,324 | 83,326 | 1,21,796 | 1,71,150 | 2,22,273 |

*Cont'd...*

*...Cont'd*

| | | | | | | |
|---|---|---|---|---|---|---|
| Karnataka | Elementary | 19,59,956 | 17,86,891 | 11,85,820 | 9,30,595 | 3,65,772 |
| | Secondary | 3,84,582 | 4,37,473 | 4,02,373 | 4,52,878 | 3,36,831 |
| | Higher | 34,403 | 34,186 | 42,609 | 79,108 | 1,03,825 |
| Kerala | Elementary | 3,60,262 | 5,58,077 | 7,23,133 | 7,29,855 | 5,59,513 |
| | Secondary | 79,480 | 1,19,921 | 3,38,572 | 3,88,794 | 4,44,239 |
| | Higher | 4,195 | 34,868 | 18,997 | 82,492 | 1,64,376 |
| Tamil Nadu | Elementary | 10,50,269 | 19,43,400 | 21,32,917 | 15,80,813 | 6,94,890 |
| | Secondary | 2,29,077 | 5,34,055 | 7,27,448 | 8,28,977 | 5,82,431 |
| | Higher | 15,191 | 24,488 | 64,141 | 1,69,630 | 2,63,146 |
| Other States | Elementary | 44,56,529 | 39,89,303 | 32,54,631 | 24,08,589 | 12,93,849 |
| | Secondary | 6,51,399 | 6,99,979 | 8,06,060 | 11,65,278 | 10,81,784 |
| | Higher | 37,062 | 40,057 | 1,16,168 | 2,39,226 | 5,53,158 |

*Source:* Author's Self-Computation from NSSO 64th Round Unit-level Data.

*Subsidy – Quintile-wise – in Crore ₹*

| | | *Quintile 1* | *Quintile 2* | *Quintile 3* | *Quintile 4* | *Quintile 5* |
|---|---|---|---|---|---|---|
| Punjab | Elementary | 76 | 93 | 110 | 91 | 4 |
| | Secondary | 78 | 164 | 254 | 474 | 590 |
| | Higher | 7 | 5 | 22 | 39 | 37 |
| Haryana | Elementary | 206 | 281 | 285 | 184 | 50 |
| | Secondary | 45 | 118 | 207 | 184 | 188 |
| | Higher | 12 | 25 | 18 | 84 | 182 |
| Rajasthan | Elementary | 841 | 986 | 711 | 404 | 107 |
| | Secondary | 182 | 364 | 388 | 389 | 259 |
| | Higher | 1 | 27 | 17 | 24 | 12 |
| Uttar Pradesh | Elementary | 2,950 | 2,280 | 1,415 | 485 | 15 |
| | Secondary | 529 | 618 | 596 | 398 | 160 |
| | Higher | 38 | 63 | 80 | 38 | 49 |
| Bihar | Elementary | 1,270 | 1130 | 565 | 211 | 30 |
| | Secondary | 177 | 215 | 188 | 98 | 59 |
| | Higher | 21 | 101 | 238 | 173 | 237 |
| | Elementary | 310 | 334 | 379 | 281 | 125 |
| Assam | Secondary | 36 | 144 | 186 | 198 | 137 |
| | Higher | 11 | 48 | 79 | 107 | 95 |
| West Bengal | Elementary | 950 | 614 | 486 | 286 | 92 |
| | Secondary | 459 | 614 | 645 | 638 | 533 |
| | Higher | 39 | 57 | 100 | 186 | 210 |
| Orissa | Elementary | 1,014 | 339 | 234 | 64 | 24 |
| | Secondary | 241 | 175 | 146 | 46 | 23 |
| | Higher | 56 | 86 | 131 | 67 | 100 |
| Madhya Pradesh | Elementary | 1,206 | 522 | 358 | 153 | 26 |
| | Secondary | 225 | 153 | 124 | 101 | 41 |
| | Higher | 30 | 24 | 47 | 39 | 84 |

*Cont'd...*

*...Cont'd*

| | | | | | | |
|---|---|---|---|---|---|---|
| Gujarat | Elementary | 512 | 749 | 645 | 582 | 224 |
| | Secondary | 111 | 241 | 266 | 396 | 441 |
| | Higher | 10 | 13 | 26 | 69 | 173 |
| Maharashtra | Elementary | 1,601 | 1,450 | 1,155 | 999 | 601 |
| | Secondary | 793 | 1,034 | 976 | 1,254 | 1,081 |
| | Higher | 55 | 99 | 111 | 317 | 172 |
| AP | Elementary | 768 | 767 | 675 | 331 | 40 |
| | Secondary | 273 | 493 | 514 | 294 | 201 |
| | Higher | 68 | 133 | 185 | 251 | 220 |
| Karnataka | Elementary | 1,144 | 1,037 | 682 | 514 | 139 |
| | Secondary | 371 | 418 | 387 | 400 | 208 |
| | Higher | 66 | 62 | 77 | 136 | 128 |
| Kerala | Elementary | 227 | 353 | 453 | 455 | 340 |
| | Secondary | 100 | 150 | 427 | 482 | 549 |
| | Higher | 7 | 72 | 35 | 162 | 249 |
| Tamil Nadu | Elementary | 402 | 736 | 806 | 569 | 131 |
| | Secondary | 209 | 485 | 654 | 721 | 434 |
| | Higher | 13 | 23 | 57 | 114 | 57 |
| Other States | Elementary | 7,246 | 6,461 | 5,241 | 3,815 | 1,817 |
| | Secondary | 1,028 | 1,098 | 1,243 | 1,739 | 1,489 |
| | Higher | 188 | 200 | 582 | 1,165 | 2,443 |

*Source:* Author's Self-Computation from NSSO 64th Round Unit-level Data.

# 17

# Participation of Mahadalit Students in Higher Education

## *A Case Study in Gaya District of Bihar*

**AMARDEEP KUMAR**

The participation of Dalit students in education in the country has remained by and large unattended over the centuries despite many slogans for equality and freedom as well as host of humanitarian revolutions down the stream of human history. This, despite all the human rights declarations and constitutional directives or commitments made particularly since the dawn of our freedom struggle under the patronage of the Father of the Nation, Mahatma Gandhi, the prophet and high priest of 'Harijans', followed of late by great Dalit *avtars* like Dr B.R. Ambedkar (the architect of the Indian Constitution) who really dreamt of mitigating the conditions of Dalits within a span of 10 years after the adoption of the Constitution on 26 January 1950. But even after nearly 65 years or so, the dream remains a dream, except that only a few among them did enjoy most of the benefits, leaving millions in the lurch and in the midst of deprivation of all kinds, rendering them to be in the most deprived or 'Mahadalit' status across the States. The participation of Mahadalits in the process of education has continued to be dismal so much so that their space for higher education seems rather at a standstill. This study tries to understand how the most disadvantaged group within the Dalits is participating in the arena of higher education in Bihar, one of the greatest 'BIMARU' states in India. 'Mahadalits' have been recognized as the most disadvantaged category on the basis of their social, economic and educational status in Bihar. Most Mahadalit castes in Bihar are still treated as untouchable, despite prohibition of untouchability throughout country. Most of the Mahadalit communities are landless and are involved in traditional forms of occupation, agricultural work or unskilled work.

Most of the Mahadalit students leave their education at an early stage and very few reach the stage of higher education. At every stage, there is high drop-out or push-out of Mahadalit students from education. Senior secondary schools being not available at the village level is reported to be the biggest constraint in access to higher education for the students of this community in Bihar. The state lacks in provision of senior secondary education in the rural areas. It is concentrated at the district headquarters or at block headquarters though mostly at the former location. This affects the ability of disadvantaged sections like Mahadalit in accessing higher education as the students of this community cannot afford higher education because of social, economic and various other forms of disability.

## In Retrospect

Scheduled Castes in India are not a homogenous group and within the Scheduled Castes, the 'Mahadalits' have been recognized as the most deprived and marginalized social category among the Dalits, especially in Bihar. The poorest Dalits are declared as Mahadalits. Although Mahadalits are not recognized at the national level despite efforts being made by states like Andhra Pradesh, Punjab and others, Bihar is the only state which has categorized the Mahadalits as a separate category comprising 21 castes from amongst the Scheduled Castes. Education in general and higher education in particular plays an important role in the growth and development of an individual and society as a whole. Higher education is extremely important for social and economic development because it opens the window of opportunities. It provides better opportunity in the labour market and helps individuals in upward mobility on the economic and social ladder. In this context, it is important to know how these Mahadalits have been able to access higher education and how the policy of positive discrimination in higher education functions with respect to Mahadalits. Despite rapid expansion in higher and technical education due to various UGC sponsored programmes for the students of Schedule Castes, they have been found to be still facing constraints in access to higher education and are not able to overcome their social, political, economic discrimination.

The present study examines the policy of positive discrimination and tries to present the impact of positive discrimination policy in higher education an across Mahadalit castes including their enrolment-pattern through a field study conducted in the Gaya district of Bihar.

## Objectives of the Study

- To study the problems involved in the process of access to higher education by the Mahadalit students.
- To study the intra-Mahadalit community variations in enrollment and utilization of programmes under policies of positive discrimination offered by the government in higher education.

## Design of the Study

The present study is descriptive in nature. It helps in understanding the whole process of access, participation and experiences of Mahadalit students in higher education. This study is empirical in nature and a Mixed Method Approach has been applied by using tools such as questionnaires, semi-structured interviews, observations, field-notes, etc. Mixed Methodology Research is a research design with philosophical assumptions as well as methods of inquiry. As a methodology, it involves philosophical assumptions that guide the direction of the collection and analysis of data and the mixture of qualitative and quantitative approaches in many phases in the research process. As a method, it focuses on collecting, analysing, and mixing both quantitative and qualitative data in a single study or series of studies. Its central premise is that the use of quantitative and qualitative approaches in combination provides a better understanding of research problems than either approach alone (Cresswell et al., 2003).

In the present study, case-study has been conducted in one institution and in-depth informations have been gathered to understand the participation of Mahadalit students in higher education. It helped in the understanding of the current phenomena in depth.

The researcher had no control over the participants of this study. Due to this fact, the data has been collected in a natural social setting of respondents without any manipulation and control and from the admission forms of the Gaya College for the year 2013–14 at the undergraduate level. The main emphasis of the study is to explore the participation of Mahadalit students in higher education in the Gaya District.

## Sources of Data

In the present study, the researcher has used both primary as well as secondary data to understand the enrollment pattern on the one hand and participation of Mahadalit students in college life on the other. The primary and secondary data has been collected to cover every aspect of the study. The primary data are related to understanding the students' point of view as well as their real life phenomena. The secondary data shows distributional pattern of enrollment and other benefits under the positive discrimination policy. These data were used in combination as per needs of the study. Despite having different merits and demerits, both types of data serves our purpose of the research study. The primary sources of data in this research are college, students, district welfare office where the researcher extensively interacted with all the stakeholders who are the target of study. The primary sources of the data have been constituted by admission forms and other documents, and appropriate techniques were used for the same to calculate and understand the enrollment patterns of students from different Mahadalit castes. Primary data were also collected through the questionnaires from Mahadalit students through semi-structured scheduled interviews.

The study has extensively used secondary resources. The secondary data includes academic writing such as articles from journals, books written by various authors, scholars and activists, etc. Secondary data has been collected from Bihar Mahadalit Vikas Mission; Bihar Government, Patna; Census data from various years; All India Survey on Higher Education, MHRD and various other central and state government reports, etc.

## Selection of Location for Data Collection

The geographical setting of the study has been selected on the basis of some of the prominent indicators like highest numbers of Mahadalit population with various groups within the Dalits. The diversity of population of Dalits in general and Mahadalits in particular was an important consideration in selection of area. Within the district, one college was selected as a case study to understand the participation of Mahadalit students in higher education. The rationale for choosing this college was on the basis of permission to gather data from various departments as well as support by the administration for the case-study, which has been mentioned in the case study section. Generally colleges do not provide admission forms to outsiders for reasons of privacy but it was a great success to be able to get the admission forms for this study. The college is surrounded by different castes of Dalits in general and Mahadalits in particular which makes the availability of data more diversified. The selection of the sampled district was based on stratified multistage purposive sampling.

## Findings

### *The Following are the Findings of the Study*

#### *Understanding the Mahadalits*

The term 'Mahadalit' has arisen due to the discourse of development in which certain castes within the Dalits have not been able to develop their selves and the basic principle of social justice is negated. Their proportional share in economic development and in the educational process has remained unfulfilled. It became a challenge for the government to look into the matter so that nobody is left out of the process of development. Articles 38 and 46 of the Indian Constitution laid great stress on bringing Scheduled Castes and Scheduled Tribes into the mainstream of society. In view of these directives of the Constitution, the government has launched several schemes for the socio-economic and cultural development of Scheduled Castes. It has been found that certain sections of Scheduled Castes have been able to take considerable benefits from these schemes and develop themselves. But it has also been seen that considerable sections of Scheduled Castes have remained socially and economically backward. The state government, after due thought, conceptualized an initiative to make special projects and earmark special funds for overall development of these most deprived sections among the Scheduled Castes. The state government decided to constitute a Commission known as the State Mahadalit Commissionin the year 2007 to identify the castes within Scheduled Castes that had lagged behind in the process of development. The main purpose of the Commission was to study the educational and social status of these castes, suggest measures and recommend actions for their educational and social uplift together with ways for their employment. For the execution of different schemes for the development of Mahadalits, the state government has established a society called 'Bihar Mahadalit Development Mission' under the Societies Registration Act, 1860.The vision of this Mission is to fulfil the basic necessities of all Mahadalit communities through their social, economic and cultural empowerment and ensure their full participation in the mainstream of development. The Bihar Mahadalit Vikas Mission has planned a number of schemes along these guidelines, thereby targetting Mahadalit sections of society in this regard. The first task of the Commission was to gather data on various Dalit castes so that policy and plan could be formulated to improve their condition from being the most disadvantaged group as Mahadalits.'Mahadalit' is, thus, a new term to represent a community that has emerged as a by-product of social engineering, and changing inclusive policy. While viewing the formation of Mahadalits within dalits from the Ambedkar perspective, it is more like a divisive policy to divide and break the unity among the Dalits.

Mahadalits in Bihar are the most subjugated in the whole process of caste hierarchy and excluded from the mainstream of society. They are landless labourers and placed unfavourably in the ownership of productive assets as well as in the distribution of assets. Inequality tends to be cumulative in their case. Mahadalits have the least ownership of assets. Landownership, for instance, is highly unevenly distributed in the state of Bihar and Dalits and Mahadalits have the least ownership of land. Bigger land holdings are in the hands of a few dominant castes. The land distribution policy of the government has not succeeded in its goal. It has left the Dalits and Mahadalits in the extreme form of slavery.

## Intra-Caste Variations in Enrollment among Mahadalits in Higher Education

On the basis of first objectives, the present Section deals with intra-castes variations in enrollment among Mahadalits in higher education. The data collected from the field shows the differences among the Mahadalits in accessing higher education. Out of 21 Mahadalit castes, six are major Mahadalit castes – namely Bhuiya, Musahar, Rajwar, Dhobi, Pasi and Chamars that have access to higher education. While looking at the data of different castes among the Mahadalits, one finds that the Bhuiyas, Musahars, and Rajwars are in the worst condition while Mehtars, Dhobis, Pasis and Chamars are somehow in a better condition on the basis of their proportion of population.

Bantar, Bauri, Bhogta, Chaupal, Dabgar, Dom, Ghasi, Halalkhor, Mehtar, Bhangi, Kanjar, Kuriar, Lalbegi, Nat and Pan have no substantive population and their participation in terms of enrollment in higher education is also very low or negligible. The Bhuiya caste is a dominant caste with around 54.79 per cent in terms of population but their enrollment proportion is very low at 6.24 per cent of the total enrollment for the current academic year. This shows the backwardness of this caste among the Mahadalits. Traditional occupation and concentration in remote rural areas hinders them from breaking the barriers of constraint in terms of either geographical location or distance from colleges which are mainly available in urban areas. Unaffordability of cost to be incurred in staying in the city as well paying room rents and other living costs apart from the educational expenditures too are factors that act as barriers. The condition of Musahars has not improved even after six decades of the country's Independence and this community is still marginalized and deprived of the fruits of the development process. Arun Kumar (2006), before establishing the recognition of Mahadalits, wrote about the Musahar as Dalit among Dalits.

Literally, Musahar means one who eats rats – a rat-eater. Most of the Musahars are still bonded labourers with the land-owners in Bihar. On the other hand, the Dhobis' proportion in population in terms of the total population of Mahadalits is 2.20 per cent, though their proportion in terms of enrollment is 25.54 per cent out of the total Mahadalits' enrollments. Data in Table 1 shows an advantageous position of Dhobis among the Mahadalit students.

**Table 1**

*Proportion of Intra-Mahadalit Castes' Population, Proportion of Enrollment and Gross Proportion of Enrollment 2013–14*

| *Caste* | *% of Population* | *% of Enrolment* |
|---|---|---|
| Bantar | 0.00 | 0.00 |
| Bauri | 0.00 | 0.00 |
| Bhogta | 0.97 | 0.00 |
| Bhuiya | 54.79 | 6.24 |
| Chaupal | 0.00 | 0.00 |
| Dabgar | 0.04 | 0.00 |
| Dom, Dhangad | 0.22 | 0.00 |
| Ghasi | 0.00 | 0.00 |
| Halalkhor | 0.00 | 0.00 |
| Mehtar, Bhangi | 0.24 | 2.99 |
| Kanjar | 0.01 | 0.00 |
| Kuriar | 0.01 | 0.00 |
| Lalbegi | 0.00 | 0.00 |
| Musahar | 5.94 | 1.01 |
| Nat | 0.13 | 0.00 |
| Pan, Sawasi | 0.07 | 0.00 |
| Rajwar | 2.67 | 0.60 |
| Turi | 0.35 | 0.00 |
| Dhobi | 2.20 | 25.54 |
| Pasi | 11.79 | 31.33 |
| Chamar | 20.55 | 32.29 |
| Total | 100.00 | 100.00 |

*Source:* Calculated from College Records – Gaya, Bihar.

Dhobis are closely associated with the so-called upper castes due to their occupation because of which often this community learns of new and modern ways which have helped them in upward mobility in education as also in the social milieu. M.N. Srinivas characterized this process as one of 'sanskritisation', which means not only the adaptation of new customs and habits but also exposure to new ideas and values which have found frequent expression in the vast body of Sanskrit literature, social as well as secular, and generally 'sanskritisation' qualifies a caste for a higher status.

Pasis are 11.79 per cent of the total Mahadalit population, though their share in enrollment is 31.33 per cent of the total enrolment. The population of

Chamarsamong the Mahadalits is 20.55 per cent whereas their enrollment (out of the total enrollment of Mahadlit students) is 32.29 per cent.

The next figure will show the geographical location of previous schools, and will enable us to understand the background from which the students are enrolling into higher education. The study conducted by PRIYA has also found that among the numerically larger castes, Dhobis have registered the highest overall literacy rate as well as female literacy rate, followed by Pasis, Dusadhs and Chamars. The literacy rate is the lowest so far as Musahars are concerned. The study has also found that among the major sub-castes, Dhobis have the higher proportion of matriculates (19.7%) whereas this proportion is the lowest in Musahars and Bhuiyas (6% each). Every seventh literate amongst the Chamars is a matriculate, whereas amongst the Dusadhs and Pasis, every sixth literate is a matriculate.

### *Distribution of Fellowships*

The distribution of fellowships was calculated on the basis of the data provided by the college authorities which the college had received from the District Welfare Department Office. Of those who apply, the fellowship is given to those whose guardian's income is below ₹ 2 lakh per-year. But in real terms, all the students who had applied were not getting the fellowship due to many other reasons.

**Table 2**

*Proportion of Mahadalit Population and Proportion of Fellowship Distribution (2012–13)*

| Castes Name | % of Population | Fellowship Distribution |
|---|---|---|
| Bhogta | 0.97 | 0.00 |
| Bhuiya | 54.79 | 6.06 |
| Dabgar | 0.04 | 0.00 |
| Dom, Dhangad | 0.22 | 0.00 |
| Mehtar, Bhangi | 0.24 | 1.02 |
| Kanjar | 0.01 | 0.00 |
| Kuriar | 0.01 | 0.00 |
| Musahar | 5.94 | 3.00 |
| Nat | 0.13 | 0.00 |
| Pan, Sawasi | 0.07 | 0.00 |
| Rajwar | 2.67 | 0.00 |
| Turi | 0.35 | 0.00 |
| Dhobi | 2.20 | 25.54 |
| Pasi | 11.79 | 31.33 |
| Chamar | 20.55 | 32.29 |
| Total | 100.00 | 100.00 |

*Source:* Calculated from District Welfare Office Report, Gaya for Year 2012–13.

Provision of fellowship application is online and this created many problems for students. Lack of online facility inside the campus forces the students to use cyber-cafés where the charges are heavy.

Like the enrollment pattern, the fellowship distribution is also divided among the six castes' students as only these Mahadalit students reach the portals of higher education. There are also variations among Mahadalits in terms of proportion of fellowship distribution.

## Location of Previous Schools and Board

Policy-makers in many countries around the world are concerned with significant proportions of youth dropping out of upper secondary education. A high drop-out rate after post-secondary generates inequality between classes, castes and within the caste itself in higher education. It also can have detrimental effects on achievement of social justice. The relatively low higher education participation-rates of people from lower socio-economic backgrounds, rural backgrounds and the apparent resistance of their participation rates to equity programmes present a major challenge for educational policy framing. The findings of this study suggest that some redirection of equity initiatives may be beneficial. Availability of post-secondary schools paves the way for entry into higher education. However, scarcity or availability of schools at a distance negatively affects the participation in higher education, especially by the poorer and the downtrodden. This Section extensively deals with the location of previous schools attended by the Mahadalit students who are now in the higher-education stage.

Becker and Siebern-Thomas (2007) find that the supply of high schools is higher in urban areas in Germany and this pattern motivates their use in urban versus rural areas during childhood as an instrumental variable for educational attainment in earnings equations. The concentration of higher schools in India is also much higher in urban area than in rural area and it determines the participation of student into the higher education. Using US data, Card (1995) finds that individuals living closer to four-year colleges attained more years of education than those living further from such institutions. The evidence from the Netherlands in Sá et al., (2006) indicates that geographical proximity to universities and professional colleges increases the probability for school-leavers to continue education at the post-secondary level. This type of research done specially in the developed world shows how the geographical location impacts students' participation in higher education. More studies on this aspect are badly needed to be done in developing countries too.

Table 3 describes the caste-wise previous location of Mahadalit students who are entering into the higher education. Majority of Musahars and Dhobis (75%) passed out from the district head-quarter schools and only 25 per cent in the Dhobi category are pass-outs from block head-quarter schools. The Bhuiya Caste was found to have 100 per cent urban background schools at the 12th or inter-mediate level. It shows not even a single student from the Bhuiya caste coming into the higher education from a block-headquarter school, indicating how the lack of availability impacts students' entry into higher education. It is also astonishing to notice that even though the Bhuiyas have a share of 54 per cent in the population of Mahadalits in the district, their participation is extremely low. The non-availability of senior secondary schools in rural areas is a major problem in access to higher education. Amongst the Pasis and Chamars too, more than 89 per cent and 78 per cent, respectively, of these students passed out from the urban background schools.

**Table 3**
*Location of Previous Schools and Board*

| *Castes* | *% of Rural* | *% Dist. HQ* | *% of Block. HQ* | *Total* | *Boards* |
|---|---|---|---|---|---|
| Bhuiya | 0.00 | 100.00 | 0.00 | 100.00 | BSEB |
| Mehtar | 0.00 | 75.00 | 25.00 | 100.00 | BSEB |
| Musahar | 0.00 | 50.00 | 50.00 | 100.00 | BSEB |
| Dhobi | 0.00 | 75.00 | 25.00 | 100.00 | BSEB |
| Pasi | 0.00 | 89.66 | 10.34 | 100.00 | BSEB |
| Chamar | 0.00 | 78.57 | 21.43 | 100.00 | 100.00 |

*Source:* Calculated from Admission forms for the Year 2013–14.

The data in Table 3 (Graph 1) shows that location of senior secondary school does play a very important role in providing access to higher education to Mahadalit students and unavailability of senior secondary school in rural areas is the biggest hindrance in their being not able to enter the portals of higher education.

**Graph 1**
*Location of Previous Schools*

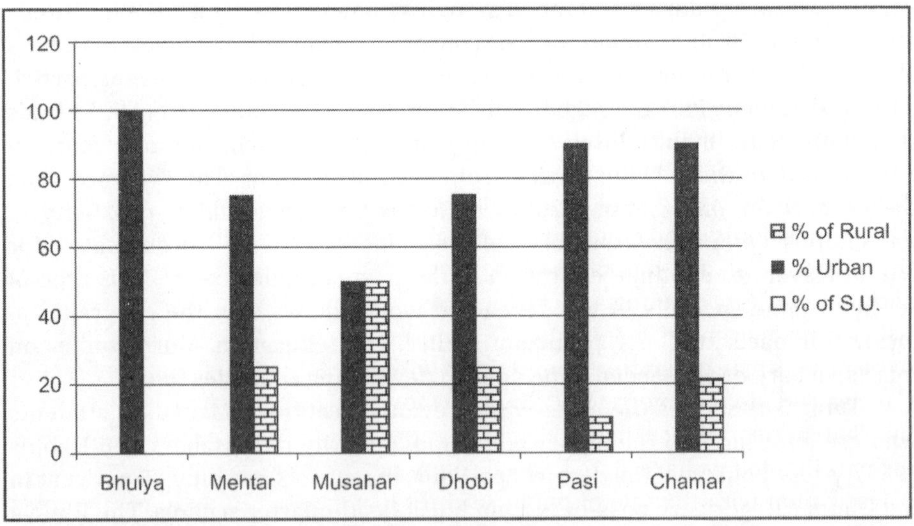


*Source:* Calculated from Admission-forms for the Year 2013–14.

The major finding of the data shows that no student has passed out from rural background schools and this clearly indicates the non-availability of senior schools in the rural areas. Students entering higher education are either in schools which are available at block head-quarters or in the urban head-quarters. Students partaking of higher education are of three categories. One category is of students who go to the senior secondary institution daily by bicycle or by sharing transport; the second category is of those whose parents or guardians have migrated to the city for work and are involved in non-agricultural activity and students are also assisting them in either their traditional work or in family work. The third category is of students living in the city on rent just for education and getting monthly expenditure from their family. It does not mean that these students are from well-off families but they manage their expenditure from various sources like family, relatives, tuitions and sometimes they also work in the city as manual workers to fulfil their needs. However, all the students enrolled for higher education from the Mahadalit community are from the Bihar School Examination Board (BSEB). Their previous senior secondary school location does impact on their access to higher education. The location of the senior secondary institution as well as the socio-economic condition of the student plays a major role in access to higher education in the case of Mahadalit students.

## Meritocracy as Barrier

Meritocracy, defined as a system that rewards according to ability or achievement and not birth or privilege, may be unfair precisely because it is blind to differences of class, wealth and social status. Meritocracy is a social system where individual talent and effort, rather than ascriptive traits, determine individuals' placements in a social hierarchy. Although popularized in Young's '*The Rise of the Meritocracy*' (1958), the concept dates back to Plato. Two defining features of meritocratic systems are competition and equality of opportunity. Meritocracy, in trying to 'isolate' merit by treating people with fundamentally unequal backgrounds as superficially the same, can be a practice that ignores and even conceals the real advantages and disadvantages that are unevenly distributed to different segments of an inherently unequal society, a practice that in fact perpetuates this fundamental inequality (Rebecca, 2009). In this way, those who are picked by meritocracy as having merit, may already have enjoyed unfair advantages from the very beginning, ignored according to the principle of non-discrimination. Meritocracy offers a 'ladder' system of social mobility, promoting a socially corrosive ethic of competitive self-interest which both legitimizes inequality and damages community 'by requiring people to be in a permanent state of competition with each other'. In Britain, neoliberal policies and ideas of meritocracy were profoundly shaped, from the late 1970s, by Thatcherism, which made a meritocratic appeal to social mobility whilst dismantling the welfare state's social safety net and initiating the long wave of privatization with the sale of public utilities like gas, tele-communications and rail (Stuart, 1988). So merit is an academic achievement.

Mahadalit students are not able to reach that level of merit to become eligible for admission into the portals of higher education which requires special academic preparation. So, merit as the process of admission may not be fair or neutral to the background of the students.

When admission to the college takes place on the basis of marks in the previous examination, it means making a distinction between those having good marks and those not having a certain level of marks. Students from the rural background as from lower socio-economic strata, may not be able to get good marks as unavailability of better facilities for classroom as well coaching may end up seeing them with lower grades, which directly hinders the participation of Mahadalits in higher education. Here the focus is to understand empirically how the policy of meritocracy impacts on Mahadalit students.

Despite a high availability of students from the Dalit category in general and the Mahadalit category in particular, institutions do not provide space to students who may have lesser marks, and this creates elitism that excludes the masses. The function of formal schooling or college is to allocate individuals their place in society based on marks, talent, ability, and achievement. It shows how this theory reinforces inequality in our society. The stipulated quotas are simply because a sufficient number do not make the threshold in terms of the much reduced minimum for Mahadalit students as their previous school was not good enough to prepare them for higher education. It was also found that college does not have any remedial classes for the Dalit students in general and Mahadalit students in particular.

**Table 4**

*Average Grades (division) of Mahadalit Students at Entry-Level in Graduation*

| *Castes* | *1st Div. (>60%)* | *2nd Div.* | *3rd Div.* | *Total* |
|---|---|---|---|---|
| Bhuiya | 66.66 | 33.34 | 0 | 100 |
| Mehtar | 50 | 50 | 0 | 100 |
| Musahar | | | 0 | |
| Dhobi | 72.7 | 27.3 | 0 | 100 |
| Pasi | 73.9 | 26.1 | 0 | 100 |
| Chamar | 87.5 | 12.5 | 0 | 100 |

*Source:* Calculated from Admission-forms for the Year 2013–14.

Higher Education is a system of meritocracy based on merit, not right. It is more a process of elimination rather than of selection. The continual testing, target-setting and recording of results seen as an attempt to keep some kind of order and policy at the national level are doomed to fail as they cannot keep up with the increasingly diverse nature of society (Moor and Hickox, 1994). The study found that six major castes among Mahadalits are entering higher education. These castes are Bhuiya, Mehtar, Musahar, Dhobi, Pasi and Chamar.

More than 66.34 per cent students among the Bhuiya caste have first class marks and only 33.34 per cent have second class in their previous qualification examination. Although this caste is involved in mainly agricultural activity and its people are situated in rural settings, these students have an urban background – migration of the guardians to urban areas for employment has played a major role in enabling them to access higher education; the guardians are involved in non-agricultural activity in the urban milieu and supporting their children in pursuing higher education. More than 87 per cent of Chamar students have first division marks in the qualifying examination and only 13 per cent have second division marks in 12th. Among the Musahars, the most disadvantaged caste among the Mahadalits, 50 per cent students are first divisioners whereas the remaining 50 per cent have second division marks. This means the Musahars have really benefitted from reservation and they need to be provided other facilities so that they can improve their overall performance. More than 72 per cent of the Dhobi and Pasi students also have first division marks in their 12th. The university silently accepts that many students did not get admission because of lower marks as colleges prepare merit on the basis of previous marks. Hence, they either do not continue their studies or assist their parents in farming or in other non-agricultural activity. There is lots of debate and discussion within the family of the Mahadalit students who enter the arena of higher education as there is a preconceived notion that it is difficult to get employment after higher education and there is fear of losing the traditional livelihood instead.

## Conclusion

The policy of social justice has been widely debated in various academic and policy-making circles. After six decades of independence, still the disadvantaged groups are at the margins and not able to come up so that they can partake the fruits of development. Policies are not reaching or covering the most disadvantaged like the Mahadalits and Dalits as a whole. The problem starts even before higher education and higher education merely perpetuates it. Lack of availability of senior secondary schools in rural areas is a major barrier and students from the Mahadalit group face major constraints in accessing even secondary schools in urban area or in semi-urban areas. Here semi-urban area is the block headquarter. High demand for higher education from Dalits and Mahadalits has given the college a chance to increase the entry marks instead of raising the number of seats. The college is using meritocracy as a tool to select only those who have relatively higher marks. There is need to give proportional representation in admission and the occupational background of parents and the rural background of students should be taken into consideration. Students' service centres should be strengthened and the mechanism for fellowship should be made easier and should also be delivered timely. Without the inclusion of Mahadalits into higher education, a true democracy cannot be imagined.

## References

Barr, N. (2004). *The Economics of the Welfare State.* Oxford: Oxford University Press.

Becker, S. and F. Siebern-Thomas (2007). Schooling Infrastructure, Educational Attainment and Earnings. Mimeo.

Beteille, Andre (1992). *The Backward Classes in Contemporary India.* Delhi: Oxford University Press.

Bhushan, Sudhanshu (2013). 'Higher Education in 12th Plan Paradigm Shift in Favour of "For Profit"'. *Economic and Political Weekly,* XLVIII(4): 17–19.

Bourdieu, Pierre and Jean-Claude Passeron (1990). *Reproduction in Education, Society and Culture.* London: Sage.

Card, D. (1995). Using Geographic Variation in College Proximity to Extimate the Returns to Schooling, Oin Aspects of Labour Market Behaviour: Essays in Honor of John Vanderkamp, L.N. Christofides et al. (eds), Toronto: University of Toronto Press.

Chatterjee, S.K. (2006). *Educational Development of Scheduled Castes: Looking Ahead.* New Delhi: Gyan Publishing House.

Chaudhuri, Ajit (2013). 'A Treatise on Participation'. *Economic and Political Weekly,* XLVIII(40): 37–42.

Creswell, J.W., V.L. Plano Clark, M.L. Gutmann and W.E. Hanson, (2003). Advanced Mixed Methods Research Designs, Handbook of Mixed Methods in Social and Behavioral Research, 209–240.

Deshpande, Ashwini (2011). *The Grammar of Caste: Economic Discrimination in Contemporary India.* New Delhi: Oxford University Press.

Govinda, R. (2002). *India Education Report.* New Delhi: Oxford University Press.

Jodhka, Surinder S. and Avinash Kumar (2007). 'Internal Classification of Scheduled Castes: The Punjab Story'. *Economic and Political Weekly,* 42(43): 20–23.

Kumar, A. (2006). Culture, Development and the Cultural Capital of Farce: The Musahar Community in Bihar. *Economic and Political Weekly,* 4281–4291.

Makwana, M.H. and Richard Pais (eds) (2011). *Backward Classes and Social Justice.* Jaipur: Rawat Publications.

Moore, R. and M. Hickox (1994). Vacationalism and Educational Change. *The Curriculum Journal,* 5(3), 281–293.

Parimala, D. (ed.) (2010). *Equity and Education in India: Policy, Issues and Challenges.* New Delhi: Kanishka Publishers & Distributors.

Rao, S. Srinivasa (2002). 'Dalits in Education and Workforce'. *Economic and Political Weekly,* 37(29), July: 2998–3000.

Rao, Yagati Chinna (2009). *Dividing Dalits: Writings on Sub-Categorisation of Scheduled Castes.* Jaipur: Rawat Publications.

Sá, C., R.J. Florax, and P. Rietveld (2006). Does accessibility to Higher Education Matter? Choice Behaviour of High School Graduates in the Netherlands. *Spatial Economic Analysis,* 1(2), 155–174.

Showeb, M. (1986). *Education and Mobility among Harijans.* Varanasi: Vohra Publishers.

Thorat, Sukhdeo and Katherine S. Newman (eds) (2009). *Blocked by Caste: Discrimination and Social Exclusion in Modern India.* New Delhi: Oxford University Press.

Thorat, Sukhdeo and Narender Kumar (eds) (2008). *B.R. Ambedkar: Perspective on Social Exclusion and Inclusive Policies.* New Delhi: Oxford University Press.

Thorat, Sukhdeo and Paul Attewell (2007). 'The Legacy of Social Exclusion: A Correspondence Study of Job Discrimination in India'. *Economic and Political Weekly,* 42(41), October: 4141–45.

Tilak, J.B.G. (ed.) (2013). *Higher Education in India: In Search of Equality, Quality and Quantity.* New Delhi: Orient Black-Swan.

# 18

# Child Nutrition in National Food Security Bill (2013)

## *Some Evidences*

**SHRADDHA SRIVASTAVA**

For ensuring food security for all vulnerable groups, the Government of India promulgated the National Food Security Ordinance in July 2013. Subsequently, the National Food Security Bill (NFSB) has been introduced in 2013 to replace the Ordinance, as 75 per cent of the rural and 50 per cent of the urban population, at the all-India level, will be entitled to receive subsidized foodgrains under Targeted Public Distribution System (TPDS). They are entitled for getting 5 kg per person per month. In the Antodya Anna Yojna (AAY) households are to be protected at 35 kg per household per month. The subsidized price for rice, wheat and coarse grain is ₹ 3, ₹ 2 and ₹ 1 present Bill seeks to address the issue of food security in a life-cycle approach - separate entitlements for pregnant women and children (from 6 months of age and up to 14 years), besides entitlements to a much larger population to receive subsidized food grains under Targetted Public Distribution System. There are pregnant women and lactating mothers to be entitled to meals and maternity benefit of not less than 6000 rupees. In this Bill, children in the age-group of 6 months to 14 years are entitled to meals under Integrated Child Development Scheme (ICDS) and Mid-Day Meal (MDM) scheme. An important thing added in this Bill is that the eldest woman of the household, of age 18 years or above, is to be declared the head of the household for the purpose of issuing of ration cards. Targetted groups are basically women, children as well as households. Children are the most vulnerable group among all targetted human groups. But no changes have been found in most important food and nutrition scheme basically for children aged 0–6 years, yet percentage of malnourished children is increasing. According to the government's own admission, 48 per cent of children younger than 5 years are stunted, indicating that half the country's children are chronically malnourished. India ranks 65 in Global Hunger Index (International Food Policy Research Institute). UNICEF (2009)[1] estimates 55 per cent of the deaths of children below 5 years of age are due to malnutrition. In India, around 46 per cent of all children below the age of three are too small for their age, 47 per cent are underweight and at least 16 per cent are wasted. Many of these children are severely malnourished. The World Bank Report (2009–10) estimated that the problem of malnutrition is largely faced by developing countries. Nutrition indicators for Indian children under five are dismal. Nearly 43 per cent are underweight, 70 per cent are anaemic, and 57 per cent are Vitamin A-deficient.

The above problem is more acute in India despite the fact that the share of malnourished children has declined in the country. Between 1992–93 and 2005–06, the percentage of malnourished children declined to 47 per cent from 53.4 per cent (NFHS, 1992–93; NFHS, 2005–06). But the figure is still high in India as compared to many Sub-Saharan countries.

Food should be full of abundant nutrients because nutrition is a basic building-block of human capital and, as such, contributes to economic development. There is a two-way relationship between nutrition and economic development (Thirlwall, 2003). Improved economic development contributes to improved nutrition but more importantly, improved nutrition drives stronger economic growth. It also contributes to productivity, economic development and poverty reduction by improving physical-work capacity, cognitive development, school performance and health by reducing disease and mortality.

Among all groups of human beings, the most focused group belongs to children. For the mental and physical development of children, and also considering the importance of nutrition, the Government of India has started the nutrition related policies to prevent society (children and women) from increasing levels of malnutrition.[2] For children, the two nutrition-based policies which are implemented in India on a broad level are Mid-Day Meal (MDM) and Integrated Child Development Scheme (ICDS). The Mid-Day Meal Scheme was started in 1960s for the children of government schools (primary and junior high school). The age of students should be above six years. On the other hand, the ICDS scheme which is India's largest universal nutrition-improvement programmewas launched in the 1970s. ICDS follows the *life-cycle approach*.[3] A child's most vulnerable period for productive development is six months to five years. In this precious time, it is required to protect children from the effects of malnutrition. Besides, pregnant and lactating mothers also need to be protected from these effects. The child's growth depends upon the health of the mother. Children and mothers are, thus, the most vulnerable groups. They always need healthy food full of nutrients.

This national scheme was launched on 2 October 1975 as a Government of India initiative in 33 blocks and slowly expanded over the years. The philosophy and approach behind it was based on the consideration that the overall impact would be greater if various services were delivered in an integrated manner, as the efficacy of a particular service depends on the support it receives from related services. For example, the provision of supplementary nutrition is unlikely to improve the health of a child, if she continues to be exposed to diarrhoea, infections or unprotected drinking water. ICDS was, therefore, developed to take a holistic view of the development of the child. Special features of the ICDS scheme are integrated package of services, maximum beneficiaries' reach, a mechanism for co-ordination, convergence of services, inter-sectoral approach, and training set-up, holistic development of children, community-empowerment, community-participation, child rights and gender equality.

After 1975, this scheme has been revised twice more and after revision, it has covered children from all over India. At present, this is the first universalized nutrition scheme in India. This scheme is taking place in the established Aanganwadi Centres (AWC) where generally one Aanganwadi Worker (AWW) and one or two Aanganwadi Helpers (AWH) are appointed. The government started this scheme for mothers; if mothers in rural and urban areas usually go for their work outside the house, their child will be engaged in and taken care of in AWC. Another reason for bringing this scheme was that every child in country could get nutritious food and always be healthy, the motive being fulfilled by the supplement-nutrition service. The services (under the ICDS scheme) provided by the AWC to children and mothers are described in Table 1. All the services except supplementary nutrition, pre-school education and growth monitoring, are provided with the help of Health and Family Welfare Organization. Children in the age group of 3–6 years get the benefit of all these services and 0–3 years' children get *Panjiri* on every Saturday, and for immunization and proper health check-up, pregnant and lactating mothers and also the children below 3 years generally come to the AWC.

One AWC is established for an area of a total population of approximately 1000 and two AWC are for those areas in both sectors where total population ranges between 1000 to 2000. One mini AWC (temporary) is for migratory/floating population (construction etc.) in settlements of more than 250 families for rural and urban areas.

The ICDS provides free, age-appropriate meals to children through its Anganwadi Centres across the country. The World Health Organization says malnutrition encompasses poor feeding practices like inadequate breastfeeding, and persistent infections like diarrhoea, which rob children of nutrients. But the ICDS works on the assumption that lack of adequate food intake is the primary driver of malnutrition.

## Impact of the ICDS Policy on Nutritional Status of Beneficiary (Field Study)

The consequences for beneficiary children of Aanganwadi Centres have been found for January–February 2011 for two villages (Usru and Satri) of Masodha block in Faizabad district of Uttar Pradesh. The nutritional status of beneficiary children in both the villages was calculated by using Z-score in the aforementioned two sample villages. The proportion of malnourished and normal children is presented in Figure 1. The figure indicates that 63 per cent of beneficiary children are malnourished in Usru village, while only 43 per cent of children under non-beneficiary category are malnourished in the same village. Similarly, numbers of malnourished children under the non-beneficiary category are also observed to be less malnourished in Satri village compared to the beneficiary children.

**Table 1**

*Nutritional Status of Beneficiaries in Usru and Satri Villages*

| | | *Satri* | *Usru* |
|---|---|---|---|
| Normal | Beneficiary | 60 | 37 |
| | Non-beneficiary | 73 | 57 |
| Malnourished | Beneficiary | 40 | 63 |
| | Non-beneficiary | 27 | 43 |

In India, due to a strong desire for a male child and family size, number of male children are increasing day by day. For this reason, it is assumed in this section that in the AWC, the female child is neglected more than the male child and, therefore, the percentage of malnourished female children has increased. From Figure 1, it is apparent that beneficiary female children have less normal nutritional status than the males in AWC of Satri village and as well as female beneficiary children are found more malnourished in comparison to the male. The same result is found in Usru AWC. Only one result is observed different in Usru village that non-beneficiary male children are more malnourished and non-beneficiaries female children have more normal nutritional status. The similar observable fact has been shown by Bharati et al., (2007), Waters et al., (2004).

**Figure 1**

*Sex-Wise Percentage of Malnourished and Normal Children*

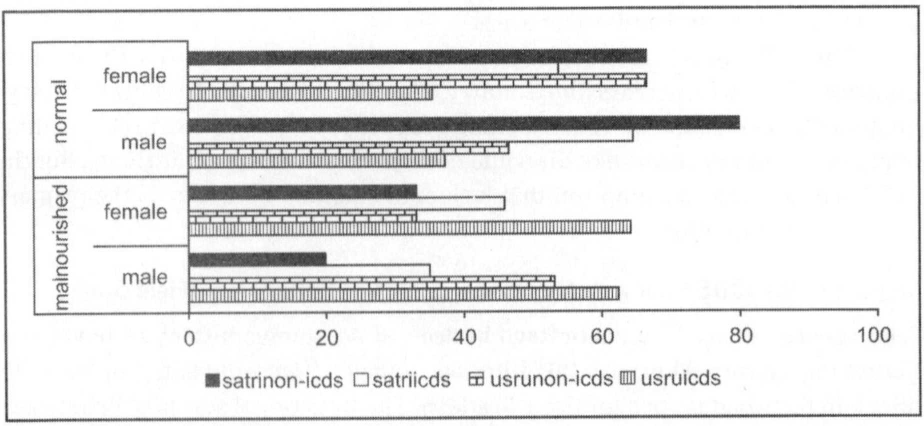


The comparison between Satri beneficiaries and non-beneficiaries showed that both the non-beneficiary female and male children are less malnourished and have more normal nutritional status than beneficiary male and female children. The result is natural as parents of Usru non-beneficiaries children pay attention more to the female girl child than the male child. Otherwise all the male children are found more dominating than female children. This suggests that after implementation of the ICDS scheme, girl-child discrimination is found in the AWCs for both villages.

**Figure 2**

*Age Group-Wise Percentage of Malnourished and Normal Children*

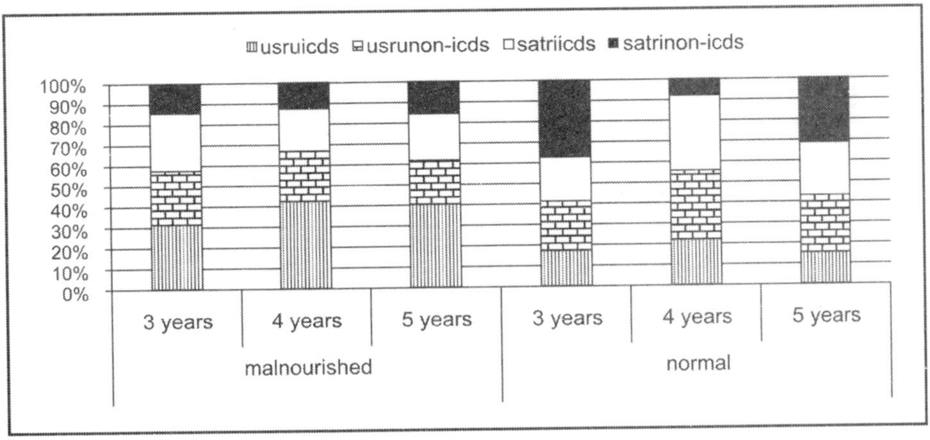


In this Section, from Figure 2, the findings show that within the 3 years' age group, Usru beneficiaries are more malnourished in comparison to others. Among all age groups, the age groups most affected by malnutrition are the 4 and 5 years' of non-beneficiaries. Mostly, normal beneficiaries are found in the 4 years' age group in Satri village. Within the 3 years' age group, non-beneficiaries in Satri village are found to be more normal in comparison to others. The overall result is revealing that percentage of beneficiaries increase more in Usru AWC than Satri AWC.

The educational level of the mother is a very important factor. It is known that if the mother is literate, she can take care of her children better than if she is illiterate. Figure 3 explains well about the children's nutritional development depending upon their mother's education level. But in this Section, the situation is found to be the reverse because the beneficiary and non-beneficiary children are malnourished in the literate mother's household. At each level of classification of the mother's education, Usru village brought out the most number of malnourished beneficiary children. In Satri village the beneficiaries' children and in Usru village, the non-beneficiaries' children are seen to have normal nutritional status. The percentage of normal children is higher in the literate mother's household than in the illiterate mother's household.

In the Figure 4, the nutritional status of beneficiaries and non-beneficiaries has been defined according to the household-types which indicates the standard of living of a household. The result shows that beneficiary children who belong to semi-*pucca* households are more malnourished in each group whereas kaccha households belong to those beneficiaries and non-beneficiaries have normal nutritional status.

**Figure 3**

*Children's Nutritional Status as Per Mother's Education Level*

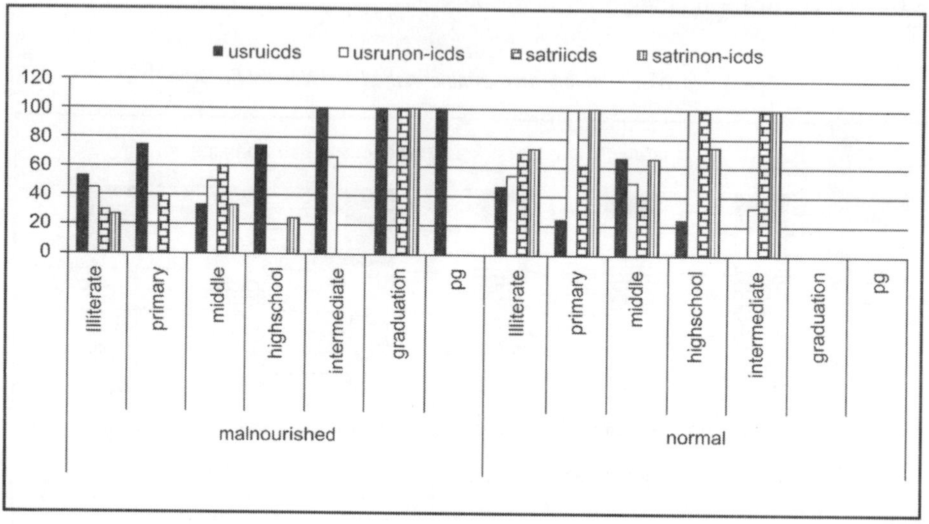


**Figure 4**

*Percentage of Malnourished and Normal Children as per Household Type*

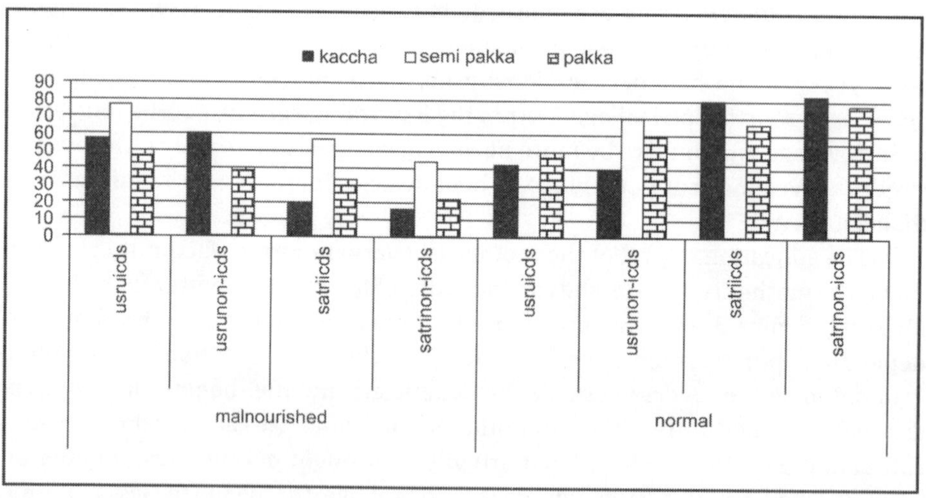


A huge number of malnourished children are found in the general category assessed in both villages (Figure 5). However, more normal children are found among the OBC category in both villages. The SC category is the next group which has a greater percentage of normal children.

Usru village has households belonging to Hindus. Therefore, for religion-wise comparison, only Satri village has been selected (Figure 6). In this village, more Muslim beneficiaries are malnourished as compared to Hindus. In both Hindus and Muslims, less percentage of malnourished beneficiaries is found. Beneficiaries amongst Hindus are found to be normal while in the non-beneficiary group, both Hindu and Muslim children are normal.

**Figure 5**

*Percentage of Malnourished and Normal Children as per Social Group*

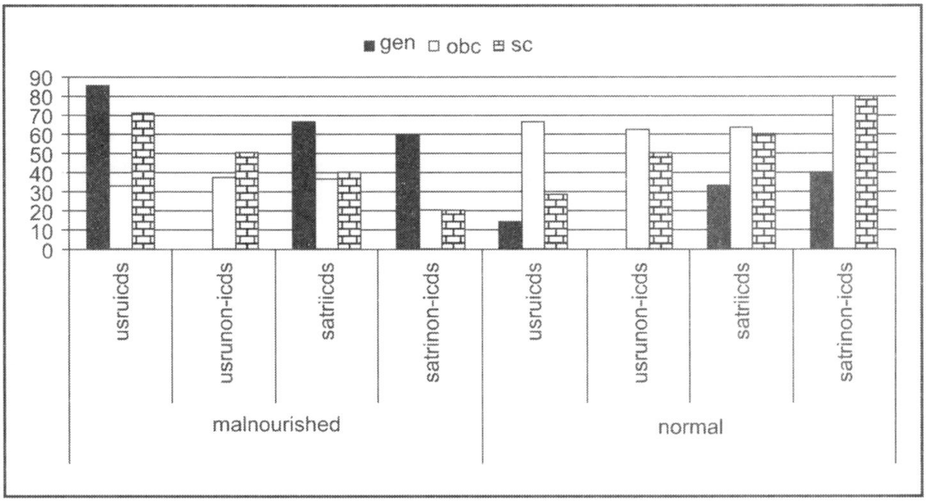


**Figure 6**

*Religion-wise percentage of Malnourished and Normal Children in Satri village*

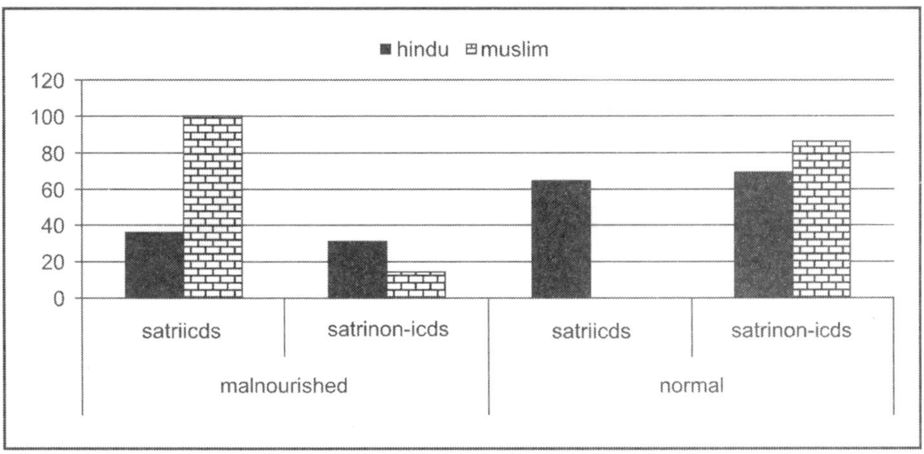


The health status of the mother always affects the nutritional status of her children. A healthy mother can make her child healthy and productive through better and nutritious food. This phenomenon is checked in Figures 7 and 8 for both villages. The findings show that in Satri village, both groups, beneficiaries and non-beneficiaries, have a normal nutritional status if their mothers' nutritional status is normal while in Usru village, mothers with normal nutritional status have more malnourished beneficiary children than normal. In Usru village, mothers with normal nutritional status have more beneficiaries of the normal nutritional status. A surprising result is seen in Satri village that the non-beneficiaries of overweight mothers have normal nutritional status. The inference is obtained that in Satri village nutritional status of mothers affects their children more in comparison to Usru village.

**Figure 7**

*Relationship between Mother's Nutritional Status and their Children's Nutritional Status in Usru Village*

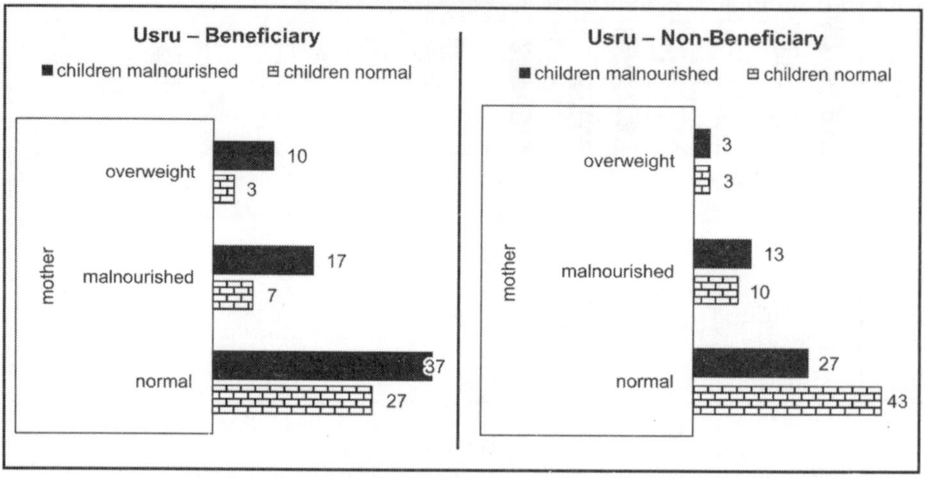


**Figure 8**

*Relationship between Mother's Nutritional Status and Children's Nutritional Status in Satri Village*

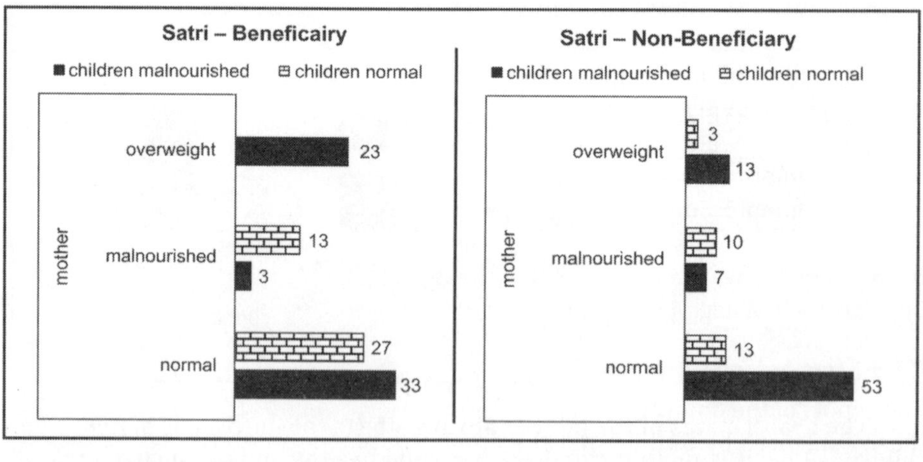


In this Section, final result of the present chapter shows the positive impact of the ICDS scheme on the nutritional status of ICDS-children in Satri village in comparison to those in Usru village. In Satri village, beneficiaries have less normal status than non-beneficiaries and in Usru village, non-beneficiaries are more in normal nutritional status than beneficiaries.

Though it would be unfair to conclude that ICDS has an adverse impact on nutritional security, it can still be said that ICDS does not have a substantial impact on the nutritional status of children. The existing literature also shows a mixed outcome of ICDS. Some studies (Saiyed et al., 2000; Vaid and Vaid, 2005) reported positive impact of ICDS, while some (Bredenkamp and Akin, 2004) reported an adverse impact. As literature reveals, the outcomes of ICDS vary region to region. Therefore, one cannot generalize observations obtained from limited areas.

## Lack of ICDS Policy: Reality from Responders

Apart from the findings from the two villages, there are also some field experiences. There were two or three Aaganwadi Centres in both villages. The infrastructure was so bad that it can't even be visualized. There was no separate kitchen for preparing food for children. One Aaganwadi helper told that the government issues cylinders for cooking but generally the Gram Pradhan captures all cylinders and this affects the cooking system of Aaganwadi Centres as Aaganwadi helpers have to make food on *chulha*. Around 30 per cent mothers in Usru and 57 per cent mothers in Satri village were not satisfied with the quality of food. The reason – sometimes *panjiri* was not cooked well and sometimes food remains infected with worms which affected children's health a lot. The situation in Aanganwadi centres is very pathetic indeed.

There were no facilities to measure the height and weight of beneficiary children. During the field visit, one witnessed an Aaganwadi worker filling the height-weight sheet for calculating the nutritional status of children. Various national and international organizations are associated with the ICDS scheme and they provided weighing machines to each and every Aaganwadi Centre, yet the Aaganwadi workers did not measure the height and weight of beneficiary children. The situation was shocking. The side-effect of this scheme is that most of the families did not want to send their children to Aaganwadi Centres. They were attracted to private schools than to Aaganwadi Centres.

The Aaganwadi workers and helpers give reason for not working in a proper manner in Aaganwadi Centres. In the hierarchy of system, the supervisor always dominates them and also pay less to them which discourages their working system to a great extent. At each step, corruption has been seen in the ICDS scheme. The observation is that the reason behind this pathetic situation is only the fault of aaganwadi centres.

### *ICDS Facts behind CAG Report*

The report of the Comptroller and Auditor General of India (CAG) has supported these evidences by finding that the number of malnourished children exceeds the 40 per cent mark in 10 states in March 2011. The audit of the flagship Integrated Child Development Services (ICDS) says 49 per cent children in Andhra Pradesh, 82 per cent in Bihar, 43 per cent in Haryana, 40 per cent in Jharkhand, 50 per cent in Orissa, 43 per cent in Rajasthan, 41 per cent in UP and 50 per cent in Delhi are moderately to severely malnourished. The number of severely malnourished children exceeded 1 per cent of the total weighed children in eight states, including Bihar, Chhattisgarh, Gujarat, Karnataka, Madhya Pradesh, Maharashtra, Uttarakhand and West Bengal. The figure was a high 3 per cent and 4 per cent in Maharashtra and West Bengal, respectively. The audit, covering 2006–07 to 2010–11, says that 52 per cent of Aanganwadis surveyed lack toilets, 32 per cent don't have drinking water and reveals 33–45 per cent gap between eligible beneficiaries and actual recipients of supplementary nutrition. Funds allocated for ICDS components are being diverted for paying salaries. As against a release of ₹ 1,753 crore to 13 states in 2008–09 and 15 states in 2009–11, the actual expenditure was ₹ 2,853 crore. Another ₹ 57 crore was diverted to activities not permitted under ICDS in five states, and ₹ 70 crore was parked in deposits blocking funds. Worryingly, while there was no data in six states on beneficiaries of pre-school kids who joined mainstream education, in five states the shortfall in the number of children who took up formal education ranged between 7 per cent and 30 per cent. Ten years after reporting that ICDS goals were not being met as health status of beneficiaries was not improving, CAG found functional weighing machines for babies and adults were not available in 26–58 per cent depending on the years surveyed in test-checked Aaganwadis.

Around 61 per cent Aaganwadis did not have their own buildings and 25 per cent were functioning from semi-*pucca* or open or partially covered spaces. Medicine kits are not available in 33–49 per cent of Aaganwadis that formed the sample. The shortfall under various categories of training ranged from 19 per cent to 58 per cent of targets and the supplementary nutrition was under-funded by 15–36 per cent between 2006 and 2011. Some 33–47 per cent children were not weighed for monitoring their growth from 2006–07 to 2010–11. Under the wheat-based nutrition programme, the Centre could allocate 78 per cent of the foodgrain demanded by states. The actual off-take by states was only 66 per cent of the total demanded by them.

## Mother's Perception about ICDS Scheme

The findings from field survey and CAG report suggest that the Aaganwadi Centres are playing an awful role in the children's life. It is obviously right that these centres are not working properly and due to this fact most of the beneficiary children are still found to be malnourished. Although the working system of Aaganwadi Centres is not as good as it should be but we cannot fully blame the aaganwadi workers for beneficiary children's malnourishment. Due to lack of awareness, parents, especially mothers, are found equally responsible for malnourishment. A mother plays an important role in making her child's life. But facts have been found from the field which show lack of awareness among mothers. Around 74 per cent mothers in Usru village and 23 per cent mothers in Satri village knew that the Aaganwadi Centres provided the food facility and more or less the schooling facility in addition. Very few mothers were, however, concerned about the facilities of the ICDS scheme. During the interview, it was asked if they were satisfied with the food menu and the response was in the negative. Further, they said that *paneer, daal-chawal, puri-sabzi* and non-vegetrian food items should be added in the food menu. They were not totally aware that the food menu contains the nutrients in substantial amount.

They think that government is only responsible to bring out their children to ICDS centres. In Usru village, only 10 per cent mothers knew about the facilities like referral services, health check-up and vaccination and in Satri village, they did not even know about these services. They were asked about the facilities related to nutrition and health education and growth monitoring, but were not aware of these facilities. Nutrition and health education is necessary to bring up children the right way. They should be sensitive about the food items which are full of nutrients and this will benefit their children. But they have no knowledge regarding the nutrients in food. The mothers did not even know the place where the Aaganwadi Centres are situated. They did not know the distance of Aaganwadi Centres from their houses.

The above information raises some points – like, there is something lacking from the Aaganwadi side or from the mother's side. Mothers not knowing about many facilities could mean either that they don't know in actual or they don't want to be aware of these or Aaganwadi Centres did not give any information related to important available facilities.

The conclusion is that we expect everything from the government but awareness should also be there. Society's problems can be eradicated only when we want to eradicate them, otherwise we cannot always blame the government for everything. My mother is a school teacher in a junior high school in Uttar Pradesh. She always teaches the children that they should wear a clean uniform. But those very children again start wearing dirty clothes. When asked as to why they did not wear clean clothes, they replied – 'Madam ji, when we reache house, our parents ordered us to help them in work and due to this we don't get enough time to study and wash the clothes.' We have to put in efforts to make better the functioning of government policies and programmes.

Amartya Sen supported this Bill and said that children's entitlements under the Food Security Bill are very weak but recent Supreme Court orders on Mid-Day Meal and the ICDS have made an important contribution to the health and nutrition of children. In this order, the Food Security Bill will bring healthy children in future. Deepa Sinha too has supported this Bill and said that the government now recognized the importance of breastfeeding and Right to Food for children younger than 6 months. The government added the Maternity Benefit Scheme.

However, the fact is that the Food Security Bill covers all necessary things except the nutrition aspect of children which is very necessary for their development. There is no change in the ICDS scheme in NFSB.

The Bill covers food items like rice, wheat and coarse grains. But according to Suneetha Kadiyala (IFPRI) and Rajiv Tandon (New Delhi-based pediatrician who are also a senior advisor on maternal and child nutrition to save children), the ordinance is too focused on calories and not on diet diversity. These food items alone do not provide adequate nutrition to people, especially micro nutrients, as there are two types of persistent hunger. The first is lack of macro nutrients and another is lack of micro-nutrients. There is no focus on diversified food basket (shifting towards non-cereal from cereal) while all focus is on the calories only. The National Nutrition Monitoring Bureau (2002) has clearly brought this out in its report on the Diet and Nutrition Status of the Rural Population. Although the rural child in 1–6 years of age group suffers from a deficiency of calories (about 40%) and proteins (about 10–20%), the deficits with regards to vitamins are truly alarming: about 75 per cent for vitamin A, 65 per cent for vitamin C, 70 per cent for riboflavin or vitamin B2, 35 per cent for folic acid and so on. The deficit of minerals are also very large. The children also need pulses, vegetables, fruits and micro nutrients. The state governments, such as Tamil Nadu, also provide *dals*, spices, oil and other commodities under the PDS system and this does help in addressing the deficiencies of the Indian cereal-dominated diet.

The ordinance currently stipulates 5 kg of foodgrain, classified as coarse grain (including rice and wheat) and millets per person per month but ICMR guidelines stipulate at least 16 kg for adults and 7 kg for children. Besides, the Food Security Bill doesn't address where this group will source its main nutrition from or how access to healthcare facilities will improve. India has a poor record when it comes to nutrition and health and the Ministry of Health Report 2011 supports the fact that 43 per cent of children below the age of 5 years are underweight, 48 per cent are stunted and 20 per cent have severe and acute malnutrition. Tragically, 1.3 million children under the age of 5 years die every year because of malnutrition and lack of access to healthcare. To absorb nutrients is an important factor but in reality children are not able to digest all food in a proper way as they are infected with water-borne diseases. Infected children fail to absorb nutrients, whatever their diet may be.

Issues related to sanitation, water and hygiene should be included in NFSB. UNICEF, the children's agency of the United Nations, says that diarrohea kills 400 young children in India every day. Two-third of Indians lack proper sanitation as some estimates suggest that 70 per cent drinking water is seriously polluted with sewage. And the last but not the least, the most significant factor which influences the development of society is lack of awareness in people related to the government's policies and programmes.

## Notes

1. UNICEF, *Tracking Progress on Child and Maternal Nutrition: A Survival and Development Priority*, New York, 2000.
2. NFHS–3: Almost half (46 percent) of all children under three are underweight (an improvement of only 1 percentage point compared to NFHS–2 (1992–93), and almost 80 per cent of children in the age-group of 6–35 months are anaemic. Only 24 percent of babies are breastfed within one hour of birth, and 46 percent are exclusively breastfed during the first six months. As many as 57 of every 1,000 children die before they reach the age of one year (IIPS).
3. A malnourished mother gives birth to a week baby and when that malnourished baby grows by the day, his/her productivity also begins to lose and he/she will be weak due to lack of proper nutrients. When he/she goes on routine work, he/she is not able to work properly and this bad condition affects the development of a country. Further, it will affect her/his baby also.

## References

Bharati, P., S. Bharati and M. Pal (2007). 'Growth and Nutritional Status of Pre-School Children in India: Rural-Urban and Gender Differences'. *Coll. Antropol*, 33: 7–21.

Bredenkamp, C. and J.S. Akin (2004). *India's Integrated Child Development Services Scheme: Meeting the Health and Nutritional Needs of Children, Adolescent Girls and Women*. Background Report for India Nutrition AAA Report, Washington, D.C.: The World Bank.

IIPS (2000). National Family Health Survey 1998–99 (NFHS–2). Mumbai: International Institute for Population Sciences.

——. (2006). NFHS–3 Factsheets, National Family Health Survey 2005–06 (NFHS–3). Mumbai: International Institute for Population Sciences.

NNMB (2002). *Diet and Nutritional Status of Rural Population*. National Institute of Nutrition, Indian Council of Medical Research, Hyderabad: Indian Council of Medical Research.

Saiyed, F. and S. Seshadri (2000). 'Impact of the Integrated Package of Nutrition and Health Services'. *Indian Journal of Pediatrics*, 67(5): 322–88.

Thirlwall, A.P. (2003). *Growth and Development*. Seventh edition, New York: Palgrave Macmillan.

Vaid, S. and N. Vaid (2005). 'Nutritional Status of ICDS and Non-ICDS Children'. *J. Hum. Ecoi*, 18(3): 207–12.

Waters, H., F. Saadah and S. Surbakti (2004). 'Weight-for-Age Malnutrition in Indonesian Children, 1992–1999'. *International Journal of Epidemiology*, 33: 589–95.

# 19

# Progressive Horizontal and Vertical Equity in Healthcare Financing in India

SWADHIN MONDAL

Catastrophic out-of-pocket spending (OOPS) for healthcare is the major determinant of inequity in healthcare financing in developing countries. It increases the poverty and inequality among households. Sometimes the costs are frequently high enough so that households are unable to recuperate them from existing resources. However, in many countries, the option of financial protection mechanisms to mitigate such burden is very limited (Xu et al., 2003; Su et al., 2006; Flores et al., 2008). As a result, protecting households from medical expenditure continues to remain a formidable challenge, particularly for countries with high levels of poverty. These issues are crucial to India because health-expenditure, especially out-of-pocket expenditure, is very high (59%) according to WHO (2011). Empirical studies (Narayanan et al., 2000; Krishna, 2006) show that the poor people in India become utterly vulnerable when they seek medical intervention for major ailments. Peters et al., (2002) estimated that every year about one quarter of the hospitalized people fall into poverty due to catastrophic payments for availing such care. Twenty-five per cent of hospitalized Indians face such level of catastrophic medical expenditure (Peters et al., 2002; Mondal et al., 2010). Also, there is wide variation in the utilization of healthcare services across the states in India. In the case of hospitalization-care, inequality within an economic group is very prominent (O'Donnell et al., 2008; Kanjilal et al., 2007; Ghosh, 2011). Also, the payment-structure for healthcare is inequitably distributed across socio-economic groups – poor people pay a higher proportion of their capacity to pay (CTP) than higher income groups (Peters et al., 2002). Therefore, vertical inequity in healthcare payment is also another crucial challenge that needs to be addressed in planning.

Many countries have already addressed these issues; their governments have set a target to enhance equity and increase fairness in health-care financing through health-sector reforms (Kanaul et al., 2006; Knaul et al., 2005; Ugalde and Homedes, 2009; Esteves, 2012). Globally, there is enormous evidence that health-sector reforms in any form – such as Conditional Cash Transfer (CCT) or Universal Health Converge (UHC), increase accessibility to healthcare services that ultimately reduce the risk of catastrophic healthcare payment (WHO, 2011; Limwattananon et al., 2011; Gao et al., 2001; Wagstaff and Yu, 2005; Lufaand Nan, 2013; Bigdeli and Annear, 2009).

Recently, India has systematically addressed the question of health financing and its inequities and vulnerabilities. First, the government has targetted an increase in health expenditure, from 1.4 per cent of GDP in 2013 to 2.5 per cent by 2017. Secondly, the central government, as well as many state governments, have developed a comprehensive strategy to improve the health status of people, especially the poorest of the poor and those in greatest need. The National Rural Health Mission, Janani Suraksha Yojana, and Rogi Kalyan Samiti are three examples of problem-focussed coping mechanisms, as is the Rashtriya Swasthya Bima Yojana, the Government of India's recently-implemented health-insurance scheme for families Below Poverty Line (BPL).[1] More recently, the government has proposed UHC to reduce inequity and improve fairness in healthcare spending.

However, does the allocation of greater resources ensure better health for the poor and reduce the risk of OOPS? How have trends in OOPS impacted household-level health equity? The consequences of these changes in health systems, for equity in terms of fairness of healthcare financing, are hardly ever discussed or considered in planning. In India, there are studies only on OOPS, and some on OOPS and poverty, but there is no systematic analysis of trends over time on equity in financing at the household level. In this study, we examine the impact of health-policy changes on equity of financing among households using four successive rounds of National Sample Survey (NSS) data on consumer expenditure, and try to find out the factors of equity in health-financing at the state level.

## Materials and Methods

This study is based primarily on the data of the national-level household survey conducted by the National Sample Survey Organization (NSSO). The NSSO, under the Ministry of Statistics and Programme Implementation, Government of India, has been conducting regular multi-subject integrated sample surveys since 1950. We have used four successive rounds of NSSO data (50th, 1993–94; 61st, 2004–05; 66th, 2009–10; and 68th, 2011–12) on consumer expenditure. In these rounds, the NSSO collected detailed information on the quantity and value of household consumption. To minimize recall errors, a detailed item classification was adopted in all consumption rounds, including 142 items of food, 15 items of energy (fuel, light, and household appliances), 28 items of clothing, bedding and footwear, 19 items of educational and medical expenses, 51 items of durable goods, and 89 other items. The schedule also collected socio-economic and demographic particulars of household members. Health expenditure included institutional and non-institutional medical care at the household level. Table 1 describes the total sample size of the four rounds of survey mentioned above.

**Table 1**

*Total Sample Size of the Four Rounds of NSSO Survey*

| *Round No.* | *Year of Survey* | *Households Covered* | | | *Populations Covered* | | |
|---|---|---|---|---|---|---|---|
| | | *Rural* | *Urban* | *Total* | *Rural* | *Urban* | *Total* |
| 50th | 1993–94 | 69,491 | 46,254 | 1,15,745 | 3,58,184 | 2,08,981 | 5,67,165 |
| 61st | 2004–05 | 79,298 | 45,346 | 1,24,644 | 4,03,207 | 2,06,529 | 6,09,736 |
| 66th | 2009–10 | 29,117 | 41,732 | 1,00,849 | 2,87,136 | 1,81,408 | 4,68,544 |
| 68th | 2011–12 | 59,695 | 41,967 | 1,01,662 | 2,85,796 | 1,79,164 | 46,496 |

To find out the determinants of equity at the national as well as state level, we consider major macro-economic variables, such as health expenditure, GDP, per capita Gross State Domestic Product (GSDP), GDP growth rate, poverty ratio, income inequality, formal health coverage and the fund utilization capacity of the State. Recent data on these macro economic indicators have been collected by reviewing secondary documents, such as central government and state government reports, budget documents, etc.

To measure the equity of healthcare financing within countries at different stages of development and health transition, the World Health Organization (WHO) developed an index of Fairness of Financial Contribution (FFC) for the health system (Murray et al., 2000; WHO, 2000; Xu et al., 2000). We used the FFC index to analyse changes over time within countries, such as the results of health-sector reforms. It can be written as:

$$FFC = 1 - 4\frac{\sum_{n=1}^{H} |HFC_n - \overline{HFC}|^3}{0.125H} \qquad (1)$$

Where,

$$HFC_n = \frac{Total\,health\,spending_n}{Capacity\,to\,pay_n} = \frac{HS_n}{(Exp + aTax - Food)^n} \qquad (2)$$

$HFC_h$ is the health financing contribution, $h$ indexes households, and $H$ is the number of households. The FFC index-value ranges from zero to one. A value of one indicates perfect equity, when everyone pays the same proportion of their Capacity to Pay (CTP), and a value of less than one indicates inequality in healthcare payment as a proportion of CTP. The index reflects both horizontal and vertical inequities. However, this index cannot explain horizontal and vertical inequities clearly when different households pay differently (Wagstaff, 2002). The value of the FFC index is less than one when households with similar CTP spend different proportions of their CTP on healthcare (horizontal inequity) or when households with different CTPs spend different proportions of their CTP on healthcare (vertical inequity), or there is a combination of the two. In other words, the value of the FFC index is different from one when the system is horizontally inequitable, or vertically inequitable, or both (Wagstaff and Doorslaer, 2001; Wagstaff, 2002).

To overcome this problem, it may be worth considering a concept in the literature on Public Finance: imposing a tax can generate horizontal and vertical re-distribution (Aronson et al., 1994; Aronson and Lambert, 1994). Horizontal re-distribution means horizontal equity (which would have obtained if the tax rate were progressive), which reduces the pro-poor Redistributive Effect (RE) associated with a progressive tax and makes a regressive tax even more pro-rich. This is the Aronson, Johnson and Lambert (AJL) approach of measuring the RE of tax on household, and has been used in health economics to measure the RE of health payment in several countries in the late 1990s (Wagstaff and Doorslaer, 1997; Doorslaer et al., 1999). The AJL method of calculating the RE of healthcare payment can be written as:

$$RE \equiv V - H - R \qquad (3)$$

Where,

$$V \equiv \left(\frac{g}{1-g}\right) K^* \qquad (4)$$

$$H \equiv \sum \alpha_x G_{F(x)} \qquad (5)$$

$$R \equiv G_{x-p} - C_{x-p} \qquad (6)$$

Where,

V = vertical redistribution,

H = horizontal inequity,

R = re-ranking,

g = average tax rate,

K* = Kakwani's index computed on the assumption that at each income level everyone spends the same amount on health-care,

V is directly proportional to g and K,

$\alpha_x$ is the product of the population share and post-payment income share of households with pre-payment income x, and GF(x) is the Gini co-efficient for post-payment income for these households.

Recently, Wagstaff suggested an alternative approach of Redistributive Effect (RE) of healthcare payment when there is no horizontal inequity and re-ranking (Wagstaff, 2002). Wagstaff also mentioned that in the FFC index (in equation 1), CTP ought to be defined as income less subsistence-expenses (food, etc.) and for equity, payment should be proportional to CTP. This has a serious limitation that after healthcare payment, the income-distribution may be more unequal, and the disposable income of some households may be insufficient for food consumption. Wagstaff and Doorslear modified it and re-adjusted it by subsistence-expenses (food, etc.) when there is no horizontal inequity or re-ranking (H=0, R=0). The Wagstaff–Doorslear approach for measuring RE of healthcare payment can be written as:

$$RE = V = \frac{g}{1-g} K_p - \frac{gf}{(1-g)(1-f} K_f \qquad (7)$$

Where, $K_P$= Kakwani index showing the progressivity of payments for payments on CTP,

$K_F$= Kakwani index showing the progressivity of subsistence-expenses (food, etc.) on pre-payment income,

f = share of pre-payment income absorbed, and

g = the average tax rate.

We have mentioned that the healthcare system in India is very heterogeneous, there is horizontal inequity in healthcare access, and that households fall into poverty after healthcare payment. Therefore, horizontal inequity and re-ranking may not be zero. By putting the value of V (Equation 7) in Equation 3, a combined index (assuming $H \neq 0$ and $R \neq 0$) for measuring RE can be written as:

$$RE = \left( \frac{g}{1-g} K_p - \frac{gf}{(1-g)(1-f)} K_f \right) - \sum_{i=1}^{n} \alpha_x G_{F(x)} - G_{x-p} - C_{x-p} \qquad (8)$$

The WHO's FFC index is computed on the same data to compare it with the approach of Aronson et al., (1994). The FFC index is straightforward to compute. The Aronson et al., decomposition is more involved. RE can be computed simply as the difference between Gpre and Gpost. In each case, the convenient covariance approach was used on household-level data (Wagstaff, 2002). The out-of-pocket share g is computed simply as mean out-of-pocket payments divided by mean pre-payment income. To compute K [or more precisely the concentration index for OOPS (Cp) and CX-P], one has to decide on appropriate groups of pre-payment equals. All the variables in the equation have been computed using the ADePT health financing software of the World Bank.

## Results

It has been seen that OOPS on healthcare in terms of household non-food expenditure has declined substantially since 1993 (NSS 50th round), but it still is more than 10 per cent of household non-food expenditure, and has increased in recent years for the lowest income group (Figure 1). Higher amounts are being spent on drugs and medicines and diagnostics than on other components of healthcare expenditure, and this constitutes the high level of OOPS; also, this OOPS has increased over the years (Figure 2). For out-patient care, drugs and diagnostics make up more than 70 per cent of the total OOPS. Also, the OOPS for drug and medicine has increased over the years. For in-patient care, medicine and hospitalization charges make up 70 per cent of the total expenditure.

**Figure 1**

*Out-of-Pocket Expenditure for Health to Non-Food Expenditure by Households*

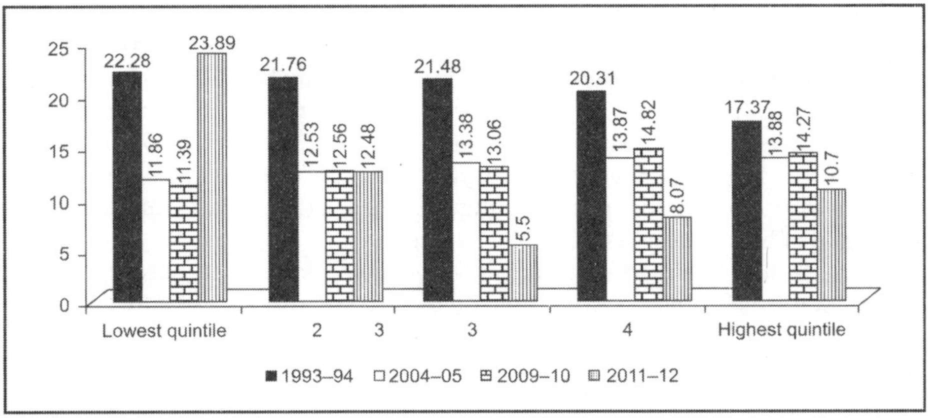


Using the WHO's FFC index, the values of FFC for out-of-pocket payment in years 1993–94, 2004–05, 2009–10, and 2011–12 are 0.8851, 0.8834, 0.8729, and 0.8512, respectively (Table 2). This indicates that the Indian healthcare payment structure produces lesser fairness of out-of-pocket payment for healthcare and offers limited protection to 'vulnerable' populations from excessive OOPS. One possible reason may be that the lowest income-group pays more than higher-income groups (Figure 1).

**Figure 2**

*Out-of-Pocket Payment for Medical Care by Type of Treatment*

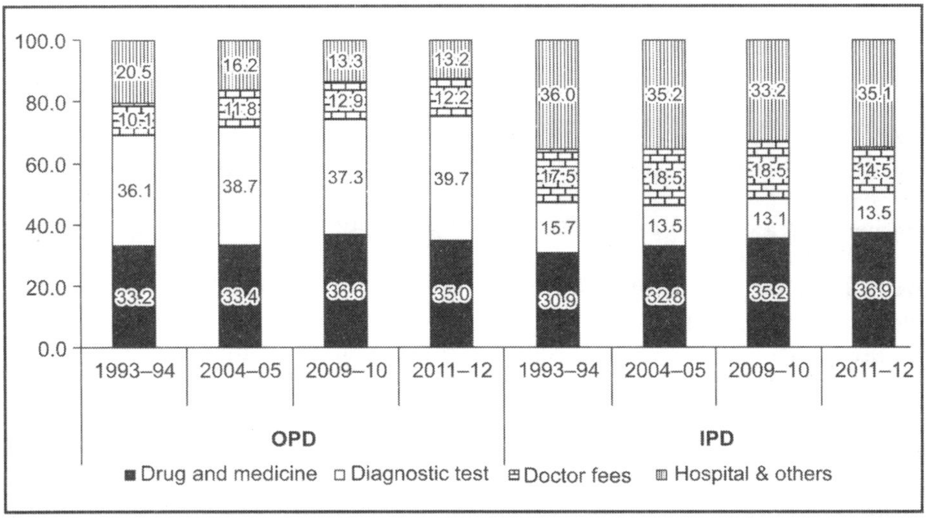


Table 3 also shows the values of the components of the AJL decomposition of re-distributive effect. The Kakwani index (assuming horizontal inequity) increased between 1993–94 and 2004–05, but suddenly decreased by 92 per cent between 2004–05 and 2009–10, and then increased. The vertical effect of OOPS had a positive impact between 1993–94 and 2004–05, but had a negative impact between 2004–05 and 2009–10 and again a positive change in 2011–12. Horizontal inequity increased in 2009–10 but decreased by 72 per cent in 2012.

The RE of healthcare payment in 1993–94, 2004–05, 2009–10, and 2011–12 was 0.0034, 0.0045, 0.0047, and 0.0017, respectively. The re-distribution effect increased over the initial 15 years but fell by 64 per cent in 2011–12. The reduction in pro-rich re-distribution was due, in part, to a reduction in the overall share of pre-payment income absorbed by out-of-pocket payments – from 1.7 per cent of pre-payment income in 2009 to 0.38 per cent in 2012, a reduction of 84 per cent during the period. This is presumably a reflection of higher user-fee at public facilities.

The Indian healthcare system is very heterogeneous in nature, because Indian states are diverse in terms of healthcare finance, healthcare infrastructure, morbidity patterns, health-seeking behaviour, utilization of healthcare services, etc. Also, under the Constitution of India, health is a state subject. Therefore, many policy interventions can be meaningfully identified and effectively implemented only at the state-level, and any generalization of an 'Indian' experience may not be meaningful. Instead, it would be more meaningful if we examine all Indian states.

**Table 2**

*FFC and Decomposition of Re-Distributive Impact of Out-of-Pocket Payment*

| *Quintiles of Per capita Consumption, Gross* | *NSS 50 (1993–94)* | *NSS 61 (2004–05)* | *NSS 66 (2009–10)* | *NSS 68 (2011–12)* | *% Change (NSS 61– NSS 50)* | *% Change (NSS 66– NSS 61)* | *% Change (NSS 68– NSS 66)* |
|---|---|---|---|---|---|---|---|
| Lowest quintile | 2.8 | 1.2 | 1.8 | 0.5 | –57.1 | 50.0 | –72.2 |
| 2 | 5.4 | 3.0 | 4.2 | 1.4 | –44.4 | 40.0 | –66.7 |
| 3 | 7.6 | 7.8 | 8.4 | 2.3 | 2.6 | 7.7 | –72.6 |
| 4 | 13.1 | 18.6 | 16.3 | 7.4 | 42.0 | –12.4 | –54.6 |
| Highest quintile | 71.1 | 69.3 | 69.3 | 88.4 | –2.5 | 0.0 | 27.6 |
| FFC | 0.8,851 | 0.8,834 | 0.8,729 | 0.8,512 | –0.2 | –1.2 | –2.5 |
| Payments as fraction of Income (g) | 0.0,171 | 0.0,199 | 0.0,234 | 0.0,038 | 16.4 | 17.6 | –83.8 |
| Kakwani index assuming horizontal equity (Ke) | 0.0,228 | 0.3,112 | 0.2,633 | 0.2,729 | 1,264.9 | –15.4 | 3.6 |
| Vertical effect (V) | 0.0,004 | 0.0,063 | 0.0,063 | 0.0,010 | 1,475.0 | 0.0 | –84.1 |
| Horizontal inequality (H) | 0.0,024 | 0.0,010 | 0.0,010 | 0.0,007 | –141.7 | 00.0 | –30.0 |
| Re-ranking (R) | 0.0,006 | 0.0,009 | 0.0,006 | 0.0,000 | 50.00 | –33.33 | –100 |
| Total redistributive effect (RE = V – H-R) | 0.0,034 | 0.0,045 | 0.0,047 | 0.0,017 | 32.4 | 4.4 | –63.8 |
| V/RE | 0.1,182 | 1.4,171 | 1.3,298 | 0.6,069 | 1,098.9 | –6.2 | –54.4 |
| H/RE | 0.7,110 | 0.2,183 | 0.2,115 | 0.3,816 | –130.7 | –3.1 | –280.4 |
| R/RE | 0.1,708 | 0.1,988 | 0.1,142 | 0.0,116 | –216.4 | –42.6 | –110.2 |

*Source:* Author's Calculation.

The overall rate of change of FFC index is negative, and the FFC declined between 2005 and 2010, and also during 2010–12. Only a few small states like Goa, Manipur, and Mizoram showed a positive change between 2005 and 2012.

Some other states like Punjab, Chandigarh, Himachal Pradesh, Jharkhand, Tripura and some North-East Indian states experienced better FFC between 2010 and 2012. The value of the FFC index improved in some major states like Delhi, West Bengal, and Odisha between 2005 and 2010, although their 'fairness' declined later.

Table 3 shows the values of the component of the AJL decomposition of re-distributive effect. Out-of-pocket expenditure exerted a disequalizing effect on income distribution in both 2005 and 2010. In many states, the impact was disproportionately high. The magnitude of RE was not very high but increased to a certain extent. States like Jammu and Kashmir, Gujarat, Manipur, Mizoram, and Punjab experienced bigger and positive changes. However, other states like Haryana, Nagaland, Arunachal Pradesh, and Assam showed a dramatic fall in RE of out-of-pocket payment for healthcare. Overall, during 2005 to 2010, there was a high impact of RE for out-of-pocket payment in India. This happened because of change in vertical redistribution (V) and changes in horizontal inequity and re-ranking (H+R). The Kakwani index in both years was positive, but declined dramatically in 2010. This means that healthcare payment structure was less progressive in 2010 than in 2005. The reduction of pro-poor redistribution was due to an increase in the overall share of pre-payment income absorbed by out-of-pocket payment. The other determinants of RE during this period are vertical effect (V), horizontal inequity, and re-ranking (H+R). Most Indian states faced the impact of large vertical income re-distribution during this period. Many states such as Jammu and Kashmir, Gujarat, Manipur, and Arunachal Pradesh, and the Union Territory of Chandigarh faced the impact of high vertical re-distribution, whereas horizontal inequity and re-ranking have had less impact.

However, in 2010 and 2012, the value of RE declined across all states, because the Kakwani index of healthcare payment indicates progressivity in the healthcare payment structure. In addition, the value of vertical effect (V) declined during this period, and the greater intensity in the decline of RE may be attributed to this decline.

**Table 3**

*Percentage Changes of FFC, V, H, R and RE of Out-of-Pocket Payment across the States*

| | FFC | | Vertical Effect (V) | | Horizontal Inequality (H) | | Re-ranking (R) | | Redistributive Effect (RE = V – H-R) | |
|---|---|---|---|---|---|---|---|---|---|---|
| | (2005–2010) | (2010–2012) | (2005–2010) | (2010–2012) | (2005–2010) | (2010–2012) | (2005–2010) | (2010–2012) | (2005–2010) | (2010–2012) |
| Andhra Prad. | 2.2 | –2.5 | 5.5 | –100.0 | –37.5 | –20.0 | 20.0 | –88.9 | 9.4 | –117.1 |
| Arunachal Prad. | –6.1 | 6.3 | 42.9 | –30.0 | 200.0 | –100.0 | 1400.0 | –100.0 | –350.0 | –170.0 |
| Assam | –0.3 | –2.1 | –82.4 | 33.3 | 100.0 | –100.0 | –50.0 | –100.0 | –116.7 | –250.0 |
| Bihar | –1.9 | –5.7 | 20.0 | –72.2 | 50.0 | –66.7 | 0.0 | –100.0 | 10.0 | –72.7 |
| Jharkhand | –2.3 | 1.4 | –70.6 | 20.0 | 100.0 | –100.0 | 0.0 | –100.0 | –127.3 | –300.0 |
| Delhi | 1.4 | –7.3 | –25.0 | –166.7 | NA | 0.0 | NA | –50.0 | –75.0 | –500.0 |

*Cont'd...*

*...Cont'd*

| | | | | | | | | | | |
|---|---|---|---|---|---|---|---|---|---|---|
| Goa | 1.4 | 4.4 | –38.3 | –88.0 | 120.0 | –100.0 | 100.0 | –100.0 | –75.8 | –68.8 |
| Gujarat | 2.4 | –4.8 | 166.0 | –97.0 | –10.0 | –88.9 | 116.7 | –100.0 | 250.0 | –96.9 |
| Haryana | 10.1 | –2.7 | 117.2 | –103.2 | –33.3 | –66.7 | –17.4 | –110.5 | –1366.7 | –105.3 |
| Himachal Prad. | –1.5 | 5.1 | 53.2 | –98.6 | 41.7 | –88.2 | –4.2 | –100.0 | 190.9 | –103.1 |
| Jammu Kashmir | –3.3 | –4.1 | 1850.0 | –98.3 | 700.0 | –87.5 | 700.0 | –87.5 | 2425.0 | –100.0 |
| Chhattisgarh | 6.1 | –3.5 | 0.0 | –103.0 | –33.3 | –75.0 | –33.3 | –133.3 | 9.8 | –101.8 |
| Karnataka | –7.2 | –1.9 | 9.4 | –97.1 | 75.0 | –71.4 | –14.3 | –100.0 | 4.8 | –104.5 |
| Kerala | 0.6 | –4.5 | –11.1 | –113.6 | 7.1 | –60.0 | –5.7 | –121.2 | –30.6 | –172.0 |
| Madhya Prad. | 3.0 | –3.7 | –53.1 | –97.4 | 20.0 | –83.3 | –37.5 | –100.0 | –59.7 | –100.0 |
| Maharashtra | –4.1 | –1.8 | –25.3 | –100.0 | 18.2 | –69.2 | 17.6 | –110.0 | –51.1 | –108.7 |
| Manipur | 0.5 | 0.5 | 133.3 | –100.0 | –33.3 | –100.0 | –33.3 | –100.0 | 466.7 | –100.0 |
| Meghalaya | 0.6 | –0.3 | –58.8 | –57.1 | 0.0 | –100.0 | –50.0 | –100.0 | –57.1 | –50.0 |
| Mizoram | 0.4 | 0.1 | 0.0 | –100.0 | 0.0 | –100.0 | –100.0 | NA | 100.0 | –150.0 |
| Nagaland | 0.1 | –0.1 | –200.0 | –133.3 | –100.0 | NA | NA | NA | –175.0 | –133.3 |
| Orissa | 4.7 | –7.8 | –15.9 | –89.2 | 0.0 | –83.3 | –57.1 | –66.7 | 0.0 | –96.0 |
| Pondicherry | –7.9 | 7.4 | –77.7 | –112.0 | 100.0 | –50.0 | 128.6 | –93.8 | –99.0 | –900.0 |
| Punjab | –10.6 | 0.7 | 88.5 | –98.0 | 87.5 | –86.7 | 116.7 | –73.1 | 79.7 | –106.6 |
| Rajasthan | –2.3 | 0.1 | 5.0 | –101.6 | 16.7 | –71.4 | –14.3 | –100.0 | 12.8 | –106.8 |
| Sikkim | –0.1 | 0.1 | –150.0 | 0.0 | NA | NA | NA | NA | –150.0 | 0.0 |
| Tamil Nadu | –3.4 | –5.4 | 42.6 | –98.7 | 100.0 | –50.0 | 33.3 | –106.3 | 42.1 | –103.7 |
| Tripura | –7.0 | 7.2 | 7.5 | –88.4 | 166.7 | –100.0 | 325.0 | –100.0 | –45.5 | –72.2 |
| Uttar Pradesh | –3.7 | –8.7 | –13.8 | –92.8 | 8.3 | –76.9 | 5.6 | –94.7 | –26.0 | –100.0 |
| Uttaranchal | –6.7 | 6.3 | 10.3 | –109.4 | 0.0 | –80.0 | 7.1 | –100.0 | 44.4 | –130.8 |
| West Bengal | 3.2 | –11.9 | 17.4 | –92.6 | 25.0 | –70.0 | –13.3 | –92.3 | 23.4 | –96.6 |
| A&N Islands | –3.3 | 6.5 | 58.5 | –92.3 | 0.0 | –100.0 | 400.0 | –100.0 | 35.1 | –90.0 |
| Chandigarh | –0.5 | 1.2 | 2350.0 | –85.7 | 200.0 | –66.7 | 100.0 | –100.0 | –1300.0 | –80.6 |
| D&N Haveli | 0.4 | –13.9 | –100.0 | NA | –100.0 | NA | NA | NA | –100.0 | NA |
| Daman and Diu | –2.2 | –5.5 | –150.0 | 133.3 | –100.0 | NA | –66.7 | –100.0 | NA | 100.0 |
| Lakshadweep | 14.4 | –14.5 | –195.6 | –102.3 | –44.4 | –80.0 | –41.7 | –96.4 | –136.1 | –109.4 |
| India | –1.2 | –3.1 | 0.0 | –84.1 | 0.0 | –170.0 | –33.3 | –100.0 | 4.4 | –63.8 |

*Source:* Author's Calculation.

## Discussions

The National Health Policy 1983 attempted to synthesize the recommendations of the earlier Bhore Committee (1946), Mudaliar Committee (1962), and Srivastava Committees (1975, 1976) with the vision of providing basic medicine, medical training, and medical education as part of social justice. In 2002, India made another change to its health policy by strengthening the health system and providing additional financial resources for health. In 2005, India made a major change to its health system by implementing the National Rural Health Mission (NRHM), which aimed to enhance equity in access to public health services and to improve health-outcomes by reducing Infant Mortality Rate (IMR) and Maternal Mortality Rate (MMR). Apart from the NRHM, India has implemented a health insurance scheme (Rashtriya Swasthya Beema Yojana), which provides direct cash transfers to the poor to protect them from catastrophic OOPS. However, even after implementing these programmes, India is still far behind its goal of enhancing equity in healthcare financing. The OOPS for healthcare has declined, but the level of expenditure, particularly in low-income households, is still very high – they spend nearly 24 per cent of their non-food expenditure, but the high-income group spends 10.7 per cent. Therefore, some inequity persists among the various socio-economic groups.

Out-of-pocket expenditure declined between 1993 and 2009, but increased suddenly between 2009 and 2012 for low-income groups. The main reason for increasing healthcare expenditure might be the introduction of user-charges in public facilities (Prinja et al., 2012). Another cause of rising health- care expenditureis the high costs of medicine and diagnostic tests, even in government hospitals. In the case of in-patient care, hospitalization and medical charges, which were already very high, have increased over time. Hospitalization charges have increased because of the introduction of user-fee in government facilities. User-fee discourages patients from filling in beds at public hospitals, This increases their utilization of private health facilities, which ultimately increases the cost of medical care. As a result, the Indian healthcare payment structure is moving towards lesser fairness in the out-of-pocket payment component. However, the value of the FFC index cannot explain the reason for these changes, as it is blind to who (poor or rich) pays more as a share of their income (Wagstaff, 2002). In other words, this index cannot explain whether the FFC is falling due to the horizontal re-distributive effect of health financing or vertical re-distributive effect of health-financing.

The vertical effect (V) of healthcare payment on income re-distribution increased from 0.0004 in 1993–94 to 0.0063 in 2004–05, and then decreased to 0.0010 in 2012. The higher value of V may be due to the greater value of g (the share of pre-payment income absorbed by health-care payment) or the lower value of K (Kakwani index). However, K showed a higher value in 2004–05. This means that the healthcare payment structure was more progressive during this period but became somewhat less progressive later on. Thus, as the value of g increases, the vertical effect of healthcare on income-redistribution increases in the corresponding year. This means that although the progressive health-care payment structure could have exerted an equalizing effect onincome re-distribution, the disproportionately higher proportion of healthcare payment (g) exerted a disequalizing effect. The value of vertical effect fell to 0.0010 in 2012 due to the greater progressivity of healthcare payment as well as the lower fraction of income absorbed by healthcare payment (g).

On the other side, horizontal inequity (H) and also re-ranking fell over the period. Horizontal difference (sum of H and R) is the inequity in post-payment income within a group. It always makes the post-payment income re-distribution more unequal than in the absence of horizontal inequity. Reduction in horizontal difference over time implies higher unequal distribution of income due to healthcare payment, which has a greater impact on RE, that also fell to 0.0017 in 2012. The main determinant of RE is V, and its value was also lowest in 2012. This implies that poor people are paying a lower share than earlier as compared to high income groups. One interpretation of this phenomenon is that government-funded healthcare services have a higher impact on the low-income group, or that government-sponsored health programmes (NRHM, RSBY, etc.) produce higher equity in OOPS on health.

However, the re-distributive impact of healthcare payment was not uniformly distributed across states. States like Jammu and Kashmir, Gujarat, Manipur, Mizoram and Punjab experienced a higher impact than those like Haryana, Nagaland, Arunachal Pradesh, and Assam, because of state-level heterogeneity in healthcare infrastructure, health-financing, morbidity patterns, and other macro-economic state-level factors. Apart from horizontal and vertical differences, rate of poverty, per-capita state GSDP, and public health expenditure (state and central) are the major factors of health inequity. Economically developed states like Haryana and Delhi and the Union Territory of Chandigarh are performing well. All North Indian states, and Union Territories like Lakshadweep and Pondicherry, are also performing well. These states are also better off in terms of Human Development Index and other health indicators, which is consistent with these results.

## Conclusions and Policy Implications

The study concludes that, overall, changes made by the Government of India to its Health Policy, especially 2005 onwards, has had a positive impact on equity in out-of-pocket payment and income-inequality (but not on poverty). Over the period, the share of pre-payment income absorbed by OOPS fell to some extent and increased the progressivity of payment structure. Over the same period, horizontal differences (H+R) have also fallen (but only a very small percentage). Thus, these were even more important sources of RE in recent years than earlier.

These results can help shape National Health Policy. The introduction of new health policies, especially the implementation of the NRHM in 2005, RSBY, direct cash transfer policy (such as RKS), and state-level health insurance schemes particularly for the poor, would increase the utilization of public health facilities and also reduce out-of-pocket payment. The high cost of medicines and diagnostic tests is still the killing field. A CCT policy can help reduce out-of-pocket payment of medicines and medical tests. The National Health Insurance Scheme for the poor (RSBY) remains small-scale; its expansion can produce better results and that, in turn, can (be expected to) reduce inequity in out-of-pocket payments and make it more progressive.

## Note

1. The Government of India has proposed the Janani Suraksha Yojana, a centrally sponsored scheme that integrates cash assistance with delivery and post-delivery care, to promote the institutional delivery of babies and thereby decrease neo-natal and maternal deaths. Rogi Kalyan Samiti, another centrally sponsored

scheme under the National Rural Health Mission (a programme for improving health-care delivery across rural India), provides financial aid to the poor for medical treatment.

## References

Aronson, J.R., P. Johnson and P.J. Lambert (1994). 'Redistributive Effect and Unequal Tax Treatment'. *Economic Journal*, 104: 262–70.

Aronson, J.R. and P.J. Lambert (1994). 'Decomposing the Gini Co-efficient to Reveal Vertical, Horizontal and Re-ranking Effects of Income Taxation'. *National Tax Journal*, 47(2): 273–94.

Bhore, J. (1946). *Report of the Health Survey and Development Committee*. Vol. I to IV, Government of India, Delhi.

Bigdeli, M. and P. Annear (2009). 'Barriers to Access and the Purchasing Function of Health Equity Funds: Lessons from Cambodia'. *Bulletin of the World Health Organization*, 87: 560–64.

Chadha Committee (1963). Special Committee for NMEP Maintenance Phase. MoHFW, Government of India, New Delhi.

Chaudhuri, A. (2012). 'Socio-Economic Inequity in Health-Care Utilization and Expenditures in Richer States in India'. *Indian Journal of Medical Research*, 136(3): 368–69.

Doorslaer, E.V., A. Wagstaff, V.D. Burg, T. Christiansen, G. Citoni et al. (1999). 'The Redistributive Effects of Health-Care Finance in 12 OECD Countries'. *Journal of Health* Economics, 18(3): 291–314.

Duggal, R. (2002). 'Health Planning in India', in *India Health: A Reference Document*. Kottayam: Rashtra Deepika, pp. 43–56. Available at www.cehat.org/go/publications/subectpublication

Esteves, R. (2012). 'The Quest for Equity in Latin America: A Comparative Analysis of the Health-care Reforms in Brazil and Colombia'. *International Journal for Equity in* Health, 11(6): 1–16.

Flores, G., J. Krishnakumar, O. O'Donnell and E.V. Doorslaer (2008). 'Coping with Health-care Costs: Implications for the Measurement of Catastrophic Expenditures and Poverty'. *Health Economics*, 17(12): 1393–412.

Gao, J., S. Tang, R. Tolhurst and K. Rao (2001). 'Changing Access to Health Services in Urban China: Implications for Equity'. *Health Policy and Planning*, 16(3): 302–12.

Ghosh, S. (2011). 'Catastrophic Payments and Impoverishment Due to Out-of-Pocket Health Spending'. *Economic and Political Weekly*, XLVI(47): 63–70.

Gupta, I. (2009). 'Out-of-Pocket Expenditures and Poverty: Estimates from NSS 61st Round'. Draft Paper, Institute of Economic Growth, New Delhi.

Kanaul, M.F., H. Arreola-Omelas et al. (2006). 'Preventing Impoverishment, Promoting Equity and Protecting Households from Financial Crisis: Universal Health Coverage through Institutional Reforms in Mexico'. Working Paper Series: Innovation for Health Financing.

Kanjilal, B., M. Mukherjee, S. Singh, S. Mondal, D. Barman and A. Mandal (2007). 'Health, Equity and Poverty: Exploring the Links in West Bengal'. FHS Working Paper 4, India. Available at http://www.futurehealthsystems.org/publications

Karami, M., F. Najafi and M.B. Karami (2009). 'Catastrophic Health Expenditure in Kermanshah, West of Iran: Magnitude and Distribution'. *Journal of Research Health Science*, 9(2): 36–40.

Kawabata, K., K. Xu and G. Carrin (2002). 'Preventing Impoverishment through Protection against Catastrophic Health Expenditure'. *Bulletin of World Health Organization*, 80(8): 612.

Knaul, F.M., H. Arreola-Ornelas, O. Méndez-Carniado, C. Bryson-Cahn, J. Barofsky et al. (2006). 'Evidence is Good for Your Health System: Policy Reform to Remedy Catastrophic and Impoverishing Health Spending in Mexico'. *The Lancet*, 368(18): 1828–41.

Knaul, F.M., O.H. Arreola, O. Mendez and M. Miranda (2005). 'Preventing Impoverishment, Promoting Equity and Protecting Households from Financial Crisis: Universal Health Insurance through Institutional Reform in Mexico'. Mexican Health Foundation Working Paper.

Krishna, A. (2006). 'Pathways Out of and Into Poverty in 36 Villages of Andhra Pradesh'. *India World Development*, 34(2): 271–88.

Limwattananon, S., V. Vongmongkol, P. Prakongsai, W. Patcharanarumol, K. Hanson, V. Tangcharoensathien and A. Mills (2011). 'The Equity Impact of Universal Coverage: Health-care Finance, Catastrophic Health Expenditure, Utilization and Government Subsidies in Thailand'. Research for Development, DFID. Available at http://r4d.dfid.gov.uk/output/188980/

Lufa, Z. and L. Nan (2013). 'Health Reform and Out-of-Pocket Payments: Lessons from China'. *Health Policy and Planning*, 29(2): 217.

Mondal, S., H. Lucus, D.H. Peters and B. Kanjilal (2014). 'Catastrophic Out-of-Pocket Payment for Health-Care and Implications for Household Coping Strategies: Evidence from West Bengal, India'. *Economics Bulletin*, 34(2): 1303–16.

Mudaliar Committee (1961). Health Survey and Planning Committee. MoHFW, New Delhi.

Mukherjee Committee (1966). Committee to Review Staffing Pattern and Financial Provision under Family Planning Programme. MoHFW, New Delhi.

Murray, C.J.L., F. Knaul, P. Musgrove, K. Xu and K. Kawabata (2000). 'Defining and Measuring Fairness in Financial Contribution to the Health System'. GPE Discussion Paper Series No. 24, EIP/GPE/FAR World Health Organization.

Narayan, D., R. Chambers, M. Shah and P. Petesch (2000). *Voices of the Poor: Crying Out for Change*. New York: Oxford University Press.

National Sample Survey (1994). 'Household Consumer Expenditure 50th Round 1993–94'. National Sample Survey Organisation, Ministry of Statistics and Programme Implementation, Government of India.

——. (2006). 'Household Consumer Expenditure 61st Round 2004–05'. National Sample Survey Organisation, Ministry of Statistics and Programme Implementation, Government of India.

——. (2010). 'Household Consumer Expenditure 66th Round 2009–10'. National Sample Survey Organisation, Ministry of Statistics and Programme Implementation, Government of India.

——. (2012). 'Household Consumer Expenditure 68th Round 2011–12'. National Sample Survey Organisation, Ministry of Statistics and Programme Implementation, Government of India.

O'Donnell, O., Doorslear E.V., R.P. Eliya et al. (2008). 'Who Pays for Health Care in Asia?'. *Journal of Health Economics*, 27(2): 460–75.

O'Donnell, Doorslear E.V., R.P. Eliya, S.R. Somanathan, S.R. Adhikari et al. (2007). 'The Incidence of Public Spending on Health-care: Comparative Evidence from Asia'. *The World Bank Economic Review*, 21(1): 93–123.

Peters, D.H., A.S. Yazbeck, R.R. Sharma, G.N.V. Ramana, L.H. Pritchett and A. Wagstaff (2002). 'Better Health Systems for India's Poor: Findings, Analysis, and Options'. Human Development Network, Health, Nutrition, and Population Series, Washington, D.C.: The World Bank, pp. 1–376.

Prinja, S., P. Kanavos and R. Kumar (2012). 'Health-care Inequities in North India: Role of Public Sector in Universalizing Health-care'. *Indian Journal of Medical Research*, 136: 421–31.

Su, T.T., B. Kouyate and S. Flessa (2006). 'Catastrophic Household Expenditure for Health-care in a Low-income Society: A Study from Nouna District, Burkina Faso'. *Bulletin of World Health Organization*, 84(1), January: 21–27.

Ugalde, A. and N. Homedes (2009). 'Health and Equity in Latin America'. *Americas Quarterly*, Fall.

Wagstaff, A. (2002). 'Reflections on and Alternatives to WHO's Fairness of Financial Contribution Index'. *Health Economics*, 11(2): 102–15.

Wagstaff, A. and E. Van Doorslaer (1997). 'Progressivity, Horizontal Equity and Re-ranking in Health-care Finance: A Decomposition Analysis for The Netherlands'. *Journal of Health Economics*, 16(5): 499–516.

——. (2001). 'Paying for Health-Care: Quantifying Fairness, Catastrophe and Impoverishment, with Applications to Vietnam 1993–98'. Policy Research Working Paper #2715, Washington, D.C.: The World Bank.

Wagstaff, A. and Shengchao Yu (2005). 'Do Health Sector Reforms Have Their Intended Impacts? The World Bank's Health VIII Project in Gansu Province, China'. The World Bank Policy Research Working Paper 3743, October.

——. (2002). 'Poverty and Health Sector Inequalities'. *Bulletin of the World Health Organization*, 80(2): 97–105.

World Health Organization (2000). *World Health Report 2000: Health Systems: Improving Performance*. Geneva, Switzerland.

——. (2011). 'Success Stories of Health Financing Reforms for Universal Coverage, Ghana', Geneva.

Xu, K., D.B. Evans, K. Kawabata, R. Zeramdini, J. Klavus and C.J.L. Murry (2003). 'Household Catastrophic Health Expenditure: A Multi-country Analysis'. *The Lancet*, 362: 111–17.

Xu, K., P. Lydon, J. Ortiz de Iturbide, P. Musgrove, F. Knaul, K. Kawabata, C.E. Florez, J. John, S. Wibulpolprasert, H. Waters and A. Tansel (2000). *Analysis of the Fairness of Financial Contribution in 21 Countries*. Geneva, Switzerland: World Health Organization.

# Part 7

## Democracy and Representation

# 20

# Democracy and Pluralism

## *Immigrant Incorporation and Citizenship*

**DIKSHA JHA**

### Theoretical Premises on Immigrants' Rights

The existence of varied theoretical debates on immigrants' rights and their incorporation provides us with an interesting lens to build an analysis and present the current status of immigrants or migrants in the context of liberal democracies. Under the restrictive view on immigrants' rights, I would begin my discussion with the work of Michael Walzer who belongs to the communitarian strand and has written widely on membership and the question of immigrants. He argues, 'Under the contemporary notion of membership, citizens are distinguished from aliens by virtue of a series of protection-rights to which they are entitled'. Walzer puts forth a dualistic explanation to differentiate the republican and liberal notions of citizenship. The former describes citizenship as 'an office, a responsibility, a burden proudly assumed'. Under the liberal conception, 'citizenship is a status, an entitlement, a set of rights that is passively enjoyed'. The republican understanding presumes the citizen as 'a primary political actor, law-making and administration his everyday business'. Under the liberal notion, Walzer argues, a 'citizen's business is private and law-making and administration are someone else's business' (Ball, Farr and Hanson, 1989).

Coming to the question of immigrants, Walzer states, 'across a considerable range of decisions that are made, states are simply free to take in strangers or not.' But the right to adopting such an admission policy is more than simply being an exercise of sovereign right of the State, as, at stake here is the community's shared understanding and self-determination. 'Self-determination', he argues, 'in the sphere of membership is not absolute as it is a right exercised most often by national clubs or families, but held in principle by territorial states'. Thus, any sort of determination of the guests and aliens by citizen-groups would not be regarded as communal independence, but a form of oppression. The citizens are free so far as to set up clubs and make membership exclusive, but such a freedom does not extend up to claiming territorial jurisdiction and ruling over the people. He calls the rule of citizen over citizens, members over outsiders as 'the most common form of tyranny in human history'. However, he does uphold the 'limited right of closure', without which there could be no communities and the 'political inclusiveness of the existing communities'. He then goes on to discuss the various categories of outsiders. One of the categories includes that of the newly-independent States that find themselves as members of territories in which alien groups admitted by the earlier imperial rule also reside. Such category of aliens often face the constant threat of expulsion due to popular hostility which even the new government cannot afford to overlook and therefore play a part in driving them out (Walzer, 1983).

Walzer argues that it may be difficult for the alien groups to be rightful members of a club or the community, but 'some form of territorial right may still be described to them'. He further states that any theory of justice 'must allow for the territorial state to recognize a collective right of admission or refusal'. Regarding the category of needy outsiders which he calls 'refugees', he argues that their need for membership is a 'non exportable good'. Admitting the refugees does not imply any kind of reduction in the amount of liberty that the members enjoy. As long as the numbers are not that large to have any significant impact on the character of the political community, allowing the refugees in might not appear a big problem. The problem arises once the numbers are too large as he describes in one of the examples involving millions of Russians captured by the Nazis in the Second World War. On forcible return to the Soviet Union, they were either shot or sent to die in the labour camps. Many of them pleaded for asylum in the West, but that too was denied to them. He argues that while it may be a morally strong reason to take them in, knowing that they would be killed anyway on returning home, there does exist a 'limit to collective liability' and therefore, 'the right to restrain such a flow remains a feature of communal self-determination' (ibid.). After having allowed admission into the territorial space, next comes the question of citizenship rights. This he calls the process of naturalization or second admission process. He argues that 'at stake here is citizenship and not nationality'. Thus, the question would then become, using Walzer's example, 'whether an Algerian immigrant to France could rightfully claim French citizenship without becoming a Frenchman'. The image of the immigrant, he argues does not look pleasant. In a way they become nothing more than resident aliens. He also draws a parallel between the resident aliens and 'metics' in the Athenian city-state as described by Aristotle. He, therefore, describes the State like 'a family of live-in servants' (ibid.).

It appears, therefore, from Walzer's understanding that he does not push too far the question of claims of the immigrants. This appears clear from his argument regarding the refugees, where on the one hand he appears sympathetic to their moral claims for membership, but at the same time allows for the closure argument to limit such claims. Thus, in Walzer's scheme of the membership-debate, the question of nationality and communal interest would take precedence over the moral or cosmopolitan claims of universal citizenship. Gary

Freeman argues that immigrants of different legal origin are treated differently, whereby the skilled category of migrants may be better placed than the unskilled category in terms of integration into the country of residence (Freeman, 2004: 950). Joppke (1999) on similar lines argues that there exist categories of wanted and unwanted immigrants. In the context of Germany and Britain, he argues, those who are formally recruited may enjoy advantages because policy-makers tend to feel a moral obligations towards them which they lack towards those who are unwanted.

Another scholarly work that I will now look into is that of Macedo and his moral-justification argument for restrictive immigration. He is looking particularly into the context of USA and immigration policies therein. His broad argument is that if a high level of immigration has had a detrimental impact on the poor citizens of US and does not address their distributive justice concerns, then there is a moral justification for a restrictive immigration policy. He states, 'Comparative standing of citizens matters in some ways that the comparative standing of citizens and non-citizens does not' (Swain, 2007: 64). He cites various empirical evidences to substantiate this claim. Further, he also uses the normative arguments of Rawls and Walzer, who are equally supportive of such a claim, that the distributive-justice aspiration has to be addressed within a bounded political community. He cites Rawls, who in 'The Law of Peoples', endorses Walzer's discussion of the moral significance of membership and borders, and argues that 'we have no obligations across borders to regulate the relative well-being of better and worse-off people'. Thus, Macedo argues that the two basic principles of justice that Rawls proposed would be chosen by citizens of modern pluralistic democracies. He argues that in shaping the immigration policies, concerns about distributive justice are urgent and important and these concerns are 'inward looking rather than cosmopolitan', emphasizing the special obligation toward fellow poor citizens (Swain, 2007).

Therefore, Macedc's arguments too are on similar lines as those of Walzer. That is, he too does not want to think beyond a particular point of sympathy, non-exploitation and humanitarian grounds and therefore considers the cosmopolitan-justice claims for the immigrants as asking for too much. The following Section takes up the theoretical grounds that provide for a moral basis and support for immigrants' rights.

## Case for Open Borders and Rights of the Immigrants

In this Section, I would look into the scholarly works that question the civic view of bounded political community and their inward-looking claims and rather, present a moral justification of cosmopolitan claims and rights' claims of the immigrants. I would begin this Section with the argument of Joseph Carens, who uses three major theoretical premises of Nozick, Rawls and the Utilitarian Theory to push forth his case for open borders and immigrants' rights. He argues that none of these three theories supports the claims of restrictive immigration. In Nozick's Property Rights Theory, he argues, the State has the role of ensuring law and order and safeguarding the individual's property rights. Any question of admitting or restricting immigration flows would hold in a scenario when the property is collectively owned, and this not being the case in modern territorial States implies that the State has no role in restricting the immigration flow. Further, any such restriction, if made, would imply interfering in the voluntary exchange among individuals and, therefore, a major violation of property rights. Also, he argues that any claims of the State's exclusion or ill-treatment of poor aliens can hold in a similar manner for the poor citizens too in a Nozickean world of property-rights (Carens, 1995: 254).

In a similar way, Carens uses the Rawlsian 'veil of ignorance' argument to advocate the rights of immigrants. While in the original Rawlsian theory, the original position was to be within the confines of a political community, Carens stretches this premise to the extent of calling it a 'global original position'. In such a global original position, the argument of nationality and belongingness to community would be as arbitrary as one's colour of skin (Carens, 1995; Benhabib, 2004). Thus, since in the Rawlsian understanding, liberty is a prior principle, any economic or moral and cultural claim for restrictive immigration would not hold under the Rawlsian scheme as well. Regarding the utilitarian argument, Carens argues that even the utilitarian claim of maximizing utility would not be anyway impacted due to immigration. Thus, the best immigration policy, he argues would be one that maximizes the overall utility and this would not take into account the preferences of individual citizens over those of the immigrants and, therefore, this too advances a claim in some manner for open borders. Thus, he argues that 'no moral argument would seem to be acceptable if it challenges the assumption of the equal moral worth of individuals'. Therefore, any restrictive migration claim has to respect this principle. He argues in the end, any striving towards making a claim for open borders would in no way threaten the communal character but only reaffirm it. It would lead towards 'an affirmation of liberal character of community and of its commitment to the principles of justice' (Carens, 1995: 271).

Thus, it very well appears from the claims made in support of open borders by Carens that he, to a great extent, made an attempt to stretch the three theoretical premises beyond a point to make them fit into his scheme of things regarding free migration and open borders. Before I move to discuss the next theorist, it is important to understand how important the right to belong to a bounded political community is for an alien and this idea is effectively put forth by Hannah Arendt, who argues:

> Because only savages have nothing more to fall back upon than the minimum fact of their human origin, people cling to their nationality all the more desperately when they have lost the rights and protection that such nationality once gave them. Only their past with its 'entailed inheritance' seems to attest to the fact that they still belong to the civilized world. (Arendt, 1962: 300)

Moving to our next theorist, Linda Bosniak has argued as to how a simplified view of citizenship as an egalitarian and democratic aspiration obscures the deep contradictions that it entails within. She further states, 'the idea of citizenship is usually invoked to convey a state of democratic belonging or inclusion, but this inclusion is premised on a conception of a community that is bounded and exclusive (Bosniak, 2006). Thus, citizenship, which looks to embody a commitment against subordination, can also represent an axis of subordination itself. Therefore, in normative terms, the boundary-focused citizenship entails not just belonging but also 'community exclusivity and closure'. She argues for the need to deepen the conversation between the inward-looking and boundary-conscious approach to citizenship. Just as one presumes the existence of boundaries, the national society is treated as the 'total universe of analytical focus and normative concern'. Citizenship, she regards, is thought as 'hard on the outside and soft on the inside, with hard edges and soft interior together constituting a complete citizenship package'. However, she asserts, the complementarity aspired to in this construct of citizenship can stand only 'so long as the hard outer edges actually separate inside from outside'. In the world of open, porous borders, real separation is often elusive. As is seen in the case of transnational migration, once the foreigner enters a bounded national space, he is assigned the status of 'alienage'. She argues, 'these non-citizen immigrants have entered into the spatial domain of universal citizenship, but they remain outsiders in a significant sense: the border effectively follows them inside' (ibid.).

Lastly, in this Section we look into Benhabib's arguments on the rights of immigrants or 'others' as she calls them. She argues that a major paradox regarding the current political developments is that while the State's sovereignty in economic, military and technological domains has been to a great extent undermined, on the political front it seems to have been strongly asserted, and while national borders may seem more porous, they are there to keep out aliens and intruders. The growing normative inconsistencies between the international norms of human rights, particularly as they pertain to the 'rights of others', and the assertions of territorial sovereignty, she argues, is a novel feature of this new landscape. The Universal Declaration of Human Rights, 1948, signalled the beginning of international norms of human rights whereby the State's sovereignty was no longer the ultimate arbiter of the fate of citizens or residents. However, such a charter of human rights does not explicitly state the rights of immigrants, refugees and asylum-seekers and despite its cross-border character, it upholds the sovereignty of individual States. Benhabib approaches the question of political membership from the standpoint of 'discourse ethics and a normative theory of deliberative democracy'. Using Habermas' idea of discourse ethics, she argues, 'only those norms and normative institutional arrangements are valid which can be agreed to by all concerned under argumentation-situations named discourses'. Since the Discourse Theory articulates a universalist moral standpoint, it views the moral conversation as potentially extending to the entire humanity. She argues, 'everymoral person who has interests and whom my actions and consequences of my action can affect in some manner, is a potential moral conversation-partner with me' (Benhabib, 2004).

Unlike the communitarians, whom she calls 'decline of citizenship theorist', who reduce the demands of morality to the claims of specific ethical, cultural and political communities, and unlike the realists and post-modernists who are skeptical that political norms can never be made subordinate to the moral ones, the discourse ethicist insists on the 'necessary mediation between the moral and the ethical and the moral and the political'. She develops the concept of 'democratic iterations' to show 'how commitments to context transcending constitutional and international norms can be mediated with the will of the democratic majorities'. These are complex processes of deliberation, arguments which contest the universal-rights' claim and have a tendency to 'transform authoritative precedents'. Through such a process, she argues, the distinction between citizen and alien can be made 'fluid and negotiable', and only then can one move toward a 'post-metaphysical and post-national conception of cosmopolitan solidarity that brings all human beings by virtue of their humanity under the net of universal rights'. She follows the Kantian tradition of 'cosmopolitan federalism' to highlight the significance of membership in a bounded community and defend the need for 'democratic attachments' that may not be directed towards existing nation-state structures alone. Thus, she argues, there is a need to respect the distinct claims of the democratic communities while strengthening their commitment to the norms of cosmopolitan justice (ibid.).

Stephen Castles and Alistair Davidson argue how globalization has emerged as an important factor in increasing international population-mobility and this in turn has given rise to the formation of distinct ethnic communities which in certain circumstances have become ethnic minorities. They argue that nation-states have an 'inbuilt tendency to create difference and to racialize minorities'. This results not just as a consequence of the discourses that ascribe difference to the others, but also through 'various forms of social and political action'. This 'otherness' becomes a justification for the differential treatment and their marginalized standing in the political community. In the era of rapid socio-economic change, they argue, 'these immigrants over a course of time become ethnic minorities who are then subject to exclusion from the legal, economic, social sphere' (Castles and Davidson, 2000).

Amid the competing claims of the communitarian school (that advocates civic republican citizenship) and the liberal school which privileges the citizen (with a shared common understanding) and the individual respectively, Chantal Mouffe offers an interesting alternative. Mouffe argues, the need is to construct an identity of a citizen and individual in a way that does not sacrifice one for the other (Mouffe, 1992: 30). She further states, 'rather than having a conception that emphasizes commonality at the expense of plurality and respect of difference, or that denies any form of commonality in the name of difference and plurality, it's important to envisage a commonality that respects diversity and gives space to different forms of individuality' (ibid.). This argument goes a long way in making the claim for immigrant incorporation in modern democracies.

## Status of Migrants in India

In the context of India and its approach towards migrants and refugees, B.S. Chimni argues that India may have implicit respect for the principle of *non-refoulement* (under International law, 'no refugee should be returned to that country where he or she is likely to face persecution or torture'), but the absence of refugee-specific legislation has created problems (Chimni, 2005: 302). Apart from the aspect of a refugee-specific legislation, Chimni points towards the aspect of civil society 'contesting the official discourse'. The official discourse or the standpoint of the State tends to view relief given to refugees as a form of charity rather than rights. This idea, he argues, needs to be contested by the civil society. That citizens are morally obliged to only fellow-citizens and not other human beings portrays a very exclusive idea of citizenship in modern democracies (ibid.: 310).

Jayal in her analysis of the 'stateless in Rajasthan' argues that 'the legal status of residence and eventually citizenship is a challenge that has to be negotiated on arrival' (Jayal, 2013: 94). She further states that 'citizenship is defined by these migrants as *suvidha* or facility or fulfillment of basic needs in the form of land, livelihood, government school, water and electricity.' It also includes getting hold of 'official documentation such as ration cards, caste certificates, and BPL cards which entitles its holders various government-initiated poverty-reduction programs' (ibid.: 94). Unlike in North America, where 'aliens do have access to certain sets of socio-economic rights, like the right of children to attend public school, property-related rights, our migrants do not enjoy even basic rights of mobility, let alone other types of social rights' (ibid.: 88).

## Conclusion

In the end, it can be argued that the model of immigrant incorporation has an underlying moral or normative substance. Current models of citizenship that exist in most liberal democracies across the world advocate an idea of the citizen as an exclusive category, thus simultaneously creating a category of 'the other'. Thus, to my mind, Bosniak's claim of citizenship rights and presence of a bounded community, presuming some sort of exclusiveness and closure giving rise to 'alienage', seems to best describe our present context. This point has been further reinstated by Jayal in the context of migrants in Rajasthan, who view citizenship as basic access to a certain set of entitlements and political rights or political membership that hold little meaning for them (ibid.). This approach as has been adopted by liberal democracies like India, needs to make way for a more inclusive idea where diversity, plurality and individuality of different kinds are given space and democracy assumes a more broad and inclusive understanding.

## References

Arendt, Hannah (1962). *The Origins of Totalitarianism*. Cleveland and New York: Meridian Books and World Publishing Co.

Ball, Terence, James Farr and Russell L. Hanson (eds) (1989). *Political Innovation and Conceptual Change*. Vol. 11, Cambridge: Cambridege University Press.

Benhabib, Seyla (2004). *The Rights of Others: Aliens, Residents and Citizens*. Cambridge: Cambridge University Press.

Bosniak, Linda (2006). *The Citizen and the Alien: Dilemmas of Contemporary Membership*. Princeton: Princeton University Press.

Carens, Joseph H. (1995). 'Aliens and Citizens: The Case for Open Borders', in Ronald Beiner (ed.), *Theorizing Citizenship*. Albany: SUNY Press.

Castles, Stephen and Alistair Davidson (2000). *Citizenship and Migration: Globalization and the Politics of Belonging.* New York: Palgrave.

Chimni, B.S. (2005). 'Outside the Bounds of Citizenship: The Status of Aliens, Illegal Migrants and Refugees in India', in Rajeev Bhargava and Helmut Reifeld (eds), *Civil Society, Public Sphere and Citizenship Dialogues and Perceptions.* London: Sage, pp. 277–313.

Freeman, Gary P. (2004). 'Immigrant Incorporation in Western Democracies'. *International Migration Review*, 38(3): 945–969.

Jayal, Niraja Gopal (2013). *Citizenship and its Discontents: An Indian History*. Cambridge: Harvard University Press.

Joppke, Christian (1999). *Immigration and the Nation-State: The United States, Germany and Great Britain.* Oxford: Oxford University Press.

Moufee, Chantal (1992). 'Citizenship and Political Identity'. *October*, 61: 28–32.

Swain, Carol M. (2007). *Debating Immigration.* New York: Cambridge University Press.

Walzer, Michael (1983). *Spheres of Justice: A Defense of Pluralism and Equality.* New York: Basic Books.

——. (1989). 'Citizenship', in Terence Ball, James Farr and Russell L. Hanson (eds), *Political Innovation and Conceptual Change*. Cambridge: Cambridge University Press.

# 21

# New Media in India

## *An Overview of Internet and Mobile Technologies*

**SANDEEP BHATT**

### Types of Indian Media

Mass media are the channels of communication – whether written, broadcast, or spoken – that reach a large audience. This includes television, radio, advertising, movies, the internet, newspapers, magazines, and so forth. Mass media is a significant force in modern culture, particularly in America. Several sociologists refer to modern culture as a mediated culture where media reflects and create the culture. Communities and individuals are bombarded constantly with messages from a multitude of sources including TV, billboards, and magazines, to name a few. These messages promote not only products, but moods, attitudes, and a sense of what is and is not important.

According to a report put out by FICCI-KPMG, 2013, India's media and entertainment industry is poised to double in size by 2017. The Report, 'FICCI Frames 2013', says that the industry, whose current size is estimated at ₹ 91,700 crores, is expected to touch ₹ 1,66,000 crores by 2017. FICCI says television continues to be the dominant segment of the sector although new media like animations, visual effects, gaming and digital advertising are expected to post strong double-digit growth during the next five years. In 2012, the television segment had accounted for 45 per cent of the ₹ 83,100 crores markets. Its share is likely to go up to 50 per cent by 2017 with a size of ₹ 84,760 crores of the ₹ 1,66,000 crore market. Print is expected to post a moderate Combined Annualized Growth Rate (CAGR) of 8.7 per cent to touch ₹ 34,020 crores from the 2012 level of ₹ 22,410 crores. The Indian film industry is slated to grow from the present ₹ 11,240 crores to ₹ 19,300 crores in 2017. The digital advertising industry in India is estimated at ₹ 2,170 crores. Followings are the prominent types of media in India:

### Print Media

The first major newspaper in India, *The Bengal Gazette* was started in 1780 under the British Raj by James Augustus Hickey. Other newspapers such as *The*

*India Gazette, The Calcutta Gazette, The Madras Courier* (1785), *The Bombay Herald* (1789), etc. soon followed. These newspapers carried news of the areas under the British Rule. *The Bombay Samachar*, founded in 1822 and printed in Gujarati, is the oldest newspaper in Asia still in print. *The Times of India* was founded in 1838 as the *Bombay Times and Journal of Commerce* by Bennett, Coleman and Company, a colonial enterprise now owned by an Indian conglomerate. The Times Group publishes *The Economic Times* (launched in 1961), *Navbharat Times* (Hindi language), and the *Maharashtra Times* (Marathi language). In the 1950s, 214 daily newspapers were published in the country. Of these, 44 were English language dailies, while the rest were published in various regional and national languages. This number rose to 2,856 dailies in 1990 with 209 English dailies. The total number of newspapers published in the country reached 35,595 newspapers by 1993 (3,805 dailies). The main regional newspapers of India include the Malayalam language *Malayala Manorama* (published from: Kerala, daily circulation, 6,73,000), the Hindi-language *Dainik Jagran* (published from: Uttar Pradesh, daily circulation in 2006, 5,80,000), and the *Ananda Bazar Patrika* (published from: Kolkata, daily circulation in 2006, 4,35,000). The Times of India Group, the Indian Express Group, the Hindustan Times Group, the Hindu Group and the Ananda Bazar Patrika Group are the main print-media houses of the country. By 2007, 62 of the world's best-selling newspaper dailies were published in China, Japan, and India. India consumed 99 million newspaper copies as of 2007, making it the second largest market in the world for newspapers.

## Broadcasting

*Radio:* Radio broadcasting was pioneered in India by the Madras Presidency Club Radio in 1924. The Club worked a broadcasting service for three years, but owing to financial difficulties, gave it up in 1927. In the same year (1927), some enterprising businessmen in Bombay started the Indian Broadcasting Company with stations at Bombay and Calcutta. This company failed in 1930, and in 1932 the Government of India took over broadcasting. A separate department known as Indian Broadcasting Service was opened. The Service was later designated as 'All India Radio' (AIR) and was placed under a separate Ministry – the Ministry of Information and Broadcasting. While the total circulation of all the newspapers in India, including both English and Indian language papers, is around 8 million, there are, according to a recent estimate, nearly 400 million (out of a total population of 625 million) potential listeners of All India Radio. All India Radio (also known as Akashvani), as a national service developed and operated by the Government of India, operates over a network of broadcasting stations located all over the country. Starting with six broadcasting stations in 1947, the AIR today has a network of 82 broadcasting stations, grouped into five zones. This is, indeed, a great improvement upon 1947 when there were only six radio stations in the country.

*Television:* Television started as a modest affair in India on 15 September 1969 when the AIR set up an experimental television service in Delhi. It was soon converted into a full-fledged telecasting station. Bombay was the second city in India to open a television centre on 2 October 1972. A television centre was commissioned at Srinagar (Kashmir) on 26 January 1973 and another was opened at Amritsar (Punjab) on 29 September 1973. A relay centre was set up in Poona (Maharashtra) on 2 October 1973. In August 1975 Calcutta (West Bengal) and Madras (Tamil Nadu) also opened centres.

The television set-up, under the name 'Doordarshan', was given the status of a full-fledged Directorate with effect from 1 April 1976. Separation of television from AIR was intended to facilitate fuller development of this medium and the specialized skills peculiar to it. Doordarshan has at present seven Kendras located at (1) Delhi (2) Bombay (with a relay-centre at Pune) (3) Madras (4) Calcutta (5) Srinagar (6) Amritsar and (7) Lucknow, besides three Base Production Centres at Delhi, Cuttack and Hyderabad. The main objective of Doordarshan is bringing on board issues of development and education, besides providing rich entertainment through varied programmes of music, feature films, etc. Intended to benefit both urban and rural viewers, Doordarshan tries to project to the people development-plans and their implementation. Doordarshan lends powerful support to the major multimedia campaigns initiated by the central government from time to time.

## Traditional Media

Apart from all the above-mentioned media, traditional media of communication like Dances, Folk Performances, Oral Traditions, Nautanki, and Puppetry still exist and are accepted in wider parts of the country. Though newspapers, Magazines and Television have greater impact than these traditional media, people still have a strong attachment to the content and contexts of such traditional media.

## Growth of Internet and Mobile in India

The web emerged as recently as in 1995 when it was available only in the metros. The real thrust to the introduction of internet was received in the initial years of the new millennium. The rapid increase in mobile and wireless connections continued to drive the growth of internet penetration in India. With better access, through cheaper and smarter devices, audiences (especially youth) are consuming more content and are getting increasingly engaged. Going forward, better uptake of 3G connections and the beginnings of the 4G roll-out are expected to spur growth further. Also, 4G technologies will enable greater uptake in services, including Live TV, HD video/audio streaming, real time online gaming, high-speed data downloads and uploads, and could enable introduction of new innovative offerings. The industry looks forward with great hope to an aggressive roll-out of this technology by the telecommunication.

Internet was born in USA in 1960s to aid defence and scientific projects. In India also, Internet was introduced by research institutes. India had 42,000,000 internet users (not subscribers) in July 2007 compared to 5,000,000 at the turn of the last century. The usage growth during the seven years ending 2007 was 83.3 per cent. Videsh Sanchar Nigam Ltd. launched a commercial internet service in 1995 for industry, trade, home-users, and so on. In February 2002, the Government of India released 25 per cent of VSNL's equity to the TATAs. The TATA Indicom and other private service providers have since been offering connectivity to the net-users in all parts of the country. Along with these developments, other private telephone operators have been spreading their markets with handsets that have camera, audio-visual add-ons and even a communicator incorporating MS Office which can send and receive e-mails. These developments have given a major push to Information Communication Technology (ICT), mostly in major cities but also in smaller places in the countryside. Government and non-government agencies, enterprising institutions, and innovative individuals have been trying to effectively use the new generation tools not only for entertainment but also for the development of society. Internet services, which were offered initially from the four metros of Mumbai, New Delhi, Calcutta and Chennai, found excellent demand and were soon expanded to cover a network of 42 nodes being operated by the Department of Telecommunications (DOT) and VSNL by 1998.

Internet growth in India mirrors the trend worldwide, with the service being the fastest growing segment of the telecommunications sector. In India, VSNL has tripled the number of internet accounts since September 1997 when it has 50,000 to over 150,000 accounts today. As per the informal policy in vogue, VSNL was allowed to operate only from six gateway nodes, while DOT took on the responsibility of operating nodes from the remaining cities in India. In the process of establishment of 42 nodes, VSNL has set up an India-wide backbone with six direct international outlets for international connectivity. In fact, 6 November 1998 was a landmark day in the history of Internet in India, when a revolutionary new policy was unveiled. The policy permits unlimited number of internet players with no licence fees for the first five years, thus setting the stage for a completely deregulated operating environment.

## Mobile Phones

Initially mobile was considered just as telephonic equipment to communicate. That was the time of monochrome-screen cell-phones. Only calling and short message services were available with mobiles almost up to the year 2000. Later on, with the advancement of the chip revolution, multimedia mobile came into existence and it changed the entire scenario in an unexpected manner. Mobiles started multimedia services, i.e. sharing of audio and visual contents. This resulted in mobile radio services and internet on mobile phones. About 94 per cent Indians now use mobile phones. There are approximately one dozen mobile phone network-operators in India. The top four national carriers are Airtel, Reliance, Vodafone, and Bharat Sanchar Nigam Limited (BSNTL is the incumbent government-owned carrier). Other smaller carriers operate in specific regions of the country.

India made rapid progress in Information and Communication Technology within a very short period of time. This has to be viewed against the backdrop that internet for private use was first available only in 1995. Within the first three years, there were 1,400,000 users while the number went up to 5,500,000 at the turn of the century though it meant a penetration of only half a per cent for a population of 1,094,870,677. There were 137,000 000 internet users in India representing 11.4 per cent of the population during mid-year 2012 to 30 June 2012, according to Internet World Stats, December 2012.

## Mobile Devices: Some Initiatives and Experiences

*Mobile Governance:* It is an excellent example of using the mobile device for social transformation. Mobile Governance is a Government of India plan similar to National Governance Plan. According to the definition given in its framework by Government of India, it is basically a strategy and its implementation to leverage available wireless and new media technology platforms, mobile phone devices and applications for delivery of public information and services to citizens and businesses. The Mobile Governance framework of the Government of India aims to utilize the massive reach of mobile phones and harness the potential of mobile applications to enable easy and round-the-clock access to public services, especially in the rural areas. The framework aims to create unique infrastructure as well as an application development ecosystem for Mobile Governance in the country.

*Public Broadcasters and Government Web Sites:* The Public Broadcasters, Doordarshan and All India Radio have continued to cover, besides spot news, Science and Technology, Agriculture and Rural Development, Women and Children, Arts/Culture/Entertainment, Education and Social sectors and so on. Those interested in the proceedings of both Houses of Parliament can watch exclusive coverage from channels dedicated for this purpose. The Union government harnessed internet technology to post these proceedings also on the web sites http://rajyasabha.gov.in/and http://loksabha.gov.in/. Similarly, state governments have set up their own websites to project the plans and achievements of the respective governments. SMS Service of News Service Division of All India Radio (MR) was launched in May 2008. The service is available for news alerts. AIR also has it application downloadable from android phones. The new technology has made it possible to provide essential contents in real time and also with very little cost.

*Centre for Agricultural Media:* Centre for Agricultural Media (CAM) came into existence in Dharwad, Karnataka, on 3 December 2000. It has been expanding its activities successfully to accomplish its objective of strengthening the farmer-friendly communication system. It is now registered as a trust under the India Trust Act. CAM supports any pro-farmer issue in all possible ways. This is the first venture of its kind in India. This forum has initiated several activities, with support from like-minded experts in farm and rural development journalising. It has been effectively using new media tools such as web activities: CAM maintains its website (www.farmedia.org). Two important issues of water and organic farming have been addressed extensively on this website. Two separate sections have been created for this purpose. Through its bulletins, CAM has disseminated related information to concerned people, which helped several people's movements considerably.

*ITGC's e-choupals (e-choupal.com): Chaupal* is an Indian concept of gathering in rural areas, specially in the northern parts of the country (i.e: Uttar Pradesh, Haryana, Uttarakhand etc.). In *chaupals*, people gather together and share concerns on common issues. ITC Ltd is one of India's foremost private sector companies. It is a leading FMCG marketeer with a market capitalization of nearly US $ 18 billion. Its e-*choupal* initiative, started in the year 2000, is claimed to be the world's largest rural digital infrastructure empowering over four million farmers. Farmers now log on to the site through these internet kiosks in their villages to order high-quality agri-inputs, get information on best farming practices, prevailing market prices for their crops at home and abroad and the weather forecast. The ITC-designed e-*choupal* is modelled specifically to tackle the challenges posed by the unique features of agriculture in rural areas – like fragmented farms, weak infrastructure and the involvement of numerous intermediaries, among others.

*MKRISHI:* Tata Consultancy Services is a leading Information Technology based company in India. MKRISHI is an initiative of this company for rural areas. It aims to reach farmers individually in order to understand their needs and enable them to use mobile technology to communicate with agriculture experts about their queries and problems via call or textual messages. Farmers can also send images of their crops via mobile camera to the experts for further consultation. They receive important information about pesticides, fertilizers and soil and water-conservation through MKRISHI and it also provides critical micro-climate weather information in order to plan farming operations. This is a good example of using mobile technologies for transformation of rural India where the mobile phone is a medium of disseminating farmer-specific important information.

*Mobile Library:* Most of the multi-media supported mobile phones have the facility of extendable memory, books and magazines in digital forms can be stored in these pocket devices. With the facility of internet, digital libraries can be accessed through these small phones. Amazon, the company behind the Kindle, perhaps the world's most famous e-reader, recently announced an international version of its digital book-reading device that will allow users to connect via 3G to download content in over 100 countries. In this manner, mobile is a helpful device to educate people.

*Reuters Market Light:* A Service to Farmers: A novel initiative to harness mobile telephone technology has been undertaken by Reuters and Maharashtra government since October 2007. Under the service called Reuters Market Light (RML) introduced for the first time in the world, farmers received through their mobile telephones local and customized prices of agro-products, news and weather updates in Marathi. The initiative, thus, acknowledges the need to combine modern technology with the tried and tested traditional postal service that reaches the remote areas.

These features of the new media have been harnessed by non-government organizations, academic institutes, co-operative ventures, and public-spirited individuals. They have set up web sites to provide details of the projects and policies or to offer advice on important issues. These web sites provide space for debates and discussions in a manner the government-hosted web sites cannot venture to do. Many of these websites have been providing great service to the people interested in issues affecting them. The convergence of mobile platforms with social networking sites is visible in Virgin Mobile India's partnership with MySpace to make the latter's social networking services available on Virgin Mobile WAP-enabled phones. There is a small but growing academic literature on mobile phone use by young Indians, especially college students (Kumar and Thomas, 2006). Chakraborty (2006) conducted a comparative study among Indian and American university students and discovered that the former relied on their mobiles more frequently as their only phone, and thus developed a different relationship to their phone than their American counterparts.

## Conclusion

The internet and mobile are considered as Conversed Media. In a single device more than one media can be accessed through mobile phones. Nowadays radio and television can be enjoyed through any multimedia-supported mobile devices. If internet is enabled in any multimedia-supported mobile, web radio, e-paper also can be had. The mobile is a medium which also provides existence to other media. It is convergence of technology. According to the internet and Mobile Association of India (IAMAI), the number of users accessing the web on their mobile handsets in India is expected to reach 155 million by March this year. This small pocket device has nowadays become an essential instrument of our daily lives. Its Information, Communication and Entertainnment (ICE) role has increased. One excellent example of this convergence is the Internet Protocol Television (IPTV). Though in its initial stage in India, on its full and final existence one can access more than 1000 television channels through a small device, i.e. the 'mobile'.

The mobile is, thus, nowadays used not only for communication but also for entertainment, education and as a tool to access many citizen services provided by the government. New media also plays an important role in democratic practices. Several examples are there, showing the importance of new media technologies for various socio-economic and political activities. During the 2009 national election, called India's 'first digital election', the Bhartiya Janata Party (BJP) used blogs, social networking communities, Twitter, and its web site to reach potential supporters. Young, urban, technology-savvy first-time voters were the most targetted groups during the election campaign, speaking to the growing power of young people and the increasing importance of urban voters. That the BJP was ultimately unsuccessful reveals, among other things, the limits of online politics. On the other hand, Dalits and other lower castes are also using the Internet as a means for organizing themselves. The organizing power of the internet emerged most forcefully during the Mumbai attacks, when individuals set up blogs to provide vital information, for example, about which hospitals needed blood donations, and to help relatives search for each other.

It was Twitter, however, that was the preferred medium of the 'citizen journalists' who provided instant and constant news-feeds and updates about the unfolding crisis. In 2012, the Jan Lokpal Movement of Team Anna was a great example of the impact of social media in the public sphere. People of small towns came to know about the demands of the masses. Social media became a common platform for Indians for sharing information and expression. Another fine example of the use of social media in India has been the Nirbhaya case of Delhi. When the news of a young student being gang-raped in Delhi was flashed, people started protests immediately. Within a day, the demand of justice for Nirbhaya became an important issue on most of the social networking sites.

In July 2008, the Indian Ministry of Human Resources Development recommended making blogging, community-radio robotic kits, and other technology devices part of public schools as academic activities. The report states that 'blogs are powerful tools to support creative writing that can be published and shared not only with the teacher but also with peers and the rest of the world.'

Before 2006, there was the concept of community web sites. Orkut became a popular community site over a short span of time. It started a race for social networks by other players. According to a Report released in February 2009, visits to social networking sites in India increased by 51 per cent during 2008, to 19 million visitors in December 2008. Orkut was followed by Facebook.

About half of the internet users access internet through mobile phones. It shows the potential of this small device. As the level of education is increasing and technology is developing, the mobile is revolutionizing our lives. New media is emerging very fast. On 8 August 2013, the Government of India announced that it would have a specialized department to take its message to YouTube, Facebook, Twitter and other social media sites after the Union Cabinet approved the Information and Broadcasting Ministry's proposal to create a new media wing. The I&B minister Manish Tewari said the officials will have the latest gadgets, including small phones, to keep in touch with the latest developments on the social media. The new media practices among Indians and the importance of mobile as new medium of communication are the focus of this paper, which situates such practices within the larger context of the role of ICT in India's economic, political, and socio-cultural life.

## References

Chakraborty, S. (2006). 'Mobile Phone Usage Patterns Amongst University Students: A Comparative Study between India and USA. A Master's Paper for the MS in Information Science Degree.

http://articles.timesofindia.indiatimes.com/2013-08-08/social-media/41200792_1_media-manish-tewari-wing

http://articles.timesofindia.indiatimes.com/2013-03-12/india-business/37650711_1_ficci-frames-media-industry-crores

Kohli, Khandekar Vinita (2009). *The Indian Media Business*. New Delhi: Sage Publications.

Kumar, K.J. and A.O. Thomas (2006). 'Telecommunications and Development: The Cellular Mobile "Revolution" in India and China'. *Journal of Creative Communications*, 1(3): 297–309.

Schwittay, Anke (2011). 'New Media Practices in India: Bridging Past and Future, Markets and Development'. *International Journal of Communication*, 5: 349–79.

19/10/2013, http://www.exchange4media.com/e4m/bottombarfiles/growth-of-new-media advertising.asp

19/10/2013, http://www.thehindu.com/sci-tech/technology/internet/india-is-now-worlds-third-largest-intemet-user-after-us-china/article5053115.ece

21/10/2013, http://www.aspeninstitute.org/policy-worldcommtmications-society/programs-topic/communications-policy/india/cs-joint-roundtable-co?c=hulwjemrk ph&b-4634691

25/01/2014, http://www.tcs.com/offerings/technology-products/mkrishi/pages/ default.aspx

29/01/2014, http://blogs.worldbank.org/edutech/a-digital-library-in-your-pocket

30/01/2014, http://www.mgoworld.org/resources/framework_mobile_governance_ 171 2012.pdf

31/01/2014, http://articles.economictimes.indiatimes.come/2014-01-01/news/ 4576 4553_1_mobile-association-iamai-rural-india

31/01/2014, http://www.avendus.com/files/fund%20performance%20pdf/avendus_report-india%27s_mobile_internet-2013.pdf

# 22

# Minorities within Autonomous Areas

**KARABI CHETIA**

This paper tries to look at the problems arising out of ethnic diversity and resource-constraints in a region due to which various groups fight among themselves to claim their ownership to the limited resources present in the region. The newly-formed Bodoland Territorial Council (formed in 2003) in Western Assam has been witnessing conflicts between the Bodos and other communities residing in Bodoland Territorial Council (henceforth BTC). Minorities in this study refer to the non-members of the autonomous region. They consist of the Assamese, Santhals (also known as tea-tribes), Koch Rajbongshis, Bengali Hindus, Bengali Muslims, Nepalis and Marwaris.

Minorities generally meant numerically smaller groups of people, but over time, this has come to refer to groups of people that are marginalized in society. These groups are formed based on shared myths and history, and certain objective features like language. Shared territory is common among the group-members. These identities transform over time and at times, the members construct them. The historical disadvantage that a community suffers is sought to be redressed through certain special rights, and State's grant of self-governance rights to these groups demanding cultural preservation and separate territory of their own. The non-members living in the same territory feel deprived of their basic rights of citizenship.

With the help of existing literature an attempt is being made to trace the roots of the conflicts in the Bodoland Territorial Autonomous District (BTAD). It has been observed that the special status granted to one group (i.e. the Bodos) is creating further problems in the region as the area is shared by many other communities settled at various points of time.

## Ethnic Groups and Identity Aspirations

Ethnicity and identity are the main issues in the mobilization of groups in the North-East. Due to its multi-ethnic character, the region is witnessing many pulls and pressures of various dimensions, tribal as well as non-tribal. Each of the communities has its own claims of being indigenous to the region. In Assam, we find various communities divided on the basis of language, race and shared history. The primordial approach to ethnicity used by Geertz, the idea being taken from Edward Shils, is considered to be of this particular view of ethnicity.[1]

Geertz emphasizes that primordial ties bind individuals together and it is on the basis of these ties that they demand recognition and progress for their group. Critiquing this view of primordialism, Eller and Coughlan argue that 'primordialism presents us with a picture of underived and socially-unconstructed emotions that are unanalysable and overpowering and coercive yet varying.'[2] They emphasize that ethnicity is constructed with time, ethnic identities are 'renewed, modified and remade in each generation'. They note that 'claims to ethnic membership arise and change according to situational variable circumstances and interests.'[3] On the other hand, Hall acknowledges both aspects of thinking about cultural identity i.e. shared ancestry with a common culture as well as 'becoming' and 'being'.[4]

Identity politics is organized around shared past or at times constructed by the oppressed groups to acquire the recognition of other groups and also to demand equitable economic distribution. It is also defined negatively, where one group sees itself as different from others.[5] Modern political theory asserted the equal moral worth of all persons, and social movements of the oppressed took this seriously as implying the inclusion of all persons in full citizenship status under the equal protection of the law.'[6] So identities are derived from a shared culture and undergo transformation over time. It is essentially a political practice which mobilizes the members on the basis of shared solidarity to achieve collective action. It has led to politicization of previously non-political aspects like sexuality, lifestyle and culture.

The other approach to understanding ethnicity is instrumentalist, proponents of which emphasize the socially constructed nature of ethnicity. They view ethnicity as a social, political and cultural resource for different status groups (Brass, 1969; Bhabha, 1990; Calhoun, 1993). Barth states that, 'ethnic groups are categories of ascription and identification by the actors themselves, and thus have the characteristic of organizing interaction between people.'[7] He stresses that ethnic groups possess different characteristics at different times and places.

Ethnic identities share a common past and, accordingly, individuals derive their group solidarity from a common culture. The boundaries of ethnic groups are not fixed, members can join if they wish to, and so it is more of a socially-constructed nature. Ethnic identities change with time and place; it is the environment in which an individual lives that determines how his ethnic identity is formed.

Ethnic groups cannot relate themselves to the identity of the larger national community and, thus, they separate themselves, stating their distinct language and culture, which is different from that of the other members of the larger community. The movement of Bodos emphasizing their distinct identity and resistance to assimilation under the bigger umbrella of Assamese nationalism has been continuing since pre-Independence. When the Simon Commission visited Assam during 1928 and 1929, 'various tribal leaders demanded reservation in the elected bodies.' Jadav Chandra Khakhlari in 1929 demanded before the Simon Commission that a separate representation for the Bodos be created. 'Besides demanding special treatment in matters of education and appointment, the Bodo community of Goalpara district also wanted a second chamber in the legislative council and urged the commission not to transfer Goalpara district to Bengal.'[8] This resonates with Eriksen's argument that the major difference between ethnicity and nationalism lies in their relationship to the State. He writes, 'Unsuccessful nationalisms therefore tend to become transformed into ethnicities whose members reside more or less uncomfortably under the aegis of a state which they do not identify with their own nationality or ethnic category.'[9]

Ethnicity and identity are the main factors of mobilization in the whole of the Northeast. Calhoun argues that both nationalism and ethnicity will exist as an identity in the modern world influenced by elites and other participants in political and social change.[10] It cannot be ignored that Bodos were marginalized since the colonial period, they were being dominated by the larger Assamese identity.[11] For long, Bodos have suffered from the caste Assamese Hindus who have been dominating other tribals and hampered the growth of their culture and religion. The seed was sown by the Britishers who had devised exclusive homelands for the tribals to control the Assam valley and the surrounding hills. A number of policies were introduced by the Britishers through the Government of India Act 1935. These were the Excluded Areas Act, the Partially Excluded Areas Act and the Inner Line Regulations to manage the affairs of the tribal people.[12]

The politicization of ethnic identity has led to several groups demanding exclusive rights to preserve their culture and heritage. Ethnic groups that have suffered some form of historical disadvantage from the dominant groups are mobilising the members of the groups to form a separate nation of their own. The preservation of culture, language and other traditional forms of lifestyle are prioritized. The leaders emphasize that this will bring in overall development for the community. This study analyses how the recognition of identity brings in development for the community.

## Historical Background

Various scholars put the blame of much of the problems arising in the North-East of India at the door of British policy. Their policy of segregating the hill population from that in the plains still finds articulation in various hill tribes demanding an exclusive homeland. The geographical boundary of Assam has changed manifold after the British conquered the north-eastern region. Certain areas of pre-colonial Assam were excluded whereas some others that did not share the cultural, economic or political values of Assam prior to its becoming a colony were included.

The British rulers segregated the hill tribes from the plains as they claimed that hill tribes were 'primitive' and therefore they were treated differently as compared to the rest of the British-controlled India.[13] Gait, writing about the 'exclusion of certain tracts from the general laws', elaborates:

> The inhabitants of the hilly tracts, however, were not yet suited for the elaborate legal rules laid down in the procedure codes and in several other enactments of the same class, and they had to be governed in a simpler and more personal manner than those of the more civilized and longer-settled districts.[14]

The location and history of Assam are significant in the articulation of a separate homeland for a particular group. Assam as a colonial province, writes Baruah, a chief commissionership to be exact, was formed in 1874 and prior to that the British ruled Assam as an 'appendage of the unwieldy province of Bengal.'[15] On 12 September 1874, the 'East Bengali district of Sylhet – historically unconnected to Assam – was included in Assam.'[16] The Bengalis and Assamese both were so engrossed in competition with each other, over language and employment opportunities, that the aspirations of the tribals, who also formed a part of Assam, were ignored.

After Independence, the north-east region grappled with a host of issues. Communication and transportation with the rest of the country have suffered a serious setback. Political self-expression, particularly among certain tribal communities, came up in the wake of Partition and the economic and political changes too came about with it.[17] The location and history of the region are among the main factors in mobilizing people to demand for recognition based on territory and ethnicity. As Smith and Hutchinson, citing Enloe, argue, 'in non-Western societies ethnicity has a much more direct influence on the creation of nations and the distribution of resources in post-colonial states. Imperialism and colonialism drew the boundaries of new states in Africa and Asia without much regard for ethnic identities, yet also encouraged the ethnic classification of population and required some ethnic communities to play special roles in the colonial polity.'[18]

## Justice for the Ethnic Groups

A person or a group's identity is partly shaped by the recognition or otherwise on the part of others in society.[19] Taylor states that to understand the relation between identities and recognition it is important to know that a 'crucial feature of human life is its fundamentally *dialogical* character.'[20] Further, Taylor argues that the change that has come with modern age is not so much about the 'need for recognition but the conditions in which the attempt to be recognized can fail.'[21] We can see in society how not every group organizes itself for recognition of its identity; it is those who are marginalized in society due to non-recognition of their identity as well as the economically backward who demand recognition. In the light of this, we can understand the debate on recognition and redistribution to see how the issue of social justice is addressed for the communities by giving a particular group exclusive rights to change its position in society.

### *Genesis of the Bodo Movement for Autonomy*

The identity assertion of the Bodos went along with the demand for a separate state for the tribals. As early as 1928, the articulation of a separate Bodo identity distinct from the Assamese had started. It was during 1928 and 1929 when the Simon Commission visited Assam that the various tribal leaders demanded reservation in the elected bodies. Jadav Chandra Khakhlari, General Secretary of the All Assam Kachari Association, submitted a memorandum to the Simon Commission, demanding separate representation for the Bodos. The Assam Kachari Jubok Sanmiloni, on 14 September 1928, at New Delhi, before the Simon Commission, stated, 'in the circumstances they appeal to the Statutory Commission to preserve their integrity and independence and grant them all sorts of facilities for making rapid studies in the path of progress'.[22] The encounter with the Simon Commission helped formulate two basic tenets centring which the Bodo politics went on evolving since then. These are:

> ... first one is the concept of reservation. Not only for assembly seats, the idea of reservation became the key word for demanding other benefits like job and land settlement. In other words, the idea of reservation became the perpetual issue that stood as a stumbling block in any subsequent attempt of reconciliation between the mainstream Assamese society and the Bodos. The second aspect that developed in the wake of Simon Commission's visit was the mechanism of projecting the Bodo demands as the demands of all plain tribals of Assam. As the most advanced group amongst the plain tribal communities of Assam, the Bodos sought to and are still seeking to establish a kind of hegemony over the other less developed plain-tribes of the Brahmaputra Valley.[23]

It is very rare that ethnic and political borders coincide with one another.[24] As Parekh states, a culturally homogeneous society whose members share and mechanically follow an identical body of beliefs and practices is today no more than an anthropological fiction.[25] Territorial and socio-cultural identities are considered as the solution for aggrieved identity groups; mainly ethnic identities and minorities who were historically disadvantaged, and hence seek for redress of their past disadvantages. Connor argues:

> the coincidence of the customary tangible attributes of nationality, such as common language or religion, is not determinative. The prime requisite is subjective and consists of the self-identification of people with a group – its past, its present and, most important, its destiny.[26]

### *Non-Bodos in Bodoland Territorial Council*

The Bodoland Territorial Council comprises areas which are also inhabited by other groups like the caste-Hindu Assamese, the Adivasis, immigrant Muslim communities and the Nepalese. With this combination of groups residing in the same area, the same apprehensions that Bodos felt vis-à-vis Assamese are felt by non-Bodos residing in these areas. Prabhakara also raises this issue while commenting on the formation of BTC – that not addressing the issues of existence of various groups in the same area is most likely to be one of the hindrances to the functioning of the BTC.[27] After the formation of the BTC in October 2003, the Sanmilita Janagosthiya Sangram Samity, which is an apex body of several non-Bodo organizations against the creation of any political structure making concession to Bodo autonomist/nationalistic aspirations, called a 100-hour *bandh* from the day the interim council assumed office. Although, the concerns are genuine, a separate homeland for a particular community does not hold ground. A particular group cannot live in isolation from the rest of the world, social change is bound to take place and with that, a separate homeland ceases to exist – this further gives rise to conflicts among different communities.

There are two competing views in helping a marginalized group to be at par with the rest. The debate between Fraser and Honneth provides a clear understanding of both the views. Honneth states that identity of a group should be given preference over other issues.[28] Fraser, on the other hand, states that the economic condition of the marginalized groups should be redressed.[29] To understand the idea of justice, the theories provided by Rawls would help us to understand the problem of social justice in a better way.[30]

In the post-socialist world, the resurgence of identity politics demanding recognition of difference has displaced material inequality as the fundamental inequality. Only in a place of material inequality, the issue of non-recognition occurs like in income and property ownership; in access to paid work, education, healthcare and leisure time. Material inequality is on the rise in most parts of the world. In the modern State, the surge for claims of recognition has given rise to the undermining of the social politics of equality. Claims for group identity are the new political imagination.

The State comes up with a certain affirmative action to provide justice to particular identity – groups demanding exclusive rights for them. Competition for resources is one of the main reasons for conflict among various groups. This is true of the Bodoland Territorial Council as well, which is a part of the Western plains and is scarce in resources. Pramod Boro, President of ABSU, in a seminar notes that control of land is an important issue because of which clashes among Bodos and other communities keep happening. According to him, Most of the conflict in the north-east region of India is taking place because of right of control over land, resources and identity issues.'[31] Apart from this factor, there are other reasons like large-scale immigration for the outbreak of violence.

To address different communities' demand for preservation of their traditions and rights, successive plans by the Indian Government have emphasized a protective development plan for the region. Policies of less interference with the cultural traditions and customs of the tribal people are being followed and additional political and administrative framework has been provided for the region. Autonomous district councils have been created under the Sixth Schedule. 'These councils are responsible for looking after the social, economic, and minor criminal and civil matters of the tribal people.'[32] The centre has tailor-made solutions for ethnic and economic grievances like this. However, the issue of the Sixth Schedule itself is controversial as this is a continuation of the British policy towards the secluded hilly areas of the region.

In the modern world when the citizenship right is extended to everyone, the question arises as to why some citizens remain second-class citizens who do not enjoy equality and social justice. Young accepts the Marxist answer to this, which states that those social activities that most determine the status of individuals and groups are anarchic and oligarchic; economic life is not sufficiently under the control of citizens to affect the unequal status and treatment of groups.'[33] Contemporary social movements 'assert a positivity and pride in group specificity against ideals of assimilation. They have also questioned whether justice always means that law and policy should enforce equal treatment for all groups. Embryonic in these challenges lays a concept of differentiated citizenship as the best way to realize the inclusion and participation of everyone in full-citizenship.'[34]

In I.M. Young's critique of Fraser, she argues that instead of separating recognition and redistribution claims, we should try to look at them together. After all, economic needs are ingrained in the claim for cultural rights.[35] On the other hand, Fraser observes that affirmative and transformative action cuts across both redistributive and recognition remedies. Affirmative remedies try to correct the inequitable outcomes of social arrangement without changing the underlying framework that generates them whereas transformative remedies aim at correcting inequitable outcomes by restructuring the underlying framework that is at the root. She notes that mainstream multiculturalism is an affirmative action, which is sought to redress unjustly devalued group identities.[36]

In opposition to the liberal view which emphasises that giving special rights to minorities creates inequality in the society, the proponents of this view claim that common rights of citizenship also adhere to cultural membership. Kymlicka opines that knowingly or unknowingly, the majority culture is forced on the entire population, and this leads to undermining of the culture of minority groups.

Rawls argues that giving economic benefit to a disadvantaged group will also help them in their cultural recognition. While talking of exclusion, Deepak Nayyar emphasizes, economic exclusion from livelihoods often creates or accentuates a political exclusion from rights. Similarly, cultural exclusion such as that of immigrant groups, minority communities or ethnic groups interacts with economic exclusion from the market. Each dimension reinforces the other to produce a vicious circle of cumulative causation. The outcome is embedded discrimination.[37]

The above discussion reflects the views of various scholars attempting to address the issue of injustice that is inflicted knowingly or unknowingly on certain communities. These communities are socially discriminated and to redress this discrimination, scholars have tried to use various methods. These methods revolve around socio-economic remedies to address the issue of inequality in wealth whereas the other view focuses on recognition-remedies to preserve devalued identity. The inequality in wealth among various members is addressed by class politics and as Fraser states, this has been replaced by the politics of recognition, which is also referred to as identity politics.[38] However,

Honneth argues that politics of recognition does not need to be understood as mere cultural recognition, it should be understood as social recognition and that it is persisting since a long time.[39] Rawls, in his theory of justice, argues that economic benefit to the disadvantaged groups also helps them to get recognition in society. Therefore, he states that rights and liberties should be equal whereas distribution of wealth and income need not be equal – however, it should advantage everyone in society.[40] As both recognition and redistribution seeks social justice, both of them have contradictory views – recognition promotes group differentiation and redistribution seeks to abolish economic arrangements and de-differentiate group identities.

The economic condition as well as cultural exclusion, both reinforce each other to create a vicious circle. In this era, where material inequality is ever increasing, the recognition of cultural identity does not seem to be a solution for various groups in conflicts. The distribution of resources among the members has to be paid attention to. As the economic resources get scarcer with the increase in population, different communities mobilize themselves into distinct identity groups to demand for a separate cultural status as well as to have a greater share of the resources.

The above Section provides the tools of analysis for the rest of the study. The debate on recognition and redistribution helps to understand how the contesting identity-groups are accommodated by the State and what impact is felt on the other communities. How can the issue of injustice for some members of society be remedied with the help of special rights for a particular group?

### *Who are the Minorities?*

To understand the claim for autonomy or other affirmative action by the minorities, we should have the knowledge of who forms the minority in a State. Kymlicka and Norman have stated that different kinds of groups face very different kinds of challenges finding their place within the larger state, and therefore demand different kinds of special accommodations. They broadly divide minorities into four different groups, which are, 'national minorities, immigrant minorities, religious groups and *sui generis* groups.'[41] Kymlicka further gives details about these minorities, as he states that national minorities are national communities that share a state with one or more larger nations.'[42]

The political liberalization legalizes the right to organize, writes Yashar (1999). The political reforms, however, restrict access to the State's resources and also limit the cultural and political autonomy of the indigenous people.[43] In the wake of this, these communities mobilize around their indigenous identity to save their local culture. They contest the present government policies and seek for an alternative in the form of self-government or autonomy. Though we cannot rubbish the claims of these groups as vague, there is a strong view from a section of the scholars that these movements help in reinforcing group differences, rendering the devalued groups different from the other sections of people.

We can understand this from the recent violence in Assam between Bodos and non-Bodos in the region. The violence of 2012 was between Bodos and

Bengali Muslim 'immigrants' of the region. Bodos were granted an autonomous council to fulfil their long-standing demand, which gives them the right to self-government. The non-Bodos in Bodoland felt deprived of their basic rights as the Bodos subjected them to domination. Hence, they are being relegated to second-class citizens. In the field study undertaken in Kokrajhar (Headquater of BTAD) it was found that the non-Bodos did not enjoy political rights in BTAD. One of the respondents stated that 'the constituencies which have majority Bodo population are kept open for all the communities residing in BTC and those with majority non-Bodos are reserved for the STs. It has to be stated that Bodos formed majority of the ST population and it is clear that constituencies with majority Bodo population are most likely to have a Bodo being elected. Hence, it is open for all the communities and those with less Bodo population are only reserved for STs so that only a Bodo candidate can be selected.'[44] This shows the deprivation faced by non-members in an autonomous region.

## Conclusion

Ethnic ideology has been playing a vital role in the disruption of normal life in the North-East. It has to be accepted that the demography of the region is heterogeneous and no single community occupies a separate territory. The North-East, and particularly Assam, consists of various ethnic groups speaking different languages; living habits, traditions and dresses are also different. It is quite obvious that if in such multi-cultural regions one group tries to subsume the others under its nationality, there will be protest. People have bitter memories of Assamese nationalism of the 1980s and now comes the Bodo nationalism that is mobilizing people to conserve the Bodo culture and identity. The leaders of the movement argue that since Bodos are not as developed as the other groups in the region due to historical disadvantages, they must be given special advantages to come to the fore. As Horowitz has put forth, that certain ideological and institutional currents have underpinned the growth of ethnic conflicts like the growth of norms of equality have made the ethnic groups compare their standing in society with other groups living in close proximity. He further adds that 'ethnic identity is often accompanied by hostility toward out groups.'[45]

In the empirical data collected it was observed that the non-Bodos area marginalized group under the BTC. They do not enjoy the right of citizenship in such arrangements. Their political rights are crushed. Even if they are in the ruling party, they are mere stooges to the government. Thus, the issue of social justice which encompasses both demands for preservation of identity and bridges the economic gap between the members of a society is not enjoyed by the non-Bodo people.

## Notes

1. J. Hutchinson and A.D. Smith (eds), *Ethnicity*, New York: Oxford University Press, 1996.
2. J. Eller and R. Coughlan, 'The Poverty of Primordialism', in J. Hutchinson and A.D. Smith (eds), *Ethnicity*, New York: Oxford University Press, 1996, p. 46.

3. Ibid.
4. Stuart Hall, 'Cultural Identity and Diaspora', in P. Williams and L. Chrisman (eds), *Colonial Discourse and Post-Colonial Theory: A Reader*, New York: Columbia University Press, 1994, p. 394.
5. Eric Hobsbawm, 'Identity Politics and the Left', *New Left Review*, I/217, May-June 1996, p. 38.
6. I.M. Young, 'Polity and Group Difference: A Critique of the Ideal of Universal Citizenship', *Ethics*, Vol. 99, No. 2, January 1989, p. 250.
7. Fredrik Barth, 'Ethnic Groups and Boundaries', in J. Hutchinson and A.D. Smith (eds), *Ethnicity*, New York: Oxford University Press, 1996, p. 77.
8. Nani Gopal Mahanta, 'Politics of Space and Violence in Bodoland', *Economic and Political Weekly*, Vol. XLVIII, No. 23, June 2013, p. 50.
9. T.H. Eriksen, 'Ethnicity versus Nationalism', *Journal of Peace Research*, Vol. 28, No. 3, August 1991, p. 263.
10. Craig Calhoun, 'Nationalism and Ethnicity', *Annual Review of Sociology*, Vol. 19, 1993, pp. 211–39.
11. Suryasikha Pathak, 'Ethnic Violence in Bodoland', *Economic and Political Weekly*, Vol. XLVII, No. 34, August 25, 2012.
12. Mahanta, op. cit.
13. Sanjib Baruah, *India against Itself*, Oxford University Press, New Delhi, 1999, p. 28.
14. Edward Gait, *A History of Assam*, Thacker, Spink and Co., Calcutta, 1963, pp. 385–86.
15. Ibid.
16. Ibid., p. 25.
17. L.P. Singh, 'National Policy for the North East Region', in A. Jacob and T. Singh (eds), *Reconstructing the Republic*, Har-Anand, New Delhi, 1999, p. 399.
18. Hutchinson and Smith (eds), op. cit., p. 13.
19. Charles Taylor, 'The Politics of Recognition', in Amy Gutman (ed.), *Multiculturalism: Examining the Politics of Recognition*, Princeton University Press, New Jersey, 1994, p. 25.
20. Ibid., p. 32.
21. Ibid., pp. 32–35.
22. Ibid., p. 175.
23. Sujit Choudhury, *The Bodos: Emergence and Assertion of an Ethnic Minority*, Indian Institute of Advanced Study, Shimla, 2007, p. 68.
24. Walker Connor, 'Self Determination: The New Phase', *World Politics*, Vol. 20, No. 1, October 1967, p. 30.
25. http://www.powerofculture.nl/uk/archive/commentary/parekh.html
26. Connor, op. cit.
27. M.S. Prabhakara, 'Bodoland Territorial Council: Going Round in Circles?', *Frontline*, Vol. 20, No. 24, 22 November–5 December 2003.
28. Nancy Fraser and Axel Honneth, 'Recognition or Redistribution? Changing Perspectives on the Moral Order of Society', *Theory, Culture and Society*, Vol. 18, No. 21, June 2001, pp. 43–55.
29. Nancy Fraser, 'From Redistribution to Recognition? Dilemmas of Justice in a "Post-Socialist" Age', *New Left Review*, Vol. 1, No. 212, 1995, pp. 68–93.
30. John Rawls, *The Theory of Justice*, Clarendon Press, Oxford, 1972, p. 54.

31. Pramod Boro, 'Conflict in BTAD, Issue of Influx and Land Alienation in Assam: Problems and Perspectives', National Seminar, New Delhi, November 2012.
32. Gulshan Sachdeva, 'Policy Framework for the North East', in *Economy of the North East: Policy, Present Conditions and Future Possibilities*, Konark Publishers, New Delhi, 2000, p. 7.
33. Young, op. cit., p. 251.
34. Ibid.
35. I.M. Young, 'Unruly Categories: A Critique of Nancy Fraser's Dual System's Theory', *New Left Review*, Vol. 1, No. 222, March-April, 1997.
36. Nancy Fraser, 'Social Justice in the Age of Identity Politics: Redistribution, Recognition, and Participation', in Nancy Fraser and Axel Honneth, *Redistribution or Recognition? A Political Philosophical Exchange*, Verso, London, 2003, p. 75.
37. Deepak Nayyar, 'Discrimination and Justice Beyond Affirmative Action', *Economic and Political Weekly*, Vol. XLVI, No. 42, October 2011.
38. Fraser, op. cit., p. 44.
39. Fraser and Honneth, op. cit., p. 46.
40. Rawls, op. cit., p. 101.
41. Will Kymlicka and Wayne Norman, 'Citizenship in Culturally Diverse Societies: Issues, Contexts, Concepts', in *Citizenship in Diverse Societies*, Oxford University Press, New York, 2003, pp. 18–19.
42. Ibid., p. 19.
43. Deborah J. Yashar, 'Democracy, Indigenous Movements, and the Post-liberal Challenge in Latin America', *World Politics*, Vol. 52, No. 1, October 1999, p. 77.
44. Interview with Muslim Community Respondent, May 25, 2013.
45. Donald Horowitz, *Ethnic Groups in Conflict*, University of California Press, Berkeley, 1985.

## References

Barth, Fredrik (1996). 'Ethnic Groups and Boundaries', in J. Hutchinson and A.D. Smith (eds), *Ethnicity*. New York: Oxford University Press.

Baruah, Sanjib (1999). *India against Itself.* New York: Oxford University Press.

Bernstein, Mary (2005). 'Identity Politics'. *Annual Review of Sociology*, 31: 47–74.

Beteille, Andre (1998). 'The Idea of Indigenous People'. *Current Anthropology*, 39(2), April: 187–92.

Bhabha, Homi (1990). *Nation and Narration*, London: Routledge.

Brass, Paul (1996). 'Ethnic Groups and Ethnic Identity Formation', in J. Hutchinson and A.D. Smith (eds), *Ethnicity*. New York: Oxford University Press.

Brubaker, Rogers and Frederick Cooper (2000). 'Beyond Identity'. *Theory and Society*, 29: 1–47.

Calhoun, Craig (1993). 'Nationalism and Ethnicity', in *Annual Review of Sociology*, 19: 211–239.

——. (2007). *Nations Matter: Culture, History, and the Cosmopolitan Dream*. New York: Routledge.

Chatterjee, Partha (1993). *The Nation and its Fragments: Colonial and Post-Colonial Histories.* New Jersey: Princeton University Press.

Choudhury, Sujit (2007). *The Bodos: Emergence and Assertion of an Ethnic Minority.* Shimla: Indian Institute of Advanced Study.

Cohen, Abner (1996). 'Ethnicity and Politics', in J. Hutchinson and A.D. Smith (eds), *Ethnicity*. New York: Oxford University Press.

Ericksen, Thomas Hylland (1999). 'Ethnicity versus Nationalism'. *Peace Research*, 28(3), August: 263–78.

Fraser, Nancy (1995). 'From Redistribution to Recognition? Dilemmas of Justice in a "Post-Socialist" Age'. *New Left Review*, I(212): 68–93.

Fraser, Nancy and Axel Honneth (2003). *Redistribution or Recognition? A Political-Philosophical Exchange*. London: Verso.

Gait, Edward (1963). *A History of Assam*. Calcutta: Thacker Spink & Co.

Hall, Stuart (1994). 'Culture Identity and Diaspora', in Patrick Williams and Laura Chrisman (eds), *Colonial Discourse and Post-Colonial Theory*. New York: Harvester-Wheatsheaf, pp. 392–401.

Hobsbawm, Eric (1996). 'Identity Politics and the Left'. *New Left Review*, I(217), May-June: 38.

Hutchinson, John (2000). 'Ethnicity and Modern Nations'. *Ethnic and Racial Studies*, 23(4), July 4: 651–69.

Hutchinson, John and Anthony D. Smith (eds) (1996). *Ethnicity*. Oxford: Oxford University Press.

Kymlicka, Will (1995). *Multicultural Citizenship*. Oxford: Clarendon Press.

Kymlicka, Will and Wayne Norman (2000). 'Citizenship in Culturally Diverse Societies: Issues, Contexts and Concepts', in Will Kymlicka and Wayne Norman (eds), *Citizenship in Diverse Societies*. Oxford: Oxford University Press.

Levy, Jacob T. (2000). 'Three Modes of Incorporating Indigenous Law', in Will Kymlicka and Wayne Norman (eds), *Citizenship in Diverse Societies*. Oxford: Oxford University Press.

Mahanta, Nani Gopal (2013). 'Politics of Space and Violence in Bodoland'. *Economic and Political Weekly*, 48(23), June 8: 49–58.

Nayyar, Deepak (2011). 'Discrimination and Justice: Beyond Affirmative Action'. *Economic and Political Weekly*, 46(42), October 15: 52–59.

Pathak, Suryasikha (2012). 'Ethnic Violence in Bodoland'. *Economic and Political Weekly*, 47(34), August 25: 19–23.

Rawls, John (1972). *The Theory of Justice*. Oxford: Oxford University Press.

Rothchild, Donald and Caroline A. Hartzell (1999). 'Security in Deeply Divided Societies: The Role of Territorial Autonomy'. *Nationalism and Ethnic Politics*, 5(3–4): 254–71.

Sachdeva, Gulshan (2000). 'Policy Framework for the North East', in *Economy of the North East: Policy, Present Conditions and Future Possibilities*. New Delhi: Konark Publishers.

Schermerhorn, Richard (1996). 'Ethnicity and Minority Groups', in J. Hutchinson and A.D. Smith (eds), *Ethnicity*. New York: Oxford University Press.

Singh, L.P. (1999). 'National Policy for the North East Region', in U. Baxi, A. Jacob and T. Singh (eds), *Reconstructing the Republic*. Delhi: Har-Anand Publishers.

Smith, Anthony D. (1996). 'Culture, Community and Territory: The Politics of Ethnicity and Nationalism'. *International Affairs*, 72(3): 445–58.

Taylor, Charles (1994). 'The Politics of Recognition', in Amy Gutmann (ed.), *Multiculturalism: Examining the Politics of Recognition*. Princeton: Princeton University Press.

Tilly, Charles (1994). 'States and Nationalism in Europe 1492–1992'. *Theory and Society*, 23(1), February: 131–46.

Yashar, Deborah J. (1999). 'Democracy, Indigenous Movements, and the Post-liberal Challenge in Latin America'. *World Politics*, 52(1): 76–104.

Young, Iris Marion (1990). *Justice and the Politics of Difference*. Princeton: Princeton University Press.

## Websites

http://www.censusindia.gov.in.

http://www.powerofculture.nl/uk/archive/commentary/parekh.html.

## Seminar

Boro, Pramod (2012). 'Conflict in BTAD, Issue of Influx and Land Alienation in Assam: Problems and Perspectives'. National Seminar, New Delhi, November.

# Part 8

## Gender, Culture and Power

# 23

# Women, Power and Culture

**RANJANA UPADHYAY**

All human beings are social being and the society, they live in, is made up by several relationships quite dependent on beliefs, laws, customs, rituals, religion and ideology. All these components of society, in their accumulative figure, make the culture of a particular society. It has been also said that society itself is a product of culture and acquired by man, as a member of it.[1] Culture makes a behaviour or pattern of living because it makes certain regularities of living style for all human beings to follow with and to defend this viewpoint that it secures the personal and social survival of an individual. So we can say that culture is socially constructed and the relations, made in the society, are power based and make a sense of subordination and domination. Gender is also a socially constructed idea and primary way of signifying the relationship of power and hierarchy.[2] Men and women are considered as culture and nature respectively, culture becomes patriarchal in its nature while women, because of their reproductive roles, are universally viewed as being closer to nature; culture dominates the nature as men to women. In the private sphere of family, where a woman passes most of her time, things occur naturally. Division of labour in the human society has also fixed the role of man and woman. Females were assigned to take care of young ones, while men were responsible to gather the food for the family. This type of division of work pushed women into the boundaries of family and made it a cultural norm and moral responsibility for women to bear. As a socialist looks at all the events by the materialistic glass, it can be said that one who controls the resources and property, will retain the authority and power. So the relations alter in the power relation. This authority and power status of male sex became a part of human culture and women remained within the private sphere, the boundaries of the house.

We see, this division of labour is not only universal but there is a matter of recognition of it. As in every known society, the work done by men is recognized whether he cooks, weaves, hunts or dresses the dolls too, it will be given importance by the whole society, by men and women, but in case of the women, it becomes less important, undervalued and recognized as their natural work. So this division of labour is also socially and culturally constructed. Women are understood as habitual for these certain type of works and remained in the private sphere. All the resources of authority and power were pre-occupied by the men. Thus, men have culturally legitimate power to dominate in the society. This division of labour continued as the civilization developed. A number of activities like collection of fodder and fuel, maintaining dairies and animals, vegetable growing, sewing, weaving are usually performed by women though these activities have no monetary value and are considered as women's household work. Further, when the new economic features emerged and new economic policies were implemented, the top-most position in organized sector, were rarely occupied by women. They only do the works, comparatively, of low wages, semi-skilled and highly laborious. They are still far behind from the skilled occupations in the lack of necessary training because they have been understood as being incapable of such type of activities. There are rare chances of holding the decisive ranks by women in corporate sectors. So they are not regarded as major contributor of the economy. But as the socialist theory says that the division of labour by which women were subjugated to the family sphere, in spite of that they were active part in the mode of production since a long period of history and contributed to the capitalist economy. They explain, when a tired employee, after his day's long work returns back and finds a comfortable atmosphere at home, everything ready food, dresses, it restores his energy to work again. If it would not be done, the employer has to pay extra or adjust for their employees commodities. So, because man is the bread-earner, brings money to home, is more authoritative and women become isolated and their whole work has been unaccounted. This notion of responsibility became a culture for women and because of household responsibilities and restrictions on their mobility, the boundaries of home became the sacred line.

## Socialization of Culture: From Birth till Death

The process of socialization of a person begins right from the childhood, as Sylvia Walby says that this is a process of recognizing the identities, masculinity and feminine. From the birth, a child is treated differently according to biological sex, colour differentiation as pink for girls and blue for boys, playing activities, pattern of wearing, level of encouragement by the family members make a different type of culture for both women and men.[3] So it is rightly said by Simon de Beauvoir that 'one is not born, but made a women'. A girl grows up according to the expected rules and traditions of her family; she learns the track, on which her whole life will proceed. How she will dress, move, play, everything has a cultural standard quite different from a boy. Women's duties as good daughters, good wives, and good mothers are well defined in Indian patriarchal society these roles are imposed on women from the culture and society. Gentle, loving, caring and sacrifices are inherited qualities of women and men's values become quite different. Juliet Mitchell argues that human beings carry the memories of patriarchal beliefs and practices and it becomes a part of culture which suppressed women simultaneously.

In India, culture, custom and religion are intertwined.[4] The religious practices performed by the people in different societies, become the part of their culture and the society approves them as the moral and ethical norms. Women have been the best conveyor of these practices and rituals yet they suffered a lot by them. In the name of *pativrat dharma* and *stri dharma*, a lot of sacrifices have been done and still continues. *Sati* and honour killing are the best examples of this *dharma*. The practice of *Sati* was also an influence of patriarchal culture and was still in practice in post-Independence India in the name of cultural rights. Sati idols are still worshiped in some areas of Rajasthan. An essay written by Sudesh Vaidya and Kumkum Sangri, 'Institutions, Beliefs, Ideologies: Widow Immolation in Contemporary Rajasthan', presents the atrocities carried out on women in the name of *Sati dharma*. Widows were forcibly thrown into the fire and a sense of sacrifice was made. This reveals the excavation of religion and custom. Honour killing in some of the Jat communities in western UP, Haryana and Rajasthan brings a threat to law and order system which rules parallel to the state functionaries. On the name of cultural rights, women have been and still are exploited by their own family and community. Festivals, beliefs, legends, food, fasting and chastity have been naturalized in the behavioural pattern of women. This became an inseparable part of women's existence.[5]

So in every society there are two different norms for human life, one for men and another for women. As women have been used as best conveyer of traditions and rituals, they attain neither power nor authority, even they have to bear several responsibilities.[6] The cultural barrier upon a baby girl are so well rooted in our society that a large number of female remained uneducated even in the 21st century. In the era of fast growing human civilization, which is landing on the surface of Moon and Mars, half of its population is inadequately educated. Where education is a tool of overall development of a person, women have been restricted to achieve this holy goal also as it would liberate them. Even today in rural areas a mother would like to stop her daughter in the house so that she can take care of the younger ones of the family. Also, lack of general facilities in the schools and distance makes it hard for girls to get their primary education. Lack of education makes them unable to know about essential information like health awareness, hygienic habits, women welfare programmes, different laws and acts to protect their rights. Beyond this, they are unable to validate the values and customs they are following. Education can play a major role to bring them out of these restrictions. Table 1 reveals the facts of women education in India.

Though the gap between male and female literacy is being narrowed since 1951 but the picture of girl education is still alarming. The increasing data of girl enrollment in the schools and female literacy is quite different from the ground realities. A girl mainly in rural areas, hardly attends the school regularly because of household responsibilities. A lot of private schools and colleges have been opened in these areas also but the girls are not permitted to get admission in these schools while a boy can. There are insufficient number of schools for secondary and higher education and available institutions are at much distance from the core rural areas and the problem of quality education yet remains pitiable. Also because of growing figure in violence against women make every parent worried about the safety of the girls. Though girl enrollment is increasing at primary level, but in secondary and higher education girl's ratio is not much encouraging. Girls are far behind in professional, scientific and technical education because of its inaccessibility and the nature of the jobs depending on these degrees.

**Table 1**
*Female Literacy Rate in India (1951–2011)*

| *Census Year* | *Total Literacy* | *Males* | *Females* | *Male–Female Gap in Literacy Rate* |
|---|---|---|---|---|
| 1951 | 18.33 | 27.16 | 8.86 | 18.30 |
| 1961 | 28.3 | 40.4 | 15.35 | 25.05 |
| 1971 | 34.45 | 45.96 | 21.97 | 23.98 |
| 1981 | 43.57 | 56.38 | 29.76 | 26.62 |
| 1991 | 52.21 | 64.13 | 39.29 | 24.84 |
| 2001 | 64.83 | 75.26 | 53.67 | 21.59 |
| 2011 | 74.04 | 82.14 | 65.46 | 16.68 |

*Source:* censusindia.org.

## Violence against Women: A Cultural Product

Sexual abuse and violence is deepening in our social structure, either in villages and towns. There is an alarming growth in the violence against women in our country. Galtung, in 'Violence, Peace and Peace Studies Research' (1969), has rightly remarked, 'When one husband beats his wife, there is a clear case of personal violence, but when one million husbands keep one million wives in ignorance, there is a structural violence.'Surprisingly 54 per cent of women and 51 per cent of men in India agreed that hitting a woman is acceptable.[7] Women are the victims of several types of violence as infanticide, child marriage, dowry, rape, domestic violence, sexual violence, trafficking and infinite numbers of the same. Women and child trafficking is increasing fast in our country, mostly in North-East states. These women and girl children are forcibly pushed into sex labour. A report from Dasra, a strategic philanthropy foundation has revealed the facts that about 60 per cent of trafficked girls, below than age of 16, are engaged in commercial sex activities. Along with other reasons, economic disparities and discriminatory cultural practices make young women and children particularly vulnerable to being trafficked.[8] Violence against women in the social structure is supported and reinforced by gender norms and values across the classes, religion and cultures.[9] In fact every violence against women mentioned above is a result of cultural belief. Amazing to see is the state's apathy towards the issue, while everything is in the knowledge of its authorities in several parts of the country. How any activity or business degrading moral values as well as status of women can be legitimized and get licence. In the same concern, the judgment given by the Supreme Court on female bar worker in Mumbai must be reviewed.

**Figure 1**

*Crime against Women (% Distribution During 2012)*

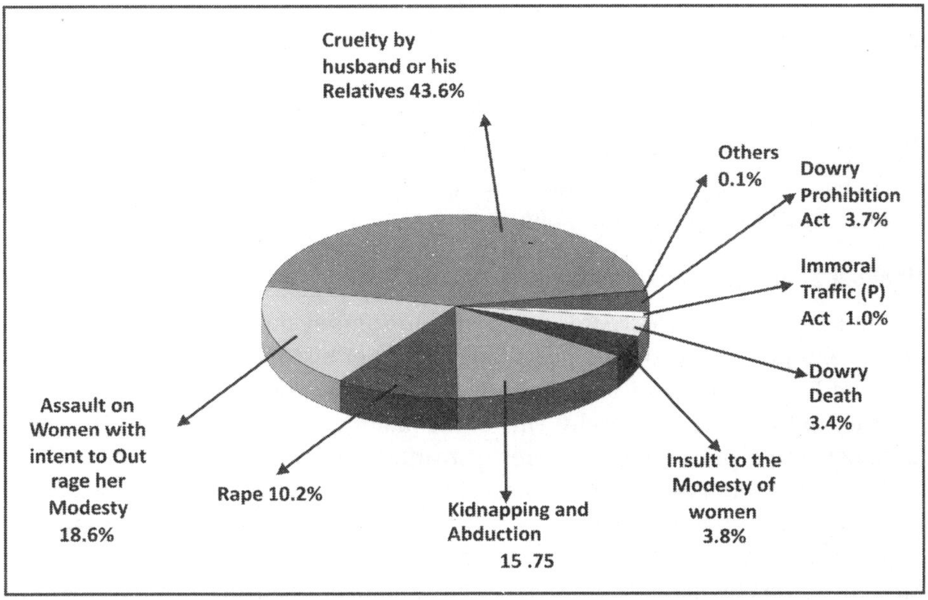


*Source:* National Crime Bureau.

Women face most of the violence from their relatives and family members according to the report of National Crime Bureau 2012 (Figure 1). Inadequate education, insecure environment, sexual abuse and assault have created a sense of less confidence in women. They find it hard to move independently, to get proper information and also to adjust in workplace. Though there have been several legal provisions to protect women from such type of problems but the implementation of these laws has been unsatisfactory. It is a mimicry to see that the legal and law-making institutions are bound to pass the hard rules against executive bodies if they don't response positively to women's problems. Here, the structural patriarchy as well as violence is deeply rooted in the implementing bodies also.

The problem of female infanticide is increasing like epidemic in India. According to the Hindu culture and traditions, marriage gives a legitimacy to enter in the family life and having a son is very important to release one from the chain of birth-death-rebirth. A girl is not eligible to perform the custom of cremation. The family runs in the name of the son, this is a big reason behind female infanticide, and the desire to avoid extra burden. It leads to a continuous decline in the child sex ratio (0–6 age group). Though the Medical Termination of Pregnancy Act 1971 had been enacted as a health measure for women and to prevent female infanticide, major proportion of illegal abortion after sex determination continues in a large scale in most parts of northern India. The Census Report 2011 shows a downfall in child sex ratio with continuity from 1951 (Table 2).

**Table 2**
*Sex Ratio in India Adult and 0–6 Age Group (1951--2011)*

| *Census Year* | *Adult Women* | *Girl Child (0–6 Age Group)* |
|---|---|---|
| 1951 | 946 | 983 |
| 1961 | 941 | 976 (–7) |
| 1971 | 930 | 964 (–12) |
| 1981 | 934 | 962 (–2) |
| 1991 | 927 | 945 (–17) |
| 2001 | 933 | 927 (–18) |
| 2011 | 940 | 914 (–13) |

*Source:* censusindia.org and india.unfpa.org.

## Unequal Share in Power-Positions

The imbalance of power creates dissatisfaction among people. Women, for being apart from power positions since a long period of history, now seek the reason of their humiliation and exploitation, either in family or in society, in their absence in the power hierarchy. One of the major reasons behind this irresponsible behaviour of the state agencies is insufficient presence of women in these bodies also. From law-making to implementing bodies, women are inadequate in numbers. Parliament, Judiciary and executive institutions, all are facing a huge vacancy of women. After six decades of Indian Independence, only four Supreme Court Justices were women. The domain of law is male centric. Women were not allowed to practice in India until 1924. Similarly, the same feature remains in the police force. Morever 13 states and Union Territories have no all women police stations.[10] While induction of more women in the police force is an essential advice from the committee formed for the Police Reform in India.

Though women are approximately 50 per cent of entire Indian population, average percentage of their representation in National Parliament and state assemblies has been very low since Independence. As they remained in the private sphere of the society, they themselves have never been concerned to reach on the power hierarchy. The civilizations, as Greeks and Romans, declaring themselves as the most developed of the ancient world, didn't regard their women as citizen. The whole medieval world was a dark age for womanhood as several restrictions were imposed on them across culture and community. In modern world also, they have to fight for a life full of dignity which has been always a dream for a large proportion of women. Because they have been regarded as a heterogeneous group and within the strata of social division, a woman of lower caste is always in worst position and remains at the last step. Though barriers in women empowerment exist in every area of the society whether social, economic, political and academic, a need for political empowerment is felt since a long time because if they achieve the power positions in the law-making bodies, it can be a catalyst for change in the status of the women. But because the nature of Indian politics is also patriarchal, it makes the political domain harassing for women involvement. They had been an active and equal participant in the Indian Freedom Movement and were an effective weapon of non-violence movement, their contribution for the revolutionary organizations cannot be ignored. Along with struggle for the Independence of the country, several women groups like Bharat Stree Mahamandal, Women's Indian Association and National Council of Women took various effective steps for bringing women on equal footing with men. They raised the issues like child-marriage, *Sati*, illiteracy, widow-remarriage, right to vote with other nationalist demands. Several times they came out of the four walls of their homes and women *satyagrahies* courted arrest. But after Independence in 1947, they were pushed back into the boundaries of the domestic life and vanished from the political stage of the country. Their presence at national and state political scenario has declined both in quantity and quality.

As the nature of politics in India has changed and has become more criminalized, violent and corrupt, it has made the situation more hazardous for women participation in politics. Though the Constitution of India provides equal opportunity and rights to its every citizen, but women are far behind from equality. The demand of getting more and more women candidates in the Parliament and Assemblies has logic that if they will be a part of the decision-making process of the country, the laws can be made more gender-sensitive; also it will be better to uplift their social status. In a country like India, where cultures norms are so deeply rooted in the society, a notion of independent women is still a miracle in the 21st century, but we all have seen how for other marginalized sections of our society, after having a legal space, provided by the Constitution, things are altering positively, though slowly. The women can also change the wave against them. We can see how the 73rd and 74th Amendment in Indian Constitution has brought a drastic change for women participation at the grassroots politics in India. But this representation has necessarily not cut the cultural chain for the elected women members. In village panchayat meetings, the women *pradhans* either become invisible or are seen accompanied by their family members. The independency culture and confidence could not be developed among them either for visiting alone or in taking independent decision. In some village Panchayat, they are bringing their experience of civic society into the government of state.[11] Though there is several other cultural barricading in their active performance at grassroot level, but the results shown by local level encouraged the demand for women reservation in Parliament and state Assemblies because their representation at this stage is very pitiable. The average percentage of women members in Lok Sabha has been below 7 per cent and in Rajya Sabha it has been less than 10 per cent since 1951. In cabinet positions also these elected women members have not found appropriate places. Table 3 depicts the whole figure:

Though some of the political parties like Indian National Congress, Bahujan Samaj Party, Trinmool Congress, All India Anna Dramuk headed by women leaders, but this leadership has perhaps not played any decisive role to emancipate and promote women leadership and women presence in Indian politics. From a long time of Indian polity, women leaders, without patronage from powerful men, found it hard to come forward in the political life. The ambiguous policies and patterns of political behaviour led by these women leaders have created a passive environment in the women movement for political space. Because of the political parties' patriarchal structure, today even the best of the female parliamentarians feel sidelined and powerless in their respective political party.[12] Almost, all the political parties in India have been very selective to grant election tickets to women candidates, they prefer only winnable candidates. Though all of them declare themselves as the best well wisher of women welfare and empowerment, but the issue of Women Reservation Bill gives a strain to their heads. The political parties against the Bill argue that because of the comparatively low level of literacy of political training, women are unable to represent the popular sovereignty. Also the ways and patterns of political life are not suitable to women because of their time and space constraints. In a culture where formal interaction with men unconnected to one's own family is frowned upon, women are severely handicapped because they cannot make even communications with men without endangering their position in the family.[13]

**Table 3**

*Women Representation in Indian Parliament*

| | *Lok Sabha* | | | *Rajya Sabha* | | |
|---|---|---|---|---|---|---|
| *Year* | *No. of seats* | *Women M.P.* | *Percentage* | *No. of seats* | *Women M.P.* | *Percentage* |
| 1952 | 499 | 22 | 4.41 | 219 | 16 | 7.31 |
| 1957 | 500 | 27 | 5.40 | 273 | 18 | 7.59 |
| 1962 | 503 | 34 | 6.76 | 238 | 18 | 7.56 |
| 1967 | 523 | 31 | 5.93 | 240 | 20 | 8.33 |
| 1971 | 521 | 22 | 4.22 | 243 | 17 | 7.00 |
| 1977 | 544 | 19 | 3.49 | 244 | 25 | 10.25 |
| 1980 | 544 | 28 | 5.15 | 244 | 24 | 9.84 |
| 1984 | 544 | 54 | 8.09 | 244 | 28 | 11.48 |
| 1989 | 517 | 27 | 5.22 | 245 | 24 | 9.81 |
| 1991 | 544 | 39 | 7.17 | 245 | 38 | 15.51 |
| 1996 | 543 | 39 | 7.18 | 223 | 19 | 8.52 |
| 1998 | 543 | 43 | 7.92 | 245 | 15 | 6.12 |
| 1999 | 543 | 49 | 9.02 | 245 | 19 | 7.76 |
| 2004 | 543 | 45 | 8.28 | 245 | — | — |
| 2009 | 543 | 58 | 10.68 | 245 | 22 | 8.98 |
| Average | 530 | 35 | 6.59 | 240 | 21 | 9.00 |

*Source:* Election Commission of India.

The present scenario is against the right to equality given by the Constitution because at every step of today's life also women face a problem of inequality, insecurity, discrimination and exploitation so the goal of our independence movement is yet far away. As CSWI (1974) stated, 'A political system can't be based on ideology alone must keep in touch with actualities of social system .... The continuing under representation of women prevents their proper participation in decision-making process in a country .... When one applies the principles of democracy to a society characterized by tremendous inequalities such special protections are only spearheads to pierce through the barriers of inequality. An unattainable goal is as meaningless as a right that can't be exercised.' So women in India, in spite of several remedies provided by laws, are still struggling to come out from the ceiling of cultural glass.

Everything has two aspects, positive and negative. Human civilization could not develop in the vacuum of ideas and these ideas in the form of beliefs and traditions makes the culture. But only positive features of any society are acceptable because it can help to develop anybody. A gender-biased culture is thrashing a huge population, stopping women from getting proper education, equal opportunity and equal status. The nation has forgotten the famous words of Gandhi, 'Educate one man, you educate one person but educate a woman and you educate the whole civilization.' As Nehru had mentioned, 'The future of India cannot consists of dolls and playthings and if you make half the population of country a mere plaything of other half – an encumbrance on others, how will you ever make progress'.[14] So giving them a life of equality and dignity will make our society a healthy and a noble society.

## Conclusion

Undoubtedly society is necessary for every human being and culture is a tool of his socialization. Culture has a wider aspect, and it won't be correct to reflect upon only its negative features. Morals and ethics may be different for different people and society but its positive sides should be traced and-adopted in a just society. The debate on cultural restrictions must not make two groups, out of their swords. Every person either men or women can easily consider the positive and negative implications of cultures, as described earlier, human being carry their earlier beliefs and customs over centuries, but if they begin to think about its rational, everything can be sorted out. It should be a universal slogan to treat everyone as a human being first; gender was socially constructed later on. Degrading ones dignity is a crime against humanity. So, if a girl is restricted from being born, treated unequally even as an innocent child, forbidden for education, there is a ban on her mobility, increasing violence against her modesty, she is made a victim of sexual assault and dowry death, then she is certainly made the most exploited creature of the world, and if all these practices are any how constructed and legitimized by our cultural beliefs, any religion, custom then that culture must be rejected. Men and women are two equal parts of the society and they should be treated equally.

## Notes

1. Taylor as cited in D.N. Majumdar and T.N. Madan, *An Introduction to Social Anthropology*, Mayoor Paperbacks, Noida, 1999, p. 21.
2. Joan W. Scott, 'Gender a Useful Category of Historical Analysis', in *Gender and Politics of History*, Columbia University Press, New York, 1988, p. 42.
3. Sylvia Walby, *Theorizing Patriarchy*, Basil Blackwell, Oxford, 1990.
4. Vasudha Dhagamwar as cited in 'Culture, Custom and Religion', in Maneesha Priyam, Krishna Mennon and Madhulika Banerjee, *Human Rights, Gender and Environment*, Pearson, New Delhi, 2009, p. 118.
5. Ibid., p. 120.
6. Julia Annas, 'Women and the Quality of Life', in Martha C. Nussbaum and Amartya Sen (eds), *Quality of Life*, Oxford University Press, New Delhi, 1993, p. 279.
7. Report Dasra: *No Private Matter*, 2013.
8. *Times of India*, December 11, 2013.
9. Ellina Samantroy, 'Structural Violence and Gender', *Women's Link*, Vol. 16, No. 4, October-December 2010, p. 28.
10. *The Hindu*, March 24, 2013.
11. Devaki Jain, *Panchayati Raj: Women Changing Governance*, UNDP, New York, 1996.
12. Report: *Women's Representation in Legislature: An Alternative to the Government Bill for Women's Reservation*, Forum for Democratic Reforms, p. 41.
13. Madhu Kishwar, 'Women's Marginal Role in Politics', *Manushi*, No. 97.
14. S. Gopal (ed.), *Selected Works of Jawaharlal Nehru*, Orient Longman, New Delhi, 1972.

## References

Association for Democratic Reforms (2012). *Report on UP Elections.*

Brettell, Caroline B. and Carolyn F. Sargent (2009). *Gender in Cross-Cultural Perspective.* New Delhi: PHI Learning Private Limited.

Committee on the Status of Women in India (1974). 'Towards Equality', Report, Ministry of Education and Social Welfare, Government of India.

Election Commission of India Reports.

Government of India (2011). *Census Report.*

Galtung, Johan (1969). 'Violence, Peace and Peace Research', *Journal of Peace Research*, 6(3): 167–91.

Jain, Jasbir (2011). *Indigenous Roots of Feminism: Culture, Subjectivity and Agency*. New Delhi: Sage.

John, Mary E. (ed.) (2008). *Women's Studies in India: A Reader*. New Delhi: Penguin.

Kishwar, Madhu (1996). 'Women's Marginal Role in Politics'. *Manushi*, 97, November-December: 16–18.

Mahajan, Gurpreet and Helmut Reifeld (eds) (2003). *The Public and the Private: Issues of Democratic Citizenship*. New Delhi: Sage.

Majumdar, D.N. and T.N. Madan (1999). *An Introduction to Social Anthropology*. Noida: Mayoor Paperbacks.

Menon, Nivedita (1999). *Gender and Politics in India*. New Delhi: Oxford University Press.

National Crime Bureau (2012). *Report Crime against Women.*

Nusbaum, Martha C. and Amartya Sen (eds) (1993). *The Quality of Life*. New Delhi: Sage.

Priyam, Manisha et al. (2009). *Culture, Custom and Religion in Human Rights and the Environment*. New Delhi: Pearson.

Ryle, Robyn (2012). *Questioning Gender*. California: Sage.

Samantroy, Ellina (2010). 'Structural Violence and Gender'. *Women Link*, 16(4), October-December.

Sharma, Kumud (1998). 'Power vs Representation'. Occasional Paper No. 28, New Delhi: Centre for Women's Development Studies.

UN Women (2011). *Country Review of Women Political Participation*.

Walby, Sylvia (1990). *Theorizing Patriarchy*. Oxford: Basil Blackwell.

## Websites

www.censusindia.org
www.india.unfpa.org

# 24

# Enabling Women Entrepreneurs through MSMEs

## *A Road Map for their Economic Empowerment*

**SUNITA SANGAR**

Economic empowerment of women opens up avenues for them to gain personal identity and social status (National Policy for Empowerment of Women, 2001). It is important to focus on women's entrepreneurship as a way to poverty alleviation and economic empowerment. Empowering women entrepreneurs is a means for achieving the goals of sustainable and inclusive economic development. Women's entrepreneurship started to gain importance in India in the wake of economic liberalization and globalization. The policy and institutional framework for developing entrepreneurial skills, providing vocation education and training has also widened the horizon for economic empowerment of women. The potential of women to be entrepreneurs has now been well-recognized and encouraged.

However, the road to entrepreneurship for women has not been easy and several barriers have been identified through various research papers, including the recommendations that emerged from the '12th Global Conference of Women Entrepreneurs' in India which was organized in New Delhi from 3–5 September 2012 and supported by the Ministry of Women and Child Development, Government of India. Besides, studies on the impact of micro-finance on women's empowerment revealed that though women experience an increase in income and consumption, they have very little control over the resources, assets and participation in household decisions. These, and a lack of entrepreneurial talent on the one hand and socio-cultural norms that impede risk-taking ability among these women on the other, are the real bottlenecks for women's empowerment. There is, thus, a need to improve upon the knowledge we have about women's enterprises, identify the key barriers hampering their growth in participation, facilitate the financing of enterprises owned by women and favour the participation of women entrepreneurs within the country as well in the international trade through encouraging policies and schemes.

## Women Entrepreneurs in India

The Government of India has defined women entrepreneurship as an enterprise owned and controlled by women having a minimum financial interest of 51 per cent of the capital and giving at least 51 per cent of the employment generated in the enterprise to women. Women have traditionally played an important role in the micro and small enterprises as owners, managers and workers. Though the entry of women into business in India is traced out as an extension of their kitchen activities, it has now spread to the modern needs of energy, electronics and engineering with the spread of education.

There has been a paucity of data with respect to the sector-wise distribution of women's enterprises in India. Some indicative trends reveal concentration of women's enterprises in the areas of traditional choices, such as in the textile and garment sector, followed by service and trading sectors and food products. However, rest of the women opt for non-traditional enterprise choices in innovative and high-technology areas like chemicals, plastics, rubber, mechanical and metal ware, and wood products.

With the dominance of women in the micro-enterprises that constitute a large percentage of working enterprises in India (as compared to small and medium enterprises), the emergence of women entrepreneurs and women-owned firms and their significant contributions to the economy is visible in India. There is a change in scenario from majority of women being in economically non-productive activities that are financially remunerative to a large number of women showing interest to be economically independent, creative and with innovative ideas to start the small and medium-sized enterprises. Women entrepreneurs can benefit from the initiatives of the micro, small and medium enterprises (MSMEs) sector which contributes significantly to the manufacturing-output, employment and economic growth of the country. Women entrepreneurship can foster the economic empowerment of women, particularly through the MSME sector by helping them to become successful entrepreneurs.

## Promoting Women's Entrepreneurship through MSMEs

The micro, small and medium enterprises (MSMEs) sector employs about 595 lakh persons in over 261 lakh enterprises throughout the country. The sector has consistently registered a higher growth rate than the rest of the industrial sector. There are over 6,000 products ranging from traditional to high-tech items, which are being manufactured by the MSMEs in India. This sector is a blend of the traditional and the modern sectors with an alarming level of informal sector enterprises. MSMEs provide good opportunities for both self-employment and jobs, outside agriculture. It is estimated that in terms of value, the sector accounts for about 45 per cent of the manufacturing output and 40 per cent of the total exports of the country. The inclusiveness of the sector is underlined by the fact that nearly 50 per cent of the MSMEs are owned by disadvantaged groups of society. This is a sector in which many women earn their livelihoods with women's entrepreneurship increasing rapidly in India. Many women support themselves and their families through income they receive from their entrepreneurial activities.

## Contribution of Women in MSMEs

Involvement of a large number of women's workforce in the MSME sector, particularly in the unorganized sector, is well known despite the non-availability of a comprehensive sex-disaggregated data on this sector. Over 60 per cent of the workforce comprises women in sectors such as handloom, chemical and plastics, food processing, and village industries that employ a large number of women.

**Table 1**

*Women's Participation in the MSME Sector*

| | | *Sector* | | | *Sector* | | |
|---|---|---|---|---|---|---|---|
| | | *Registered* | *Unregistered* | *Total* | *Registered* | *Unregistered* | *Total* |
| Number of women's enterprises | | 2,15,036 | 17,04,938 | 19,19,974 | 13.85 | 6.95 | 7.36 |
| Number of enterprises managed by women | | 1,56,753 | N.A. | 1,56,753 | 10.10 | N.A. | N.A. |
| Employment by male and female | Male | 76,19,234 | 4,17,00,391 | 4,93,19,625 | 76.43 | 83.99 | 82.72 |
| | Female | 23,49,525 | 79,50,377 | 1,02,99,902 | 23.57 | 16.01 | 17.28 |
| | Total | 99,68,759 | 4,96,50,768 | 5,96,19,527 | 100.00 | 100.00 | 100.0 |

*Source:* Extracted from the table based on the Summary Results of Fourth All-India Census of MSMEs.

The Fourth All India Census of MSMEs provides the latest available data (Table 1) on women's enterprises, enterprises managed by women and sex disaggregated data on employment, for both registered and unregistered units. The proportion of women entrepreneurs is, however, quite low as per the MSME Annual Report 2011–12, with only 13.72 per cent (2.15 lakh) of the enterprises in the registered MSME sector being women's enterprises, whereas the share of enterprises actually managed by women is also 13.72 per cent. There is a dominance of males in the ownership of MSMEs with few units reported as women's enterprises as compared to enterprises owned by men. Comparison between the third and the fourth Census reveals that the share of women's enterprises has not increased significantly!

As is clear from Table 2, there is no significant deviation in the pattern in urban and rural areas, although the dominance of women-managed enterprises is slightly more pronounced in rural areas (15.27%) as compared to the urban areas (12.45%), indicating their greater involvement in rural enterprises.

It becomes evident from Table 3 that the share of women enterpreness in view, small and medium declius with the increase in size of enterprise while opposite side the case with male owned enterprises. This indicates that women and layely during micro enterprises and too that too in rural onces.

**Table 2**

*Percentage-Distribution of Ownership of Enterprises by Gender in Rural and Urban Areas*

| *Sector* | *Women (%)* | *Men (%)* |
|---|---|---|
| Rural | 15.27 | 84.73 |
| Urban | 12.45 | 87.55 |
| All | 13.72 | 86.28 |

*Source:* Fourth All India Census of MSMEs.

**Table 3**

*Percentage Distribution of Enterprises by Gender of Owner and Sector*

| *Sector* | *Women (%)* | *Men (%)* |
|---|---|---|
| Micro | 14.19 | 85.81 |
| Small | 5.06 | 94.94 |
| Medium | 4.21 | 95.79 |
| All | 13.72 | 86.28 |

*Source:* Fourth All India Census of MSMEs.

## Problems Faced by Women Entrepreneurs

Women entrepreneurs may not be experts in all the functions involved in the development of an enterprise. They need sufficient time to understand and learn activities involved in the development of an enterprise. Several problems faced by the women entrepreneurs in India have been identified by researchers. These range from shortage of finance, marketing problems, shortage of raw materials, stiff competition, limited managerial ability, high cost of production, and absence of entrepreneurial aptitude. The high cost of production, low risk-taking ability, family conflicts, patriarchal society, lack of entrepreneurial training, legal formalities and travelling are other major hurdles. Lack of access to credit facilities too is a major problem. Women are often denied credit by bankers on the ground of lack of collateral security. Their access to risk-capital is, thus, very limited. The complicated procedure of bank loans, the inordinate delay in obtaining the loans and the running about involved do deter many women from venturing out. However, despite all these hurdles, women have made a mark in the enterprises. They have been able to make their presence felt and contributions recognized, despite adversities and the myriad problems they face.

Various policies and programmes have been formulated, incentives and schemes introduced and institutions established to give momentum to the emergence of growth of women entrepreneurs in India, specifically by the Ministry of MSMEs. Emphasis to women was given under the thrust on 'special category' when the Ministry of Micro, Small and Medium Enterprises (MSMEs) came into being in 1999. Initiatives of the Government involve Micro, Small and Medium Enterprises Development (MSMED) Act, 2006 that recognized the concept of 'enterprise', and Task Force constituted by Prime Minister in 2009 to identify issues inhibiting growth of the sector that gave several recommendations to unshackle the Indian MSMEs. In addition to the MSME, other initiatives of the government may also be utilized to the maximum extent. In this context Prime Ministers 'National Council on Skill Development' was also constituted in 2008, for the creation of 500 million skilled people by 2022 with emphasis on inclusiveness. The new, ambitious National Manufacturing Policy, 2011, that aims to make India a manufacturing hub and increase the sectoral share of manufacturing in GDP to 25 per cent in the next decade would also require substantial support from MSMEs and a quantum jump of the sector's growth rate from existing level of 12–13 per cent per annum. This necessitates convergence of efforts and resources that should involve effective participation by the target beneficiaries of which half of the population constitute women. Not many years back, the Ministry of MSMEs submitted a report to the Planning Commission based on the recommendations of the Working Group on MSMEs'Growth for the 12th Five Year Plan (2012–17) and the Public Procurement Policy for MSMEs was also announced in 2012 under the MSMED Act, 2006.

The MSME sector can help solve some of these problems through its programmes and schemes and has the capability to generate opportunities for self-employment and wage employment for women. The promotion of enterprises of home-based workers, self-employed workers and small producers is an essential component of the 12th Plan and is of particular relevance for women. The 12th Plan strategy aims to support their enterprises through setting up of common facility centres to ensure all important services including technology and skill training, entrepreneurship training, market information, access to institutionalized credit, power and other infrastructure, and related facilities. The MSME sector has emerged as a highly vibrant and dynamic sector of the Indian economy over the last few decades.

The efforts of the government and its various agencies are ably supplemented by NGOs that are playing an equally important role in facilitating women's empowerment. However, the government-sponsored development activities have benefitted only a small section of women i.e. the urban middle class women. Since women occupy nearly 45 per cent of the Indian population, effective steps are needed to provide entrepreneurial awareness, orientation and skill development programmes to women. The MSME sector which is known as the 'engine of growth' by way of contributing significantly to the national manufacturing output and exports can play an important role in giving a boost to women entrepreneurs.

## Current Schemes for Women Entrepreneurs

MSMEs are an effective tool to expand employment opportunities, help ensure equitable distribution of the national income and facilitate effective mobilization of private sector resources of capital and skills (Annual Report, MSME, 20011–12). The policies and programmes implemented by the Ministry of MSME span across different areas of operations of MSMEs, covering credit, marketing, technology, skill-development, infrastructure-development, fiscal matters and legal/regulatory framework. These programmes are implemented through various organizations under the Ministry, commercial banks, Small Industries Development Bank of India (SIDBI) and the State/UT Government. Besides, the Ministry also runs three training institutes, namely National Institute for Micro, Small and Medium Enterprises (NIMSME), Hyderabad (successor to the Central Industrial Extension Training Institute), National Institute for Entrepreneurship and Small Business Development (NIESBUD), Noida and the Indian Institute of Entrepreneurship (IIE), Guwahati, with the objective of training and development of human resource relevant to small industries as also entrepreneurship. It has also supported setting up of a large number of Entrepreneurship Development Institutes (EDI) in various states. The organization is supported by the office of the Development Commissioner (Micro, Small and Medium Enterprises), a Public Sector enterprise called the National Small Industries Corporation Limited (NSIC), Khadi and Village Industries (KVIC), Coir Board and Micro, Small and Medium Enterprises Institutes in nearly every state.

Some of the schemes being currently run by Ministry of MSMEs that would help in the promotion of women entrepreneurs are:

**Table 4**

*Current MSMEs' Schemes Promoting Women Entrepreneurs*

| *Sl. No.* | *Name of the Scheme* | *Women's Component* |
|---|---|---|
| 1. | **Trade Related Entrepreneurship Assistance and Development Scheme for Women (TREAD):** This is a scheme for economic empowerment of women, specially illiterate and semi-literate women of rural and urban areas for the development of entrepreneurial skills in the non-farm activities. | Assistance in the form of a Government of India Grant of up to 30 per cent of the total project cost, as appraised by the lending agency, is provided to the NGOs for promoting entrepreneurship. Remaining 70 per cent of the project cost is financed by the lending agency as loan to women entrepreneurs for undertaking activities as envisaged in the project. |
| 2. | **Micro and Small Enterprises Cluster Development Programme (MSE-CDP):** This scheme aims at holistic and integrated development of micro and small enterprises through soft interventions (capacity building, marketing development, export promotion, skill development, technology upgradation, etc.), hard interventions (setting up of Common Facility Centres) and infrastructure upgradation in the new/existing industrial areas/clusters of MSEs. | In this, for the North Eastern and Hill States, in clusters with more than 50 per cent women-owned enterprises, the GOI grant will be 90 per cent in soft as well as hard interventions. Also, infrastructure, grant will be 80 per cent for projects in case 50 per cent are women-owned. Scheme also provides scope for putting up exhibition centres by Associations of Women Entrepreneurs for display and sale of products of women-owned Micro and Small Enterprises at 40 per cent of the project-cost. |
| 3. | **Credit Guarantee Fund Scheme for Micro and Small Enterprises (CGMSE):** Support for Entrepreneurial and Management Development through EDPS/MDPS, etc. | To ensure better flow of credit to micro and small enterprises by minimizing the risk perceptions of financial institutions and banks in lending without collateral security.<br>The scheme covers collateral free credit facility – 80 per cent for MSEs owned/operated by women. |
| 4. | **Entrepreneurship Development Programmes (EDPs):** Entrepreneurship development is one of the key elements for promotion of micro and small enterprises particularly, the first generation entrepreneurs. These are conducted through MSME–DIs to impart skills relating to trades such as electronics, electricals, food processing etc. that enables the trainees to start their own ventures. | 20 per cent of the targetted EDPs are conducted exclusively for weaker sections including women for which no fee is charged. Besides, a stipend of ₹ 125 per week per candidate is provided. |
| 5. | **Mahila Coir Yojana** is the first women –oriented self-employment programme in the industry | Under the scheme, women coir-workers are given subsidy to the extent of 75 per cent of the cost of the motorized spinning ratt or a motorized traditional ratt. |

*Source:* Compiled from, *A Guide to Self-Employment: Schemes & Programmes of the MSMEs*, Ministry of MSMEs, Government of India, 2011.

Various issues which are impacting women entrepreneurs could be enabled through programmes/schemes of the MSME sector along with the schemes of other Departments/Ministries also.

## Recommendations

Despite a large presence of MSMEs in India, women entrepreneurs make a very meagre proportion of it. An overview of the key publications/schemes/policy papers/reports related to MSMEs reiterates a greater role of women entrepreneurs in MSMEs sector. Some of the specific suggestions towards enabling the achievement of this inclusiveness include:

### Convergence among Existing Schemes/Policies

There is a need to bring more women into the fold of government schemes. Here, MSME schemes can play an important role. Enabling women entrepreneurs would also help achieve other targets as committed through other policies such as Public Procurement Policy for MSMEs Order, 2012, under MSMED Act, 2006 that calls for overall procurement of a minimum of 20 per cent of the total annual purchases of products produced and services rendered by MSMEs in a period of three years. This has a special provision where 4 per cent out of this 20 per cent shall be earmarked for procurement from micro and small enterprises owned by SC or ST entrepreneurs. However, there is no special provision for women entrepreneurs. One would imagine that least 5 per cent could be earmarked for procurement from MSMEs owned by women entrepreneurs. Also, within the 4 per cent already provisioned for SC or ST in the Public Procurement Policy, at least 2 per cent of allocation should be from women SC and ST entrepreneurs. This will go a long way in enabling and recognizing the role of women entrepreneurs in the national economy.

Increase in employment in the subsidiary status category, particularly in urban areas, that is largely occupied by women is indicative of their potential to be a part of the organized sector. The Government of India has announced a National Manufacturing Policy, 2011, with the objective of enhancing the share of manufacturing in GDP to 25 per cent within a decade and creating 100 million jobs. It will be crucial to increase the share of women in the total employment in the Indian manufacturing sector which has remained stagnant at 10.9 per cent between 2000 and 2007. With feminization of labour largely in the unorganized sector, it is important to bring more skilled women under the ambit of the organized sector by reaping the benefits of this policy that envisaged 10–12 per cent increase in job opportunities. Convergence between the Ministry of MSMEs and Ministry of Commerce and Industry to take forward initiatives for ensuring increased participation of women entrepreneurs will be crucial – for example, by bringing more women into the fold of the National Manufacturing Competitiveness Programme of the Ministry of MSMEs.

### Role of Research: Evidence for Policy-making

There is a need for researchers to take up pertinent issues related to the promotion of women entrepreneurs in order to create enough evidence for policy-making as also formulation of need-based schemes for women entrepreneurs. Some of the key research areas include steering gender analysis for all entrepreneurial support programmes;examining differential impacts of governmental policies, programmes and actions; gathering data on female and male entrepreneurs, studying the impact of existing and new instruments on female entrepreneurs and identifying instruments that act as barriers to their expansion and growth. Besides, it will also be useful for making full use of data gathered to inform new policies, programmes and supportive actions ensuring synergies between various ministries having programmes to promote women entrepreneurs. For example, continuation of the TREAD scheme of the Ministry of MSMEs in the 12th Five Year Plan period with the budget allocation of ₹ 100 crores was done on the basis of working-group recommendations. An evaluation of the earlier women beneficiaries would be helpful in understanding the difficulties faced by women entrepreneurs as also help to widen the reach to a large number of women.

Since collection of national-level data on the number of units owned by women as also the number of women employed in MSMEs is of recent occurrence, it will be important to collect sex-disaggregated data on a regular basis that would help design and target policies and programmes to attract women entrepreneurs in specific categories for their entrepreneurship development. Holding regular consultations to review progress and identify new bottlenecks impacting women entrepreneurs as also encouraging and rewarding dynamic women entrepreneurs is also important.

## Promoting Women's Entrepreneurship in Rural Areas

Encouraging women's entrepreneurship for women involved in agriculture and allied activities can create opportunities for income-generation in rural areas in the era of increasing feminization of agriculture in the country. The Report on Conditions of Work and Promotion of Livelihoods in the Unorganized Sector (2007) revealed a large disparity in work participation across rural and urban areas among women. While half of the adult women have participation in workforce, only a little more than one-fifth of urban women participate in the workforce. A higher rate of participation in work *per se* among women in rural areas is because women in these areas are mostly engaged in agriculture and allied activities, with other opportunities for work being restricted. This does not mean that their economic condition is better than that of their counterparts in urban areas.

Women's entrepreneurship in rural areas through capacity building in the key areas such as finance, literacy skills, marketing, production and managerial skills, etc. could play a crucial role (Mehta and Mehta, 2011). However, it may not always target their inclusion in the formal sector.

It is evident that government initiatives can play an important role in enabling women's entrepreneurship in the country. Even though agriculture has largely been viewed as a non-entrepreneurial traditional activity in the past, emergence of women entrepreneurs in agriculture and allied activities can play the role of a catalyst to propel the rural population into the fold of sustainable inclusive development.

## References

A Guide to Self-Employment: Schemes and Programmes of Ministry of MSMEs. Ministry of MSMEs, Government of India, New Delhi.

Annual Report (2011–12). Ministry of Micro, Small and Medium Enterprises. Government of India, New Delhi.

Chander, S. and D.D. Arora (2013). 'Study of Financial of Women Entrepreneurs'. *International Journal of Social Science and Interdisciplinary Research*, 2(4): 103–21, http://indianresearchjournals.com/pdf/ijssir/2013/april/12.pdf

Chaudhary, R. (2013). 'Problems Faced by Women Entrepreneurs in India'. *4D International Journal of Management and Science*, 3(1): 128–39, http://4dinternationaliournal.comijournal/pdf/problems-faced-bv-wemen-renu-chaudhary.pdf

Eleventh Five Year Plan (2007–12). Vol. III, Planning Commission, Government of India, New Delhi.

Final Report (2011). Fourth All India Census of Micro, Small and Medium Enterprises, 2006–07: Registered Sector. Development Commissioner, MSME, Ministry of Micro, Small and Medium Enterprises, Government of India, New Delhi.

GOI (2001). National Policy for Empowerment of Women, 2001, Ministry of Women and Child Development, Government of India.

Kaur, G. and S. Singh (2010). 'Women Entrepreneurs in India: Problems and Prospects'. *Third Front: Journal of Humanities and Social Science*, 1(1): 63–73.

Kaushik, S. (2013). 'Challenges Faced by Women Entrepreneurs in India'. *International Journal of Management and Social Science Research*, 2(2): 6–8, http://www.iriciournals.org/iimssr/feb2013/2.pdf

Kumar, L. (2013). 'Illusion of Women's Empowerment in Micro-finance: A Case Study'. *Economic and Political Weekly*, 48(15): 70–76.

Lal, A.T. 'Women's Enterprises in India Over the Years'. Social Science Research Network, pp. 1–17, http:thapers.ssrn.comisol3/delivery.cfm/ssrnid2177746 code1931965 .pdf?abstractid=2176377&mirid=4

Mehta, A. and M. Chandra Mehta (2011). 'Rural Women Entrepreneurship in India: Opportunities and Challenges'. International Conference on Humanities, Geography and Economics (ICHGE), 1–18th December, Pattaya, Thailand.

Mishra, S.P. (1996). 'Factors Affecting Women's Entrepreneurship in Small and Cottage Industries, India'. ILO and Sida, 91 pages.

National Manufacturing Policy (2011). Department of Industrial Policy and Promotion, Ministry of Commerce and Industry, Government of India, 30 pages.

Ramani, S.V. et al. (2013). 'Women Entrepreneurs in the Informal Economy: Is Formalization the Only Solution for Business Sustainability?'. UNU-Merit Working Papers–018, UNU-Merit, The Netherlands.

Report of Prime Minister's Task Force on Micro, Small and Medium Enterprises (2010). Government of India, 172 pages.

Report of the Working Group on MSMEs, Growth for 12th Five Year Plan 2012–17 (2012). Ministry of MSMEs, Government of India.

Report on Conditions of Work and Promotion of Livelihoods in the Un-organized Sector (2007). National Commission for Enterprises in the Un-organized Sector, Government of India.

Saurabh, S. (2012). 'Issues and Challenges Faced by Women Enterprises and Their Training Needs'. *International Journal of Multi-disciplinary and Academic Research*,

1(2): 1–8, http://ssiimar.in/vol.%201%20no.%202%20pdf%20for%20website/sweta%20saurabh.pdf

Shankar, P. (2013). 'Women Entrepreneurs in India: Opportunities and Challenges'. *International Monthly Refereed Journal of Research in Management and Technology*, January: 14–18.

Summary Results of Third Census (2001–02). Development Commissioner, MSME, Ministry of Micro, Small and Medium Enterprises, Government of India, New Delhi, http://dcmsme.gov.injssiindiaicensusisumryres.htm

Vijayakumar, A. and S. Jayachitra (2013). 'Women Entrepreneurs in India: Emerging Issues and Challenges'. *International Journal of Development Research*, 3(4): 12–17.

# Index